Esotericism in African American Religious Experience

Aries Book Series

TEXTS AND STUDIES IN WESTERN ESOTERICISM

Editor

Marco Pasi

Editorial Board

Jean-Pierre Brach
Andreas Kilcher
Wouter J. Hanegraaff

Advisory Board

Allison Coudert – Antoine Faivre – Olav Hammer
Monika Neugebauer-Wölk – Mark Sedgwick – Jan Snoek
György Szőnyi – Garry Trompf

VOLUME 19

The titles published in this series are listed at *brill.com/arbs*

Esotericism in African American Religious Experience

"There Is a Mystery"...

Edited by

Stephen C. Finley
Margarita Simon Guillory
Hugh R. Page, Jr.

BRILL

LEIDEN | BOSTON

Cover illustration: Untitled, c. 1977 by Martin Green. Graphite and poster paint on poster board
22" × 28" from the collection of Robert Tannen and Jeanne Nathen. Reproduced with kind permission.

Library of Congress Cataloging-in-Publication Data

Esotericism in African American religious experience : "there is a mystery"... / edited by Stephen C. Finley,
Margarita Simon Guillory, Hugh R. Page, Jr.
    pages cm. -- (Aries book series. Texts and studies in Western esotericism, ISSN 1871-1405 ; VOLUME 19)
    Includes bibliographical references and index.
    ISBN 978-90-04-28309-1 ((hardback) : alk. paper) -- ISBN 978-90-04-28342-8 ((e-book)) 1. Occultism--
United States. 2. African Americans--Religion. 3. United States--Religion. I. Finley, Stephen C., editor.
    BF1434.U6E86 2014
    200.89'96073--dc23

                                                            2014033846

This publication has been typeset in the multilingual "Brill" typeface. With over 5,100 characters
covering Latin, IPA, Greek, and Cyrillic, this typeface is especially suitable for use in the humanities.
For more information, please see www.brill.com/brill-typeface.

ISSN 1871-1405
ISBN 978-90-04-28309-1 (hardback)
ISBN 978-90-04-28342-8 (e-book)

Contents

PART 3

Late 20th Century to Present-day

Foreword

"Listening to the Esoterica Africana"

Jeffrey J. Kripal

It is a great pleasure, indeed a delight, to see this volume appear. I cannot help but think that it signals something genuinely new and something truly promising. It is certainly long overdue for the shared and overlapping fields of study that gathered in the twentieth century under the umbrellas of those three heterodox – isms: Gnosticism, Esotericism, and Mysticism, or "GEM," as we have come to call them affectionately here at Rice, where a number of these young essayists were trained. It is certainly time for those of us who have labored in these same historical fields for decades now, with little or no awareness of these African religions and these African American esotericisms, to put down our theories and books and ponder what appears in these pages—*to listen.*

It is time to listen to our colleagues, as they move the study of African American religions from the margins to the center of the professional study of religion, and as they liberate that study from the traditional assumptions of denominational history, congregationalist identity, and the Black Church, indeed even from Christian theology, the Bible, and the category of race itself. There are multiple precedents to and ancestors of this project, of course. One thinks, for example, of those distinguished European intellectuals who carved out the new field of Western esotericism for us in the last decades of the last century and the first decade of this one: individuals like Antoine Faivre, Wouter Hanegraaff, and Kocku von Stuckrad. One also thinks of all of those American intellectuals who have pioneered the study of black religion in America, prominent figures like Charles Long, who has blazed exactly these sorts of intellectual paths in the history of religions and the study of black religion for over four decades now, and my own colleague here at Rice, Anthony Pinn, whose words appropriately conclude the present volume. More on Tony in a moment.

The present volume represents the work of the next generation of scholarship, as it consists of a collection of essays that are performed, for the most part, by younger intellectuals, many of whom are looking at figures and movements that are either poorly known or hardly known at all. As a developing new school of thought, the essayists write against the common assumptions that black religion and the Black Church are the same thing, and that African Americans are more or less equivalent to their socially constructed racial identities. Put more positively, without ever taking their eyes off the crucial concerns of race and social justice, the essayists are able to show in exquisite detail how such complex, conflicted human beings also know extraordinary moments of vision and myth-making, paranormal power and psychic capacity, and numinous states of temporal, spatial, and cultural transcendence: "Why your Knockings are so accurate they can chart the course of a hammerhead shark in an ocean 1000s of miles away. …Why, when the seasons change on Mars, I sympathize with them."

These essayists thus demonstrate for the reader that African Americans, like everyone else, are *more* than their communities, *more* than their cultures, *more* than their race, *more* than their relative places in space and time, even as, of course, they always also express themselves in the terms and images of their space and time and communities. If I might venture a personal reading here, I would suggest that there is a kind of double vision implicit in this volume, a sophisticated both-and that has the potential to drive the field forward into a truly sophisticated history of African American religions—and here is where it gets very personal—not backwards into the same-old constructivisms, relativisms, materialisms, and flatland Marxisms of our profession's most recent past ("Marxism is acceptable, esotericism is not," as someone with whom I am acquainted so beautifully puts it). There is material history and politics aplenty here, of course, but there is also vision, mystical experience, and transcendence. There is *both*. There is always, always *more*. Or, in the words of the editors, "there is a mystery."

Having said that, the essayists never take their eyes off what we might call the sociology of esotericism. They understand that such visions and states often come into serious conflict with the religious and social orthodoxies of the day, be these the underlying racist structures of American society or the theological assumptions of the Black Church (or the normalizing, domesticating effects of academic materialism and constructivism). They also understand that it is this very challenge, this high strangeness, that in turn calls for and then shapes the various forms of esotericism that are the focus of their essays. Secrets, after all, are only necessary if there is a reason to keep a secret. Secrets are not necessary for the ordinary, the uncontroversial, and the banal. Secrecy implies the presence of something extraordinary, something strange, something that does not fit in, something that transcends or transgresses the social or cognitive register in place. Hence, the sociology of secrets.

If I might add my own voice here for a moment (again), this is precisely why intellectuals should be so fascinated by the phenomenon of esotericism in the history of religions. The connections between esoteric truths and the intellectual life are profound ones. Both call into question the status quo, the social consensus, the ordinary, the assumed. Both stand against (and yet in deep concerned conversation with) the orthodox and the public. The intellectual is often also the esoteric, and the esoteric is often also an intellectual. They *have* to be. Both the intellectual and the esoteric visionary also insist that the appearance is not the reality, that the truth of things is deeper, more complex, more complicated, and more strange. They thus both exemplify different forms of what my colleague Tony Pinn has called for in the study of black religion: a study of the search for "complex subjectivity."

Complex, indeed! I mean, exactly how does one introduce a collection of essays like this? Here we encounter: an Arkansas monastic community of purple people seeking purple transcendence; African American New Thought as a form of modern Gnosticism; a Louisiana Easter Rock Ritual performed exclusively by women; the Spiritualist, erotic occultist, Rosicrucian, clairvoyant, radical Republican, novelist, and defender of women's rights, Pascal Beverly Randolph, who was the founding figure of African American esotericism and one of the true prophets/founders of the New Age; a man named Jungle Cat pole dancing for Jesus; Astro-black mythology and Space Age esotericism; the pop singer Erykah Badu and the men and women who are Gods and Earths; Haitian Vodou as human-spirit interaction channeled and shaped by African-based practices hybridized with the history of slavery and colonialism, Native American beliefs, and Catholic hagiography; magickal notebooks and grimoires as at once material artifacts and conduits of real spiritual power; Afro-Cuban religion on the South Side of Chicago; the "fourth dimension" of the Gurdjieff-Ouspensky School and the superman doctrine of Theosophy in the Harlem Renaissance; numerology, Free Masonry, and conspiracy theory in the history of the Nation of Islam; trance possession and speaking with the dead in white and black Spiritual Churches; conjure practices in the African Diaspora; the African American mysticisms of Howard Thurman and Langston Hughes through the Spirituals and Blues of black embodiment and the key notion of writing reality; a treatise on the magical machines—from treasure finding and cursing machines to conjuring wheels—of Hoodoo, Rootwork, and Conjure; and Sufism, Egyptian symbolism, Nazi occultism, UFO religion, and Caucasian reptilian extraterrestrials from the Orion constellation in the United Nuwaubian Nation of Moors, the "Nu" Nation.

Where, exactly, does one draw the line in all of this? And which line? Where to start? Where to end? Clearly, we are only at the beginning here. This volume is more of a call and a provocation than an end or conclusion. So *listen*...

Preface

The original title of this volume was "There Is a Mystery"..., and it remains the secondary title. The expression "There is a mystery" is a phrase that is derived from Howard Thurman's *The Luminous Darkness* (1989, 73) in which Thurman explores what he suggests are mysteries surrounding those who have been oppressed, that they sometimes appear epistemologically enigmatic to those who injured and segregated them even while their eyes project a hidden yet critical gaze. Thurman suggests that the interpretation of the content surrounding the mysteries of the oppressed was supplied by those who had the power to construct and control the metanarrative, which then interacts with images and caricatures that support and stabilize systems of domination. He intimates that while such misrepresentation supplies false content and meaning to the *mystery* surrounding the lives of marginalized communities—in particular, Africana communites—these distortions of reality function as forms of capital or what he calls "currency" that shape discourses, practices, and interpretations though the meanings, under conditions of marginalization, may remain obscured to those who maintain such systems.

"There Is a Mystery"...implies an exploration of the discourses and practices that resist and defy totalizing narratives and power constructs that shape fields of practice—in particular religious ones—which then participate in the policing of the boundaries of those fields. The essays in this collection destabilize dominant tendencies in multiple scholarly fields and disciplines including the Study of African American Religion, Western Esotericism, and other cognate arenas. More specifically, the contributors to this volume interrogate hidden, secretive, muted, and excluded religious discourses and practices that are located in persons and communities that posit direct access to secret knowledge, contact and interaction with some transcendent or invisible force that may pervade nature, and symbolic or actual correspondence between realms or worlds. Such perspectives are most often relegated to the margins in society and academia. By examining the interplay between scholarship and the data of those religiosities that are often structured as heretical, impossible, and pathological by religious groups that are considered mainstream and authoritative, the co-editors and contributors scrutinize the ways in which their (re)inclusion may affect the shape of African American religious history and theory of African American religion, and how the particularities of African American religion may speak to broader notions about the nature of religion, indeed, the nature of the world. In the words of the late Howard Thurman, the essays "probe the mystery" in order to ascertain what the data may signify about the world in which we live.

At the same time that this anthology can be considered groundbreaking because of the historical and theoretical implications of the essays it brings together, the disciplinary commitments out of which the contributors write and the methods used in their investigations of these religious discourses and practices will serve as the markers in the mapping and inauguration of a new scholarly endeavor—in close relationship to Religious Studies and Africana Studies and in conversation with Western Esotericism—that we call Africana Esoteric Studies (AES) as a broader category about esotericism in Africa and the African Diaspora. In the case of this particular volume, the focus is on African American esotericism. This inaugural project also features additional contributions from eminent scholars—a Foreword by Dr. Jeffrey J. Kripal and an Afterword by Dr. Anthony B. Pinn—that explore the implications of the volume for the discipline of Western Esotericism and the fields of African American religion and Religion in America.

The twenty articles constituting the core of this volume—including those we have contributed as co-editors—explore complex and diverse appearances of Esotericism, Gnosticism, and Mysticism in African American religious experiences and cultures as well as the ways that the hegemony of dominant religious discourses and scholarship often obfuscate, silence, or render invisible expressions of religiosity that lie at the margins of mainstream conversations and practice.

"*There Is a Mystery*"..., indeed, and our work serves as the initial phase of what we trust will be an ongoing investigation of esotericism(s) throughout the Africana world—secrets that are selectively made known and carefully guarded because of their life-giving essence. In many ways this volume challenges conventions, both social and disciplinary. It critiques traditional ways of obtaining and producing knowledge. We hope the pages of this collection *speak* and *reveal* as they *initiate* readers into the mysteries they disclose.

The Co-Editors

Acknowledgements

Esotericism in African American Religious Experience: "There Is a Mystery"... has quite an interesting genealogy. Most immediately, the project represents the coming together of three streams of influence. The first is the Gnosticism, Esotericism, and Mysticism (GEM) program at Rice University, which grew out of the interests of several faculty at Rice, including Dr. Jeffrey J. Kripal and Dr. April D. DeConick. Their influence in this area—especially that of Dr. Kripal—precedes the GEM program, given that Dr. Kripal's work was significant for Drs Guillory and Finley, and he was on the dissertation committee of Dr. Finley. More specifically, it was at the "Hidden Histories, Hidden God" conference organized by Dr. DeConick and other important scholars and hosted by Rice in April 2010 that this project was really born. It was in this setting, during the second or third day of the four-day symposium (April 16th or 17th) that Drs. Guillory and Finley committed to producing a volume on African American esotericism. Two significant events happened at the conference to begin this process. The initial one was that both Drs. Guillory and Finley presented papers, which began to formulate their thoughts on African American esotericism that were later published in Dr. DeConick's and Dr. Grant Adamson's edited volume *Histories of the Hidden God: Concealment and Revelation in Western Gnostic, Esoteric, and Mystical Traditions* (Acumen Publishing 2013). The other significant event was meeting Dr. Kocku von Stuckrad, who was the keynote lecturer for the conference. Dr. von Stuckrad was an early and sustained supporter of our work and this project, and, for that, we owe him a debt of gratitude. This project would also not have been possible without Drs. Kripal and DeConick. We are grateful for their support and encouragement. It was shortly after this conference that Drs. Finley and Guillory quickly developed a short list of scholars who would be able to contribute to such a project that explored African American esotericism. Dr. Hugh R. Page, Jr. was at the top of this list, which leads us to the second stream of influence.

Dr. Hugh R. Page, Jr., whose work on theories of esotericism and Africana esotericism(s) had been ongoing prior to meeting Drs. Finley and Guillory, was a scholar at the University of Notre Dame in 2007 when Dr. Finley was on campus as a finalist for Notre Dame's Erkine A. Peters Dissertation Fellowship program. Dr. Page was one of the conveners of the meeting. It was in these initial encounters with Dr. Page that Dr. Finley learned of his already-well developed work on esotericism, and it seemed only fitting that he should join Drs. Finley and Guillory as co-editor. Without his professional experience, deep intellect, and kind heart this book would neither have the depth nor richness that it has.

The third stream of influence can be attributed to Dr. Anthony B. Pinn, who advised both Drs. Finley and Guillory in their doctoral work at Rice University. In another intriguing connection, Dr. Page was a graduate teaching assistant for one of the classes in which Dr. Pinn was enrolled at Harvard Divinity School. Dr. Pinn's emphasis on looking at traditions that are in the margins for the ways in which they inform theory and method in the study of religion (generally) and African American religion (in particular) can clearly be seen in this project. This volume would look very different, if it existed at all, without Dr. Pinn, who has continued to be a mentor and friend.

We also wish to thank others, who played significant roles in this volume coming to fruition. We held a session at the annual meeting of the American Academy of Religion in Chicago, on November 17, 2012, which highlighted some of the contributors to this volume, and the co-editors moderated and were panel respondents. It was at this meeting that we met Dr. Marco Pasi, the Editor-in-Chief of the *Aries Book Series: Texts and Studies in Western Esotericism* with Brill. Dr. Pasi was exceedingly enthusiastic and invited the co-editors to submit a book prospectus for this eminent series. We could never adequately express our gratitude for what he has done. Nevertheless, we thank Dr. Pasi, the Editorial Board and the Advisory Board, especially Allison Coudert of the University of California, Davis, for their support and belief that ours was a project that was worthy of publication in such a series. We also want to thank Brill Religious Studies Editor, Maarten Frieswijk, and Maaike Langerak, who have led us expertly and professionally through the entire publication process.

As can be expected in a project such as this, the contributors are really the ones who make this book what it is. Most of them were our friends prior to this project, which made pulling the pieces together much easier. They were already doing the expert scholarly work that is published in these pages. We did not have to issue a call for papers. We knew who they were. All they had to do was say "yes," which they did without question. We thank them all for the relationships and labor that they shared with us, and we are happy that our names are associated with theirs in this work.

A word must be said about the art that appears on cover of this volume and those who made its use possible. Martin Green was the artist who created the untitled piece emblematic of the book's major themes. He was an African American artist from New Orleans, who, tragically, was killed in his home by a robber in 1987, ransacking his home and destroying valuable artwork in the process. Some of his remaining works, more than a hundred, were destroyed by Hurricane Katrina in 2005. Prior to his death, he had given about a dozen of his original works to artists Robert Tannen and Jeanne Nathen. Fortunately, this handful survived, and Dr. Finley was privileged to see some of them exhibited at the Ohr-O'Keefe Museum in Biloxi, Mississippi in 2013, and he remembered them when Brill asked the co-editors to consider art for the cover. The pieces resonated with the co-editors, especially the selection that we chose containing images of planets, stars, Africa, and a volcano. Something about this constellation of features in a work by an African American artist from New Orleans and his "visionary paintings of the other world" bespeak the intent of this volume. We honor the memory of Martin Green by featuring his art on the cover. We wish to thank Barbara Johnson Ross, curator of the Ohr-O'Keefe Museum, for facilitating our request to use this image and the owners of the collection, Robert Tannen and Jeanne Nathen, for graciously granting us the permission.

In addition, Stephen C. Finley would like to thank Drs. Page and Guillory for being professionals, visionaries, and friends. *Esotericism in African American Religious Experience* would never have happened without their insight and effort. Members of the Society for the Study of Black Religion have been a wonderfully supportive community since 2006, as has the Association for the Study of Esotericism, more recently. He also thanks his colleagues at Louisiana State University in Religious Studies and African & African American Studies. They have always believed. Particular individuals deserve special notice, although these are certainly not all of them: Dr. Joyce Marie Jackson, Dr. Eldon Birthwright, Dr. Solimar Otero, Dr. Devyn Benson, Dr. Cassandra Chaney, Dr. Lori Martin, and Martha Pitts. Thanks are also due to Dean Gaines Foster and the School of Humanities and Social Sciences at LSU, which awarded a Summer Research Award in 2011 to work on the early planning stages of this book. Moreover, many of his fraternity brothers of the Omega Psi Phi Fraternity, Inc. have been more than friends. Special thanks to the Theta Chi Chapter, especially Isaac Jones, Donald Pipkins, Cliff Hodrick, Harold "Tex" Allen, as well as George "Tino" Prince, Gregory "GAP" Parham, Rev. Dr. Bobby Joe Saucer, Nathan Lawson, Damon Powell, Dr. Juan Barthelemy, and Dr. Michael Joseph Brown. Lastly, his wife, Dr. Rachel Vincent-Finley, has been especially supportive as have his sister, Sonja Finley-Adams, his cousin Glenn I. Anderson, best friend, Christophe L. Beard, his mother, Hattie Fuette, and his step-father, Herman Fuette.

Margarita Simon Guillory would like to extend thanks to Linus Joseph, Jr. for his loving support throughout this entire process and Linus Joseph, III for teaching her that the creative process is organic in its nature. She is also appreciative of the encouragement that she received from her colleagues in the Religion and Classics department at the University of Rochester. Lastly, she would like to thank the contributors of this volume for their courageous act of recapturing voices, traditions, and methodologies that have often been overlooked in African American religious studies.

Hugh R. Page, Jr. would like to thank his editorial collaborators—Drs. Stephen C. Finley and Margarita Simon Guillory—for sharing the rich and rewarding journey leading to the conceptualization and completion of this remarkable project; his colleagues in the First Year of Studies as well as those in the Theology and *Africana* Studies Departments at the University of Notre Dame for their support; his grandparents (the late Arnett and Deacon Virginia Brown and the late Dr. George C. and Patricia B. Page) and parents (the late Deacon Hugh R. Page, Sr.; and Dr. Elaine B. Page) for instilling in him an insatiable curiosity about the subtle textures of *Africana* life; and his wife, Dr. Jacquetta E. Page, for her inspiration, support, love, and unfailing belief in the importance of this volume.

List of Contributors

Julius H. Bailey
is a Professor of Religious Studies at the University of Redlands. He has written two books, *Race Patriotism* and *Around the Family Altar* on the African Methodist Episcopal Church, as well as other publications on various aspects of the study of religion.

Justine M. Bakker
completed the two-year research master program in Religious Studies in 2013 at the University of Amsterdam, where she also earned her BA in European Studies (2010) and Religious Studies (2011). She is currently a graduate student in the African American Religious Studies program at Rice University.

Yvonne Chireau
is Professor at Swarthmore College, where she teaches courses on comparative religions. She is the author of *Black Magic: Religion and the African American Conjuring Tradition,* and co-editor of *Black Zion: African American Religions and Judaism.* Her current project is an online research blog, *The Academic Hoodoo* (academichoodoo.com).

Mary Ann Clark
is the author of several books on African-based religions in the Americas, most recently *Then We'll Sing a New Song: African Influences on America's Religious Landscape.* She is an independent scholar, who teaches religious studies at Yavapai College in Prescott, Arizona.

Paul Easterling
holds a Ph.D. and a M.A. in Religious Studies from Rice University, with specialization in African American religious and a M.A. in Africana Studies from SUNY Albany with specialization in Pan-Africanism and Black Psychology. He is currently an Adjunct Professor of History and Government at Bowie State University. Dr. Easterling's research interests include: African American Religious Culture, History of African American Religion, 20th African American Islam, African American Religion and Popular Culture.

Lana Finley
received her PhD in English at the University of California, Los Angeles, in 2012. Her dissertation traces the history of early American esotericism through

its appearance in the "occult novel" tradition, a subset of the gothic. She studies several branches of Hermeticism and has taught at UCLA.

Stephen C. Finley

is an Assistant Professor in the Department of Religious Studies and the African
and African American Studies Program at Louisiana State University. An
Executive Committee member of the Society for the Study of Black Religion,
he is completing his book, *In and Out of This World: Material and Extraterrestrial
Bodies in the Nation of Islam*.

Margarita Simon Guillory

is an assistant professor of religion at the University of Rochester. Her research
interests include American Spiritualism, identity construction in African
American religion, and social scientific approaches to religion. In addition to
contributing essays to several edited volumes, she has published articles in
Culture and Religion and *Pastoral Psychology*.

Biko Mandela Gray

is a fifth-year doctoral student in religious studies at Rice University,
working on a dissertation tentatively titled, "Making-Life-Matter; a
Philosophical Theory of African American Religious Experience." His current research interests are African American religion, religious experience,
embodiment with/in religion, continental philosophy, and religion and
popular culture.

Barbara A. Holmes

is president of United Theological Seminary of the Twin Cities. She is
the author of five books and is widely known as a dynamic leader in theological education and inspiring lecturer on African American religious thought, Art Activism, Diasporan Religions, Science and Liberation
Theology.

Joyce Marie Jackson

is Director of the African & African American Studies Program and an Associate
Professor in the Department of Geography & Anthropology at Louisiana State
University, Baton Rouge. She earned her Ph.D. from Indiana University in folk-
lore and ethnomusicology. Her key research interests center on African and
African Diaspora performance-centered studies and cultural and community
sustainability. She has authored *Life in the Village: A Cultural Memory of the
Fazendeville Community*.

Alisha Lola Jones

is a post doctoral fellow in the Department of Folklore and Ethnomusicology at Indiana University. Her research focuses on black men's performance of gender and sexuality in gospel music. She is a graduate of the University of Chicago (Ph.D.), Yale Divinity School (M.Div.) and Oberlin Conservatory (B.M.).

Jeffrey J. Kripal

holds the J. Newton Rayzor Chair in Philosophy and Religious Thought at Rice University, where he chaired the Department of Religious Studies for eight years and helped create the GEM Program, a doctoral concentration in the study of Gnosticism, Esotericism, and Mysticism that is the largest program of its kind in the world. His full body of work can be seen at http://kripal.rice .edu/.

Mambo Vye Zo Kommande LaMenfo

(Patricia Scheu) is an avid collector of Afro-Caribbean art and music. A long-time interest in the artwork of Haiti led her to Jacmel, where she was ordained as a Mambo Asogwe in 2003. Mambo leads Sosyete du Marche, Inc., a 501c3 Vodou church in Pennsylvania.

Darnise C. Martin

holds a doctorate from the Graduate Theological Union in Berkeley, California. Dr. Martin is also the author of *Beyond Christianity: African Americans in a New Thought Church* (NYU Press, 2005), and coeditor of *Women and New and Africana Religions* (Praeger, 2009).

Aundrea L. Matthews

is a PhD candidate in African American religious studies. She received a BS and MA from Texas Christian University and an MTS from Brite Divinity School. Her area of interest is African American quilting and material culture and their significance in the study of African American religion.

Hugh R. Page Jr.

is Associate Professor of Theology and Africana Studies as well as Vice President, Associate Provost, and Dean of the First Year of Studies at the University of Notre Dame (Notre Dame, IN). He is general editor of *The Africana Bible: Reading Israel's Scriptures from Africa and the African Diaspora* (Fortress, 2009) and author of *Israel's Poetry of Resistance: Africana Perspectives on Early Hebrew Verse* (Fortress, 2013).

Elizabeth Perez

is assistant professor of religion at Dartmouth College. An historian and ethnographer of Afro-Diasporic traditions, she earned her doctorate at the
University of Chicago Divinity School. Her first book is based on research in a
predominantly Black community of Lucumí, Espiritismo, and Palo Monte
practitioners on Chicago's South Side.

Chad Pevateaux

specializes in Christianity and comparative mystics, and works on theories of
gender, race, class, and species. Having earned a PhD from Rice University and
MDiv from Harvard Divinity School, he currently teaches at Mary's College of
Maryland, the public honors college, as a Visiting Assistant Professor.

Anthony B. Pinn

is Agnes Cullen Arnold Professor of Humanities, professor of religious studies
and Director of the Center for Engaged Research and Collaborative Learning at
Rice University. He is the author/editor of thirty-two books, including
Introducing African American Religion (2013) and Terror and Triumph: The
Nature of Black Religion (2003).

Marques Redd,

a graduate of Harvard University and PhD recipient from the University
of California-Berkeley, devotes his life to reviving ancient Egyptian metaphysical sciences and using Egypt's powerful spiritual technologies to uplift the
lives of those around him. More information can be found about him at
www.goldenbeetleastonomy.com.

Stephen Wehmeyer

holds a doctoral degree in Folklore and Mythology from UCLA, and specializes
in the study of the vernacular material and ritual arts of the Afro-Atlantic
world. He is an Assistant Professor in the Core Division of Champlain
College (Burlington, Vermont) where he teaches interdisciplinary Humanities
courses.

Jon Woodson

is the author of *Oragean Modernism: a lost literary movement, 1924–1953* (2014);
*Anthems, Sonnets, andChants: Recovering the African American Poetry of the
1930s* (2011); *A Study of Catch-22: Going Around Twice* (2001); and *To Make a New
Race: Gurdjieff, Toomer, and the Harlem Renaissance* (1999).

Africana Esoteric Studies
Mapping a New Endeavor

Stephen C. Finley, Margarita Simon Guillory and Hugh R. Page, Jr.

One of the more important goals that the essays included in this volume seek to achieve is to inaugurate Africana Esoteric Studies (AES) as a new scholarly endeavor closely aligned with, though not subsumed by, Religious Studies and Africana Studies—a field also in conversation with Western Esoteric Studies and other cognate disciplines, including Afrofuturism. While we view AES as complex, diverse, continental (i.e., inclusive of the African experience) and diasporic, this first collection of essays has focused on Africana esotericisms in the United States. This introductory essay will map the disciplines and methodologies that constitute this nascent sub-field and then suggest possible implications that such a novel universe of discourse and research arena may have for the study of African American religion and culture, as well as Religion in America, more generally.

In a recent essay, published in the *Journal of Africana Religions*, scholars Dianne M. Stewart Diakité and Tracey E. Hucks argue for a transdisciplinary theoretical and methodological approach to what they call Africana Religious Studies or ARS (Diakité and Hucks 2013, 31). The history of ARS, they contend, has been incontrovertibly influenced by discursive traces of early debates over African survivals and retentions or the notion that African practices, ideas, and sensibilities survived the Middle Passage and appear in the cultural practices of the African Diaspora, particularly in religion. The authors revisit this discussion in a lengthy exploration of the ramifications of it for the study of ARS. The primary figures in this great debate from the 1930s and 1940s were Sociologist E. Franklin Frazier and Anthropologist Melville Herskovitz. Diakité and Hucks assert that as a result of the denial by Frazier that African American life retained any African culture—in part due to his focus on America rather than other parts of the Diaspora—the study of Africana religions has focused on and privileged Christianity, which has had detrimental and limiting effects on the methodological development of the field. The logic, they assert, is that if the gods of Africa "died," that is, they did not survive the Middle Passage, as Chapter 2, "Death of the Gods," of Albert Raboteau's monumental *Slave Religion: The "Invisible Institution" in the Antebellum South* contends, then it follows that studies of African diasporic religion should begin with Christianity, which was a primary religion that Africana peoples "inherited" from their

European slavers (Raboteau 2004, 43–92; Diakité and Hucks 2013, 36–40). Consequently, they seek to disentangle ARS from this incessant centering of Christianity as well as from respectability politics that sought, by way of an apologetic and theological study of black religion, to assert black people's humanity vis-à-vis white supremacy and colonialism (Diakité and Hucks 2013, 29–66).

Instead, Diakité and Hucks seek to push the field to consider phenomenological methods much more reminiscent of the lineage of Historian of Religions Charles H. Long's monumental work, *Significations: Signs, Symbols, and Images in the Study of Religion* (Long 1984). Indeed, we submit, the work of Anthony B. Pinn, who contributed the Afterword to this volume, has also been important in pushing the boundaries of the study of Black religion in a similar way, both by endorsing a theory- and method-based approach to the study of Black religion and for de-centering Christianity in the study of religion. His *Varieties of African American Religious Experience* (1998), *Terror and Triumph: The Nature of Black Religion* (2003), and most recently, his writings on African American Religious Humanism (2004, 2008, 2012, 2013), are sensitive to all of Diakité's and Hucks' major concerns. Namely, Pinn locates his work in the phenomenological tradition of Long's *Significations*, de-centers Christianity, and pushes for a nuanced and complex methodology (Pinn 2003, 177–188). His *oeuvre* is massive, including more than thirty books and dozens of essays that expand the academic study of Black religion beyond its historical boundaries that Diakité and Hucks describe so vividly.

Along these lines, Diakité and Hucks suggest a transdisciplinary method, drawn from the Humanities and Social Sciences, that escapes the limitations of traditional Religious Studies—a field that often overlooks religious groups and phenomena such as those represented in *Esotericism in African American Religious Experience*, which represent a broad range of esoteric, Gnostic, and mystical phenomena. They remark:

> The transdisciplinary scholar transgresses all relevant disciplinary boundaries to interlace varied tools, methods, frameworks, and datasets in pursuit of a research problem. She responds to the problem-based questions driving her research as opposed to unidisciplinary questions and predispositions that impose limits upon her conceptual options based upon her principal discipline's preferred methods, theories, and tools. Inter/multidisciplinary scholarship leans toward transdisciplinarity but does not necessarily proceed from problem-driven inquiries that demand consolidated research methods in the pursuit of comprehensive proposals.
>
> DIAKITÉ and HUCKS 2013, 39

Such transdisciplinarity is why AES constitutes a completely new kind of enterprise whose disciplinary contours are intentionally porous. Advocating transdisciplinarity in his essay on Africana Esoteric Traditions (AETs) that appears in this volume, for example, Marques Redd argues that Africana esotericism necessarily defies strict disciplinarity. His groundbreaking essay on the cosmic poetry of Sun Ra suggests that Africana esotericism requires trans-disciplinarity because no one discipline—Ethnomusicology, Religious Studies, Art History, or Sociology, for instance—can account for the incredibly complex mixture of poetry, jazz, philosophy, cosmology, Gnosticism, and so on, in the practices and incredibly complex thought of Sun Ra's Africana Esotericism. We concur.

Indeed, the historic approach to the study of Black or Africana religions— one that tends to privilege Christianity as both dominant and normative—is narrowly theological in nature; fails to consider the distinctive character of Africana religion and culture; and has marginalized esoteric, Gnostic, and mystical religious groups, ideas, and phenomena. Needless to say, such neglect has been to the detriment of the study of religion as a *topos* as well as to research on African American religion and religion in America, generally.[1] One could argue that AES has much to offer Religious Studies and that it captures something distinctive about religion in America that is often missed because African American or Africana Religion in America is not viewed as American religion, as such. Instead, it tends to be viewed either as a religious subset or something non-normative, derivative, or—for some—aberrant. Harold Bloom's (2006) often-overlooked text, *The American Religion*, argues the opposite—i.e., that American religion gains its distinctive character from African influences and particularly African American religions and cultures.

Originally published in 1992, Bloom proposes both a theory and method for engaging American Religion by arguing for a "religious criticism" that seeks to locate what is irreducibly religious or spiritual in religion much in the same way, he explains, that literary criticism functions in relation to aesthetics in and of texts (Bloom 2006, 11–12). In so doing, he argues not only that American religion is experiential, individually and internally focused, immanent or immediate in its relation to the divine forces, and Gnostic—all features that are derived from Africa; but that African American religion is paradigmatic for "the American religion." That is to say, what makes American religion

---

1 A more inclusive vision of the theological enterprise allows room for a broader spectrum of conversation partners and has, as part of its central agenda, the deconstruction and de-centering of its ascribed privilege.

unique from the religious landscape of Europe, Bloom ascribes ironically to African cultural influences (Bloom 2006, 261–282), and more aptly, to African Americans' religion and culture. Bloom remarks, "I find that this confirms my own intuition that the American religion is born about 1800, and that African American religion was a crucial element in this origin," which itself relied upon "African spiritual formulations," especially the Baptists. (Bloom 2006, 263). Though African American religion is marginalized in the professional study of religion in America and seen as something other than a manifestation of religion in America proper, Bloom, implies that African American religion should be central to the methodological formulations and musings in the field.

Mary Ann Clark (2012), who also has an essay in this volume, agrees. In her book, *Then We'll Sing a New Song: African Influences on America's Religious Landscape*, Clark agues for a distinctly American religious sensibility that she ascribes to the population of Africans, primarily representing "Kongolese and Angolans from the Angolan Coast, the Yoruba-speaking people of West Africa, and the Fon peoples from Lower Guinea" (Clark 2012, 7), who were brought to the United States to serve as slaves, and their African American descendants. Many of these "sensibilities" share resonances with Bloom, particularly his understanding of American religion as Gnostic, a point that is not lost on Clark. Her insight on this is poignant:

> However, today few Americans outside of seminaries or schools of theology can articulate the differences between one denomination and another, as religiosity has moved from a focus on beliefs to a focus on a type of gnosis or religious knowledge—not theological knowledge but a personal intimate knowledge of God...This was a radical change in Christian religiosity. We can trace this change back to the religious revivals of the early nineteenth century, that period when African Americans had an important influence on the developing American religious sensibility.
>
> CLARK 2012, 112

This Gnosticism and a particular focus on religious knowledge and intimate experiences of divine transcendence, which both Bloom and Clark apprehend as an essential characteristic of American religion, have their roots in African American religion, the influence of which has remained largely concealed in popular discourses about national religious character and religiosity. Religion in America is not the only problem, however. Scholarship on African American Religion obfuscates the extent to which Africana esoteric, Gnostic, and mystical traditions, which may be the most paradigmatic forms of

American religion, are an essential part of our religious landscape, partially due to an incessant disciplinary focus on Christianity, which obscures many of the religious traditions that are the focus of this volume (Diakité and Hucks 2013, 43).

In the context of the academic study of religion, then, the study of Africana esotericism(s)—specifically, the critical examination of African American esoteric, gnostic, and mystical phenomena—is an enterprise doubly marginalized. The causes are two. The first has to do with disciplinary short sightedness—i.e., because these manifestations of the esoteric are "African American," they tend not to be viewed as fully "American" or as part of the landscape of religion in America. What's more, one could argue that the designation "Western" in the field devoted to the examination of Western Esotericism functions in a manner similar to "American," which structures discourses and disciplinary boundaries. Thus, the implicit bias marginalizing the study of Africana life prevalent as a global phenomenon remains undisrupted in the academic study of religion in America, and a non-Black norm functions as the unacknowledged and invisible center that structures the production of knowledge in the field. This center, grounded in the presumed social and intellectual supremacy of European culture and its congeners, functions through concealment and complicity, given that scholars rarely, if ever, justify or interrogate it. Philosopher George Yancy would mark this predisposition of whiteness as the universal center in the study of religion in America as "speaking from this invisible (or unacknowledged) center" (Yancy 2004, 2). Yancy contends that concealment of and failure to acknowledge what we might think of as the [white] elephant in the room is an essential feature of the social ontology of whiteness that reinscribes and maintains the social, economic, political and cultural benefits of—and investments in—whiteness (Yancy 2004, 4).

The second has to do with what might be termed the ontologies and epistemic foundations of Africana esotericisms themselves. Since this vast constellation of belief systems, life ways, and practices is neither exclusively nor narrowly Christian, efforts to study it are relegated to the margins of African American religious research where older paradigms for Black Church Studies shape its disciplinary architecture and agenda. Esotericisms remain relatively concealed (except for a few prominent exceptions, such as the works of Jacob Dorman (2007) and Tracey Hucks). Stephen C. Finley (2013) and Margarita S. Guillory (2013), likewise, contributed essays, "Hidden Away: Esotericism and Gnosticism in Elijah Muhammad's Nation of Islam" and "Conscious Concealment: The Repression and Expression of African American Spiritualists," respectively, that explicitly explored AETs in the compilation, *Histories of the Hidden God: Concealment and Revelation in Western Gnostic, Esoteric, and Mystical Traditions* (DeConick and Adamson 2013). Moreover, Hugh R. Page, Jr.'s forthcoming essay, "The Bible and Africana Esotericism—Toward an Architectonic for Interdisciplinary Studies," is sure to advance AES. Because the cosmological foundations and basic premises of Africana esotericisms differ, in some respects radically, from those considered normative in the black religious mainstream—and given that a critical mass of scholars studying these phenomena has yet to coalesce—the body of research conducted and published to date is modest at best.

In addition to the aforementioned reasons as to why Africana Esotericism(s) may not have been more substantially known and studied, a further and more mundane, issue may participate in the configuring of legitimated discourses that ignore these realities. Following Donald Matthew's *Honoring the Ancestors: An African Cultural Interpretation of Black Religion and Literature*, Diakité and Hucks attribute this to what has been termed the politics of respectability. (Diakité and Hucks 2013, 48; Matthews 1998).[2] That is to say, the relative invisibility of esoteric, Gnostic, and mystical religions in public consciousness and scholarship to date is not simply due to political pressures encouraging conformity to mainstream values, disciplinary structures that police the boundaries of acceptable work, or discursive practices that configure—almost out of existence—phenomena that defy or contradict prevailing opinion about the tasks to which a given academic field should be dedicated (von Stuckrad 2005, 10). What is also the case is that all of these factors work together to overdetermine the ways that individuals talk about (or consciously ignore) their religious experience if it is of an esoteric, gnostic, or mystical orientation. The very language that is invoked to describe one's experience and reality is filtered so as to conform with more acceptable religious narratives. That is, the politics of respectability often exert force on people, and their desire for social inclusion leads them to ignore or deny that such religious experience plays a meaningful role in their lives (and sometimes their scholarship). This may in fact be the case within Africana communities in which adherents of esoteric belief systems within and outside of the academy negotiate pressures in public and professional spheres that provide substantial incentives for assimilation.

---

2   The term, "politics of respectability," however, first appears in Evelyn Brooks Higginbothams' (1994, 14, 185–230) book, *Righteous Discontent: The Women's Movement in the Baptist Church, 1880–1920*, to describe modesty, thrift, sexual purity, polite manners, and cleanliness as a means of countering racism, which was supposed to make Black women, and Black people generally, more acceptable in the eyes of white communities.

Mitch Horowitz (2009), author of *Occult America: The Secret History of How Mysticism Shaped Our Nation*, illustrates this notion in a particularly poignant way. As indicated by the title of the book, Horowitz argues that secretive and hidden religious practices and traditions have helped to shape American life, religion, culture, and politics in ways that escape acknowledgment in public discourse (Horowitz 2009, 2). Rather, when such religiosities surface in public conversations, they receive short shrift and pejorative characterization. Adherents of these traditions are at times framed as fanatical or naïve. To a certain extent, one could argue that concealment of these individuals, groups, practices, and experiences protected them from a larger culture that may have looked upon them suspiciously, being generally unaware of their own cultural and religious indebtedness to them.

"Go Tell Pharaoh: The Rise of Magic in Afro-America" is a lively and lucid chapter of *Occult America* in which Horowitz documents an alternate narrative of African American religion that, instead of excluding Africana esotericism(s), defies the pressure to cloak their existence in respectability language (Horowitz 2009, 117–146). In doing so, he documents their prominence and salience within both American religious history and African American culture. In sum, Horowitz makes clear that they have always been with us, have co-existed alongside and within so-called "mainstream" religion, and—in many cases—were more significant than more tame accounts of the evolution of the American religious landscape would allow. This is a point that Yvonne Chireau (co-author with LaMenfo of an article in the current volume), makes brilliantly in her book *Black Magic: Religion and the African American Conjuring Tradition* (Chireau 2003). She notes that "religion" and "magic" (or Christianity and conjure) were often indistinguishable from one another and could not be viewed as discrete in a way that is helpful theoretically (Chireau 2003, 1–7).

One very telling example of the politics of respectability documented by Horowitz is found in the self-representational narratives of Frederick Douglass, expressed in his "memoirs," where Douglass narrates his encounter with the infamous slave breaker, Edward Covey, to whom he had been loaned out for a year. The 1834 scenario has become famous and Philosopher Lewis Gordon cites it as a pivotal existential moment in which Douglass became acutely self-conscious of his humanity in spite of the violence he experienced as a slave (Gordon 1999, 207–226). The Africana esoteric readings of the story, however, are lesser known. To be sure, Covey had become notorious for his cruelty, brutality, and his ability to "break" unruly slaves, one of which Douglass had come to be viewed. Covey had beaten and bruised Douglass so badly that Douglass returned to his slave master, begging for mercy. Notwithstanding his pleadings, his owner, Thomas Auld, turned him away. Before returning to the Covey farm,

Douglass hid away in the woods one dark night, where he met Sandy Jenkins, a conjure man and root worker, who had given him an amulet, a root charm, shaped like a testicle (Horowitz 2009, 120), so as to give Douglass the fortitude to face his tormentor and protect him from violent attack. Sandy encouraged him to return to Covey and the rest is history, or is it?

The legendary account details how, upon his return, the young Douglass fought with Covey for two hours. Covey proved incapable of subduing him. It was in this moment, facing certain death because of his physical resistance to a white man, that Gordon contends Douglass became self-consciously human—alive—exalting himself above the order of the animals, to which enslaved Africans were relegated (and often worse). In his later memoirs, Douglass downplayed the significance of the root and the African American worldview that it signified, as perhaps does Gordon—cf., Stephen Wehmeyer's essay in this volume, which argues that Brown (1990) does the same thing—in the irruption of self-conscious awareness of his humanity and confidence in that fateful encounter with Covey. By 1855, Douglass had greatly redacted his story of this confrontation from one that emphasized a "spirit" of unknown origins that imbued him with strength and courage that allowed him to confront death, to one that attributed his strength curiously to a "remembered" pledge that he made to "stand up" for himself (Horowitz 2009, 121). Horowitz notes that, while Douglass distanced himself from Sandy and root work, he "proved resolute in his unwillingness to slam shut the door on the matter or to qualify the veneration that he felt for Sandy" (Horowitz 2009, 122). Indeed, however, Douglass was careful not to be misunderstood as one who relied on "superstition." Instead, he wanted to emphasize the education and inward conversion of consciousness that led to his triumph.

What is at stake in similar redactions, linguistic erasures, or hidden religious histories? One could argue that a great deal is lost that could tell us about the complexities of human experiences and perhaps about ourselves. Moreover, what esoteric, Gnostic, and mystical religious experiences may offer us is a new way of looking at the world, a new metaphysics and epistemology that challenge the ways in which religion and science are constituted (as opposites), and in particular, a distinct challenge to the hegemony the sciences enjoy in the minds of some as the only legitimate sources of knowledge about the world. This is what Jeffrey J. Kripal, whose Foreword opens this volume, contends in his *Authors of the Impossible: The Paranormal and the Sacred* (Kripal 2010)—i.e., that such "impossible" religious experiences (that happen, nevertheless), which are structured "out of existence" by mainstream religion and science, have something profound to reveal about the nature of reality and most importantly, about consciousness. In many respects science is just beginning to catch up to religion when it comes to such matters, and quantum physics, considered the "new science," is on the cutting edge of this "new" (new to science, that is) frontier. One example is Bruce Rosenblum's and Fred Kuttner's *Quantum Enigma: Physics Encounters Consciousness* (Rosenblum and Kuttner 2006). While denying the existence of the paranormal that Kripal affirms, they note that "physics can look like mysticism" (Rosenblum and Kuttner 2006, 4). They go on to state that, "Quantum mechanics challenges each of these intuitions by having observation actually *create* the physical reality observed" (Rosenblum and Kuttner 2006, 4). This "science-mysticism," as Kripal calls it (Kripal 2010, 9, 123–124), is what the religions have been saying for centuries and is exactly what is revealed when one looks at the intersection of science and religion in the context of the paranormal, a field that, for Kripal, belongs squarely in Religious Studies.

However, more is at stake for Africana communities that have generally recognized the existence of a hyper-consciousness that some African Americans have euphemistically referred to as "feeling" (Pinn 2003, 173–175) or an unnamed "something" in the world to which they believed themselves to be connected; a power or force they considered capable of being harnessed. Whether or not one "believes" in the efficacy of practices such as conjure, for example, a worldview at once scientific and mystical makes room for a reality in which things resonate with and subtly influence other things; a cosmos in which the world can be and is affected by—and *created* through—the action of human consciousness. And this is precisely why Africana esoteric thought would be a primary source for emerging fields such as Afrofuturism, whose proponents should make an explicit move toward Africana esoteric ideas or black religious thought as source material in their attempts to re-envision race, the cosmos, and new world consciousness. The essays in this volume explore all of these matters.

As fantastic as all of this may sound, scholarship at the intersection of race, religion, and the sciences has some less than salutary implications. If not undertaken with an appreciative gaze toward those for whom the esoteric is the bedrock on which hope and meaningful living are built, it can render Black bodies invisible and Africana voices mute. Such is almost certain to occur unless, as Elizabeth Perez's chapter in this volume insists, we "re-center" AETs or what used to be known pejoratively as "the [black] cults and sects." Horowitz gives us a good illustration of what the sciences, Religion in America, African American Religion, Western Esotericism, Afrofuturism, and related universes of discourse could gain if we were to re-conceptualize religious history at the margins.

Horowitz points to important implications at this intersection, as do others. One such illustration is that of Robert T. Browne, a follower of Marcus Garvey, whose historical significance also changes when one re-engages Garvey's metaphysical religious inclinations in the way that Darnise Martin does in her essay, "The Divine Self: Know Ye Not That Ye Are Gods?" A friend of the famed Arthur A. Schomburg, Browne was a futuristic thinker—what Kripal might call an "author of the impossible"—who was compelled to conceal his identity in his work because of his race and the ideas he espoused. Hugh R. Page, Jr. uncovers a similar concealment of race in his essay for this anthology, "Post-Imperial Appropriation of Text, Tradition, and Ritual in the Writings of Henri Gamache." Once again, in the work of Browne, we see the politics of respectability at work—this time in response to the marginalization of Black voices in mainstream religion and science. Browne's 1919 book, *The Mystery of Space*, prefigured modern quantum mechanics, as Horowitz explains:

> Browne's book—an inquiry into hyperspace, mathematical theory, and unseen dimensions—would today be called 'new science' or 'quantum theory'. In it, Browne posited that matter and space are products of the one truly limitless resource: the human mind. He surveyed ideas from Egyptian geometry to the thought of Kant to argue that mind is the ultimate reality.
>
> HOROWITZ 2009, 144

Egypt, here and in the work of other Africana Esoteric Traditions (AETs), is a recurring trope. For some, it is the symbolic—and for a few, the actual—place from which all esotericisms flow. Within this *milieu*, Africana esotericism(s) and African American esoteric thought are pivotal epistemological resources with the power to facilitate human advancement and potential. Quantum theory aside, Browne—and others in his vein—offers but one instance of the would-be world altering possibilities that should not be separated from African American esoteric, Gnostic, and mystical religious experience that lift the proverbial veil on a heretofore unexplored treasury of metaphysical musings by peoples of African descent.

Related to his religious vision with the potential to impact humanity, Browne became a hero to thousands of Americans and other inmates when, in 1941, he was rounded up in a World War II Japanese prison camp in the Philippines, where his visualization techniques—similar to those taught by Marcus Garvey—saved thousands from death by starvation (Horowitz 2009, 144–145). Browne and others were rescued in 1945, but the media failed to mention the ways in which his lectures on metaphysical religion, while encamped, saved many of his comrades.

Browne and his wife went on to found the Hermetic Society for World Service, a theosophically inspired organization that survives to this day (Horowitz 2009, 146). Browne is but one of many exemplary figures whose roles as architects of the esoteric in the Africana world have been overlooked.

What emerges is a picture of Africana esotericism(s) that has enormous implications for the study of religion, African American religious history, African American religion, Western Esotericism, Africana Studies, Afrofuturism, and the pure and applied sciences. AETs, in many respects, are more paradigmatic than scholarly and popular accounts would have us believe. It is for this reason that *Esotericism in African American Religious Experience* has such enormous ramifications. It reveals and centers a discrete set of traditions, communities, and practices that have traditionally been silent partners in the all too human endeavor of "meaning making." They have been essential to those quests for freedom and self actualization undertaken by Africana peoples throughout the world. They have provided the lexicon, grammar, and syntax for the language of concealment and selective disclosure through which people in Africa and the African Diaspora have "whispered" their understanding of lived experience and unseen (quantum) verities. AETs call into question the *status quo* in the academic study of religion in ways that implicate race, religion, and disciplinarity in the muting of alternative epistemologies that have important truths to convey about the worlds we inhabit. Such should encourage us to consider the ways that disciplinary boundaries are inscribed and maintained. It should also call into question those presuppositions and values that govern 21st Century knowledge production. What *Africana Esoteric Studies* advocates is the embrace of a new paradigm for thinking about the material and ethereal dimensions of the world as encountered and charted by peoples of African descent.

Mapping the Terrain, Delineating a Field

However, such a task is accompanied by an ethical conundrum. The many esoteric tributaries through which Africana life is nourished have long been sequestered to protect them from those that might be inclined to exploit them for profit or make use of them in ways that are harmful to the very women and men these traditions were created to protect. Therefore, one of the major issues with which those hoping to understand more deeply the esoteric impulse among peoples of African descent must wrestle, particularly those hoping to use their research to benefit the Africana community worldwide, is whether some elements of AET should be off limits and not subject to the critical and at times exploitative tendencies of the academy. Another equally important issue concerns both the *gaze* and the tools most appropriately utilized in this kind of research. Adoption of *friendship* as the paradigmatic metaphor for such investigative work, and that of *initiation* for the intellectual metamorphosis to which the responsible researcher should be open, seem at this point to be most appropriate. The former establishes kinship. The latter is the gateway to epiphanies and revelatory experiences—some of which may verge on the uncanny. To be friend and initiate is to stand in solidarity, and more often than not, on the margin, with those into whose extended family one has been grafted and to whose secrets one has been made privy. Moreover, one must honor the customs—formal and informal—governing the disclosure of esoteric lore. Together, the metaphors of friend and initiate present an opportunity for scholars to develop methodologies for the study of esotericism that allow one to study and maintain a healthy respect for the women and men who have stewardship of them.

The essays in this volume amount to an partial exposé of cherished yet hidden African American religious ideas and practices (not strictly as *forms or patterns of thought*) that are esoteric, not simply due to the nature of those ideas and practices, but as responses to cultural repression that has been and continues to be impacted by racism, the politics of respectability, and disciplinary exclusion. Africana Esoteric Studies (AES) is unlike Western Esoteric Studies, which understands itself as a singular discipline—despite utilizing the language of a *field* (Bogdan 2007; 6–8; Hanegraaff 1998, 7; von Stuckrad 2005, 6–7)—with pronounced emphasis on textuality, social history, and empirical agnosticism (Hanegraaff 1998, 3–7; Faivre 2010, 8–10). To be sure, the field of Western Esotericism has as its bedrock a definition of esotericism that delimits it as a largely European construct.

The disciplinary boundaries of AES are more porous. It is not simply a multidisciplinary, inter-disciplinary, or trans-disciplinary endeavor. It is an epistemological orientation to Black life. It is a set of investigative habits that, while not *exclusively* empirical, places a premium on the collection and analysis of data from the worlds peoples of African descent inhabit. It is an experiential and at times autobiographically driven encounter with the material culture, *àshe* (power), and *itutu* (coolness) of *Africana* existence (on these concepts see Thompson 1984, 5–12; 2011, 16–17). It is an *axial* endeavor under the tutelage of the Yoruba and Black Atlantic deity *Eshu*—a revelatory and healing pilgrimage for which the *Philosopher's Stone* is Jazz; the *Elixir Vitae*, the Blues; and the place where truth is negotiated, that intersection of expressive culture and the footnote laden expository prose that is the academy's *koine* and currency. AES makes the peripheral zones of Religious Studies and Africana Studies the *interstices*—the metaphorical Crossroads—at which discovery occurs. AES is a *poetics of discovery* rather than strictly a field or discipline. Those involved in it are *makers* (poets) and in some instances *devotees* rather than mere scholars (those with the leisure to study). They are comfortable in the discourses of the arts, humanities, sciences, and theological disciplines. Many are also fluent in the languages of several uninvited guests to the academic banquet (e.g., Africana Studies, Ethnic Studies, Womanist Studies, Cultural Studies, and Queer Studies). More than a few are also at home in the esoteric idioms of the Black Atlantic. As for the questions that animate this project—they are as varied as the initiates who cross the threshold beyond which are the warp and weft of the *Communitas Africana*. Such an enterprise defies strict disciplinarity.

Frustrated by the politics and blindness to broader perspectives that the disciplines promote in the study of similar religious phenomena, Jacques Vallee, astrophysicist, computer scientist, and UFO researcher who was, at least in part responsible for development of the internet, noted the problem of language and disciplinary hegemony when he concluded that "The language of each discipline has become an esoteric jargon that cannot be penetrated even by someone with an advanced education in another field" (Vallee 1979, 17). Likewise, methodologies *conceal* even as they *reveal*, and while some are better at uncovering and making sense of data than others, AES pushes for a broader use of approaches and a wider set of conversation partners than the norm.

Those included in this volume exhibit remarkable intimacy with their subject(s). Participant observation is a method central to several of these essays. Again, one observes *friendship* and *initiation* in several of their approaches. The prominence of this standpoint honors the *kinship* (with people, ideas, and physical artifacts) that has made their research possible and the initiatory experiences that inform the methodologies used in their work. Reflexivity is not eschewed. Self-awareness is celebrated as a virtue, as is open acknowledgment of the places from which these scholars write. Much more remains to be seen and heard of the "mystery" that is the soul of Africana life. This volume is an invitation to those with a hunger to commune with that indescribable "something"; the courage to become kin of those who are its inheritors; and the boldness to become initiates entrusted with its timeless secrets.

Chronological Scheme and Content of the Volume

Although recognizing the role that religion has played as the central organizing paradigm thus far in research on Western and *Africana esoterica, Esotericism in African American Religious Experience* leaves open to debate the taxonomies used to classify the constellation of phenomena being examined, while calling attention to several things. The first is the role of methodology and authorial location in the study of African American *esoterica*. The second is the relationship between esoteric texts, aesthetics, and popular culture. The third is the importance of being attentive to embodiment and ritualized performances of the esoteric. The fourth is the role of symbol, number, and language in the transmission of esoteric teachings. The fifth is the experiential dimensions of African American esoteric traditions.

As a collection, these essays seek further to: (1) identify and define a distinctly *esoteric milieu* within that part of the *Africana* world situated in North America; (2) focus on particular manifestations of esoteric thought and practice in the African American cultural landscape; (3) lay the groundwork for future research on these and related *realia*; and (4) advance dialogue about the many *manifestations of the esoteric* in the Black Atlantic world and beyond; and (5) overturn or disrupt dominant meta-narratives that structure the study of religion, African American religion, and the study of esotericisms. These topical concerns have suggested a particular arrangement of the essays within this anthology.

The context for the volume's three major chronological sections—"(Pre-) 19th Century" (Part I); "Early to Mid 20th Century" (Part II); and "Late 20th Century to Present-day" (Part III)—is established respectively by Jeffrey J. Kripal's "Foreword" and Anthony B. Pinn's "Afterword."

In *Part I* "(Pre-) 19th Century," Yvonne Chireau's (Swarthmore College) and Bon Mambo Vye Zo Kommande LaMenfo's (Independent Scholar) "Esoteric Writing of Vodou: Grimoires, Sigils, and the Houngan's Notebook" contends that New insights on writing practices in Africana religious traditions can greatly enhance understandings of ritual, spiritual communication, and the vernacular literacies that form and articulate theological and metaphysical concepts, particularly those that develop and flourish in marginalized communities. Both Haitian *Vodou* and the Western mystery tradition known as *ceremonial magic* are predicated on longstanding occult practices, philosophical tenets, and metaphysical assumptions. Furthermore both are oriented toward pursuit of a divine connection or mystical enlightenment in which spiritual development and the inner quest for knowledge are paramount to the individual's journey. But some of the most explicit and interesting analogues between Vodou and Western magical practices, they conclude, center on writing practice.

Lana Finley (University of California, Los Angeles) writes on the enigmatic Paschal Beverly Randolph in her essay, "Pashal Beverly Beverly Randolph in the

African American Community." Finley declares that Randolph is *the* foundational figure of African American esotericism. She contends that he was a controversial African American celebrity whose legacy was not preserved by the black community because of his radical spiritual beliefs and questionable racial politics. While Randolph proved heavily influential on such white occultists as H.P. Blavatsky, Aleister Crowley, and R. Swinburne Clymer, Finley professes, his visionary genius would seem to have had no memorialist in the late nineteenth or early twentieth century black communities.

In her essay, "The Divine Self: Know Ye Not That Ye Are Gods?," Darnise C. Martin (Loyola Marymount University) proposes that African American New Thought religion can be considered Gnostic insofar as it requires followers either to possess or actively grow toward specialized knowledge, and it is esoteric insofar as it promotes spiritual practices that both lead to said knowledge and allows an individual to expand in consciousness and/or transcend into as yet unnamed realms of knowledge or being for ultimate fulfillment. New Thought, for Martin, represents a "revealed esoterica." She seeks to work from the margins of African American religion, which is dominated by Christian studies, to push for New Thought inclusion there and in relationship with Western Esotericism.

Part II, "Early to Mid 20th Century," begins with the essay by Elizabeth Perez (Dartmouth College), "Working Roots and Conjuring Traditions: Relocating Black 'Cults and Sects' in African-American Religious History." Perez argues that along with the phenomenon of storefront churches, the Great Migration fostered a strategy of ambiguation, or tolerance for diversity, among African-Americans that met their pressing need to balance conflicting social relationships and associations. Furthermore, she explains that it is imperative to de-center the Black Church in order to appreciate the heterogeneity and richness of lived religion, throughout the twentieth century and in our own time.

Mary Ann Clark's (Yavapai College) "Spirit is Universal: Development of Black Spiritualist Churches" maintains that just as metaphysical religion has often been discounted as an important influence on American religious history, the influences of the African and African-inspired beliefs and practices underlying these traditions have been little recognized in either the standard view of American religious history or that subset focused on African American traditions, especially the Black Church. Yet, it is these traditions, Clark asserts, that can provide a deeper understanding of contemporary American, especially African American, esoteric traditions.

The work of Jon Woodson (Howard University) observes the impact of G.I. Gurdjieff's thought on Jean Toomer and the Harlem Renaissance. His essay, "The Harlem Renaissance as Esotericism: Black Oragean Modernism," contends that the intrusions of literary theory into literary scholarship, the literary politics of the black arts movement, limitations in the numbers of scholars, teaching positions, and opportunities for publication, and the inferior quality of the research that examines African American literature have contributed to a skewed narrative in which it is virtually impossible for literary critics to concede that an African American esoteric movement might have existed within the Harlem Renaissance. He concludes that "without the propelling and sustaining influence of esotericism the Harlem movement would have been bereft of most of its most characteristic and most highly acclaimed literary achievements."

Next, the contribution of Stephen C. Finley (Louisiana State University), "Mathematical Theology: Numerology in the Religious Thought of Tynnetta Muhammad and Louis Farrakhan on Numerology in the Nation of Islam," first, argues that particular numbers, in this case, 19 and 30, are used to ascribe meaning and coherence to a world of abstractions that enables the NOI to navigate life in existential and epistemological certainty. Second, such a quest for *theosophical empiricism*, a form of Gnosticism that makes religious experience verifiable, assures and authenticates the persistence or *material perpetuity* of black bodies after "death"—the ostensible cessation of biological functioning of the human body.

Justine M. Bakker's (Rice University) "On Knowledge of Self and Others: Secrecy, Concealment, and Revelation in Elijah Muhammad's Nation of Islam (1934–1975)," pushes against the narrative that esotericism is European or non-black. She contends that much of the religion of Elijah Muhammad's Nation of Islam can be explained by many of the ideas of Western Esotericism, particularly, given that Elijah Muhammad claimed access to secret knowledge, via his relationship with Fard Muhammad, his God. Such secret knowledge helps the NOI to transcend the negative meanings that white supremacy ascribes to African Americans.

Hugh R. Page, Jr. (University of Notre Dame) argues, in "Post-Imperial Appropriation of Text, Tradition, and Ritual in the Pseudonymous Writings of Henri Gamache," that one of the distinguishing traits of these works is that they democratize access to the *numinous* through the abrogation of power typically vested in institutional hierocracies. By making readily available biblical texts, Judeo-Christian hermeneutical traditions, and selected data on indigenous religious rituals from around the world, Page notes, these books provide non-specialists with the practical knowledge and expertise to create personal liturgies for healing and canons for appropriating the Bible that resist hegemony and promote individual and communal self-empowerment.

Chad Pevateaux's (St. Mary's College of Maryland) "Mystery Matters: Embodiment and African American Mystics" argues that embodied and visceral, yet preceding and exceeding bodily limitation, a mystery exists between Howard Thurman's Spirituals and Langston Hughes's Blues that reveals an epistemology that is not dualistic but embodies a both/and, neither/nor, a/ theistic aspect to much African American religious experience. Moreover, his analysis of embodied African American mysticisms illuminates the (in)capacities we share with nonliving matter, and how this matters. He seeks to bring attention to African American mysticisms that are otherwise ignored, seen as indistinct from other mysticisms, and, through them, to correct Western epistemologies.

Biko Mandela Gray's (Rice University) "Show and Prove: Five Percenters and the Study of African American Esotericism" builds on these themes in his examination of two key authoritative texts within the *milieu* of the 5% Nation of Gods and Earths—the *Supreme Mathematics* and the *Supreme Alphabet*. Gray's major claim is that the Five Percenters are a distinctly esoteric current within African American religion. Furthermore, he argues that the esotericism of the Five Percenters can be understood in terms of what he calls a *demonstrative* phenomenological disposition—a mode of being grounded in the *inseparability* of what is traditionally understood as ontology and epistemology.

Paul Easterling (Rice University) researches Malachi Z. York and the United Nuwaubian Nation of Moors, in his essay, "The 'Nu' Nation: An Analysis of Malachi Z. York's Nuwaubians." Easterling explores written texts, audio recordings, and videos from the group and concludes that York's and the Nuwaubians' alien mythology, secret texts, and practices function to give new meaning to African-descended people in the face of white supremacy in America. Their secret knowledge and mythology locate the origins of white and black people as extraterrestrial with a moral distinction, however, that can help to explain historic white violence that is directed at black bodies.

Julius H. Bailey's (University of Redlands) essay, "Sacred not Secret: Esoteric Knowledge in the United Nuwaubian Nation of Moors," asserts that Black new world religions have had to face racial and religious prejudices as well as deal with racial matters in their sacred narratives. In this context, the UNNM's narratives of a secret, hidden, and glorious origin portend a brighter future. Bailey is concerned that Black new religious movements (NRM) are over-determined by race, which veils the complexity of their esoteric knowledge as a means of offering solutions to contemporary African American problems. Hence, their sacred narratives are seen through racial lenses and not religious ones. Therefore, even in scholarship on the group, they face racial and religious prejudices.

Part III, "Late 20th Century to Present-day," begins with Marques Redd's (Marquette University) "Astro-Black Mythology: The Poetry of Sun Ra." Redd declares that Sun Ra's Astro-black mythology causes us to "upturn all conventional thinking about the history, development, and ideal construction of knowledge" and challenges our reading of texts as objects rather than "texts of initiation" that thrust us toward cosmic consciousness. Moreover, Redd demonstrates that Sun Ra's metaphysical notion of blackness has meaning that is particular to African Americans and Africana Esotericism, and universal Soteriological significance as well. Sun Ra deconstructs national identities, loyalties, and disciplinary boundaries. He also renders race and blackness as metaphysical.

Stephen Wehmeyer (Champlain College) contributes "Conjurational Contraptions: Techno-hermeneutics, Mechanical Wizardry, and the Material Culture of African American Folk Magic" in which he maintains that Black vernacular esotericism is pigeonholed as an essentially rural, organic, and ethno-botanical phenomenon, that is, as a hyper-natural essentialism. Wehmeyer seeks to correct this trend through a critical engagement of Rootworkers or their clients, who describe complex *machines, gadgets, and technological paraphernalia* employed for various esoteric operations—including treasure hunting, exorcism, love magic, hexing, and forcing thieves to return stolen goods. In light of the substantial lacunae in the scholarly treatment of Black vernacular esotericism, he examines some of the descriptions of magical machinery found in the Hyatt collection, exploring an aspect of Hoodoo's material culture that has been underemphasized, if not plainly ignored by prior researchers.

Utilizing Lacanian psychoanalysis, Margarita Simon Guillory (University of Rochester) and Aundrea Matthews (Rice University), in their essay "Portraying Portraits: The Intersectionality of Self, Art, and the Lacanian Gaze in the Nahziryah Monastic Community," contend that the Nahziryah Monastic Community, known popularly as the Purple People, use art to convey an esoteric understanding of selfhood. Specifically, self portraits act as objects of reflexivity affording members and non-members the ability to experience an expansion of consciousness i.e. self-progression. Their essay examines how an African American monastic order employs material culture to articulate a convoluted conception of selfhood, an ego independent view of self that transcends societal constructs of race, gender, and sexuality.

In his second contribution to this volume, "Those Mysteries, Our Mysteries: Ishmael Reed and the Construction of a Black Esoteric Tradition," Marques Redd (Marquette University) critically engages Ishmael Reed's literary masterpiece, *Mumbo Jumbo*. Reed, he maintains, makes a masterful move to relocate the origins of the study of esotericism. Reed does not theorize Africana Esotericism as a sub-field within the supposedly larger territory of Western Esotericism. In a profound geographical, intellectual, and disciplinary inversion, Redd notes that Reed subsumes Western Esotericism as a sub-field within the study of the more primal field of Africana Esotericism.

Joyce Marie Jackson (Louisiana State University) contributes a piece on the Easter Rock ritual in a northern Louisiana African American Baptist Church. Her essay, "Rockin' for a Risen Savior: Bakongo and Christian Iconicity in the Louisiana Easter Rock Ritual" draws upon Africanist cultural resources and contends that the symbols and practice of the Easter Rock ritually center black women as the responsible agents in the continuance of cultural and religious rituals that challenge patriarchy in black churches. Jackson shows how black women have reconfigured the ritual icons from Bakongo symbols to Christian images to make the ritual palatable to Christian beliefs and—due to the fact that it is a pre-emancipation ritual as well as esoteric—to Baptist norms and for Christian faith in general.

Alisha Lola Jones (University of Chicago) utilizes "virtual ethnography" in her contribution, "Pole Dancing for Jesus: Negotiating Movement and Gender in Men's Musical Praise," which highlights her investigation of the mysticism of the internet sensation, Jungle Cat, an African American male religious "pole dancer." Jones argues that Black male pole dancing represents a form of homoerotic mystical religion that seeks a union with God's body. She contends that it is a rejected form of religious practice because of the racialized and gendered black male body. She uses this transgressive form of worship to indicate the complex nature of worship and mysticism in the Black Church.

Barbara A. Holmes (United Theological Seminary of the Twin Cities) writes on the reclamation of the mystical dimensions of Africana spiritual practices in Christian settings. Her essay, "Wonder Working Power: Reclaiming Mystical and Cosmological Approach to Africana Spiritual Practices," contends that the idea of "wonder working power" is an important and retrievable legacy in the African American community and that it is an essential element of the mysticism necessary for the wellbeing of humanity and especially for oppressed people. By reconnecting with the mysteries of life as seen in the lives and practices of the ancestors, Holmes explains, African Americans can find healing and flourishing that elude them in this materialistic Western culture. She seeks to correct the modern materialistic worldview that does not consider the existence of a meaningful and purposeful energy and power that animate the cosmos.

The aforementioned essays bring together for the first time exemplary research on the topic of Africana esotericism(s), and they invite critical examination of basic terminology, definitions, primary sources, and methodology. To this end, contributors were also asked to respond to and address three additional issues in their essays: (1) the academic field/disciplinary location(s) from which they were writing, the theories and methods that informed their contribution, and how they came to their interest in this work; (2) how their research had been shaped by dominant disciplinary meta-narratives—i.e., how their research represents a response to prevailing views about African American religion (e.g., that African Americans are Christians, that esotericism and New Age religion are European, etc.); and (3) the projected and/or desired outcomes for their contribution both within and beyond the academy. The writers were instructed to exercise their own discretion with respect to how and where in their essays they located these conversations. Readers will note these discussions in each of the chapters, as well as the rich intertexuality in which writers *invoke* the research of other contributors and bear witness to the intentions and potential of this project.

From a metaphorical standpoint, the essays are, as it were, both a *mosaic* representing the diversity and unity of work conducted thus far and a *map* indicative of the landscape in which future forays into this new and largely uncharted disciplinary territory might take place. They demonstrate that the *Africana milieu* in North America and elsewhere has been and continues to be endlessly generative of esoteric, Gnostic, and illuminist thought and practice. *Esotericism in African American Religious Experience: "There is a Mystery"...* makes clear that there is much to be learned about and from these phenomena concerning the larger human experience. It also demonstrates that the hidden portals through which these most profound mysteries can be accessed is, in fact, the lore that many *Africana* peoples consciously conceal. That eclectic and constantly evolving body of secret tradition is the source through which freedom, life, and hope in the Black Atlantic are both manifest and preserved.

PART 1

(Pre-) *19th Century*

∴

CHAPTER 1

Esoteric Writing of Vodou
Grimoires, Sigils, and the Houngan's Notebook

Yvonne Chireau and Mambo Vye Zo Kommande LaMenfo

Introduction

Jacmel, Haiti: Houngan Jean Vale was smoking hard and bent over, lost in thought. The lacey artwork on the floor was not done. Grunting, he crossed over to the row of rickety chairs and picked up a tattered notebook. The priest flipped through several pages until he found what he was looking for. Grunting again, he checked the page against the grainy patterns in cornmeal on the ground. Satisfied, he dropped the book onto the seat, and crossed back to survey his work. The piece was magnificent, spanning almost the entire room: a large heart edged in scalloped loops; twin snakes framed with stripes and wavy lines; a large palm tree, branched with feathery leaves and dots. Jean carefully scooped up another handful of cornmeal and traced further embellishments on the interior of the heart. A couple of extra flourishes, some final edge details, and the drawing was finished. The old man stood up, stretched, and called for rum. A bottle appeared, and he reverently saluted the four directions before spraying his creation with a fine mist.

"*Fini,*" he declared, and sat down to smoke yet another cigarette. I quietly moved to his side and pointed to the notebook.

"*Jean, mwen gade livre la?*" May I see the book? He smiled and proudly handed the worn journal to me. I flipped through pages filled with neat drawings in pen and pencil. There were dozens of *vèvès*, the sacred signs and figures of the Vodou religion. Beneath some were written prayers in a language I didn't recognize. I pointed one out to Jean and handed him the book back. He studied the writing, then looked at me again.

"I speak to the spirits. These are their words," he said. "Tomorrow I will teach you." And with that, he gathered his book, his ever-present cigarettes and departed. Jean Vale did not return the next day, and I never saw him again. But I remember that journal and recognized the treasures that it held. It was a magical notebook, a personal grimoire of *Vodou.*

LAMENFO/SCHEU, HAITI field notes, July 2003

© KONINKLIJKE BRILL NV, LEIDEN, 2015 | DOI 10.1163/9789004283428_003

A *houngan* creates and recreates the world using ritual practices and techniques to invoke spiritual forces. Such is the way of priests, magicians, and devotees on the paths of mystical knowledge and enlightenment the world over. Although universally conceived as tools of power and intellectual prestige, the use of writing and inscription is generally overlooked in studies of African American ritual, even as attention to scripture and sacred literatures is deemed critical by scholars of religion. Generally, research on Africana religions has focused on the *oral* aspects of religious expression, such as the vast repository of sacred songs, prayers, sayings and sermons that have given rise to the extraordinary spiritual legacy of black Atlantic cultures. However, an extensive variety of styles and forms of writing also occur within African American traditions. These include visionary- and spirit-writing, drawing, coding, and marking for purposes of divination, invocation, protection, creating inspirited objects, trance possession, and other performances of the body. In this essay we use *esotericism* as an organizing framework to discuss writing as a form of religious expression with symbols, signs, and embodied meanings in the ritual practices of the African-derived tradition known as Haitian *Vodou*.[1]

We approach this topic comparatively, using ethnography and history, in consideration of some tentative intriguing speculative relationships between religion and writing in Africana religions. Our sources include grimoires, journals, and occult notebooks, as well as original documentation of graphical regimens involving the translation of supernatural signs in Haitian *Vodou* and the Western mystery tradition known as *ceremonial magic*. Both traditions are predicated on longstanding occult practices, philosophical tenets, and metaphysical assumptions. Furthermore both are oriented toward pursuit of a divine connection or mystical enlightenment in which spiritual development and the inner quest for knowledge are paramount to the individual's journey. But some of the most explicit and interesting analogues between Vodou and Western magic practices center on writing practices. For not only is writing understood to be a vital technology of communication, but in both traditions writing is also considered an esoteric mode of symbolic representation.

---

1   We are indebted to recent investigations that place writing and reading at the fore of theorizing meaning in comparative religions, a phenomenon that Vincent Wimbush has called "scripturalizing" as an agenda for scholarly critical practice. See Wimbush, *Theorizing Scriptures: New Critical Orientations to a Cultural Phenomenon*, 2008; see also William Graham, *Beyond the Written Word: Oral Aspects of Scripture in the History of Religion*, 1987. On the use of alternate scripts and literacies in African American traditions see especially Gray Gundaker, *Signs of Diaspora, Diaspora of Signs: Literacies, Creolization, and Vernacular Practice in African America*, 1998.

The intersections and overlaps of these practices are discussed below, with a specific emphasis on *vèvès* in Haitian Vodou and sigils in ceremonial magic, and the creative processes by which sacred formulations and figurations are ritually inscribed. We consider these practices, along with practitioners' journals, notebooks, and grimoires, to comprise a distinct body of esoteric literature that demands further explication and analysis (On vèvè, see Clark, 1991; Brown, 1976; Rigaud, 1974; on Vodou and magic, see Cosentino, 1995; McAlister, 1995; Rigaud, 1953).

In situating Haitian Vodou and western ceremonial magic within the framework of *esotericism*, our investigation, though preliminary, has implications for the general study of religion in the black Atlantic world. A critical analysis of esoteric writing (and reading) practices can reorient scholars' acquiescence to discourses that conceive of the dominant European and European-American modes of literacy as exemplary markers of civilization – a value, we believe, that is not shared or embraced universally by practitioners in African American traditions. The tendency to relegate African and African-American styles of expression into fixed categories, such as "oral" or "spoken," can obscure the presence of alternative modes of communication, knowledge transmission, and literacy in these traditions. Furthermore, the hierarchical assumptions implied in the use of these categories constitute what Grey Gundaker has called "ideologies of literacy," which, when unexamined, affix a kind of primacy to dichotomies that privilege the "literate" against the "illiterate" (Gundaker, 1998). Consideration of the ways, historically, that African and African American religions have defined, engaged, and performed writing in ritual contexts allows us to destabilize essentialist notions of a natural, categorical nexus between Africana religions and a static "orality" that serves as the primary vehicle for spiritual expression in these traditions. Unearthing and investigating esoteric and occult forms of writing in Africana religions allows scholars to reframe the classifications of "oral" versus "written" as reciprocal expressions of meaning that utilize the mechanisms of literacy, yet do so by unconventional means. New insights on writing practices in Africana religious traditions can greatly enhance understandings of ritual, spiritual communication, and the vernacular literacies that form and articulate theological and metaphysical concepts, particularly those that develop and flourish in marginalized communities.[2]

---

2 Attainment of conventional literacy, of course, is a prominent theme throughout African American narratives of the diaspora, a source of shared identity, equality, freedom, and social advancement. In Atlantic world colonial contexts, anti-literacy was a weapon of oppression, as well as an enduring ideological condition under which oppressed peoples suffered.

Vodou, Western Magic, and Esotericism

Haitian Vodou is a religion with multiple influences that reach broadly across time and place. Like other African-derived religions, Vodou is the product of sustained encounters between Africans, Native/indigenous Americans, and Europeans that began as early as the 16th century. These encounters were shaped by historical circumstances, most notably, colonization, the institution of slavery, and the twelve-year war of independence that resulted in Haiti's unique status as the first free black republic in the western hemisphere. In Haiti, interactions between diverse peoples led to the ongoing processes of adaptation, transformation, and assimilation of a wide variety of ideas, experiences and practices. These processes, culminating in what scholars have called the *creolization* of New World societies and cultures, were nowhere seen and felt more strongly in Haiti than in the realm of religion (Bellgarde-Smith and Michel, 2006; Edmonds and Gonzalez, 2010; Braithwaite and Glissant, 2000).

While much scholarship on New World and African-African religions has examined the appropriation of western religions and theologies by Africans under slavery, studies have also highlighted the persistence of pre-colonial or indigenous cultural expressions and artifacts by which sacred knowledge and ritual practice was preserved (Edmonds, 2010; Murrell, 2009; Thompson, 1984). Scholars view the development of New World religions as the dynamic products of contacts between cultures that were forged by conflict and negotiation in an Atlantic world arena, in which Africans, Europeans and others participated in the creation of hybridized forms and styles. This complex weaving of multiple cultural strands is amply demonstrated in the religion of Haitian Vodou:

> Although the African is deep and prominent, Vodou also combines elements from the colonial plantation era into its *bricolage*. The plantation owners were French, Spanish and Dutch, and came out of a time when the Enlightenment was just beginning to make its mark in thinking,

---

In Haiti, literacy was severely proscribed during the formative eras of colonization and slavery, and magical and esoteric literacy was suppressed by the Catholic church and the government in periodic denunciations of "unauthorized practices" such as Vodou. In these recurrent periods of iconoclastic destruction it is likely that untold numbers of magical journals and notebooks were destroyed, resulting in what has been called an "irreparable loss" to Haitian national culture, to the detriment of the historical record. On suppression of African American literacy, see Janet Cornelius, *When I Can Read My Title Clear 1992*, 1991; on *dechoukaj* and Vodou suppression, see Sidney Mintz and Michel-Rolph Trouillot, "The Social History of Haitian Vodou," in Donald Cosentino, *Sacred Arts of Haitian Vodou*, (1995, 142–147).

in science, and in mystical practices such as Kabala. Catholicism added its own touches through the synchronicity of Catholic hagiography... British sailing lore lent the use of model ships and colorful flags...the occultism of European Masonry, the mysticism of the Spanish Cabalists and European folk practices....all seasoned the brew that became modern day Vodou.

LA MENFO 2011: 15

Writing is fundamental to both ceremonial magic and Haitian Vodou practice. Both traditions utilize different forms of writing to mark the starting point for narrations, encounters, and transmission of information. Both use writing to keep an account of proceedings of the work; and both hold to the idea that the physical inscription of the magical call is the principal action to be taken in invoking spirits to be present. *Esoteric writing* is the name that might be given to the discipline as it is employed through the use of sigils, or the drawing of pentagrams, or inscribing the quarters during a ceremonial service. In some cases, the writing might be purely figurative, such as the marking the crossroads in the air by the *LaPlas* (a Vodou ritual assistant) with his machete. Esoteric writing might also encompass the gestures of consecration by the Magus over water in the ceremonial work or in concert with vibrational energies, or with the houngan, who with his *asson* (sacred rattle) blesses the altars and drums during the advent of a Vodou ritual. In both traditions, esoteric writing can also be interpreted geometrically, transformed into three-dimensional symbolism by which one creates a "temple not made with hands." The culmination of the ritual process of esoteric writing is the arrival of "the mysteries" or spirit forces into the ritual space, which has been set, purified and created for sacred manifestation. Esoteric writing is therefore a primary method of engaging metaphysical energies through ritual performance (Kubick 1986, Krippner 1997).

Like Vodou, Western ceremonial magic has a long and verifiable history. The "golden age" of magic began with the period of the Renaissance, with scholars such as Marsilio Ficino (1433–1449), who disseminated the *Corpus Hermeticum* of ancient Egyptian religion; Pico della Mirandola (1463–1494), who did the same for the Hebrew Qabbalah, joining it with Hermeticism; and Henry Cornelius Agrippa (1486–1535), who combined the threads in his *Three Books of Occult Philosophy* (vonNettesheim, 1992). Renaissance practitioners understood magic both as a philosophy and science of the natural order of the world and as a spiritual tradition. These men utilized *theurgy*, also known as the "good work." Golden Dawn adept Chic Cicero describes *theurgy* as the practice of elevating one's soul toward heaven by communicating with the various levels of deity. The historian Ioan Culianu viewed Ficino's theurgy as intersubjective, "meant to direct spiritual influence upon the subject himself," by which the magus "could obtain a clean, elastic and firm spirit, which would open to him the gates of superior contemplation" (Cicero, 2003; Culianu, 1985). Glossed as the "art of calling something other to oneself," evocation is understood to be at the heart of theurgic performance (Bardon, 1970; Butler, 2001). The presumed ability of magicians to summon forth a Being that can move through time and space was based upon a practice that incorporated observation and detailed record keeping for its replication and continued success. Hence the emphasis upon writing as a powerful and essential technology that allowed for continuity, documentation and preservation of magical protocols under most conditions and in all environments (Lindberg, 1992).

One might say that physical books themselves are artifacts of magical power in a ritual context, even as they contain and reveal magical knowledge. British occultist William Gray states that in order to truly create a proper evocation, one must have copiously detailed notes in a "black book of magic." And Richard Kieckhefer writes, "a book of magic is *a magical book.*" This corresponds with the idea of text-as-magical artifact that underscores many African and African-American cultural traditions, especially in the use of books and literature for religious and supernatural mediation between the material and the spiritual worlds (Gray, 1980; Kieckhefer, 1998; Smith, 1995).

Despite the suppression of literacy in various periods of its history, books and literature flowed into Haiti in clandestine streams in the middle passage, facilitated by plantation owners, priests, sailors, and African slaves themselves. As Le Grace Benson notes:

> Qur'an and Bible traveled on the ships bound from Africa to St. Domingue. So did tracts of the European Enlightenment; copies of the *Declaration of the Rights of Man*; abolitionist letters from the Abbot Gregoire; Christian catechisms; grimoires full of instructions for magic rituals to insure love, good fortune, and victory. This print material was spare and simple compared to the complex intellectual environment carried around the minds of the people on board.
>
> BENSON 2006, 155

Because reading and writing were seen as exceptional technologies of power, multiple literacies – including oral, musical, and physically enacted forms of expression – became prevalent styles of communication for Africans in the New World, including practitioners of Haitian Vodou. The extraordinary value given to writing remained a constant in the magical world across cultures.

Be they seals, talismans, spirit writing, cosmographs, mystical scripts or gylphs, the rich variety by which esoteric writing has been utilized presages powerful human interactions with mystical, otherworldly, and transcendent forces (Gundaker, 1998; Thompson, 1978; Mullen, 1996; Flint, 1991; Fanger, 1998; Meyer and Mirecki, 1995).

Human-spirit interaction, or evocation, is at the heart of esoteric writing in most magical systems. Both Vodou and western ceremonial work employed esoteric writing with special materials; both used invocation to enliven the ritual; and both utilized consistent methods for engaging the spirit realm. Parallels in style and intent can be seen in the use of *vèvès* and sigils. The drawing and methodology of *vèvès* in Haitian Vodou, for example, is virtually identical to that of sigil writing in the western ceremonial tradition. A brief examination of the origins, functions and contexts of use for *vèvès* and sigils follows, with an emphasis on their use in evocation and consecration, further demonstrating the underlying intersections of Vodou and western ceremonial traditions of magic.

Vèvès, Sigils and Esoteric Writing

Vèvès are ideographic signs or blazons that serve as the core graphic symbols in the religion of Vodou. Created in slave-era Haiti, vèvès descend conceptually from the cultural and religious orientations of West and Central Africa while utilizing the representational styles and visual traditions of indigenous America and Europe. Like all Vodou art creations, they are the products of improvisation, appropriation, and innovation. "Fragments of Africa, certainly," notes anthropologist Donald Cosentino, "but also bits and pieces from the Taino, from Celtic and Enlightenment France, from the Jesuits and the Masons," as well as other roots. Arguably, the vèvès reveal a multiplicity of sources. Art historian Robert Farris-Thompson maintains that vèvès were adopted directly from Kongo ground drawing traditions, while the scholars Rachel Dominique-Beauvoir and Patrick Bellegarde-Smith have both alluded to a lineage that includes esoteric writing systems from Hinduism and native Taino Indians (Thompson 1984; Dominique-Beauvoir 2007; Bellegarde-Smith, 2005; Cosentino, 1995).

Like the vèvè, the ceremonial sigil in the western magical tradition is a graphic statement of intent. The most popular sigils derive from the *Lesser Key of Solomon*, a collection of images and evocations that tradition ascribes to the legendary king of Israel for the building of his spectacular holy temple (Peterson, 2001). Solomonic practitioners put a tremendous amount of care and preparation into their sigil work. Along with special materials such as virgin parchment and special color inks, sigils are written during specific hours of the day relating to their final usage, as well as being consecrated in specific incenses and perfumes. A sigil to the god Mercury, for instance, written in green ink during the hour of Mercury, on Mercury's day, is considered far more efficacious than something jotted down in the moment of need. Sigils can be worn on the body as amulets, placed on the altar as a plate or a working surface, or cast in precious metals for continual usage. The material of sigils could be adapted so as to be both temporary as well as long-lasting. For example, sigils could be made for a single act of magic or for a longer working that might involve many days of concentrated evocation. The desired result directed the length of time that a sigil was employed. The intent of the sigil is its true power (Frater, 1990).

Vèvès in Haitian Vodou are also conduits of intent. The rationale behind *vèvè* drawing is to call forth the energy corresponding with a specific lwa (the divine beings of the Vodou religion) in order to bring forth its presence, and, a desired result. In both cases (vèvès and esoteric sigils) the act of writing the symbol is the same as speaking the title of the spirit out loud. To evoke the spirit one only need know its name and its sign to capture the mystery; but *vèvè* are not simply drawn. *Vèvè* are traced, an allusion to their mystical property as the insignia of the lwa. Lwa are believed to exist on the astral plane, waiting for the Vodou practitioner to awaken their latent power by tracing them out upon the earthly realms in profane space. Created as a focal point for practitioners, vèvès offer a unified view of intent for everyone present at a Vodou service and function as doorways to realms within the mind and heart of practitioners. Undertaken with skill and devotion by their designers, the elaborate drawings also contain hidden messages for the assembled crowd to interpret and express through the songs sung and the prayers offered (Brown, 1976).

> *New Orleans, Louisiana*: Houngan Edgar carried a tin plate through the crowded kitchen with a slow gracefulness born of living in cramped quarters. Someone placed a chair for him and he folded himself into a small figure. His fingers distractedly stirred the yellow cornmeal in the plate as he studied the floor. With a steady hand, he began to trace grainy snakes and a fancy heart. Turning his wrist, he drizzled spirals and whorls, stars and dots, transforming the clean floor into an astrological drama. The beings *Danbala* and *Aida Wedo* rose in dual curves above an ornate heart with a large "M" in the center. The image was accented with stars and more curves, flairs, and lines. At last pleased with his work, Edgar put down the plate and reached for the bottle. He stood up and dropped three dashes of rum

around the piece. Nodding, he handed off the bottle, called for his asson, and sat down. The *vèvè* was thus consecrated and service could begin.

LAMENFO/SCHEU, New Orleans field notes, July 2004

The *Notary Arts* of sigil writing, a major component of Western ceremonial work, parallels the tracing out of vèvè at the beginning of a Vodou service. The very act of drawing the sigil is to "speak" to the angel that the sigil represents. The ceremonial sigil must be carefully sketched out in single strokes, the paper held a specific way so as not to actually touch the sigil itself. It is noteworthy that each *vèvè* begins the same way – with a lateral line drizzled out with *fleur ginen* between the fingers. *Fleur ginen* is a special mixture of cornmeal and herbs dedicated to the particular mystery associated with the vèvè. When it comes time to make additional lines, the priest must move carefully around the design, drawing clockwise to create a mirror image, taking extreme care to avoid any line that has been traced out already. Thus the vèvè develops into the structure of a Cartesian grid, from "two mutually bisecting lines" that function as "the gestalt of the crossroads" (Brown, 1975). Around and around the priestly artist works, bent from the waist, a pan of *fleur ginen* in one hand, the other tracing the lwa's signature. When the *vèvè* is completed, the priest also salutes the directions, using his own body to ground the tracing into temporal space. Similarly, when a ceremonial sigil is completed, it is saluted to the four directions of the temple. Both gestures, by the ceremonialist and Vodousant, add an extra push of energy to "ignite" the sign on the astral planes. At the proper time in a ceremonial magic ritual the magus will reveal the sigil by uncovering it, and then consecrating it by passing it through smoking incense or holding it above a candle flame, while in a Vodou ceremony or ritual, the *vèvè* is sanctified by the priest by blowing rum over it. The houngan or mambo will then call the congregation up to press their thumbs into the vèvè, thus impressing their own energy into the emblem. Accordingly, at the conclusion of the ceremonial working, the sigil is either covered and put away for future work or destroyed to release the angelic entity called forth by it. Ultimately in a Vodou service, the *vèvè* will be danced upon, the participants' feet scattering the energy of the drawing, thereby releasing the lwa from their earthly call sign.

As in Vodou, visual language is a central component of ceremonial work in the Western magical tradition. The Golden Dawn, for example, utilizes a series of twelve signs for their Lesser Banishing Pentagram, the quintessential ritual of invocation and consecration of a sacred circle: six to open the quarter directions of a ceremony and six to close them. These ceremonial signs are intended to help consecrate the space, align the work with the higher intent of the magician, and invoke the angels to come down and participate in the service

(Greer, 1999; Cicero, 1979). Consecration is literally defined as "to associate with the sacred." Consecration in ceremonial magical work is accomplished by signing the figure of a cross over an object, in a space, or on a person. In Vodou, it is much the same, with an equal arm traverse signed over the item or in the space. A houngan might use a piece of ginger leaf or some other sprig dipped into water before making the sign of the cross in blessing (This is a parallel practice to the holy aspergillum of Solomonic fame or the sprinkler of the Bible made from hyssop, as noted in the biblical Psalm 51). Having gathered the necessary components, the ceremonialist physically arranges his materials. These same paradigms are played out in Vodou work as well. The houngan or mambo will lift their bowl of *fleur ginen* to align it with the mythic cosmos in which they stand centered. To consecrate the physical space, the Vodou priests perform the *vire,* a ritualized set of turns and dips before the four directions. In ceremonial work, consecrating space is known as "calling quarters," an act performed before each direction. Each of the four directions is assigned an attribute, traditionally established through trial and error, which has a specific pattern that can be invoked. Each attribute has a specific pentagram that represents that energetic pattern. Each time the magus draws those pentagrams, the energy in the room shifts, as the action of his hand performing the pentagram creates a charge of energy in the space. In a Vodou service, the physical act of saluting the quarters is done in much the same way:

> *Belair, Haiti*: I watched Houngan Edgar each time as he consecrated a vèvè or set a candle on the pe. First, he would do the *vire*, the ritual gesture that orients the body into consecrated space, holding a candle in one hand and a cup of water in the other. Genuflecting at the poto mitan, he would move to the doors, the altars and the drums, marking a cross as he did so. With a slight dip of his legs, he turned counter-clockwise, crossing his left hand over his right. He'd then turn back to the right, repeating the transverse. Then, once more, to the left, each rotation smooth, ending with a slight bow. When he was completed, Edgar placed the water container on the ground and knelt down. Gently touching the earth, he slowly bent down and kissed the back of his hand: *we come from the earth and to it we will return in death.* Next, he would pick up the water, and again, perform the *vire* to complete the salute. Three turns, a kiss on the ground, three turns again, each punctuated by the crossed arms. The houngan then called for his asson and sat down. Reverently, deliberately, he drew a cross over the vèvè and then motioned for us all to sit. He began to speak the ancient words that commenced the Priye and we bowed our heads, softly answering him in response. This little sacred dance of flame

and water would be performed again and again as we sang for each lwa; sang for the vèvès as they were drawn; and sang for the Spirits as they made themselves known throughout the night.

LAMENFO/SCHEU, HAITI field notes, July 2006

As noted by the Robert Farris Thompson, *vèvès* in Haitian Vodou are permanently displayed on walls, houses and other spaces as protective guardian signs that re-appropriate sites as "spiritualized minefields," marking physical places as mystically powerful and dangerous (Thompson, 1984). *Drapo* or Vodou flags adorned with vèvè, can be seen as analogous to temple decorations in the ceremonial tradition, like those those of the neophyte banners in the Golden Dawn, or the lodge banners featured in the ritual settings of the Servants of the Light. The lotus cup from the Golden Dawn tradition is inscribed with angelic sigils, similar to the pentacle in the Servants of Light, which is marked by Qabbalistic symbols, designated according to the scripts and languages of spiritual representation. These esoteric writings are meant to further enhance, uplift and mobilize the work each item performs within a ritual space (Cicero, 2003; Ashcroft-Nowicki, 1984).

Finally, there is a consistent *"mystery"* in Vodou ritualism contained within the tracing of vèvès and the drawing of signs. The esoteric writing of a Vodou ceremony entails creating a metaphoric image of the lwa or angels themselves. Each element of a vèvè narrates a story. Ayizan's vèvè, for instance, displays both her initials with its inverted A and V, as well as forming the palm frond, which bears witness to her earthly symbol in nature. Ogoun's military origin is displayed in the triangle base of the Nago vèvès, with their flying pennants and the crossbar of the forge at the top of the illustration. Each lwa is also signified with pictorial and abstract stylizations. The vèvè, then, becomes something of a personal signature of the spirits that is placed in direct visual communion with their servitors. In both Vodou and ceremonial magic, mythological and esoteric narratives are not only represented by lines and circles – drawn either in cornmeal on the dirt floor or with ink upon a piece of parchment – but in their very presentation, they hold the key to calling for the *mysteries* to enter into the mundane world.

Jacmel, Haiti: Houngan Jean Vale reaches far across the ground as the tambor pounds out a great drum rhythm, accompanied by the voices of the congregation. He is drawing Ayizan's *vèvè*, assisted by two men holding candles and pans of fleur ginen. Jean lays down large, long lines, in the shape of two intersecting V's. Off the main lateral line, he runs several short stripes, the design resembling the huge fronds of a palm tree.

He surrounds these markings with dots, eight-armed stars, and swirls aside the main letter formation. Urgently, the voices of the crowd rise with the drums as one of the elderly mambos begins to show signs of possession. Two chairs are quickly placed over the completed vèvè and a large white sheet is draped over the entire arrangement, with four candles placed beneath. Lit in this way the covered seats billow like a large luminary, and the effect is that of a royal throne that glows from within. Suddenly, the mambo seizes a shredded bundle of palm leaves and briskly sweeps them past the vèvè and chairs, spreading them out over the back of the luminary throne. Ayizan has arrived! The priests move forward to mark the vèvè, but do so privately as the mambos spread their skirts around them, shielding their work from profane eyes. After Ayizan's vèvè is consecrated, she moves to the djevo for further blessings.

LAMENFO/SCHEU, HAITI field notes, July 2003

Notebooks, Grimoires and Magic Books

Sigils and vèvès are embedded in a venerable tradition of esoteric writing that is shared by western ceremonial magic and Haitian Vodou. To call forth an angel in ceremonial magic, the adept gathers together virgin parchment and consecrated ink. To summon the lwa in Haiti Vodou, the servitor sweeps a section of the peristyle's earthen floor smooth and gathers fleur ginen, a special mixture of flour and other ingredients. A knowledgeable Vodou priest will have the individualized formulae written out in his personal notebook, along with diagrams and instructions on how to trace the vèvè for a particular spirit. The journal or notebook of the houngan is filled with ceremonial details that have much in common with the European practice. And the organization and methodology of the houngan's notebook, filled with vèvè and *langaj* prayers, is not unlike that of the grimoire, the ceremonial magician's literary resource par excellent (Cosentino, 1995; Brown, 1976).

In focusing upon the esoteric significance of the "book," one cannot overstate the importance of the grimoire. The word "grimoire," derived from the French "grammaire," originally referred to a work of Latin that was legible only to those with access to arcane religious knowledge. In Europe, these texts would become infamous through their popular associations with alchemists and practitioners of the black arts. By the eighteenth century, the term "grimoire" was widely used to refer to any collection of occult writings. These texts were made more widely available through the advent of the printing press in the sixteenth century and the ease of paper reproductions. Considered a true danger by the Catholic Church, grimoires were notorious for containing demonic knowledge and dangerous spiritual *maleficium*. It is suggested that their real purpose, however, was to create a record of private occult information available only to adepts and initiates.[3]

The classic grimoire is a magical book for beginners. The most popular among English-speaking occultists, the *Key of Solomon*, was a register for helping a practitioner to understand the greater mysteries of a celestial nature. It was not, however, a recipe book with formulas for everyday use. Grimoires were the means and method of calling forth and binding one's personal Guardian Angel. In this sense, the work adopted from a grimoire was performed to help the practitioner align herself with a higher consciousness. Such instructions were readily available to help the petitioner achieve magical skill, to acquire health and power, and to coerce Goetic entities so as to engage them for advice and consolation (Meyer and Smith, 1994). Following a grimoire's formula of invocation meant bonding with an angel for life, similar to the Vodou ceremony of *maraj lwa* or the kanzo ceremony of initiation. The materials used are special, hard to obtain and never used for mundane writing. As Elizabeth Butler has said about the materials called for in papyri of antiquity, the instructions are not difficult to follow but they are frequently demanding of both mental and physical efforts on the part of the practitioner (Butler, 2001). The obscure language, scripts, and arcane materials contained within the grimoire may have been little more than old language blinds to keep the less than faithful from fulfilling their commitment to the works contained within the book. Still, a dedicated seeker would find hidden treasures if willing to follow the instructions with a pure intent. As noted by magic historian John Michael Greer, "if evocation is defined as something you perceive, the invocation is something you become" (Greer, 1997).

This open perspective on the grimoires stands in opposition to their less obvious usage – the acquisition of conscious communion with the highest possible aspect of oneself. Initiates in the ceremonial magical traditions have inferred that this communion might be obtained through spirit manifestation or what is also known as *spirit conjuring*. Contemporary adepts of magic generally understand that the grimoires offer methods for invoking spirit entities into manifestation. But few realize they held the formula for invoking and "marrying" one's own guardian entity, what is called the Holy Guardian Angel. Spirit conjuring, of course, is a ubiquitous practice in New World African religions as diverse as Vodou in Haiti, Lucumi in Cuba, Quimbanda in Brazil, and

---

3   Although grimoires contained numerous charms and rituals that had been passed along orally, they would ultimately become repositories of knowledge that could not be entrusted to oral forms, due to the corruptible nature of spoken secrets. See Alan Leitch, Secrets of the Grimoires, 2005.

many forms of revivalist Christianity. In all of these religions, in varying modes, the invocation of spiritual powers serves as the focal point of community service and ritualizing. Particularly in the African-based traditions, the idea of fostering human-spirit interdependence by "making" the spirit – what scholar Joseph Murphy calls "a spirituality of incarnation" – stands at the heart of personal and group practices (Murphy, 1988).

Likewise, in western magic, it is expected that one would work toward having knowledge and conversation of their Holy Guardian Angel (resignified as the *met tet* or "master of the head" in Vodou). The practices of consecration, invocation and evocation are the proven methods for reaching that goal. Similarly, if a Vodou ceremony is successful in calling forth the lwa, then one expects to speak directly to the lwa invoked. Here, the combined protocols of prayer, songs, movements, vèvès, and drumbeats are the most proven and efficacious procedures for bringing heaven down to earth (Clark, 1983; Brown, 1976; Thompson, 1984).

As the religious practices of persons of African descent merge worldwide emerge with greater visibility, some European magicians have begun to reflect upon the shared idioms and parallel structures between their traditions, in order to elucidate their own work within both temple and text. Solomonic occultist Aaron Leitch, for example, has used Afro-Cuban *Lucumi* as a model for understanding the methodology employed in the grimoires of Europe, concluding that the true application of grimoires was for the mage to establish regular contact with beings that might relate to a devoted practitioner, as with *orisha* worship practices in the New World. British necromancer Jake Stratton-Kent discovered many similarities between the Afro-Brazilian tradition of Quimbanda and the *Grimorium Vernum*, a controversial text of demonic ritual magic (Leitch, 2005; Stratton-Kent, 2010). In other instances, contemporary ceremonial magicians have found that the roots of the African-American religions reflect deep streams of esotericism that run through the rituals, thought, and material cultures of indigenous traditions. Students, scholars and practitioners have thus turned to African and African-American faiths to help to illuminate the obscure meanings of their own practices, sometimes placing the traditions in conversation with each other and creating interpretive models and methodological paradigms that embrace the ancient traditions as valid and credible resources in a newer context. In doing so, they have found that esoteric currents in African derived religions can help them to achieve an acceptance of the greater, transcendent truths to be mined within their own traditions, thereby solidifying a bridge of understanding between the two.

CHAPTER 2

Paschal Beverly Randolph in the African American Community

Lana Finley

Introduction

Because I happen to differ from the Boston standard, I am, forsooth, everything that is bad!...Yet whenever opportunities occur, in or out of the pulpit, I shall be found doing still in my own quiet way for the race whose blood, as well as that of the Anglo Saxon, fills my heart.

   – P.B. RANDOLPH, 1858 (RANDOLPH 1858)

How often do we look in wonder at the course of other men's lives, whose paths have diverged so widely from the beaten track of our own, that, unable to comprehend the one spring upon which, perhaps, the whole secret of the diversity hinged, we have been fain to content ourselves with summing up our judgment in the common phrase, 'Well, it's very strange; what odd people there are in the world to be sure!'

   – PAULINE HOPKINS, 1903 (HOPKINS 2004, 37)

Texts, Contexts, and Canonicity

Paschal Beverly Randolph (1825–1875) is one of America's most important occultists, and he is *the* foundational figure of African American esotericism. That Randolph did not primarily minister to the African American community should not preclude historians from ascribing to him such an exceptional title. This essay argues that Randolph was a controversial African American celebrity whose legacy was not preserved by the black community on account of his radical spiritual beliefs and questionable racial politics. While Randolph proved heavily influential on such white occultists as H.P. Blavatsky, Aleister Crowley, and R. Swinburne Clymer, his visionary genius would seem to have had no memorialist in the late nineteenth or early twentieth century black communities. However, a 1903 novel by Pauline Hopkins pays tacit homage to Randolph, thereby contradicting the assumption that Randolph's occult career

© KONINKLIJKE BRILL NV, LEIDEN, 2015 | DOI 10.1163/9789004283428_004

made no impression on his African American peers. Hopkins (1859–1930), an accomplished African American writer and editor, honors Randolph's particular spiritual innovations in *Of One Blood*, a text which claims that ancient Africa is the wellspring of all occult arts.

Little known today, P.B. Randolph was that rarest of beings: a man who consistently saw and lived beyond the limitations imposed on him by his times. His impressive erudition shines through the forty-five publications he is known to have authored, and he was a popular orator in Spiritualist circles. Randolph was one of a small number of nineteenth century African Americans to travel independently overseas, first to Europe as an emissary of Spiritualism, and then to the Middle East to learn the occult secrets of Egypt and Syria, in imitation of the fabled Christian Rosenkreutz. He was an unabashed proponent of women's sexual rights, and it was Randolph who ushered in the New Age in advance of the pugnacious H.P. Blavatsky, by articulating the transition from passive to active mediumship in the spiritual sub-culture. Randolph accomplished all this during an age when the color of his skin was thought to render him intellectually stunted, morally degraded, or otherwise inferior. It is no wonder that P.B. Randolph has acquired a superhuman status among the occult groups that lionize him; that he largely avoided the violence and persecution perpetrated on black bodies that dared to defy their lot of second-class citizenship, is in many ways miraculous.

Because Randolph's status as an occult innovator has been well-documented in the biography by John Patrick Deveney (Deveney 1997), I focus my attention here on Randolph's lesser-known activity as a "race man." Randolph may have been consternating and contradictory on the subject of race, but that he advocated for black emancipation and spoke out against racial oppression both before and after the Civil War are facts too often neglected in his biography. Establishing Randolph as a celebrated African American orator, one known to both the abolitionist and Spiritualist communities whose memberships frequently overlapped, can mitigate the perception that he somehow evaded identification, and involvement, with others of his race. To be sure, Randolph offended both black and white abolitionists by endorsing a gradualist approach to slavery's end at an 1858 Philanthropic Convention in Utica. He also constructed his own fantastic racial identity, claiming at times to have seven different bloodlines running through his veins, while denying that any of these were black (Randolph 1939, 72). Such assertions do not accord with our current ethic of political correctness, nor did they suit the nineteenth century emphasis on racial solidarity as the surest road to racial uplift. Yet Randolph is the same man who, as a youth, wrote to prominent white abolitionists in inquiry of how he might use his considerable talents to best serve his race. As a middle-aged man, he moved to Louisiana on behalf of the Freedmen's Bureau, where he ran a school for newly freed slaves. These tensions in Randolph's biography do not reveal a man who forsook his identity and his community, but, rather, suggest that he vacillated between placing his hope in political (and inevitably materialist) solutions for transforming the world around him, and putting his faith in transcendental ideas as a means of circumventing an omnipresent oppression.

My own interest in Randolph is framed by my studies in nineteenth century American literature. The first African American novels appeared around the mid-point of the nineteenth century, that period dubbed the "American Renaissance" for giving us such classics as Melville's *Moby-Dick*, Hawthorne's *Scarlet Letter*, and Whitman's *Leaves of Grass*. Though Randolph's two novels of 1863, *Tom Clark and His Wife* and *The Wonderful Story of Ravalette*, qualify as the fifth and sixth African American novels ever published, and only the third and fourth to be published in the United States, no critical study of early black literature has ever included Randolph's works (for a standard chronology, see Bell 2004, 95–96). This neglect of a talented black author is rendered all the more noteworthy by the fact that there seems to be a growing cultural hunger for early fictional works by African Americans. For instance, in 2002 Henry Louis Gates, Jr. created a bestseller out of a rediscovered African American manuscript, *The Bondswoman's Narrative*, by Hannah Crafts. Though no authoritative editions of Randolph's novels have been published, *Ravalette*, at least, is available to read in facsimile format. The failure of literary scholars to embrace Randolph as a relevant voice in African American letters points to a willful cultural blindness which has held sway since the nineteenth century.

In the eras of Civil War and Reconstruction, leaders in the African American community worked to define themselves and their race in opposition to the prevalent stereotype of black people as bestial and unrefined. Randolph's enthusiasm for florid occult mysteries and his endorsement of a robust sexuality flew in the face of their enforced allegiance to Victorian propriety. While the promotion of Christian mores by nineteenth century black leaders executed a necessary political function in the battle for civic equality, now, 150 years since *Ravalette's* initial publication, it seems high time to lift the taboos which have prevented Randolph from receiving his due as an impressive and foundational figure in African American letters.

Let it not be imagined that *Ravalette* (a more crafted and complex work than Randolph's other extant novel, *Tom Clark and His Wife*) has been excluded from the canon of African American literature on the basis that it is lacking in style or quality. Of the four African American novels which precede it, *Ravalette* is the most ornate and erudite. *Ravalette* is certainly the first work of science fiction by an African American author, and that it is partly autobiographical does not bar it from inclusion in the canon. Harriet Wilson's *Our Nig* (1859), the first novel published by an African American woman, also blends the genres of fiction and autobiography (Wilson 2009). *Ravalette's* bizarre subject matter constitutes its only deterrent to a wide readership, then as now; the story of a man's quest to wed a pre-Adamite woman in order to undo an ancient curse, a quest which forces him to untangle the various transmutations of a dueling vampire and the real identity of the Rosicrucian, can hardly be claimed as hallmarks of nineteenth century black experience. The critical disregard for *Ravalette* articulates a bias in the African American literary canon which has survived in some form to our own day: novels which thematize racial injustice and call for social reform are lauded and claimed as high literature, while more imaginative works by African American authors escape notice for failing to conform to an obligatory – and uniform – political consciousness.

Reclaiming P.B. Randolph's place in American letters does more than simply add to our growing knowledge of nineteenth century black authors. Randolph's occult presence amongst the predominantly Christian collective of writers upsets the whole terrain. We may install Randolph as the literary forebear to writers like Zora Neale Hurston and Ishmael Reed, African American authors who alike celebrated esoteric religious practices and a full-bodied sexuality, to the disdain of their more politically-minded peers. More broadly, reviving Randolph's literary legacy serves to awaken consciousness of a minor but never-the-less persistent genre which has traversed centuries of Western literature: that of the occult novel. To date, more scholars in religion than in literature are sympathetic to this phenomenon, which refers to fiction's power to provoke personal gnosis. In *Restoring Paradise*, Arthur Versluis argues that esoteric initiation in the West has been effected more often through a text than through a teacher (Versluis 2004, 12). Jeffrey Kripal has developed the idea of fiction's primacy in religious experience, claiming that the paranormal always has a narrative dimension and that texts, in turn, can engender mystical revelations which transcend the content of the book being read (Kripal 2010, 26). Here he describes how the act of reading may function as a vehicle to gnosis:

> We need to recognize that the act of reading, far from being a mechanical, disembodied exercise of vocabulary and grammar, is in fact an immeasurably complex psychophysical event in which two horizons of meaning and being (the reader and the read) are "fused" and transfigured in a mysterious process that we do not, and perhaps cannot ever, fully understand.
>
> KRIPAL 2008, 61

Paschal Beverly Randolph's novel *Ravalette* reads perfectly well as a piece of science fiction; the implication that it is also the man's autobiography is far more unsettling. A book which blurs not only genres but the line between fantasy and reality, human and god, is a dangerous text indeed. Critics attempting to understand Randolph's banishment to the literary hinterland should not fail to take into account the gnostic risks such reading entails.

Paschal Beverly Randolph in the African American Community

What follows here is a consideration of Randolph's involvement with the African American community, a background intended to serve as counterpoint to portraits of the man which martyr him as the beleaguered prophet of the New Age, or alternately denigrate him as a hapless huckster who fell victim to the worst delusions of his era. In this endeavor I am somewhat answering the call put forth by Scott Trafton in *Egypt Land*: "The only major scholarly work on Randolph places him almost exclusively in the context of white colleagues, peers, and enemies...but it makes equal sense to place him in a context of mostly black intellectuals working from within the spaces of Egyptology, ethnology, and abolitionist activism" (Trafton 2004, 28). Randolph was born in New York City in 1825, the son of a white father and black mother. His father took no hand in raising him, and his mother died when he was only five. For a time he was cared for by his half-sister Harriet, but while still a child he joined an ad hoc family made up of a prostitute and her boyfriend, and was forced to beg his supper from the streets (Deveney 1997, 1–3). It is something of a myth that Northern free blacks enjoyed a better quality of life than Southern slaves. The Five Points ghetto where Randolph grew up was the most dangerous place in the city, and in 1834, race riots erupted among the immigrant Irish and free blacks who crowded its unwholesome tenements (Harris 1999, 195–199).

Randolph received no more than two years of formal education, and in the 1840s he relocated to Portland, Maine, where he learned the trades of barber and dyer (Deveney 1997, 4–8, note on 376). But apparently it was the job of cabin boy which enabled him to escape the pressure-cooker of Five Points. Randolph's entree into print dates to 1846, when he placed this advertisement for a "New Work" in William Lloyd Garrison's abolitionist newspaper, *The Liberator*: "Now in press, and soon to be published, an original work entitled Beverly Randolph, or Life in the Galley, by P.B. Randolph. Its object is to show the many hardships suffered by sea cooks and stewards, a profession which the writer has followed the greater part of his life" (Randolph 1846). The short blurb is fascinating for what it reveals about young Randolph. Randolph's mythic sense of himself and instinct for self-fashioning underlie this attempt to write himself out of his lowly circumstances, by transforming a life of hardship into literary gold. Even more interesting is Randolph's choice to advertise in *The Liberator*. The paper remained a notorious organ of the radical abolitionists through the Civil War, and boasted a high number of African American subscribers. Associating with *The Liberator* at all registered political support for enslaved African Americans and their plight, and yet Randolph here does not identify as black. But neither does he disclaim his black ancestry. Was the omission of his race intentional? Perhaps *Life in the Galley* could tell us more, but no copies have surfaced. *Ravalette*, however, narrates Randolph's suicidal desperation as a sailor, and describes how a Rosicrucian transmission of hope and courage arrested him in his attempt to throw himself over the ship's taffrail (Randolph 1939, 91).

Randolph wrote a letter to the anti-slavery Congressman, Horace Mann, in 1851, desiring his opinion on "the proper course to be pursued by the free Blacks of the North towards Ameliorating their own condition [sic]"(Deveney 1997, 8). That Randolph sought such high-level patronage is evidence that he was aware of his intellectual gifts, and hoped to use them to better the prospects of African Americans above the Mason-Dixon line. But he was in something of an awkward position; as the abolitionist movement heated up in the 1850s, less energy was directed toward raising the circumstances of Northern black people in favor of addressing the more pressing outrage of the millions toiling under chattel slavery in the South. It's probable that Randolph's eccentric opinions about race and slavery were forged out of the inconvenient truth that his own upbringing amid grinding poverty and virulent racism in the most notorious ghetto in New York had been more degraded than that of many Southern slaves. In any case, Randolph soon found a venue for his talents which allowed him to evade the political hot potatoes of race and slavery and to pursue more ethereal concerns. He first appears as an occultist in the Utica City Directory of 1853, where he lists himself as a "clairvoyant physician and psycho-phrenologist" (Deveney 1997, 8).

One exception to the rule that abolitionists focused their philanthropy solely on the South can be found in Gerrit Smith, Randolph's wealthy patron of the 1850s. Smith was a supporter of the radical abolitionist, John Brown, and one of the "Secret Six" who funded Brown's raid on Harper's Ferry, the incident which polarized sectional feeling and sparked the Civil War (Frothingham 1909, 239). Sometime in the late 1840s or early 1850s, Randolph received a land grant from Smith in the neighborhood of Peterboro, where he lived with his wife and three children (Deveney 1997, 8). Randolph may have moved to upstate New York for any number of reasons, but to accept the largesse of such an extremist reformer was to league himself with a faction of individuals utterly committed to black emancipation and suffrage. Anyone with a fervent desire to "pass," or a wish to escape the political predicaments of the black race, would not have done so. Finances may have been a factor in Randolph's decision to take the farm, and yet until the very end of the decade, the 1850s were a prosperous time for him. He made two tours of Europe as a Spiritualist, one in 1855 and one in 1857. He also seems to have found regular work as a trance speaker in the states; he engaged the Boston Music Hall for a series of six lectures in 1855, and charged a fifty cent admission (Deveney 1997, 60).

Randolph's fortunes took a sharp turn in the fall of 1858, when he alienated both of his natural audiences, the Spiritualists and the abolitionists. In his first notable appearance in the black press, he was accused of being both a thief and a traitor to the African American cause. The trouble had begun in 1855, when William Wells Brown identified a charlatan named Randolph as having stolen collection plate money from both himself and Sojourner Truth on the lecture circuit. William Wells Brown is familiar to students of American literature as the author of the first African American novel, *Clotel: Or, The President's Daughter*, a fiction about Thomas Jefferson's real-life children by one of his slaves (Brown 2000). Brown described the man in question as, "A rather tall, slim, wiry-walking, empty-headed, thin-faced, cunning-looking colored man," who introduced himself as, "John Randolph, son of John Randolph of Roanoke"(Brown 1855). It is beyond me to determine whether this "John" was the same man as P.B. Randolph, yet P.B. also claimed throughout his life that he was descended from the hot-tempered Virginia Congressman. Other details in Brown's account are equally damning, such as his depiction of Randolph's officious manner, his handkerchief "highly scented with musk, rose water, or something else," and the fact that this Randolph "calls himself a doctor, and attempts to lecture on Phrenology." The controversy was reignited following P.B. Randolph's ill-considered comments to Parker Pilsbury, a leading abolitionist, regarding the call for an immediate and uncompromising end to slavery (Pilsbury 1858). Randolph's more moderate, gradualist stance was considered a particular piece of lunacy, coming from a black man, and Pilsbury's outraged letters to *The Liberator* reminded another reader of the shady dealings of the phrenologist Randolph from a few years back (Grandin 1858). Throughout the fall of 1858, an editorial war raged in *The Liberator* over the questionable character and real identity of P.B. Randolph.

Randolph's recantation of Spiritualism in this same period would also negatively impact his future as a public speaker. Renunciations of the upstart religion were not rare, and were often exploited by trance speakers seeking to revivify a flagging career. Yet Randolph endured particularly harsh criticism for his turn-coating; the latent racism of the Northern Spiritualists was surely a factor in this, as was Randolph's bitterness toward Andrew Jackson Davis, Spiritualism's unofficial leader. Though Randolph's apostasy of 1858 damaged a potentially fruitful career as a public medium, the ensuing years, 1859–1863, were the most productive of his life. The ostracism of the Spiritualists forced him deeper into himself and to the creations of his pen in order to make a living. To these years belong two lost novels by Randolph, the surviving novels *Tom Clark* and *Ravalette*, and a number of pamphlets on topics as diverse as the wrongs of Spiritualism, the benefits of hashish, clairvoyance and magic mirrors, and occult methods for sexual satisfaction. In 1863 he published the extensively researched tome, *Pre-Adamite Man*, a fascinating compendium of nineteenth century ideas about racial origins, blended with proto-Theosophical ideas about descent from godlike races.

Randolph owes his reputation as an occultist to the projects he seeded in these Civil War years. His wanderings in Syria and the Middle East of 1861–62 were the basis for the later *Ansairetic Mystery*, a privately circulated document detailing his method for sex magic. Randolph's most sophisticated work of occult philosophy, *Dealings With The Dead; The Human Soul, Its Migration And Its Transmigrations* (1862), explains the process of "blending" or remaining conscious when channeling disincarnate entities. By distinguishing between different types of Spiritualistic phenomena, specifically between those produced by the spirits of the dead and those produced by benevolent angelic presences, Randolph "became the forerunner of the rise of occultism in the nineteenth century" (Deveney 1997, 97). Randolph's identification of a *hierarchy* of disincarnate entities is key, since Blavatsky would cite this same invisible pantheon to differentiate her own communications with "ascended masters" from the Spiritualists' possession by mere ghosts. In her monumental text, *Isis Unveiled* (1877), Blavatsky dedicates a sub-section of a chapter to the idea, "Mediumship totally antagonistic to adeptship" (Blavatsky 1988, 487–493). She asserts that the adept's conscious mediation with spiritual guides is superior to the unconscious channeling of lesser spirits performed by the Spiritualists, and this iconic distinction has led religious historians to understand her as the chief reviver of that old-time medieval magic, in some sense the "Mother of the New Age." Yet Blavatsky clearly knew Randolph's work and was also an inveterate plagiarizer. The revisions to the Spiritualist worldview that Randolph proposed in *Dealings With The Dead*, first appearing as a series of magazine articles over a decade before *Isis Unveiled*, justify Deveney's claim that Randolph was the unsung father of the occult revival.

Perhaps with the end of Civil War and the passage of the Thirteenth Amendment, Randolph felt emboldened to throw his lot in with African

Americans. It must be remembered that the outcome of the Civil War was not a foregone conclusion for those who lived through it, and all along Randolph was hedging his bets, alternately touting his black ancestry, his white ancestry, and the wonderful enigma of the "*sang mêlée*" (Randolph 1939, 72). Randolph's brief but spectacular career as a "race man" in the years 1864 through 1866 should permanently put to rest any sense that the activities of "the Rosicrucian," as he called himself, existed outside the notice of the larger black community. Yet because he endorsed the illicit pleasures of sex, drugs, and the occult, he was disowned by the black community. He was an embarrassment to the proponents of racial uplift who sought to prove that mores among the races were essentially the same, and thus his public record and accomplishments were functionally erased. His second fall from grace in the 1860s cemented this erasure which has persisted until the present day. By cataloguing Randolph's considerable accomplishments within the African American community, we gain a sense of how thoroughly his legacy has been expunged.

As early as 1863, Randolph was appointed chairman of a New York committee to recruit black soldiers for the Union Army. Perhaps this noble effort helped his peers to forgive his excesses as an occultist, because in 1864 he was asked to serve on the business committee of the National Convention of Colored Men. Five hundred black leaders attended, including Frederick Douglass, who sat as president (Deveney 1997, 155–156). Randolph next became involved in the Freedmen's Bureau, the agency erected in the aftermath of Civil War to serve the needs of four million newly freed saves. He relocated to New Orleans where he set up a school for black adults, and for the first time in his life he cultivated black audiences for his occult lectures. Randolph hoped to found a normal school in Louisiana for black teachers, and in this endeavor he received the backing of General Howard and the endorsement of President Andrew Johnson, who described him as "an educator of his people, a true philanthropist, and a gentleman of very rare and unusual attainments as a scholar and orator" (Deveney 1997, 168). Randolph was even received at the White House. By all accounts, his progress as a humanitarian had been quick and stellar, and he augmented his fame by going on tour with a radical contingent of politicians, sponsored by the National Union Club, in 1866. The mixing of black and white orators on the same stage was considered so controversial that the traveling convention was snidely dubbed a collection of "Wandering Miscegens" by *The New York Herald* (Deveney 1997, note on 462).

Randolph's talent as an orator prompted comparisons in the press to that "dean" of African American speechifying, Frederick Douglass, who was also part of the convention. *The Chicago Tribune* reported that "the little Octoroon" outdid Douglass in "description, word-painting, language, apostrophe, appeal,

[and] denunciation" (Deveney 1997, 170). Leading newspapers reprinted his speeches in full, and the black press also lauded his efforts. *The Christian Recorder*, arguably the most important African American newspaper of the nineteenth century, and one which is still extant at the time of this writing, gave Randolph high praise throughout 1866. He is referred to as, "that strangely gifted author and eloquent orator," the "prince of orators," "world-renowned," and "one of the most able colored men on the continent" (Highgate 1866; "News" 1866; Strother 1866). Both *The Liberator* and *The Christian Recorder* printed Randolph's letters about his educational efforts in Louisiana (Randolph 1865 and Randolph 1866).

Randolph's star was on the rise, but he was not cut out for a politician. The phrenologist returned with a vengeance when Randolph ruffled his new champions by comparing black men's skulls unfavorably to those of white men's at a lecture he gave in Quincy, Indiana. The irritated editorialist for *The Christian Recorder* also noted that Randolph ranked himself higher in cognitive power than the full-black because he, as an octoroon, possessed more white blood (Brown 1866). Similar to his apostasy of 1858, Randolph's alienation of initially positive audiences following 1866 was attributable to gaffs on both political and religious fronts. While he had previously angered the Spiritualists by recanting their beliefs, now he damned himself before all Christians by publicly denying Jesus, and claiming that God was instead to be found in electricity, motion, and light (Deveney 1997, 171). This completed the fall of his star in the eyes of the black community. Christianity was practically a prerequisite for black leadership in the nineteenth century, and Randolph's erstwhile supporters could not abide such heathen wildness. The next time his name appeared in *The Christian Recorder*, he was described, simply, as "the infidel" ("Communications" 1873).

Beacon Hill, Black Boston, and Pauline Hopkins

In 1867, Paschal Beverly Randolph moved to the Beacon Hill area of Boston and established "Rosicrucian Rooms" at 29 Boylston Street. Deveney describes Randolph's Boston years as the most prosperous of his life:

> He had obviously become something of a celebrity, lionized in a small way by Boston society. He was consulted on the stock market by Horace Day, a prominent financier (and spiritualist) and achieved some notoriety for correctly predicting the gold panic of 1869, the appearance of a comet, and the fall of Napoleon III. His books were selling well.
>
> DEVENEY 1997, 176

Beacon Hill, a long-established black neighborhood with a rich tradition of political radicalism and a thriving cultural life, is also where the novelist Pauline Hopkins spent her youth. Born in 1859, Hopkins probably knew something of the controversial Rosicrucian who lived in her neighborhood; her father ran a barber shop at 1 Cambridge Street, making him "one of the most visible members in the community," and her mother took in boarders (Brown 2008, 65). In 1872, the same year Hopkins turned thirteen, Randolph was arrested and jailed on obscenity charges for his possession of free-love literature (Deveney 1997, 195–199). Never one to miss an opportunity for publicity, Randolph quickly issued a salacious pamphlet entitled *The Great Free-Love Trial*, even though the charges had been dropped (Randolph 1872). One can almost hear the collective groan uttered by the black community: instead of offering his considerable talents to help the less fortunate of his race, P.B. Randolph was promoting sexual smut. Given the politically fraught climate of Reconstruction, it's reasonable to assume that the moral guardians of Beacon Hill simply refused to acknowledge Randolph's glaring presence, both as a method for discouraging publicity, and also as a means for disassociating themselves from his embarrassing pursuits.

Randolph continued to develop his mature magical systems until his death in 1875. The Boston fire of 1872 devoured what little he had acquired over the years, and he spent his last years in Ohio. *The Christian Recorder* reported his suicide – that final apostasy of his life-affirming, occult beliefs – without comment ("Personal Items" 1875). In 1902, Pauline Hopkins issued the first chapters of a novel entitled *Of One Blood; Or, The Hidden Self*, in the *Colored American Magazine*. Much of *Of One Blood* is concerned with "establishing the primal existence of the Negro as the most ancient source of all that you value in modern life, even antedating Egypt"(Hopkins 2004, 87), and to that end the novel takes us on a journey to an ancient Ethiopian city. Hopkins also makes tacit reference to the early psychologists, William James and Alfred Binet, two theorists who were attempting to plumb the "unclassified residuum" of phenomena traceable to the human mind (Hopkins 2004, 2–6, 35). Perhaps Hopkins had noticed that the occult resurgence which unofficially began with *Isis Unveiled* was now receiving the attention of Harvard professors and serious, scholarly organizations like the American Society for Psychical Research. And perhaps she remembered, then, that an American black man had boldly championed such psychic technology many decades before.

The similarities between P.B. Randolph and *Of One Blood's* protagonist, Reuel Briggs, are too striking to be considered mere coincidence. The novel introduces Reuel as a suicidal student of esoteric medicine who is successfully passing for white (Hopkins 2004, 4). Randolph made mention of his suicidal urges throughout his many works, and he also frequently denied his black ancestry. Some of Hopkins's critics have suggested that the influential race leader, W.E.B. DuBois, was the model for Reuel, simply because both were students at Harvard. Other than this small detail, however, the character and the man have little in common. For example, Reuel's first major act is to bring a beautiful woman back from the dead, using only his mesmeric powers and an alchemical powder. Dr. Randolph had long claimed this ability (Randolph 1939, 104), while revivification seems something of a stretch for the sociologist, Dr. DuBois. Significantly, the protagonist's initials are R.B., probably a sly reference to Randolph's initials, B.R. (he often dropped the Paschal from his name). This seemingly minor detail takes on more importance following a reading of Randolph's novel, *Ravalette*; in characteristic occult fashion, cryptography, anagrams, initials, and the like are all invoked as clues in tracking the morphing identities of the novel's main characters. So, for example, "Ettelavar" in *Ravalette* is clearly an alternate identity of the enigmatic title character. The name Reuel Briggs may even be an anagram, perhaps for "rules bigger," which he does by the novel's end. He is crowned King of the ancient Ethiopian city of Telassar, a magical realm of immortal sages whose society has resisted the encroachments of time.

Of One Blood performs a complex recuperation of Randolph and his doctrines. Reuel's suicidal melancholy is shown to be a direct result of his alienation from his black lineage. Reuel hangs his head in shame before Ai, the wise counselor who welcomes him as the prophesied King of Telassar, and admits "that he had played the coward's part in hiding his origin"(Hopkins 2004, 129). Here Hopkins manages to chide and correct Randolph's chief sin in the eyes of his peers through the medium of fiction. Elsewhere *Of One Blood* functions to redeem Randolph by validating his (and Reuel's) occult claims, and by shaming the unfeeling world which could not recognize his greatness. For example, the other medical students "resented [Reuel's] genius," and "viewed him coldly as we are apt to view those who dare to leave the beaten track of conventionality." Reuel, like Randolph, contributes "scientific articles to magazines on the absorbing subject of spiritualistic phenomena," and also eloquently defends the mysteries of the unconscious mind: "[T]he wonders of a material world cannot approach those of the undiscovered country within ourselves – the hidden self lying quiescent in every human soul" (Hopkins 2004, 28–29; 4; 7). Perhaps the hardest evidence we have (if you will forgive the dreadful pun) that Hopkins wrote *Of One Blood* as a paean to Randolph's teachings is the scene in which Ai prepares a magic mirror for psychic viewing. Randolph published frequently on this topic and sold mirrors in a mail order business; the not-so-secret ingredient for magically charging them was semen (Deveney

1997, 79–80). Readers may now cringe at the depiction of Ai preparing his remote-viewing mirror with a "liquid mixture," on which "a film of sediment instantly formed" (Hopkins 2004, 146).

By keeping the spatial and temporal qualities of Telassar intentionally vague, Hopkins can symbolically crown Randolph with the glory and prestige he never achieved on the material plane. Importantly, both Reuel and Randolph travel to Africa where they are initiated in esoteric rites, leading to personal redemption for both the fictional character and the man. Some critics find Reuel's kingship in the fantasy realm of Telassar unsatisfying, noting that any redemption he experiences is purely imaginary and not translatable to the harsh realities of lynch law and Jim Crow legislation in post-Reconstruction America. Yet by taking Reuel's spiritual conversion seriously, whether it's conceived as a past-life memory, an alternate plane of existence, or a vision of the afterlife, Hopkins subtly validates the strange worlds P.B. Randolph wrote of following his travels in Egypt. Before journeying to Egypt, Randolph was a disaffected Spiritualist, but he returned from abroad a sophisticated mystic with a coherent and highly influential vision. Outside the framework provided by esoteric history, this vision can easily appear insane, as when Randolph describes his "blending" with the ancient Egyptian king, "Thotmor," in *Dealings With The Dead* (Randolph 1862, 200). *Of One Blood's* genius is that it ventures into such epistemologically risky territory with no authorial apology, valuing Reuel's Randolph-esque visionary experiences for their redemptive power and refusing to subject his spiritual coronation to conventional psychological scrutiny. In *Of One Blood*, Hopkins constructs Reuel's journey to Ethiopia (explicitly described as the cultural predecessor of Egypt in the text) as both healing and fruitful, and never implies that the black kingdom of Telassar is an oppressed man's delusion.

Randolph's homage by Hopkins, heretofore unknown, is of inestimable value in claiming a position for him in African American history. That Hopkins, a high-profile, politically active, and ostensibly Christian black woman, should dedicate a whole novel to Randolph's enigma, and yet cloak the portrayal in obscure references and coded language, serves as positive proof that Randolph's impact on the nineteenth century black community was much wider than previously thought. Imagining a place for him in African American history demands that we rethink our assumptions about how the black community responded to his flagrant occultism and flexible racial identification; perhaps many recoiled at these things, but not all, and doubtless Randolph's colorful activities and publications made an impression, for good or ill. Much future scholarship can begin from this simple premise: P.B. Randolph was influenced by participation in the black community and the community, in turn, was influenced by him.

The "Western" Tradition and the Future Life of Randolph

Randolph's originality in fields that have long been considered beneath the notice of the academy creates some difficulty in locating him within larger narratives of African American religion. Hugh Urban calls Randolph "the first and most influential figure in the history of modern sexual magic" (Urban 2006, 265), a topic with a very short history of formal scholarship. Randolph's influence is visible in both the popular occultism pioneered by Blavatsky, and in the various twentieth century recastings of ceremonial magic within secret brotherhoods, most often associated with Aleister Crowley (Godwin, Chanel, and Deveney 1995, 67). Yet traditional definitions of "religion" have excluded the undocumented, secretive, and transitory modes of practice favored by occultists, so that even such seminal figures as Blavatsky and Crowley are often unjustly ignored in the history of modern religion. Randolph's blackness upsets the embedded notion that "high Western" occultism was the exclusive province of the white elite, thereby adding yet another wrinkle to the already vexed question of where to locate occultism in our collective cultural history. Volumes such as the present one explicitly press the issue of how the Western esoteric tradition fared in the melting pot of American culture.

P.B. Randolph's significant contributions to the modern religious landscape prompt us to challenge the largely uncontested idea of Western esotericism's European lineage. For example, some of Afrocentrism's more speculative claims might be grounded in the foundational figure of Randolph, an African American man who stands at the forefront of the modern occult resurgence, and who received esoteric teachings in North Africa. Furthermore, Randolph's success as a Spiritualist and his identification as "the man with two souls" suggest the context of African religious survivals in the Americas. Randolph became fascinated with Voodoo while living in Louisiana, and though his class bias might have prevented him from perceiving the African-derived religion's similarities to his own talent for spirit possession, contemporary scholars should not make the same oversight.

Broadening the definition of "religion" to include vernacular forms like Conjure and Voodoo, social institutions like Freemasonry, and the gnostic potential of the occult novel, opens up arenas where Randolph appears less like an anomalous outlier and more like an African American pioneer existing on a continuum with other African American pioneers. For example, Randolph's contemporary, Martin Delany (1812–1885), was like Randolph an important early novelist and a physician with an interest in occult ritual. Delany was an active and powerful voice within Prince Hall Freemasonry, and he also published an esoteric ethnology, replete with Ethiopian hieroglyphs and symbolic heraldry (Delany 1879). Randolph's most obvious influences in occult fiction, the white writers Edward Bulwer Lytton and Edgar Allan Poe, reveal the genres to which he aspired, yet future literary assessments might examine Randolph's shaping by a tradition of African American oratory and the extent to which black experience figures in his texts. Randolph may have killed himself off in his novel, *Ravalette*, but the inscription on his fictional tombstone reads, "Beverly, The Rosicrucian. *Je renais de Mes Cendres*" (Randolph 1939, 267). Meaning "I am reborn from my own ashes," the phrase connotes the revolutionary power of African America: Randolph no doubt borrowed these words from the military insignia of the Haitian King, Christophe. Reclaiming the African Americanness of P.B. Randolph serves not only to more accurately contextualize his unique vision, it also works to explode many long-standing and narrow ideas of the contours of African American religion. Scholars may contribute to Randolph's desired renaissance by allowing his legacy to rise, phoenix-like, from the ashes of an unjustified obscurity.

CHAPTER 3

The Self Divine
Know Ye Not that Ye are Gods?

Darnise C. Martin

Introduction

We affirm the inseparable oneness of God and humankind, the realization of which comes through spiritual intuition, the implications of
which are that we can reproduce the Divine perfection in our bodies,
emotions and in all our external affairs.

ANDERSON and WHITEHOUSE 1995, 5

I come to this project as part of my ongoing scholarship in the area of African
American religious diversities. My work contributes to the growing array
of scholars who seek to move African American religious practices from the
margins. The discourse, with only a few exceptions, notably Islam, is usually
dominated by Christian theologians who discuss matters of church and
Jesus, and too often those conversations that happen outside of Christian nor-
mativity are excluded as foreign, false, other or even demonic. My intent is to
portray the multi-vocal nature of African American religious practices, where
all voices are welcome within the discourse, and appreciated as legitimate,
valid religious expressions. As the body of research continues, we all begin
to see that these presumably foreign doctrines are in fact not so foreign to
people of African descent. Parallels and spiritual points of continuity can be
found between African traditional religions and the ways in which African-
Americans practice various forms of religions including Christianity (Spence
and Adofo 2011).

I employ ethnographic methods of research such as participant-observation
and direct interviewing to examine not only the visible, exoteric religious practices of New Thought beliefs, but also to uncover the esoteric meanings and
practices that these believers have constructed, and from which they derive
ongoing purpose and meaning. Furthermore, by adding African American
voices to the traditionally Eurocentric focus of Western Esotericism, the borders of that disciplinary discourse are likewise expanded. Even a casual glance
through the table of contents or bibliographies of a leading scholar such as
Antoine Faivre reveals a limited and narrow perspective in terms of what
makes up the study of esotericism (Faivre 2010). While the case may be made

© KONINKLIJKE BRILL NV, LEIDEN, 2015 | DOI 10.1163/9789004283428_005

that these scholars qualify their research as being focused upon the West, it would nevertheless be important to acknowledge esoterica within other cultures, and that perhaps there are some mutual influences among them. Such a work as *Esotericism in African American Religious Experience: "There Is A Mystery"*...allows for a broader perspective of the esoteric presence throughout the African Diaspora as critically important and necessary for the more comprehensive education of students in the fields of religion, antiquities, and anthropology to name a few.

Thus, in this essay I focus upon *African American New Thought* in an effort to broaden the discourse. I propose that New Thought can be considered Gnostic insofar as it requires followers to either possess or actively grow toward specialized knowledge, and it is esoteric insofar as it promotes spiritual practices that both lead to said knowledge and allows an individual to expand in consciousness and/or transcend into as yet unnamed realms of knowledge or being for ultimate fulfillment. In this project, I am exploring the Gnostic and esoteric teachings within New Thought religions with a particular eye to discovering how such teachings function for African-American followers. Given the traditional models of Christianity that most African-Americans have followed since the massive conversion efforts of the Methodists and Baptists during the slave era and the later Pentecostal revivals, it is a matter of considerable curiosity and importance how some African-Americans find their way to a seemingly inaccessible, cerebral, metaphysical religious system full of eastern mysticism and delivered through the legacy of White 19th century New Englanders.

I begin with some explanation regarding how I apply the terms Gnosticism and esotericism within this essay. Gnosticism is an elusive term. It is often used to describe those amorphous 2nd to 5th century religions that the early Christian theologians saw as doctrinal corruptions to their own burgeoning true religion. Although these religions were numerous and varied, they have been categorized together by ancient heresiologists such as Irenaeus and Tertullian as false gnosis or false knowledge in their efforts to distinguish true Christianity from what they considered heretical threats (Unger and Dillon 1992; Roberts and Donaldson 1896). Their mission was not to define such groups accurately, but to identify them collectively as false and illegitimate. Later scholars have generally continued this collectively arbitrary category in the discourse of Gnosticism, which only further complicates the matter into the present because much of what we know of these Gnostic religions is actually through the heresy hunting lens of early Christian apologists. Thus, it has been rather difficult to sort out the actual teachings of such groups, as their teachings have been distorted and maligned by the earliest Christian theologians as far back as Paul's biblical admonitions to be wary of teachers of a different gospel (Galatians 1:6–9, NRSV).

However, since the 1945 discovery of the Nag Hammadi texts, a collection of 4th century religious documents attributed to followers of so-called Gnosticisms, contemporary scholars are now able to peer back into antiquity and understand more directly what Gnosis or knowledge these believers may have actually affirmed. The correlation of the word "knowledge" with the ancient religions is, in the proclamation of these teachers and believers to have *special knowledge*, revealed by God or other gospels revealed by Thomas, Peter or Mary Magdalene for example. These believers understood themselves to have an alternative knowledge about many of the same events as the new Christians. Thus, the crucifixion and resurrection might have entirely alternate meanings than what the young Christian church was affirming. These "Gnostic knowings" were alternative epistemologies and although ultimately deemed heretical, they, nonetheless, reveal important religious diversity, a diversity that would suggest an alternative ultimate authority to Christianity or its understanding of God. Such diversity was, of course, unacceptable to early Christian theologians, and that knowledge was henceforth marginalized as "sectarian, esoteric, mythical, syncretistic, and parasitic" (King 2003, 3). As such the very word Gnostic has been synonymous with illegitimacy and heresy.

However, in this essay, I reclaim the specialized knowledge aspect of Gnosis in my application to African American New Thought practices. My focus here is to set aside much of the scholarly discourse over what constitutes Gnosticism as a whole or even to flesh out the individual religions which have been categorized as Gnostic, in favor of employing the barest meaning of the word, knowledge. More specifically, this is a specialized knowledge that emphasizes "enlightenment resulting from overcoming ignorance and suffering" (King 2003, 1). In contrast, those who are without this knowledge are deceived and live lives of unnecessary pain and strife. As we will see in New Thought religions, it is specialized knowledge that liberates believers from an unfulfilling, monotonous life, and prepares them for ultimate awakening into the infinite expansion of consciousness.

The natural question emerges, what are New Thought religions? New Thought is a religious system that is inherently pluralistic, being infused with many philosophical and religious teachings. New Thought does not refer to any one religion but to a particular category of metaphysical religions that affirm such teachings as monism –the oneness of all things, and idealism—the nature of reality is thought or idea, which themselves have diverse origins from both eastern and western religious traditions, notably the Vedanta Hindu tradition and various mysticisms, which began to influence American culture following the 1893 World Parliament of Religions in Chicago (Narayanan 2004, 19).

New Thought consists of three major denominations and many sub-denominations, and numerous independent churches, study groups and bodies of literature. The main denominations are Unity School of Christianity, Divine Science, and Science of Mind also known as Religious Science, all of which stem from the 19th century teachings of Phineas P. Quimby, who is generally noted as the founder of New Thought (Harley 2002; Harley presents a minority opposing view in her work). However, each of these sects has its own historical origins, leaders and specific texts and teachings.

While New Thought is not a system requiring allegiance to any formal creeds or doctrines, there are some shared beliefs generally referred to as the "declaration of principles," foremost among these as noted above is the foundational belief in monism, that is, all is one. All of creation is created of the same substance, often understood as consciousness itself, the "stuff" essence, or ground of all being. This belief underlies the teaching of divine-human unity. New Thought religions make the audacious, and yet esoteric, statement that human beings are indeed divine beings, made in the image and likeness of their creator, God, because, indeed, there is no other substance. The esoteric and Gnostic truth that New Thought affirms is reflected in the opening quote above, which I paraphrase here: There is an inseparable oneness of God and humankind, and the realization of this through mystical or intuitive knowledge is the key to a life of fulfillment and perfection in the human realm. It is incumbent upon the human being to awaken to this truth and pursue it. Ernest Holmes, the founder of Religious Science, states it thus, "There should always be a recognition of the absolute Unity of God and [Human]: the Oneness, Inseparability, Indivisibility, Changelessness...This is the recognition which Jesus had when he said I and the Father are One..." (Holmes 1938, 331). New Thought offers a particular religious path to this awakening.

Like many religions, perhaps all, the primary questions that New Thought seeks to answer for its believers are: Who am I? What is the nature of reality? Why am I here and/or how do I live a fulfilling life? What happens when I die? New Thought responds by affirming, You Are That! And you have the power to create your own experiences. To the extent that you awaken or expand your consciousness, you live a fulfilling life in the knowingness of your identity and power. Ernest Holmes further states:

> Since I know the Truth of my being, I will no longer hinder or retard my good from coming to me. I will expect and accept all that I need to make life happy and worthwhile; for I am a child of the Spirit, and every attribute of it--every attribute of Good is my inheritance.
>
> HOLMES 1984

Although New Thought teaches specialized knowledge or *Gnosis*, that knowledge is not, strictly speaking, hidden or withheld from anyone. Each believer understands that he or she must seek it out and explore the depths of it. It is an interior, personal spiritual journey that can only be done for oneself. It is the esoteric path. The particular religious denominations, myriad teachers, study groups, books, etc offer pathways to help the seeker attain the knowledge and then to practice it in their everyday lives. Thus, I affirm that New Thought religions represent what may be called a *revealed esoterica*, in the sense that anyone can find their teachings and literature, but the true esoteric nature of New Thought is in the proper Gnosis of *self as divine* and a practice of continual expansion of this consciousness, such that unity is not understood as the absorption of the human into the divine but the complete unity with the Divine (Braden 1956, 128–143). The expanded consciousness understands that God is individualized within each human being. Jesus' statement that "I and the father are one," is understood in this context, and therefore, Jesus stands as a model or "way-shower" for everyone. As a distinct human being and yet one with God, he became enlightened and thus aware of his "Christ-consciousness" or inner divinity, and was able to accomplish what the Biblical record reports. Jesus is not savior, one who does something for another, he is teacher and example, for the esoteric path is a personal and interior one. The one who sees Jesus' divinity as particular to him only, does not grasp the esoteric meaning of the Jesus event. New Thought makes the bold monistic claim, all things are one, there is no separation, and you and "the father" or source are one. Because New Thought is such a syncretic set of religious beliefs, individual teachers or texts routinely borrow the language from specific traditions, such as in the above example with the use of the term "father." Followers are reminded, and understand such language in metaphysical ways that transcend the ordinary or literal meanings of unenlightened believers. To go further still New Thought claims that the highest and truest knowledge that humans can attain is that we are God. This knowledge, though openly shared, is not properly understood by the masses. Indeed, it is the most egregious heresy according to orthodox religious institutions. Thus, the knowledge of divine-human unity is underground knowledge, but freely revealed to those who are true seekers. Those who seek the expansion of their consciousness into higher realms will understand it properly and pursue the esoteric practices necessary to facilitate the ongoing expansion.

I have also affirmed that New Thought is esoteric in practice, and I will offer some contextualization here regarding my use of the term. I consider esoteric in light of its Greek etymological origins to convey that which is obscure, mystical, hidden from public view, secret, generally only available to a select group of seekers or initiates. Noting that there is now an established tradition of Western esotericism legitimized by leading scholars of the discipline Antoine Faivre and Wouter J. Hanegraaff, and that they have given us descriptive language and working definitions for the study of esoterica, I find similarity with some of the defining categories that Faivre interrogates (and he sometimes finds inadequate) in his work *Western Esotericism: A Concise History* (Faivre 2010, 1–5, 24). Some of these I find to be helpful descriptors at least in terms of understanding ways in which groups might self identify, or ways in which groups might remain marginalized by these categorizations.

What I find more helpful, however, in terms of a definition comes from the Association for the Study of Esotericism which defines esoteric as "any teachings designed for or appropriate to an inner circle of disciples or initiates. In comparison with exo- which refers to the outer teachings, eso- refers to the inner teachings" (www.aseweb.org). Thus, I understand and employ esoteric religious practices to be those that reflect an expanded understanding of exoteric doctrine, beliefs or practices that a general public may only casually observe; such practices require an internal methodology by which the believer anticipates personal transformation and/or enlightenment with the assistance of proper guidance and/or knowledge; these practices are understood to be individually effective that is, each person must work out his/her own salvation; and these practices are made known to those who seek of their own accord. There are no saviors, gurus or saints who can achieve and somehow transfer enlightenment or salvation to another. Although some teachers may rise in popularity, regionally, nationally or even internationally, individual seekers understand that true transformation happens along the road less traveled, and thus tutelage under such a teacher can only be a part of the process. Esoteric practices dictate a solo journey. Esoteric religions can be further described as:

> alternative or marginalized religious movements or philosophies whose proponents in general distinguish their own beliefs, practices, and experiences from public, institutionalized religious traditions. [Encompassing such practices as] alchemy, astrology, Gnosticism, Hermeticism, Kabbalah, magic, mysticism, Neoplatonism, new religious movements connected with these currents, nineteenth, twentieth, and twenty-first century occult movements, Rosicrucianism, secret societies, and Christian theosophy.
>
> http://www.aseweb.org/?page_id=6

Inasmuch as New Thought is often described as belonging to "new religious movements of the nineteenth century occult movements," it is well situated by this description. Moreover, I add that these practices require the application of intuitive epistemologies that allow the believer to bypass the material, external aspects of life in order to attain their own personal experience. Here I refer specifically to the Sufi Muslim mystic who described this desired experience as the difference between being told by another that a flame is hot, and personally being burned by a flame. These types of mystics long to be burned by the flame of Allah (unnamed Sufi scholar). They seek direct, unmediated divine encounter.

Esoteric religious worship is in considerable contrast to the practices of institutional forms of religion that require allegiance to an ecclesial body or figurehead who stands as mediator between the individual and the divine. Esoteric practices generally lie outside of institutional forms of religion, encouraging direct spiritual experience variously described as divine union, enlightenment, awakening, or as in New Thought it is described as the expansion into infinite consciousness, or by some as attaining Christ-consciousness. This terminology follows the understanding that when the man Jesus became awakened, the phenomenon allowed others to see, in some respect, his divine unity. In esoteric circles (aka Gnostic) of the early Christian era, it was believed that Jesus became Christ at his awakening to this inner truth. He was liberated from the illusion of duality and separation (Steiner 1940, 55, 73). Thus, the esoteric exegete may say that the name Jesus Christ is a legacy and a testament to divine human unity that has been modeled before us and is attainable for all who seek it. Consequently, I am describing New Thought as esoteric in its practice due to the interior nature of rituals and styles of worship designed to assist the believer in transcending the visible world and awakening the follower to the oneness which culminates in divine unity.

Moreover, New Thought esoteric practice is supported by the doctrine of Idealism, in which it is believed that all things in the universe begin in the mind as an idea, and thus the nature of reality is not material as it may seem to our physical senses, but ideal. It is affirmed by idealists that the universe was first created in the mind of God, a concept that fits with the aforementioned belief in Monism, that all is one—all created by the same creator out of the same substance, God itself. Idealism then leads into the proper application of these tenets in that New Thought teaches that as God created, so do humans. Humans have the power to create through the power of our minds to imagine, to envision, to visualize, to co-create. In an idealistic universe all that is begins in mind. Those who have correct Gnosis understand this, and utilize the esoteric practices proscribed by New Thought teachings to be deliberate creators, not simply as reactors as the uninformed masses are, but as proactive, conscious actors. These actions are understood as esoteric in that they require an interior focus, sometimes in stark opposition to that which the material world would present as real or true. The New Thought believer practices rituals that allow him/her to see beyond the physical or *metaphysically* into what is considered true reality—the divine as the ground of all being, and one's own unity with it. Some of these practices include but are not limited to deliberate creation, meditation, saying affirmations, and performing or receiving spiritual mind treatment—a specific type of prayer ritual designed to remind the believer of his/her unity with the whole, perfect and complete divinity, and thus allowing the believer to acknowledge only the good in any situation or circumstance.

Moreover, New thought practices such as these are further explained in doctrine and literature of the varying denominations. For example, *The Science of Mind*, the seminal reference book for the Science of Mind/Religious Science denomination, is designed to support the believer in understanding and proper technique for practicing the religion. The book is arranged in categories according to: The thing itself; The way it works; What it does; and How to use it. In this usage the term "it" refers to divinity alternately referred to as God, Universe, or Divine Mind. The book is a teaching tool for believers to systematically (or scientifically) experience the expansion of consciousness with the right beliefs and practices. Religious practice for New Thought believers is applying the knowledge of divine unity. Religious services remind believers of their inner divinity and reinforce practices such as meditation and visualization that lead to the experience of oneness, and freedom from fear or worry about any current circumstances such as illness, financial or personal problems. Understanding oneself as Divine means that one also understands how to be a deliberate creator, that is, one who can create desired circumstances through the correct use of the mind. Seekers are taught that humans create the same way that God creates. In order for this to be conscious and deliberate one must start with the correct Gnosis, otherwise life seems haphazard, chaotic and even capriciously cruel. Each challenge or problem is to be considered as simply another opportunity for charting a new course in the direction in which one would like to go. Experiencing what you do not want helps to clarify what you do want. However, only those with proper knowledge and teaching will understand correctly. Without the knowledge one experiences oneself to be a victim of circumstance, helpless to create anything different for oneself. New Thought teaches self empowerment steeped in principles of monistic idealism. Thus, correct practice is critical in order to experience that most desirable aspect of New Thought, *the consciousness that ye are gods.*

African Americans and New Thought

Now with some understanding of New Thought religions contextualized within Gnostic and esoteric systems, I continue with exploring how African Americans employ these beliefs and practices. The cultural and religious experiences of African-Americans have been varied and syncretic. Too often the history of African Americans has been told as if it was singular and monolithic. However, this has never been an accurate representation. Specifically, the story of African American religiosity has been told as if all African Americans are Christians, and within the tradition, it has been commonplace to think of them as primarily Methodist, Baptist, or Pentecostal. Not only is this classification too narrow, it does not begin to give voice to even the diverse ways in which African Americans practice Christianity let alone other belief systems that have in fact been present (good). There is much scholarship discussing the eclectic and syncretic religious practices of enslaved Africans throughout the Americas (Raboteau, [1978] 2004; Washington 1964). We know that enslaved populations throughout North America, the Caribbean and South America found themselves in cultural contact with Catholic Europeans, British Protestants, and a multitude of indigenous peoples with their own particular beliefs. We know that enslaved people found it necessary to blend their own African loa with the gods of other populations. Religions such as Santeria, Vodun, Candomble are examples of the ways in which African traditional religions were syncretized with the Catholicism largely present in the Caribbean and South America. The African American Christianities that we encounter in North America reflect a blending with British Protestantism which did not allow for the kind of expression visible in other areas of the New World. Thus, each of these religions represents a syncretism that reflects varying needs for secrecy within which the practitioners in their respective regions and enslaved conditions had to live and worship.

We also know that this syncretism did not end with emancipation. Free Black people were more able to express themselves religiously, but certainly the pervasive Christian norm had shaped even the African-descended person's view point about what constitutes religious practices. Many of the Africanisms had been so well blended as to be lost in effect. Moreover, the desire of free African Americans to "assimilate" left many with a desire to distance themselves from anything that seemed "heathen" or "savage." The institutionalized African American churches were Christian, and African American religious people largely aspired to those traditional forms of Christianity that we can see reflected today by the large numbers of African Americans in the Baptist and Methodist denominations.

However, we know that African American religious diversities have always been alive. From the traces of plantation Islam that have been uncovered (Diouf 1998), and remixed in 20th century urban communities to form a variety of Islamic practices, to the many permutations of Catholic/Protestant/ African syncretisms throughout the Americas up to and including more contemporary Holiness and Pentecostal religions. These latter two religions in particular are practiced with great emphasis upon the activity of the Holy Spirit, an affinity which is visible in the rituals of traditional African religions who regard the Loa or Orisha in much the same way as Holiness and Pentecostal doctrine regard the Holy Spirit.

From the beginning of the African American experience in the Americas, African descended people have been creating esoteric forms of worship via covert practices that obscured or kept secret the true meaning of rituals and beliefs in which they were engaged. From the perspective of the larger White society African Americans were practicing Christianity in much the same way as they were, but on closer investigation those who were initiates understood the full complexities of their spiritual truths and experiences. They understood and maintained relationship with a deity far beyond what White slaveholders or White people in general dared to imagine. Primarily, this knowledge of the divine enabled or required African Americans to imagine and conjure a world that did not as yet exist for enslaved people. To conjure an alternative world for themselves depended upon secrecy that existed under cover of subversive language, African gods in Catholic clothing, and forms of praise that meant more than just singing and dancing. People of African descent could spiritually see beyond existing circumstances into an ultimate reality in which they could place themselves. The literal practice of conjure itself is a ritualistic blending of disparate components toward the manifestation of a new reality that only a few would properly understand in its full context. Such rituals have been passed down among African American families as folklore and old wives tales, and yet they remain legitimately active in some communities (Hurston [1942] 1991; Chesnutt 1992). However, it is more common that in traditional Christian communities such rituals and beliefs are scorned and even considered devil worship, thus esoteric practices in African American communities are forced underground. They do not align with the "legitimate" Christian church, and such people are likewise maligned and marginalized.

New Thought is one of those religious systems that is syncretistic, esoteric, and Gnostic, and thus marginalized by mainstream Christianity, the religious context within which most African-Americans still find themselves. However, this marginalization is to be expected of a religious system that (1) integrates the teachings of a variety of religions, (2) rejects notions of vicarious salvation, and

(3) encourages its believers to transcend the exoteric or conventional under-standings of any religions' concepts, doctrines, teachings, etc. For these reasons, I argue that New Thought is more than esoteric Christianity. New Thought is offered as one pathway toward esoteric truth that at once transcends religion, and yet also situates itself alongside mainstream religions such that seekers may find the deeper pathway. Popular or mainstream religions may serve as a gate-way to the inner realms of enlightenment where true freedom may be found.

Not surprisingly, African Americans who practice New Thought often find themselves on the fringes of legitimate religion. I have discussed the particular blended beliefs and practices of African Americans in a Religious Science denomination in my previous ethnographic work, *Beyond Christianity: African Americans in a New Thought Church* (Martin 2005). In that book, I describe a Pentecostal influenced kind of New Thought church with a minister and wor-ship style reflective of that tradition. Here, I have intended to discuss the role of Gnosis and esoteric practice within New Thought, and thus explore how effec-tive/practical/accessible such beliefs are for its African American believers. To assist me with this task I have interviewed Rev. Israel Malik Esters, an African American New Thought minister who leads an African American congregation, called Awakening Light, in the Virginia Beach, Virginia area. I have consulted with him because I know that he is a minister who deliberately incorporates esoteric practices and rituals in the way that he teaches New Thought and leads his congregation. Rev. Israel, like many New Thought ministers has come to the tradition from another religion. He grew up in what is often referred to by New Thought believers as "the old church," which for him was the Baptist and Pentecostal churches. For him, and other Pentecostal transplants to New Thought, the idea of the Holy Spirit who is active in human affairs can function as a bridge to New Thought in which believers understand that the universe or divinity itself is responsive to human request and/or ritual.

I have been curious about how Rev. Israel's church members have responded to these "deeper" teachings, and whether they actually incorporate them as he recommends. I have wondered if there has been resistance to teachings in astrology, tarot card reading, or numerology that he offers as alternative episte-mologies. And, I have inquired whether or not he believes these beliefs and concepts are effective in the lives of African American practitioners. The fol-lowing is excerpted from our phone conversations conducted over three ses-sions on June 22 and July 3, 2011, and January 15, 2012:

Author: How do you understand/define esotericism?
Rev. Israel: I understand esoteric as a study of those things that are within us. Eso means within, reaching inward to know, moving us to discover the

many hidden worlds to know man and mind. It means to seek knowledge of who we are at the core of our being of our minds and experiences. Esoteric is always through personal experience, not the exo-external, but a deep personal knowing. It leads us to layers of mystery, which has a very complex nature because it is about unending questions about who we are and where we came from. Esoteric practices and beliefs allow us to deeply explore. In traditional teachings the mystery is solved, questions are not welcome. Esoteric is about unfolding the mystery—we sleep collectively, we must awaken individually.

Author: Do you see an affinity or commonality between New Thought and the esoteric traditions? Would you define New Thought as essentially esoteric or simply that they are compatible with one another?

Rev. Israel: I think it can be more compatible in definition than in practice. New Thought signifies an attention to thoughts that take you deeper, into more complexity. Depending upon the individual, any thought that does not grow or expand is not esoteric, the more we discover, the more we know there is to discover. New Thought flirts with esotericism, but many believers in individual New Thought churches don't continue the depth. Those who limit the beliefs according to the founders of their denominations are in a locked system, not esoteric. Some have not changed or grown much since the early days of the founding of Unity or Religious Science. Those who do not want to go any deeper are not practicing the deeper, and are not esoteric. Individuals and individual churches can be esoteric, but in order for New Thought itself to be able to be called esoteric, there must be a specific intention.

Author: What esoteric practices do you find you incorporate most in your ministry? Has this evolved, expanded over time?

Rev. Israel: Astrology is easiest to teach and get across even if they think of it as "entertainment," they are already familiar with it. I also use numerology and teach reincarnation and astral projection as tools to use alongside of visualization. I use tarot with people who come to me individually.

Author: Any other practices?

Rev. Israel: I have tried to incorporate medium-ship in the past, and may do so if particularly led by Spirit to do it again, but I pretty much don't get into it anymore. I don't want to promote dependence [upon myself].

Author: Why have you incorporated these practices into your ministry?
Rev. Israel: I wish people would become fully expressed spiritual beings, because it is a necessity for the next phase of universal spiritual evolution.

A lot of what these esoteric practices teach has their origin in African practices. [There is a great affinity] with the religions of African cultures. It is very powerful for our people to know that. It helps us better know ourselves and not be so afraid of anything that seems different from traditional Christianity. Christianity has not been good at letting us know that we are equals. We haven't known anything else. I began teaching this to Black people because our people are always the last to get it. Other ethnic groups grow with success principles but Black people are stuck in "old religion" and pariochialism. I do it because it has to be done. The world cannot go forward until we all awaken.

Author: Are you aware of any other New Thought ministers or teachers in any era who have deliberately or covertly included esoteric practices or beliefs?
Rev. Israel: The Spiritualists are known to work with candles, healing, spells, astral traveling. The Metropolitan Spiritual Churches have incorporated esoteric practices; they read palms. They demonstrate a reliance upon the holy spirit with a metaphysical and catholic influence. Of course in New Thought, Johnnie Colemon (Rev. Dr. Colemon is considered a paragon in African American New Thought leadership) has taught on reincarnation, astrology, numerology; She has been good at reaching people wherever they were. Johnnie Colemon was about getting the lessons in classes, so that she could include it in her weekly sermons, taking people deeper into the teachings. More people just want the surface, they don't want to go deeper down the rabbit hole. Discipleship is key to becoming well versed in the teachings, not just about feeling good in the moment of a church service.

Author: How do African Americans generally respond to your ministry? Especially to the more explicitly esoteric teachings that you mix in?
Rev. Israel: Those who are afraid to go deeper than traditional Christian themes have an obstacle to receiving these teachings. Older people have been more resistant, coming from stricter, Pentecostal or Holiness backgrounds. The people of the "blackberry age" have an openness and a curiosity that leads them to want to know more.

Author: How do you think these practices serve those who receive them?
Rev. Israel: The key is being able to receive them in the first place. For those who can, they become empowered to become the sons of God; it serves them marvelously, people comment that their lives have changed, others who cannot receive it stagnate. Those who receive the teachings become better people knowing themselves better and deeper than they have before. [Here Rev. Israel quotes one of his congregants]: "I thought of what it could do for me originally, but I have learned things about myself that have shifted things that I couldn't have done in 20 yrs." People are happier, freer, more motivated, empowered. They come alive again because they have the tools to navigate through life's obstacles, illusions and distractions. Now they have the tools to master their lives.

Author: Is it too intellectual?
Rev. Israel: That maybe true, but I am not dumbing it down, or churching it down anymore. Those who want to get it, will get it, we are not for everybody. They'll go on down to somebody else's church if they can't get it.

It resonates with people a lot more than people often initially realize. I just invite people to keep coming and listen. The concepts are so foreign because we've had milk for so long. There is work that needs to go along with these teachings. When Jesus did it all for you, you are not challenged to seek and find for yourself. I remind people that Jesus did it for himself. You have to do it for yourself. I'm not looking to pacify black people which many black preachers/pastors have been doing for decades. I tell people you have to show up, if you don't you miss it.

There is an awakening to these ideas among some African Americans due to an emphasis on the desire for success through positive thinking. If that's the door by which they come that is ok. It makes sense for most people because that is the nature of their need. When people have nothing, they will listen when someone says you can have it. Of course that message is attractive to us as largely being people who have not had a lot materially. Black people realize that success is possible. It appears dismal sometimes, someone has to come in with knowledge. Having a Black man in the White House has not been able to inspire a significant change in the ghettoes that surround the White House. Slavery has left an impact on the African American collective consciousness, so self-knowledge is crucial.

Author: Many New Thought churches say they teach a "practical Christianity." Do you find New Thought to really be practical for African

Americans, both in terms of the origin of New Thought and African American history?

Rev. Israel: That depends upon the denomination; Unity has a lot of African Americans. [Charles and Myrtle] Fillmore's doctrine is much more palatable because it is focused upon the Bible more than the other denominations. Black people want more grounding in the Bible, so they don't come into Religious Science so much, which I think is due to an "old consciousness" that black people still have from the Christian church. I teach from many sources which throws some people off. Sometimes it is too much for our people, but I meet the people where they are.

The African American population is getting New Thought through secular success teachings coming forth in some forms of Christianity such as Word of Faith. This allows Black people to remain in the fold of Christianity and still use New Thought teachings. I say that New Thought per se will remain for the real hardcore people, and Word of Faith continues to give many Black people a comfortable alternative.

Author: There seems to be so much to learn in New Thought. Is New Thought really accessible for people? Or is it really too esoteric to be accessible, and thus in some ways ineffective for the masses?

Rev Israel: At this time that could be true for Black people, and it is a revelation that I have recently come to painfully. Black people remain so rooted in their Christianity that they may not make this effective for themselves. Our people have a long way to go in certain parts of the country, particularly the south. Many southern Blacks remain in the consciousness of an inflexible type of Christianity. Our people are often the last to get it. The general population is certainly more open, and they [White people] are able to make it effective.

Thus concludes the interview segment I conducted with Rev. Israel. The particular questions were selected as a way to discuss the esoteric in light of New Thought, and more specifically how receptive African Americans tend to be toward the inner practices. I considered that Rev. Israel has direct relationship with an African American congregation who are seeking to go beyond what they have previously known about religion and spirituality, but who also largely have roots in traditional Christian denominations that at least sometimes present challenges to their continued application of New Thought practices and understandings. I was curious to know if these church members were actively using the tools he teaches, or if and where they may experience resistances despite their stated desires to go deeper. I think that it is apparent from Rev. Israel's responses that individuals have to decide how much of the inner walk he or she is willing to do, which ultimately determines the esoteric value of any spiritual practice.

Rev. Israel also conveyed that it is especially important to him not to encourage people to become dependent upon him as their pastor. He views that role as someone who directs "sheep." He wants to awaken people and enable them to stand on their own spiritual feet. He uses and encourages esoteric knowledge and practice so that individuals come to know themselves as powerful spiritual beings, not those who continue to need direct shepherding. He calls himself a master teacher, raising people up toward their own knowledge of self. This is what he believes the esoteric systems encourage, that seekers can always go "deeper down the rabbit hole," because there is no limit to spiritual knowledge.

Conclusion

As I conclude, I reflect upon the interview with Rev. Israel in light of understanding New Thought religions as both Gnostic and esoteric. I have asserted that New Thought is Gnostic in belief and esoteric in practice for the following reasons: New Thought is a religious system that calls the individual to a particularly bold kind of self-knowledge, and likewise encourages the seeker to infinitely deeper levels of divine knowledge; New Thought has a particular worldview that affirms the necessity of the individual's multi-layered interior practice; and it is a system that requires personal commitment and deliberate action toward one's desires, whether it is a material circumstance or ultimate enlightenment. As Rev. Israel noted, "we sleep collectively, but must awaken individually." The ultimate desired outcome for a believer, divine consciousness, is thus dependent upon deliberate actions or rituals predicated upon correct Gnosis, both of which are more than they seem to casual observation, but apparent to "initiates."

Secondly, I reflect upon the ways in which African Americans have historically practiced religions in subversive ways as a matter of survival. I consider how they have syncretized religious elements in covert ways as a matter of empowerment and attempts to retain cultural identity. We see this in very extroverted ways in Black Nationalisms that attempt to provide identity, empowerment and religion, for example. And, I consider those African Americans who choose to practice New Thought religions in light of these elements, and conclude that these religions are well situated in the milieu of

African American religious expression alongside African American folk Christianities and Black Nationalist religions. As I have described at some length in my previous work, *Beyond Christianity*, the ways in which African Americans actually practice New Thought are diverse, and largely informed by Pentecostal understandings of the power of the Holy Spirit. Metaphysical interpretations of the Holy Spirit as the indwelling God, allow many African American believers to dive into the esoteric realms that lead to the Great Truth of Oneness, that indeed, ye are gods. It is this wisdom that is most esoteric of all, and most transformative in that it provides the specialized knowledge that ultimately frees humanity from bondage of all sorts. For African Americans, forms of bondage take on an even more nuanced importance, given the historical context of life in the United States from slavery to the current time, when many still ponder the ways in which, as DuBois said, we are still consumed with the problem of the color line. Thus, a religious teaching that offers freedom from bondage has additional and particular benefit for African Americans.

Moreover, some African Americans who practice New Thought do so as a means toward attaining and embodying personal power in contrast to life circumstances that may be difficult and limiting. As New Thought teaches a system of esoteric tools by which one can overcome such difficulties, African Americans find it to be a system for both practical and spiritual liberation. The knowledge that "ye are gods" emboldens followers to be active agents in their own lives. For African Americans this also means being able to draw upon esoteric resources to overcome institutional and systematic forms oppression towards personal, communal and spiritual success. Much like the aforementioned religious innovations and syncretism from earlier historical eras, African Americans understand and implement New Thought religions in culturally specific ways as well. Thus, New Thought religions are in some ways familiar to a people accustomed to mixing and obfuscating their religious practices. On the other hand New Thought remains foreign to African American Christian traditionalists. Practically speaking, I refer again to Rev. Israel who said, "It's not for everybody...those who can get it will, and those who won't will go somewhere else" (Personal interview, January 15, 2012). This places New Thought directly in the company of other esoteric religious practices—available and practical to those who will commit themselves to it, but closed, mysterious and possibly threatening to those who do not.

PART 2

Early to Mid 20th Century

∙∙

CHAPTER 4

Working Roots and Conjuring Traditions

Relocating Black 'Cults and Sects' in African-American Religious History

Elizabeth Pérez

Introduction

I want to tell a story that begins on the South Side of Chicago, and I invite you to board the bus with me, leaving from a stop next to the Red Line train, going west. It is the year 2006, and I am conducting ethnographic research among practitioners of the Afro-Cuban religion Lucumí, or Santería, organized around the worship of the Yorùbá-derived spirits called *orishas*. I am visiting my main interlocutor and mentor, the orisha praise-singer, diviner, Spiritist medium, and adept of the Bantu-inspired Palo Monte tradition Nilaja Campbell, initiated since 1986. I pass a dozen churches with names teased from scripture, one unfolding after another for miles like the verses of an extraordinarily ambitious exquisite corpse: *Believe in Thine Heart, the Holy Rood, Lively Stone, Repairer of the Breach, Sweet's Holy Spirit Free Will, First Anvil Baptist, Baptist Church Without Wrinkle or Spot Inc., the Purchased Church of God.*[1] Already running late, I skipped breakfast and see food everywhere: *Uncle Remus Chicken Shack, Kiki Chop Suey, Seven Star Foods.* The names mounted on the façades of shops also present unmistakable allusions to African-American history and culture: the avuncular ur-narrator of Black folklore, more of a trickster than the wily heroes of his eponymous tales; the defiant survival of Southern regional cuisine in the industrial North; the Black encounter with immigrant groups and embrace of Asian philosophy and foodways; the astro-numerical symbolism of the Nation of Islam, Moorish Science Temple, and Gangster Disciples (Poe 1999, Ho and Mullen 2006).[2]

---

1 I have not put these houses of worship in order of appearance on my journey so as not to give away the precise location of Ilé Laroye.

2 My interlocutor Hasim Washington became a Lucumí priest in 2005, and I learned in an interview that—as in the case of many young male members of Ilé Laroye—Hasim's first exposure to religious disciplines of the body and devotional memorization came when he was introduced to Islam through recruitment by a local street gang. The El Rukns, or Almighty Black P. Stone Nation, had once been closely affiliated with Chicago's Moorish Science

© KONINKLIJKE BRILL NV, LEIDEN, 2015 | DOI 10.1163/9789004283428_006

Nilaja's community is called called Ilé Laroye, in tribute to her patron Eleggua, a fierce warrior and remover of obstacles.[3] Laroye is one of Eleggua's epithets, and ilé means "house" in the Yorùbá language. As in the case of "church," ilé denotes both a religious fellowship and architectural edifice in the Lucumí tradition. There are approximately fifteen separate Lucumí communities in Chicagoland; Nilaja's "house of ocha" is only one. Increasing numbers of Caribbean and Latin American converts to the religion have added to the ilés established by Cuban exiles. But most members of Ilé Laroye are not Latinos or immigrants; they are U.S.-born African-Americans. Several of Ilé Laroye's elders are the children and grandchildren of those propelled North during the Great Migration, and the extremely heterogeneous religious culture to which it gave rise would go on to condition current members' receptivity to Lucumí. As numerous scholars have shown, the civil rights and Black Power movements coincided with a reassessment of African-inspired religious forms, leading to greater Black American involvement in Diasporic traditions, such as Brazilian Candomblé and Haitian Vodou (Hucks 1998, Gregory 1999, Henderson 2007). In reevaluating their collective past, many African-Americans began to associate Christianity with a history of enslavement, colonization, and forced conversion. In the Midwest, separatist groups flourished, and Black theology led many to question the worship of a white-faced Jesus.[4]

While it would be difficult to overstate the importance of this historical turning point and the trails it blazed in the Black religious imagination, the foundation for Ilé Laroye was laid decades earlier, in the midst of what historiographers still, for the most part, dismiss as "cults and sects." In this chapter, I want to *relocate* African-American religion in those very same cults and sects that conventional narratives of the Black experience have been organized to exclude. Taking Chicago as my geographical point of departure and the history of religions as my disciplinary center of gravity, I argue that, along with the phenomenon of storefront churches, the Great Migration fostered a

---

Temple; allied gangs continue to expose Midwestern youth to Arabic phrases and Islamic practices.

3   Her son Santi is the second 'godparent', or leader, of this community. Most subsequent ethnographic references to Ilé Laroye are based on four years of IRB-approved fieldwork, 2005–2009. I have changed the name of this community and all my interlocutors for reasons of confidentiality.

4   See, for example, the Nation of Islam and Albert Cleage's Shrine of the Black Madonna in Angela D. Dillard, *Faith in the City: Preaching Radical Social Change in Detroit* (Ann Arbor: University of Michigan Press, 2007), and Edward I. Blum and Paul Harvey, *The Color of Christ: The Son of God and the Saga of Race in America* (University of North Carolina Press, 2012).

strategy of ambiguation, or tolerance for diversity, among African-Americans that met their pressing need to balance conflicting social relationships and associations. I begin by offering an overview of the religious landscape rearranged by the Great Migration, in order to provide cultural context for the advent of such communities as Ilé Laroye. I then briefly characterize Ilé Laroye as a site of inquiry that can give rise to a more expansive understanding of what is religious in the African-American experience (Long 1986, 7). In closing, I explain that it is imperative to de-center the Black Church in order to appreciate the heterogeneity and richness of lived religion, throughout the twentieth century and in our own time.

Religion in the "Street Universities" of Canaan-land

The landscape of Chicago's South Side, dubbed the "Black Metropolis" in the early twentieth century, is the work of many authors. Above all, its contours were hewn during the Great Migration, in what was actually a wave of migrations between 1915 and 1940 that carried tens of thousands to Chicago in search of new beginnings. African-Americans in the u.s. South faced lynchings, Jim Crow, and chronic economic problems that combined with environmental crises—including natural disasters that became human-made tragedies due to the apathy, incompetence, and woefully inadequate emergency response of the federal government—to render their everyday hardships impossible to bear (Tolnay and Beck 1990, Griffin 1996, Rivera and Miller 2007). As Milton C. Sernett writes, "The city became the critical arena in which the struggle of African-Americans to find the 'Promised Land' took place" (Sernett 1997, 3). For those steeped in the Biblical imagery of sermons and Spirituals, the South was an Egypt tormented by plagues and the scourge of bondage—or, at best, a desert in which they were condemned to wander. Migration acquired the aura of a religious pilgrimage, with the journey itself compared to "crossing over Jordan," a reference to the Israelites overcoming the last major, seemingly insuperable, barrier between themselves and the land of milk and honey. Southerners discerned the hand of Divine Providence in the synchronized movement of so many kinspeople. Urban areas with established Black populations, such as Harlem and Detroit, beckoned like electrified Zions. Their "second Exodus" would also be a "second Emancipation," an act of eschatological redemption for the entire race, one 'chosen' family at a time (Reed 2005, 52; Drake & Cayton 1993 [1945], 8–9).

Countless blues and vaudeville songs extolled "sweet Chicago" as a taste of paradise; poets and painters celebrated migrants' exhilaration, solidarity, and resolve to succeed. Chicago thus emerged as a Black Metropolis with distinctively African-American institutions and forms of association. But there is no doubt that the most important of these were religious. Prior to the First World War, Chicago was already "a religious mecca for African Americans," with historic African Methodist Episcopal (A.M.E.), A.M.E. Zion, and Baptist congregations that remained dominant social and political forces well into the twentieth century (Sernett 1997, 156). During the Great Migration, these churches grew exponentially (Tuttle 1970, 98; Grossman 1989). Since the mid-nineteenth century, A.M.E. churches in Chicago had enjoyed a reputation for their proclamation of the Social Gospel and progressive activism. However, their tentative embrace of migrants cost them dearly, as ministers sympathetic to the Southerners' plight abandoned the denomination to establish Community Churches (Sernett 1997, 165–166; Denino Best 2005, 134–135). Having let a golden opportunity for congregational growth slip through their fingers, A.M.E. churches steadily increased in size, but their gains lagged behind those of the Baptists.

For many Southerners, joining these churches upon arrival in Chicago formed part of a strategy of upward mobility, as they availed themselves of the social connections available to them within women's auxiliaries, choirs, men's clubs, and lay ministries.[5] Yet Pentecostal churches and newly minted charismatic denominations made impressive gains. In 1933, 144 of the 344 churches in Chicago were Baptist, but there were already 86 Holiness churches (Sanders 1996). The expressive and participatory character of Pentecostal, Apostolic, and Sanctified church services stood in stark contrast with mainline Black Protestant congregations' high-church formality and "high-brow pretensions" (A. Philip Randolph, quoted in Taylor 2002, 30). Many migrants clamored for revival-style services with "foot-stomping and hand-clapping up-tempo songs," rousing chants, ecstatic shouting sessions, and an immediate connection with a communally defined source of divine power, made manifest through speaking in tongues, faith healing, and the ritual dissociation, or "slaying in the spirit," of congregants, collectively called saints (Cusic 1990, 87). Pentecostals adopted strict prohibitions on behavior, dress, consumption, and spectatorship, practicing corporeal disciplines intended both to purge their flesh of worldly desires and to prepare it to serve as a medium for God's salvific purpose. But their rituals allowed for a much greater acceptance of the Southern body's materiality than did those of more established Black churches.

---

5   Roman Catholicism among Black people in Chicago rose steadily during the same period (See, Sernett 1997, 94).

Residential segregation intensified in Chicago during the Great Migration, and it was with considerable disenchantment that many heart-sick migrants in the "Black Belt" of the South Side realized that they had delivered themselves into another type of captivity, that of the modern ghetto (Ruble 2001, 258). Yet migrants turned to religion not only as a refuge from the "vice districts, gambling houses, unemployment, and racial tensions" of Chicago.[6] They also wished to engage in fellowship with others similarly affected by the sojourn North, with comparable experiences of dispossession from their land, vulnerability to mob violence, and race, gender, and class-based prejudice (Baldwin 2007, 166). Out of necessity, migrants from a host of smaller denominations convened in spaces designed for business purposes, and in the process gave birth to a new institution: the storefront church. Storefront churches were not always housed in former retail shops, but also in empty houses, garages, and theaters. They were pedestrian yet approachable, promising a spontaneous, unaffected, and visceral style of worship in a modest space reminiscent of the humble one-room church buildings of the South.

The clapboard sign fought the spire on corner after corner of Chicago's Black Belt, as poured concrete competed with stately edifices for the loyalty— and incomes—of Southerners. Although mainline denominations ultimately attracted more migrants than the storefronts did, theirs was a Pyrrhic victory, due to the latter's wholesale overhaul of the city's religious and cultural landscape. Interwar Chicago and its environs served as a "gate of tradition" for African-inspired narrative, plastic, and ritual arts, particularly from the Gulf Coast (Wehmeyer 2008). Storefront churches acted as "institutional bases for conjuring traditions" also called hoodoo or rootwork: the medical and magical techniques developed by plantation slaves that combined West and Central African, Amerindian, and colonial European ethnopharmacopeias, folklore, and ritual knowledge (Chireau 2003, 139). In Northern homes, hoodoo doctors, also called rootworkers, became Professors, Teachers, and "God sent healers"; in church, the same individuals were rechristened Prophets, Reverends, Elders, Fathers, or Mothers (Chireau 2003, 139). The clairvoyant, curative, and entrepreneurial abilities of such migrants were mobilized liturgically in Pentecostal and other churches, with scriptural foundations for their "spiritual gifts" cited chapter and verse if textual legitimization was called for.

---

6   On the "Red Summer of 1919," when race riots flared in twenty-five cities and whites lynched seventy Blacks, ten of whom were uniformed soldiers, see Tuttle.

Working the Roots of "Cults and Sects"

In search of a moral-ethical community in which to address the here-and-now, those with a longer history in the urban North also rejected mainline denominations and contributed to what has been called "the rise of cults and sects" (Gallagher 2007/2008, 205–220). Among the Black bourgeoisie—whom we may define as cultural elites in the demographic upper-middle class, yet not exclusively those employed in white collar professions—the churchly self-assertion of their "country cousins" was nothing less than a scandal (Dorman 2007). African-American religious historiography has reproduced the mainstream critique of storefront churches as merely colorful and idiosyncratic, their leaders as flamboyant charlatans, and their followers as gullible, hapless rubes (Denino Best 33–34).

In fact, despite the stereotype of the migrant as a rural peasant, Southern migrants had a relatively high rate of literacy, and they tended to be skilled and semi-skilled artisans from urban areas.[7] The "vibrant experimental religious scene" they ushered in incorporated a variety of far-flung influences from both material and print culture. African-Americans of every economic and educational level availed themselves of communal settings in which to explore Western esoteric traditions—such as Freemasonry—interpreted in light of local trends (Nance 2002, 125). Completely new religious movements gaining a foothold in Philadelphia, Baltimore, and Harlem, such as the Black Hebrew Israelites, appealed to Chicagoans conversant with scripture, responsive to Garveyite claims of the African-American *volk* as a new Israel, and disposed to view themselves as a Lost Tribe. Committed to the ideals of racial equality and integration, Father Divine's Peace Mission broadcast a message of prosperity, self-sufficiency, and cooperative living, along with the gospel of a flesh-and-blood Messiah (Primiano 2004, 3–26).

In *Black Metropolis: A Study of Negro Life in a Northern City* (1945), authors St. Clair Drake and Horace R. Cayton noted that "spiritual advisers and readers" living in Chicago's Bronzeville numbered in the hundreds (Drake and Cayton 1993[1945], 642). Among them was an "Astro-Numerologist" named Professor Edward Lowe, a seller of policy numbers, oils, herbs and roots, such charm ingredients as the magnetic ore called lodestone, and a selection of occult books, including his own *Key to Numerology*. While Lowe was not typical, he was far from unique. Occult publishing of such volumes as *The Egyptian Secrets of Albertus Magnus* (ca. 1725) blossomed in Chicago during the Great Migration

---

7   They were also young, between the ages of 24 and 34. See Carole Marks, *Farewell—We're Good and Gone: The Great Black Migration* (Bloomington: Indiana University Press, 1989).

(Long 2001, 16). It may seem hard to believe that Southerners with grade-school educations could find anything of value in these texts. Yet there is ample evidence for their use as how-to manuals throughout Harry Middleton Hyatt's monumental five-volume *Hoodoo-Conjuration-Witchcraft-Rootwork*, and in narratives told to the Federal Writer's Project by Black "doctors". "It becomes obvious," Carolyn Morrow Long writes, "that they were borrowing and interpreting charm formulae," even in liturgical contexts (Long 2001, 122).

Chicago was one of the cities, including New York, New Orleans, and Philadelphia, with a dense concentration of manufacturers specializing in healing and magico-religious products such as charms, talismans, candles, and hex-removing items, sold primarily through mail order. Newspapers like the *Chicago Defender* advertised the graphically flamboyant and exuberantly worded mail-order catalogs produced by Chicago-based supply companies, including Doctor Pryor's Japo-Oriental Company and Lama Products. These catalogs capitalized on the associations of Gulf folkways with home for migrants by highlighting the "voodoo" qualities of their wares, elaborating on the concept of mojo (Long 2001, 194). These products also appealed to Northerners by connoting the tantalizingly mysterious, and harnessing the symbolic power attributed to 'authentically' Black cultural forms considered debased in other circumstances. Whether out of curiosity or sheer need, mainstream church members regularly crossed denominational lines for consultations, divinations, and therapeutic treatments.

The same social and cultural currents that buoyed the popularity these products—the desire for self-improvement and refashioning; insistence on this-worldly solutions for problems in the here-and-now; the discovery of the autochthonous in the exotic; the impatience with white models of religiosity and grands récits—also combined with a thoroughgoing critique of the political status quo in the African-American encounter with Islam. The Nation of Islam moved its headquarters to Chicago from Detroit in 1934, and enjoyed considerable success among new migrants (Lemann 1991, 64). The foundation for the NOI's success had been laid in the 1920s, with the establishment of the Moorish Science Temple by Noble Drew Ali.[8] Born in South Carolina, Drew Ali began his career as an "Angel of Allah" in Newark, instructing his Black followers that they were descended from the same exalted racial heritage as the urbane and accomplished Moors. Turning the Orientalism of his day to his

---

8 One of Noble Drew Ali's disciples was Wallace Dodd Ford, renamed Ford-El, to whom he entrusted the Chicago Temple before his death. Ford-El later relocated to Detroit, began to go by the names Wallace D. Fard and Wallace D. Fard Muhammad, and organized the Nation of Islam.

advantage, Drew Ali argued for Islam's superiority to Christianity largely on the basis of its association with Egypt and wisdom from the East (Deutsch 2001, 193–208). By redefining fellow African-Americans as "Asiatics", he strove to distance them rhetorically from the stereotype of the sub-Saharan savage, swinging from jungle vines. In Chicago, he inspired a large number of converts and sympathizers, many of them Southerners such as himself.

Derided as "primitive", "hysterical", and "frenzied", the worship styles of the storefront churches violated middle-class models of female virtue, restraint, and decorum (Higginbotham 1993, 15). Yet churches were often among the few "safe spaces" available to migrant women, in which their humanity as both Black and female was acknowledged.[9] The Black Spiritual Church provided perhaps the greatest degree of authority and prestige for women, as well as gay men (Dianteill 2006, 177–178). Born in Chicago, Alethea 'Leafy' Anderson, called Mother Anderson by her followers, founded Eternal Life Christian Spiritualist Church on the South Side in 1913. About seven years later, she relocated to New Orleans, where she established a second, racially integrated, church. Spiritual Churches spread to Chicago and throughout the Midwest along with Southern migrants. From the beginning, they incorporated key aspects of Roman Catholic material culture and popular religiosity, including holy water, crucifixes, votive candles, statuary, and brocaded ceremonial vestments for ministers. Catholic devotional practices, including praying the rosary, genuflecting, and blessing oneself with the sign of the cross were performed in church, yet worship services bore strong traces of Pentecostalism, such as an emphasis on conversion experience, ritual anointing, a declamatory mode of preaching, and a "verse by verse" exegetical style (Wehmeyer 2007, 15–74). Musically, members added another set of references, preferring to sing Dr. Watts hymns of the Methodists and Baptists from the late-nineteenth-century revival period.

Such aesthetic and religious bricolage was controversial. It also became a sensation. By 1938, one in every ten churches in Chicago was a Black Spiritual Church. Its healing practices and spirit idiom responded to a range of needs felt by migrants. Another aspect of the Spiritual Church that distinguished it from mainline Christian denominations was its acceptance of spirit possession, most famously by Native American personages (Jacobs 1989, 46). For this reason, among others, it has been held up as the quintessential storefront, devoid of theological rigor, redeeming social value, and cultural merit (Baer

---

9 This definition of "safe space" reflects Griffin's gloss of the term, coined by Patricia Hill Collins, 9. See also Anthea D. Butler, "A Peculiar Synergy: Matriarchy and the Church of God in Christ" (PhD diss., Vanderbilt University, 2001), 2.

1984, 10). Yet corporeal wellness and physical welfare through healing have been central to the Spiritual Church from the outset. White and Black followers alike seek sought the mixed-race leader Mother Catherine Seals out for cures; in the origin myth of Seals' congregation, race, gender, and the importance of healing are inseparably intertwined ("Physicking Priestess" 1931, 63–64). Some Spiritual Churches have sponsored hoodoo nights, and in bless services, ministers have conducted public divinations for individual congregants, sometimes as a prelude to private consultations. As Stephen Wehmeyer writes, in both their communal rituals and domestic routines, members wove together "a rich pharmacopeia of herbs, sacred oils, incenses and other materia sacra" derived from both Afro-Diasporic and European sources (Wehmeyer 2007, 18).

Religious Ambiguation in the Black Metropolis

Black Chicagoans can lay claim to an extensive embodied and cognitive cultural patrimony of discursive practices that arose in the context of the Second Exodus. Chief among them, and most germane to my argument here, are those associated with the attitude and technique of ambiguation. Citing Sidney Mintz's observation concerning the Caribbean "learned openness to cultural variety...an openness which includes the expectation of cultural differences," Huon Wardle writes, "[A]mbiguation typically comes into play in an attempt to negotiate, evade, in some cases to explore without extreme cost, the volatile interface of social formations and cultural values" (Wardle 2002, 498). Ambiguation as a rhetorical device involves strategically blurring the semiotic content of an utterance in order to ensure that its import is not entirely clear, often by emphasizing one possible social meaning while not explicitly denying that others exist (Lessig 1995). This decrease in denotative specificity acts to obscure the precisely correct interpretation of an interlocutor's statement, and thereby neutralize antagonisms that may result from the awareness or unequivocal expression of disagreement. Ambiguation as a linguistic technique has had a social corollary in the willingness to enter unfamiliar situations; belong to groups whose aims are at variance with one another's; conceal identifying traits for the purpose of harmonizing with others; and maintain seemingly incompatible relationships.

Ambiguation in the Black Metropolis has been not a luxury, but a daily necessity, for almost a century. Despite its depiction as parochial and insular, the Black 'ghetto' has served as a nexus point of intellectual sophistication and urbanity, borne of a vibrant print and material culture blossoming in the midst of economic disparity and racial discrimination (Nashashibi 2007, 123–131). The South Side bred cosmopolitan virtues such as tolerance and ecumenism, partly as a by-product of cultural heterogeneity in a context of racial segregation and marginalization (Turner 2000, 129–147; Zorbaugh 1929, 151). Ambiguation at the level of everyday social interaction and linguistic exchange has been most crucial, and perhaps most conspicuous, in the religious arena due to the distinctive role of Christianity in African-American life. To put it bluntly, it has seldom been an option to declare oneself completely 'unchurched', for the Black Church has traditionally been a semi-involuntary institution (Hunt and Hunt 2000, 569–594). Despite the formality and ubiquity of religious distinctions that seem categorically exclusive, ambiguation has tended to mitigate the rigidity of moral valuations—a discourse of 'good' versus 'evil'—that leads to the calcification of religious identifications and the erosion of racial solidarity (Wardle, "A Groundwork," 577).

Both anecdotal and sociological evidence suggests a widespread exchange of tropes, techniques, materials, and personnel between religious communities in the Black Metropolis as a result of ambiguation. Religious variation and intercourse within a given Black community is not a twentieth-century development; among African-Americans, writes Charles Long, "extra-church orientations" such as conjure have historically offered "great critical and creative power" as a complement to regular participation in mainstream Christian congregations (Long 1986, 7). Tracey E. Hucks has described African-American religion more generally in terms of "religious coexistence and dual or multiple religious allegiance" (Hucks 2001, 90). To offer one example, religious ambiguation in Black Chicago has gone hand in hand with African-American "therapeutic pluralism," as in the case of those used to consulting both hoodoo doctors and licensed physicians in cases of illness. The heterogeneity of the religious sphere has been an accepted part of the cultural landscape, facilitating dialogue and energetic activity across denominational lines, as well as augmenting the number of resources for crisis management, emotional satisfaction, intellectual stimulation, and corporeal well-being that African-Americans have had at their disposal.

Ambiguation has also opened a way for Afro-Atlantic traditions such as Lucumí to make significant inroads among African-Americans. I found in the course of my research that many members of Ilé Laroye had been christened as Roman Catholics, yet an equal number began their religious lives as followers of the Black Spiritual Church or the Black Nationalist Pan African Orthodox Christian Church established by theologian Albert Cleage in 1967, founded as the Shrine of the Black Madonna. For the most part, my interlocutors in Chicago had pursued the worship of African spirits after the Mariel boatlift of

1980, when large numbers of Cuban-born practitioners of Lucumí, as well as Palo Monte and Espiritismo, emigrated to the United States. Initiated and prepared for leadership by a Havana-born Lucumí elder, Nilaja has negotiated the survival of Ilé Laroye in a complex urban landscape. She has rallied to the standard set by the storefronts in reconceiving her home's floor plan to capitalize on every square foot of available space. And just the storefronts have, Nilaja's "house of ocha" has converted impediments into conditions of possibility. This has been accomplished in part by relying on neighbors to adopt the ambiguating attitude of the 'G' or 'gangster' code—"I didn't see nothing, I ain't saying nothing...I ain't ratting anyone out"—that was glossed as "a cultural thing in the Black community."[10]

Today, those in search of a Lucumí community in Chicago today need only type these words into an internet search engine to find Ilé Laroye. But arriving there has not been merely a matter of traversing the South Side and reaching a fixed address, but of first becoming sympathetic to a reappraisal of Afro-Diasporic religious forms. This is the context in which ambiguation has become of vital importance for social organization, for it was in the religious atmosphere of groups judged to be cults and sects that the future members of Nilaja's house of ocha developed their religious sensibilities, and their family histories run parallel to those of the storefront churches' faithful. (Pérez 2010) During one of my first conversations with an African-American Lucumí practitioner, a priestess named Frances said, "I *love* me some Jesus!" She had decided long ago, however, that serving the Jesus she adored was not enough to secure her well-being. On another occasion, Nilaja condensed the complex matter of her disaffiliation from Roman Catholicism into a sentence, musing on her childhood as a "wannabe nun," her short adult career as a catechism teacher, and continued participation in her local parish choir. Nilaja told me, *"If they could've handled me, I would've stayed."*[11] Nilaja's experience was representative of many whose disaffection from the religious traditions of their births occurred as a reaction to limitations placed on their ministry and full membership. For several of Ilé Laroye's members, Christianity became their extra-church orientation.

Relocating Cults and Sects

While Lucumí would seem to be a stark divergence from the traditions of practitioners' upbringings, like the storefronts, this tradition recognizes the

---

10   Personal communication, October 8, 2005.
11   Personal communication, September 22, 2006.

enfleshment of the religious subject in a particular historical moment and demands the cultivation of moral-ethical 'potentialities' through corporeal disciplines (Asad 2003, 92). Lucumí also affirms the leadership of women and gay men as only fitting, if practitioners are redefined as the brides and wifely helpmeets of their deities in initiation (Clark 2005). As in the storefronts, in Ilé Laroye folks seek resolution for real-world problems, embrace the materiality of the sacred, and seek the succor of intercessors between themselves and an ultimate source of divine power, for whom they act ritually as vehicles. In fact, within Ilé Laroye, pioneers from the South are called on ceremonially as ancestors and in everyday conversations as living repositories of wisdom—including, for instance, Nilaja's father, still called "Geechee [Country] Joe" as an octogenarian. The oral traditions, cultural contributions, and social practices of Southern migrants have continued to mold their descendants' attitudes, forms of association, and religious sensibilities well into the twenty-first century, and deserve serious consideration in any account of Ilé Laroye's membership and ethos.

This argument for the importance of cults and sects within the Black experience challenges dominant understandings of the Church's role in African-American religious history. The project to situate mainline denominations at the center of the Black religious experience began as a retort to those who claimed that Africa had no religion—only fetishism, as in G.W.F. Hegel's *Lectures on the Philosophy of History*—and that "the Negro" has no history or past (Pietz 1988, 105–123). But it has operated to silence traditions that have fallen outside regnant post-Enlightenment understandings of religion as "faith," and models of religious subjectivity that conceptualize the self as multiple and materially constituted. This has meant that, for the better part of a century, African-American religion has been deemed synonymous with Christianity, and the institutional Black Church in particular (Lincoln and Mamiya 1990, 6–7). The literature on twentieth-century African-American religious practice teems with hostility to what have been termed cults and sects—relatively new movements that, by and large, sought to render gods too concrete for the comfort of bourgeois Northern elites heavily invested in the politics of respectability. Scholars have shared a prejudice against Southern migrants, denying them agency in the making of their own history, favoring economically and politically deterministic explanations for their attraction to non-mainstream religious groups (Denino Best 2005, 33–34). W.E.B. DuBois was one of the first to refer to the "the Negro Church" in the singular, in 1897, and since that time, this entity has governed the discursive production of Black identity.

It is perhaps to be expected that theologians would define the Church as normative, sealing the boundaries of what may be called religious within the constructive dimensions of their prophetic agenda. But examples of bias against counter-hegemonic Black religious expression in African-American history are legion, with analyses driven by complementary ideological and 'ultimate' concerns.[12] Official accounts of the Black Church's formation and development have tended to elide regional and class differences, as well as erase moral-ethical practices and liturgical regimes not deemed sufficiently liberatory. The recognition of Black religious heterogeneity has been perceived as threatening to the unity of the African-American *volk*; its embarrassment of riches has been viewed simply as an embarrassment, an excess that must be excised if it is to be demonstrated that Black people are civilized citizens of the modern nation-state. In fact, one could say that African-American religious historiography has defined the Black Church against cults and sects, setting them up as foils for its idealized self-representation. It bears recalling that when the *American Journal of Sociology* published its first article about the Nation of Islam in 1938 it was called, "The Voodoo Cult among Negro Migrants in Detroit" (Beynon 1938, 894–907). Such groups have been construed as Black Christianity's Other, although members of new religious movements have also frequented the most venerable of established churches, and practices of ambiguation have encouraged African-Americans to consider themselves at home—or at least welcome—in different communities at once.

As an historian of religion and ethnographer, I train my analytic lens not on the deeds that religious subjects ought to perform—from the perspective of a particular tradition—but on the things they actually do. Rather than treating religion as a realm separate from politics or sui generis—that is, so private as to lie beyond empirical scrutiny and therefore uniquely inexplicable—I am intent on accounting for religious phenomena in terms of the social, cultural, and ideological contingencies that both enable and foreclose human action in a given historical moment.[13] My concern with the quotidian affairs and every-day reality of religious communities determines both my programs of research and engagement with the body of scholarship on Africana religions. The inescapable fact that Afro-Diasporic traditions have seldom numbered among the major world religions or appeared on syllabi in university religious studies departments cannot be understood apart from the racial, ethic, and gender bias at the foundation of religion as an academic discipline (Masuzawa 2005). This chapter is one small attempt to move Africana and African American

---

12 For only one example, see James H. Cone, "They Sought a City: Martin's Dream or Malcolm's Nightmare," in *Liberating Eschatology: Essays in Honor of Letty M. Russell* (Louisville: Westminster John Knox Press, 1999), 98, 99.

13 My comments are informed by the contributions of Bruce Lincoln, Russell T. McCutcheon, and Jonathan Z. Smith to the history of religions, in too many volumes to enumerate here.

religious studies in a direction of inquiry less indebted to assumptions about what religion should be, and toward the investigation of ordinary, lived religious experience.

To return to the title of this chapter, what I mean by suggesting that we 'relocate' cults and sects is to reconsider what is religious in the African-American experience, and to think twice about where we seek religion as scholars—and not to look merely where there is the greatest available light. Studies of congregational practice have trumped the study of religion within the home, and ignored the street as a site for the formation of religious subjectivity. Historians of religion are not usually trained to linger on the corner or in the kitchen— the part of Nilaja's home that ultimately became the micro-site of my ethnographic research. Yet it is on the bus and at the stove that we find the bricolage or polyculturalism of Black religious expression and the diversity of its influences, growing more numerous by the day as novel technologies and processes of mediatization enable local, deterritorialized traditions to go transnational. We are only starting to fathom the extent to which African-American religious practice has been inspired not just by Islam, but also Judaism; Buddhism; Freemasonry; widely disseminated occult texts such as *The Sixth and Seventh Books of Moses* and *The Aquarian Gospel of Jesus the Christ*; Midwestern spiritualism; Afro-Caribbean initiatory traditions; and a strain of Orientalism that runs zig-zag from Noble Drew Ali to the Five-Percenter anthems of the Wu-Tang Clan (Miyakawa 2005).

If we wish to understand the relationships between the traditions I have mentioned above, we have to reevaluate the grand narratives of African American religion and entertain the thought of de-centering the Black Church. This remains an almost heretical notion, bearing in mind the role of prominent pastors, deacons, and devout in not only the civil rights and Black Power movements, but also in the crystallization of African-American religious history as a field of study. Perhaps some clarification on the idea of "de-centering" would be useful. Rather than pushing the Black Church to the periphery, I would advocate viewing it as one of multiple historic centers for African-American religious expression. In fact, we can extend the study of mainline congregations well beyond our present knowledge of them by leaving the pews and listening for its cadences at the kitchen table and on the pavement, in front of the barbershop and basketball court. Traditions that have blossomed outside mainstream Protestantism—such as "Sweet Daddy" Grace's United House of Prayer for All People, the Black American Yorùbá Movement, and now-burgeoning Kemetic[14] Reconstructionism—have borne complimentary

---

14   That is, Egyptian.

fruit, and continue to be irrigated by the subterranean longing for suffering to have meaning and for the divine to assume concrete form.

The types of ambiguating social practices and forms of religious transformation I have outlined above go against the grain of the notion that religious affiliation is definitive and predictive of future religious activity. One of the implications of this approach is pedagogical. In the classroom, we can present African-American religion not according to a chronology of congregational development—beginning with the invisible institution, slave religion, the Second Great Awakening, and so on, up until the present day—but instead, examine undertheorized themes in African-American religion through their geographical sites and conditions of emergence. We can challenge the teleology of Black emancipation through Christianity that has undergirded Africa-American history and racial identity formation. We can conceptualize "cults and sects" as traditions that merit intersectional analysis, and favor genealogical accounts over the quest for stable origins. And in our scholarship, we can investigate the way that religious practitioners have aggregated mutual identifications in order to enlarge their resources for everyday living. I have taken pains to dwell on the specificity of Chicago as my point of departure, yet in analogous urban centers we also find religion in unaccustomed guises. To understand the transformation of Black religious subjects, it may be necessary to revise our understanding of religion, and in the process, embrace the possibility of unsettling ourselves.

CHAPTER 5

Spirit is Universal
Development of Black Spiritualist Churches

Mary Ann Clark

Introduction

Although little known or studied today, Spiritualism was one of the most significant of the religious movements to sweep through the United States in the early to mid-nineteenth century. This was during a pivotal period in the history of religion in the United States when Americans developed their own distinctive form of religiosity, a form that eventually set them apart from their European cousins. Significantly this new form of religiosity was built on a foundation of religious individualism, a new view of the place of the dead in the sacred cosmos, and a new relationship between the living and the dead—all of which were highlighted in Spiritualism. It is these views that have continued to be influential into twenty-first century American religious culture.

Nineteenth-century Spiritualism was an important movement among white American of all classes. Thousands of people became involved with spiritualism either as mediums or their clients. It was reported that in 1854 there were three hundred Spiritualist clubs in Philadelphia alone and one scholar has estimated that nearly one-third of the American population was somehow involved in the movement by 1867 (Cox 2003, 237n2). Significantly, it also gave members of the African American community a way to continue many of their own spiritual beliefs and practices, especially those focused on the relationship between the living and the dead. Although during the earliest history of Spiritualism black and white spiritualists worked together, eventually Black spiritualists split from the mainline National Spiritualist Church to form their own National Colored Spiritualist Association. However, even though both groups may have forgotten the contributions they made to each others' religious sensibilities, the ideas of both groups about the dead and the afterlife have never been the same. Just as metaphysical religion has often been discounted as an important influence on American religious history, the influences of the African and African-inspired beliefs and practices underlying these traditions have been little recognized in either the standard view of American religious history or that subset focused on African American traditions, especially the Black Church. Yet it is these traditions that can provide a

© KONINKLIJKE BRILL NV, LEIDEN, 2015 | DOI 10.1163/9789004283428_007

deeper understanding of contemporary American, especially African American, esoteric traditions.

Theory and Methods

In her groundbreaking survey of what she calls American metaphysical religion Catherine Albanese proposes three different view of American religious history. The first of these, based on William McLoughlin's *Revivals, Awakenings and Reform* (McLoughlin 1978) lays out what became known as the evangelical thesis: that the four "great [evangelical] awakenings" were the most important factors shaping American religious history. The second viewpoint, espoused by the Yale historian Jon Butler in his *Awash in a Sea of Faith* and other works, instead stressed the role of European state churches. According to this view, it was the development of a state-church/denominational tradition that became the most important force in the development of religion in America. Albanese, without discounting the importance of these two threads, argues that what she calls metaphysics or metaphysical religion has also had, and continues to have, an important influence on American religiosity (Albanese 2007). In fact she says that the forces represented by these three viewpoints have all been important in the development of an America religious sensibility. They each developed in relationship with each other and participants in one movement were also participants in the other two such that "(e)vangelicals could also be mainstreamers; mainstreamers could have their metaphysical side; and so, too, could evangelicals" (Albanese 2007, 17). Albanese argues that although these three viewpoints are each important in understanding American religious development, the third strand, the metaphysical religious viewpoint, has often been ignored or devalued in spite of its important influences on American religious sensibilities (Albanese 2007, 5).

Albanese also posits four themes that typify the American metaphysical movement. First is a pre-occupation with the mind and its powers. In this view, the mind is not limited to the purely rational but also encompasses the intuitive and poetic, and such capabilities as visionary, auditory, tactile, kinesthetic, gustatory and olfactory extrasensory manifestations, telepathy, trance and mediation. In fact, "the mind" includes all the ways that one can communicate between the material and spiritual world and all the ways one can cause both material and spiritual transformation. This communication depends on Albanese's second theme, a tendency to develop and use one or more theories of correspondences between the material and spiritual worlds, an idea that is also important in Fairve's definition of esotericism. These theories incorporate ideas from any number of traditions from Europe, Asia, Africa, and the Americas. The third theme suggests the tendency to think in terms of energy and movement. Every part of the material and spiritual worlds are believed to be joined together by energy that is in constant flux so that the mind that understands these correspondences and linkages is capable of not only perceiving the movement but also using its own energy to affect changes at all levels. Finally, Albanese's fourth theme has to do with the types of changes that are important in these traditions. She suggests that there is a "yearning for salvation understood as solace, comfort, therapy and healing" such that religious practice serves to benefit as much in the here-and-now as the forever-after (Albanese 2007, 13–15).

As we shall see these metaphysical themes have important influences from African-heritage peoples and continue within African-American communities through Spiritualist congregations.

American Spiritualist Tradition

The American Spiritualist tradition is generally considered to have stated in 1848 when the Fox sisters of Hydesville, New York were awakened by a series of loud rapping noises they, their parents, and neighbors interpreted as the work of a spirit presence. However, they were not the first to have such experiences. Anglo-American Shakers who also engaged in sacred dance and other types of ecstatic behavior were contacting spirits for many years before the Fox sisters had their spirit encounter. In fact the New Hampshire lawyer and rationalist William Plumer visiting the Shaker community in Harvard, Massachusetts in 1782, recorded spirit contact there. Like the Spiritualists that followed, the Shakers communicated not only with their own dead members and founders but also such important personages as George Washington, Napoleon, Queen Esther, Queen Isabella, as well as the Heavenly Father, Holy Mother Wisdom, and Jesus. There were also reports of communications with both Native American and Black spirits (Albanese 2006, 184–186). The flamboyant mixed-race Spiritualist and trance medium Paschal Beverly Randolph suggested that his mother was speaking to the dead before the advent of the Fox sisters and the movement they started. Randolph became a prominent occult theorist, Spiritualist, and trance speaker who was not only influenced by the great lights of the Spiritualist tradition but was also an important influence on the movement. It is also likely other people of African heritage also continued their own traditions of communications with the dead within the confines of the Spiritualist movement.

When the Fox sisters moved to Rochester New York shortly after their encounter with "Mr. Splitfoot," they entered into an environment that was not only a hot bed of radical ideas but was also the home to a thriving free African American community that appears to have maintained many of their own religious rituals and customs (Sweet 2006, 74–76; Stuckey 1999, 171–173). Although there was no explicit documentation of African-American influence on the Spiritualist movement, we can trace suggestive correspondences and similarities between African ideas about spirit communication and those that developed within the Spiritualist community.

The Spiritualist movement certainly opened up American ideas about the spirit world. Until this time Euro-American theology placed the spirits of the dead beyond the reach of the living so that they were unable to cause any change in their loved ones' conditions. It is important to realize that at that time any communication received from the spirit world was understood to be from demonic sources, not the benign dead relatives and influential figures of the later Spiritualist cosmos. Even the Fox sisters first named their spirit partner "Mr. Split Foot." "Old Split Foot" was one of the many euphemistic names commonly used for the devil and may indicate that the girls originally thought that they were conversing with a demonic being. However, they quickly determined that this invisible entity was the spirit of a peddler who had been murdered and buried in the cellar by previous owners of their house.

While such disquiet spirits were sometimes thought to hang around their death or burial sites, it was more commonly believed that once separated from the body one's spirit was completely disconnected from the world of the living. The Spiritualist movement was generally credited with "proving" not only that the individual consciousness continued to exist after death but also that the dead maintained interest in the world of the living and that the living could gain knowledge of that afterlife from them. Spiritualist mediums generally worked with two types of spirits: the beloved dead of their audience and great persons from previous ages. Friends and relatives who died unexpectedly could be contacted by mediums in order to provide comfort for their survivors. Both Horace and Mary Greeley and Abraham and Mary Lincoln repeated visited Spiritualists in order to contact their young sons who died in childhood, for example. Spiritualists also channeled messages from the great men of the past including George Washington, Lincoln himself, and others.

In spite of the fact that there were many male theorists attempting to explain and explicate the spiritualist tradition it was uneducated young girls who formed the bulk of the mediums who brought the messages from the "other side" to audience throughout the country. Mediumship provided an opening for women to develop careers that enabled them to travel and support themselves freed from the oversight of husbands and fathers. There were also African American mediums that attracted audiences within both the black and white communities including Randolph and the Shaker Spiritualist Rebecca Cox Jackson. Black mediums shared with their white counterparts the stereotypes of being more "intuitive, inspirational, religious and altogether mediumistic" and religious scholars suggest that there was a close connection between African American communities and the Spiritualist movement. Ann Braude even says that the Spiritualist movement served as a bridge between European spiritual ideas and what she calls African American folk practices (Braude 2001; Levine and Gleig 2009, 266–267). In fact enslaved Africans brought with them from their homelands many of the elements Albanese attributes to American metaphysical traditions including a focus on the powers of mediumship, a system of correspondences between the material and spiritual worlds, and techniques for influencing changes in the material world through the influence of spiritual beings.

African Traditions of Speaking with the Dead

The indentured and enslaved Africans that were transported to American shores brought their own cosmological viewpoints with them across the Atlantic. Although they came from different cultural areas and spoke different languages, their languages and worldviews were not completely alien to each other. Thus their related backgrounds provided commonalities that individuals were able to use to explain and attempt to control their new environment. The bulk of the enslaved came from coastal areas between present-day Senegal to the north and along the West African coast to the central African kingdoms of Kongo and Angola in the south. Most lived within 100 miles of the coast and few came from the interior or areas of southern or eastern Africa. People in the societies most affected by the slave trade did not live in isolation from each other. In fact the African scholar John Thornton has said that there were only three major cultures and seven subcultures that contributed African peoples to the New World. The enslaved generally came from societies that traded with each other, sometimes exchanged their children in marriage, migrated back and forth and often spoke similar languages, learned each other's language, or had developed a mutually understandable trade language (Thornton 1992, 186).

In terms of worldview we can find threads of commonality among these cultures including a belief in some sort of supreme deity as well as a myriad of lesser deities, ancestors and other spirits. There was also an understanding that the living and the dead formed a single assemblage with individuals moving back and forth between one condition and the other through a cycle of birth, death and rebirth. Most groups held the elderly in a high esteem that continued and grew after they passed from the world of the living to that of the dead. Members of these cultures valued both personal and collective identities and had methods for balancing the responsibilities for oneself with those for one's family and larger society. There was a veneration and respect not only for the dead but also other types of spiritual powers who could influence and be influenced for the betterment or detriment of human kind. Many if not most of these societies had rituals and techniques for communicating with these spiritual beings both directly and indirectly including ways of embodying spiritual beings through the practice of possession trance. Thus we can see that members of these cultures already had the experience of the type metaphysical techniques Albanese describes before being brought to the Americas.

Among those who study possession phenomena world wide, the West and West Central African variant tends to be of a form called trance possession. During these events gods, spirits and ancestors temporarily inhabit the bodies of select individuals in order to communicate with their living devotees and descendants. During the possession event, the consciousness of the individual is replaced with that of the possessing spirit who is thus able to interact with the observing community, eating, drinking and most importantly advising and healing those present while imparting knowledge about both the material and spiritual worlds. In general these possession events happened in the public arena, often the marketplace or town square where, through drumming and dancing, spiritual entities were invited into the bodies of the living. We have every reason to believe that these types of activities were continued in the Americas during events like the Pinkster Festival that was popular in eighteenth century Albany, New York. Even though the earliest American colonists did not recognize any religious activity among their bondspeople, they often reported the drumming and dancing that Africans in both the North and South engaged in during their personal time. Given the close relationship that existed between music, dance and possession events in Africa it would be completely surprising if these so-called "devil dances" didn't turn into religious ceremonies complete with spiritual possession, especially in the North where strong free African American communities existed for generations. These events not only gave African-heritage people the opportunity to engage in public drumming and dancing according to their own preferences, they also exposed non-African peoples to these types of celebrations and the possession events embedded within them (Sweet, 74–76, Stuckey 171–173).

The Dead Are Not Dead

Changes in the European view of the dead and their place in the afterlife are detailed in Philippe Ariès' history of death, dying and burial practices, *Hour of Our Death*. At the time of the colonial and early Revolutionary periods these practices reflected the Calvinistic understanding that the ultimate resolution of one's soul rested solely on the decision of God who had predetermined each individual's fate from all eternity. This notion of predestination meant that there was no assurance about one's ultimate fate before death and that no ritual or ceremonies afterward could change one's fortune. In addition, having achieved their eternal reward or punishment, it was believed that the dead maintained no interest or concern about those left behind. Consequently, the most important ritual site was the deathbed, and burials were unimportant and perfunctory. Most people were buried in common, unmarked graves carried there by workmen. The family and friends didn't usually accompany the body to its final resting place and in several place laws had to be passed requiring that bodies actually be interred, rather than dumped along the way.

In Europe, this disregard for the remains of those who have died has lead to a preference for cremation that efficiently made "the body disappear, in a respectable way of course, but quickly and completely" (Ariès 1974, 154). However, in the United States, ideas about death, dying and burial changed, perhaps influenced by the burial practices of the thousands of African brought to this country.

In most of the societies of West and West Central Africa whose members were enslaved and brought to America, individual gravesites and complex funeral rituals were the norm. In the prevailing cosmologies of these societies it was believed that the gravesite served as a gateway between the worlds of the living and the dead, a gateway that allowed communication and aid to pass from one world to the other. Families that performed the appropriate burial rituals and made ongoing offering at the gravesite could expect their beloved dead to return and speak to them through the mechanisms of possession trance, dreams and the like. It was also expected that the dead could smooth the way of the attentive individuals and family members. In this way the living and the dead maintained their relationships through continuing cycles of birth, death and rebirth.

Research shows that once they reached America the enslaved continued to follow their own burial customs rather than adapting those of the master class (Butler 2008, 93). It appears that slave funerals and burials were so important that even the most hardened master allowed for some sort of funeral and interment rituals. Whereas the moment of death was the focal point of white customs, among blacks the handing of the body after death, including the interment, and the subsequent embellishment of the gravesite was of premier importance. Robert Ferris Thompson's work highlighting burial practices in the South as well as excavations such as the African Burial Ground of New York highlight the ways that African burial customs were continued in the United States (Thompson 1984, 132–142; Blakey 1998; Roediger 1981).

Religious Individualism

In the analysis of religious sensibilities, *individualism* is the tendency to construct one's own religious beliefs and a preference for a personal experience of the holy. The Protestant Reformation that began in the sixteenth century Europe and continued into eighteenth century America encouraged individual believers to consider for themselves the doctrines to which they would give their assent and then to join together with others with similar ideas of religiosity to form new congregations and denominations. Africans, too, brought their own ideas about which religious doctrines and forms that they would follow. Many Africans came from societies where a multiplicity of deities and spirits were available for worship and veneration and where families and individuals often participated in the worship of specific deities as well as their own ancestors. In addition, among most of the African societies that contributed the bulk of the African-heritage peoples in the Americas, a tradition of continuous revelation was the norm. Within the European worldview, revelation was generally considered enclosed within the Christian scripture and, in some cases, the writing of the church fathers. In general, the Bible was the ultimate authority against which any new revelation had to be evaluated. New ideas and views that were not consistent with orthodox understandings of the Bible had to be rejected and the "prophet" persecuted. Much of the long history of the Inquisition in both Catholic and Protestant regions dealt with personal revelations that were rejected because they didn't conform to clerical understandings of the Bible.

However, in the West and West Central African societies of the same time it was believed that deities and ancestors regularly spoke to their followers and descendants through dreams and visions as well as through the word of trance mediums and other inspired members of society. Within this environment contemporary revelation was more compelling than ancient texts. Changes and revisions, or special revelations to individuals or small groups were readily accepted based on local standards of efficacy. New revelations that made lives better were accepted while those that did not provide such relief were rejected and forgotten. Even among the Kongolese who were converted to Catholic Christianity before the discovery of the Americas, on-going revelations held an important place within society and new revelations were evaluated, not against a standard of biblical conformity but one of efficacy and immediate accuracy.

Americans' acceptance of new revelations has waxed and waned over the course of its history. Especially during the first centuries of colonization and revolution new religious views proliferated and an acceptance of diverse religious views was written into the first of the amendment to the country's constitution. The periods known as the First and Second Great Awakenings, between the early 18th century and the late 19th century, accelerated the tendency of Americans to depend on personal revelations and their own experience of the sacred. It was also during this period that African-Americans with their own understandings of prophesy and revelation were widely converted to the evangelical Methodist and Baptist tradition that were on the forefront of the revivals of the times.

Spiritualists helped change the worldview that continues to underlie American religiosity, and moved Americans from a European-style viewpoint to one that was more consistent with African ways of viewing the world. For example, Spiritualists were religious individualists who did not define their faith according to any prescribed set of ceremonies or specific creeds. Instead each person was encouraged to seek their own inner light and to work for their own spiritual development under the leadership of their spirit guides. That the advice presented by different guides might not be consistent was not a concern as each person was seen as on their own personal spiritual journey. This is very similar to West African ideas of destiny that we find most strongly articulated among the Yoruba who believe that because each person has a unique destiny, each must have a unique way of being in the world. Consequently, there was an understanding that the advice and both positive and negative recommendations for spiritual development had to be tailored for each individual rather than being based on some universal requirement. This individualist tendency continues to be an important part of the American religious character.

Black Spiritualist Churches

Spiritualism gave to members of African American communities a way to continue many of their own spiritual beliefs and practices about the relationship between the living and the dead, and spiritual individualism. In many ways these ideas came full circle from that of the earliest enslaved Kongolese people to arrive on these shores to the development of independent Black Spiritual churches of the early twentieth century.

The idea of universal brotherhood, so cherished in early Spiritualism, was challenged after the Civil War when white Spiritualists had to find a way to include not only non-white mediums but also the Black and Native American spirits who where showing up in séance rooms, while maintaining their racist prejudices. Like Christian preachers who told their enslaved or newly freed African-American converts that they would continue to be separated from the white master class in heaven, many Spiritualists suggested that whites and Blacks would occupy different levels of the heavenly realm. Eventually African American spiritualists would feel that they had to separate from their white co-religionists to form their own spiritual communities.

Like many religious groups in the Black community, the Spiritualist movement underwent a tremendous growth in the 1920s and 1930s especially in the northern cities of Chicago and Detroit. According to one account by 1938 there were fifty-one Black Spiritualist Churches in the Chicago area, including one with over two thousand members (Baer 2001, 22–23). In 1922 the black members of the white-controlled National Spiritualist Association of Churches separated to form the National Colored Spiritualist Association headquartered in Detroit. The association had congregations in the Detroit area as well as Chicago, Columbus, Miami, Charleston, St. Petersburg, Phoenix, and New York City. As the term "spiritualist" took on negative connotations in the 1920s and 30s, black Spiritualist congregations began to rename themselves "Spiritual" rather than "Spiritualist." Identifying Spiritualism as communication with the dead, séances and fortune-telling, Voodoo, hoodoo and using Spiritual work "for the wrong reasons," Spiritual people prefer to focus on communicating with God in the form of the Holy Spirit.

Many Spiritual congregations also began to de-emphasizing the séance or other arenas where mediums provide messages from the spirit world. While such messages continue to be an important part of mainstream Spiritualist religious services, many Spiritual congregations began to relegate them to special blessing or prophesy services. Spiritual people also denied any association with Voodoo or "hoodoo" although outsiders often accuse them of engaging in such practices and some Spiritual people even accuse other Spiritual people of the same thing. Because both Voudou and many Spiritual churches developed in New Orleans in the late nineteenth century, many people attribute the use of amulets, talismans, charms, sprays, incenses, baths, floor washes, perfume oils, special soaps, powders, roots, and herbs by some Spiritual people as evidence of the influence of Voodoo among them. In spite of the fact that there may be other explanations, it is probably more likely that this parallel development came about because New Orleans Voudou and the Black Spiritual churches have many influences in common.

Although there were black Spiritualist circles in the mid-to-late nineteenth century especially in the New Orleans area, most of the Black Spiritual groups trace their beginnings to the early twentieth century. This was one of the many religions that emerged between 1890 and the Second World War as African Americans responded to their status shift in American society. The West and West Central African traditions of spirit possession and a strong veneration of ancestors with its ideal of continued community attachment to kin after death have provided a foundation for the development of Spiritual traditions within Black communities. Like many other American religious traditions, Spiritual people have always been willing to incorporate beliefs and practices from a wide range of other traditions. In addition to the influence of Spiritualism, we can see elements of Black Protestantism, Roman Catholicism, and Voodoo as well as New Thought, Islam, Judaism, Ethiopianism and astrology within the Spiritual tradition. The most obvious examples of this syncretism are the Catholic accouterments commonly found in Spiritual church including crucifixes, statues of the Virgin Mary and other saints, and holy pictures. Catholic rituals such as making the sign of the cross, genuflecting and burning incense and candles are often interspersed with activities like testifying, hymn singing and shouting more often found in typical Black Protestant congregations (Baer, 120, 122). And like many of the other unconventional religious groups described in this text, these groups are relatively invisible even within the community itself. While many people know of the Spiritual church "down the street," these congregations are seldom included in discussion of Black spirituality.

Many of the storefront churches established in the black community in Chicago in the first two decades of the twentieth century, whether or not they called themselves Spiritualist, believed in communication with spirits and used mediums to relay messages between their members and the spirit world. However, it appears that the Spiritualist groups in New Orleans had the most significant impact on the development of the Black Spiritual movement nationwide. Mother Alethea "Leafy" Anderson, a woman of Black and Indian ancestry, is credited with starting the first Black Spiritualist church in New Orleans around 1920 having migrated from Chicago where she organized churches from as early as 1913. In New Orleans she trained women, both Black and White, who established other congregations in the New Orleans area. Eventually her association of churches had congregations in Chicago, Little Rock, Memphis, Pensacola, Biloxi, Houston as well as some smaller cities. Although initially persecuted by the establishment religious organizations her churches were wildly successful. In the 1920s and 1930s Spiritual churches figured prominently among the religious organizations of New Orleans and their leaders were popular and well known. Indeed by the 1940s one in six of the New Orleans churches listed in the *Directory of Churches and Religious Organizations in New Orleans* were Spiritual. This followed a nation-wide trend of similar statistics in Chicago, Harlem, Houston, Detroit, Baltimore and Philadelphia (Jacobs and Kaslow 1991, 1). Mother Anderson died in 1927, but she was still appearing to the women who carried out her work and giving instructions from the spirit world as late as the mid-1940s (Baer 2001, 18–20).

Mother Anderson brought a "rich blend of mediumistic practices, faith healing, folk-herbalism and charismatic sacred performance" with her from Chicago (Wehmeyer 2010, 45). However, spiritual beliefs among the people of New Orleans did not begin with her. According the research of Claude Jacobs and Andrew Kaslos, there were Spiritualist organizations in New Orleans from as early as the 1850s (Jacobs and Kaslow 1991). As one of the most cosmopolitan cities in North America, the people of New Orleans participated in a culture that supported an interplay of beliefs, symbols, and rituals not only from France, Spain and the United States but also from the various Native American and African ethnic groups that made the city their home. Today this cultural interplay had incorporated many so-called "new age" beliefs and practices. Some popular Spiritual Ministers have renamed themselves "life coaches." They call the blessed oils they use "aromatherapy" and have substituted "Reiki" for the more traditional laying on of hands for healing. Contemporary spiritualists are not just appropriating these new terms; they are learning these new spiritual technologies and legitimately incorporating them to their spiritual work (Wehmeyer 2010, 56).

Spiritual Praxis

According to Hans Baer, Spiritual churches tend to consist of four different types of participants. The core members are the most involved, those who typically attend services regularly and hold most of the religious offices. The peripheral members while, considering themselves members of the congregation, attend services less often and do not hold any religious offices preferring to be merely rank-and-file members. The third type of participants is the visitors who may or may not attend services regularly and who have made no commitment to the congregation. Some regular visitors may actually be members of other churches in the area. Finally, the last category is that of clients who do not participate in the public activities of the church but engage the services of the mediums or healers associated with the church (Baer 2001, 48). Generally the pastor is a medium but congregations may include other mediums as well. Within these churches mediums function very much as the mediums found in West and West Central African societies. Like their African and Spiritualists forerunners, Spiritual mediums have the ability to "'read' people or tell them things about their past, present, and future." These mediums work both during the public services when they include séances and in private sessions with individual clients. Many churches also include healers, who may or may not have the gift of prophecy (Baer 2001, 50–51).

As in white Spiritualist churches, the centerpiece of the some of the services in many Spiritual churches continues to be a séance during which participants receive messages from deceased friends and relatives, the beloved dead, as well as Catholic saints, indigenous spirits, the deceased enslaved and other noteworthy personages. In keeping with the this-worldly orientation of the churches, the messages received from the other world are generally concerned with the well being of the congregation and focus on such issues as the search for employment and resolving strained marital relationships (Baer 2001, 30–31). Although white Spiritualist churches are generally modeled on mainstream Protestant traditions, the churches that were formed in New Orleans also draw upon the local Roman Catholic traditions. Thus many black Spiritual churches with a New Orleans lineage use such Catholic practices as the sign of the cross, genuflecting, votive candles, holy pictures, holy water and water sprinklers, containers of holy oil, elaborate altars and statues. It is also common for ministers and mediums to incorporate Catholic religious gear, such as vestments similar to those worn by Catholic priests, in their religious regalia. Many Spiritual people include both the spirit of the Native American hero Black Hawk and various Catholic saints such as the Virgin Mary, Joseph, and Francis of Assisi among their favorite spiritual intermediaries.

Most prominent among the images found in Spiritual churches has been the Indian chief Black Hawk. Indian spirits in general and Black Hawk in particular are credited with making a "right of way" for spiritualists by controlling the link between interior domestic spaces and exterior public spaces. Often altars to these spirits are placed near doorways where they can control the movements between these two types of spaces (Wehmeyer 2010, 49). In his 2000 article "Indian Altars of the Spiritual Church" Stephen Wehmeyer suggests that a Kongolese aesthetic has been incorporated into the Native American-themed Spiritualists altars especially those associated both Black

Hawk and another Indian spirit known as "Uncle," "Kind Uncle" or "Uncle Bucket" (Wehmeyer 2000, 63). Reminiscent of what Robert Ferris Thompson calls *minkisi*-of-the above, the martial character of these altars emphasizes their themes of aggression and righteous retribution. The figures on these altars, which may include St. Michael in addition to Indian spirits and the so-called Uncle Bucket, are armed, feathered and swathed in red "as visible expressions of the kinds of spiritual forces" used among the Kongolese for "protection or spiritual attack, law giving, oath taking and administering divine punishment" (Wehmeyer 2000, 63–64).

Spiritual people exhibit great flexibility in their beliefs and practices. However, they generally are more concerned with discovering solutions to their day-to-day difficulties than preparing for any focus on "other-worldly" concerns. Like their white counterparts, Spiritual people reject the mainstream Christian idea of a fixed afterlife. Instead they teach that heaven and hell are states of mind in the present day world. Heaven is a state of peace, joy, happiness and success, which is the result of a satisfied mind while hell is the opposite. The afterlife is understood as a series of levels through which one might progress even after death. The less spiritually developed may begin their afterlife in one of the lower levels but with the guidance of the more advanced spirits and they can develop and progress to one of the higher heavens. Spiritual people also share the belief that their departed friends and relatives are still interested in their lives and can communicate their regard through mediums. Many Spiritual people also maintain belief in some sort of reincarnation.

The American idea of religious individualist is a prominent feature of Spiritual Churches. Many congregations hold special classes for their members to provide esoteric knowledge and techniques for acquiring blessings or "power." These classes are often surrounded with an aura of secrecy as they are specifically for spiritual development and are only open to select members of the congregation. Members of Spiritual churches also attend classes in the many schools of the occult and the esoteric sciences offered throughout the larger American cities. Many founders and pastors of Spiritual churches have attended these schools in order to learn the "secrets" they teach. Spiritual people also study astrology and such esoteric texts as *The Aquarian Gospel of Jesus Christ* (Dowing 1908), which is the purported account of the life of Jesus between the time of his early childhood and the beginning of his ministry when he supposedly traveled to India, Tibet, Persia, Assyria, Greece and Egypt to learn the esoteric traditions of those cultures (Baer 2001, 75). Today leaders of Spiritual churches may become certified as a Reiki master, a life coach or a Psych-K instructor (Wehmeyer, 2010, 56–57). More important than the specific techniques used is invocation of the spirits to help one "lead a happy, moral, successful life in the face of constant struggle," (Wehmeyer 2000, 69).

Spiritualist people are different from many other congregations in the black community in that they also have a very flexible and tolerant code of conduct. While many more mainstream congregations condemn card playing, dancing, the "sporting life" (prostitution, gambling, drinking, boxing—all around partying), movie-going, smoking, drinking and other such "things of the world," Spiritual leaders tend leave the decision to engage in such behaviors up to the discretion of the individual as long as they do not interfere with church affairs. Rather than establishing a rigid moral code, Spiritual pastors tend to permit people to "find themselves," make their own moral decisions while searching for the truth. This is very similar to the West African view that each individual is born with his or her own destiny. Each individual must discover their destiny for themselves and live out that destiny in their own unique way (Clark 2007, 68–72). While such religious individualism is a characteristic of Americans in general, Spiritual congregations, where individuals may be guided by different spiritual entities, value such uniqueness much more highly than many other religious organizations.

Conclusion

Black Spiritual Churches have formed an important part of the esoteric African American experience and the continuation of African religiosity into the twenty-first century. Although nineteenth-century Spiritualism provided an important catalyst moving Americans away from the Calvinist religiosity of the seventeenth century, it also made it possible for African Americans to incorporate their own spiritual beliefs and practices into a uniquely American tradition. Scholars have long recognized the syncretism that can be found in the religious traditions of the Caribbean and South America, but there has been little recognition of a similar process in Black religious institution in the United States. Instead histories of African American religions have focused on an extremely narrow view of black spirituality. This short overview of the history of Spiritualism in general and the Black Spiritualist movement in particular ought to provide a springboard for a wider scholarly investigation into the influences of diverse religious traditions on contemporary Black religiosity as well as the hidden, esoteric examples of contemporary African American spirituality.

Another area that deserves more study are the correspondences between European, Asian, and African esoteric traditions and how they have come together in the Americas, especially the United States, to form new, expanded metaphysical traditions. Just as we have seen how some Spiritual ministers have incorporated new age spiritual techniques into their religious practices, a more focused study of Black esoteric traditions has the potential to show how West and West Central African spiritual technologies been integrated not only into these traditions but into the wider American metaphysical world. Of all the religious viewpoints that have influenced American religious sensibilities, these African traditions, especially their esoteric practices, are among the most hidden.

CHAPTER 6

The Harlem Renaissance as Esotericism
Black Oragean Modernism

Jon Woodson

Introduction

And if out of a wholesale allegiance to Communism the Negro could
develop just a half dozen men who were really and truly outstanding the
result would be worth the effort.
    WALLACE THURMAN 1992, 219

Sometimes the Harlem Gallery
is a harvesting machine without binding
twine; again, a clock that stops
for want of winding.
    TOLSON 1965, lns. 4136–4139

According to Tom Hodd, "scholars have grossly ignored any relation the
Modernists held to pagan religions, and in some instances, have blatantly
denied the existence of a 'secret tradition' in Modernist literature" (Hodd 2010).
This essay examines the incorporation of that secret tradition of esotericism—
Spiritualism, Theosophy, Hermeticism, Kabbalah, and Alchemy—into the literary texts of Harlem Renaissance writers. And it argues that the esoteric
teachers G.I. Gurdjieff and his New York agent A.R. Orage were directly responsible for the infusion of occultism into a new form of black writing. Hodd further comments that "occult scholarship is highly specialized and demands
considerable foreknowledge from its readers (perhaps this is part of the reason
why occult scholarship has remained on the periphery of Modernist criticism)"
(Hodd 2010, 115). What this means is that the evaluation of literary texts that
are situated in occultism requires that scholars have a deep knowledge of
occultism as well as literature and criticism. While I have placed the Harlem
Renaissance texts in the context of Modernism, I have supplanted Modernist
criticism. In order to explicate the Oragean Modernist texts, I have taken a
comparativist approach. I treat the Gurdjieff Work comparatively as an off-
shoot of Theosophy in order to establish the broad background. I also compare
the Oragean version of the teaching to Gurdjieff's version, as Orage was
present in New York and differed in emphasis from what Gurdjieff taught in

France. On another level, I treat the novels written by the Harlem Renaissance esotericists comparatively by showing their relationship to the development of the realist novel. And I also compare the novels as discrete performances of the Oragean esoteric realist ur-novel.

In addition to the problems entailed in examining the relationship of the Harlem Renaissance to occultism, there are the problems arising out of the parallel blind spot of race. Khem Guragain states that "Mainstream hegemonic discourse always undermines black's presence in the making of American literature and culture" (Guragain 2009). African American literature is a non-canonical body of writing that has only been moved out of marginality in the 1970s. The intrusions of literary theory into literary scholarship; the literary politics of the black arts movement; limitations in the numbers of scholars, teaching positions, and opportunities for publication; and the inferior quality of the research that examines African American literature have contributed to a skewed narrative in which it is virtually impossible for literary critics to concede that an African American esoteric movement might have existed within the Harlem Renaissance. Thus, Aaron Douglas's lifelong practice as an esoteric painter is trivialized as a "flirtation with Gurdjieffian teachings" (Ragar 2008, 141), while his enigmatic and inauthentic career as a Marxist is rationalized and ratified. Similarly, faced with evidence of Wallace Thurman's participation in the Gurdjieff Work, Amritjit Singh, one of the major scholars of the Harlem Renaissance, shifts the emphasis to the temporary nature of this influence, stating that Thurman "took Gurdjieff quite seriously for a while" (Singh 2008, 10) and supports this assertion by quoting Thurman's admission to Langston Hughes that "Thus I could never make a good Gurdjieff disciple" (Singh 2008, 24). Thurman and his associates had wished to recruit Hughes, and once Hughes had turned his back on them, they countered by behaving as though they had also lost interest in Gurdjieff. Throughout the writings of the Harlem Gurdjieffians there are indications that they successfully misled Hughes and that they carried on their esoteric activities without his awareness of them.

It is the Harlem writers themselves who give testimony to the falsity of Hughes's assertions about the collapse of Jean Toomer's esoteric school. In *Seraph on the Suwanee*, Zora Neale Hurston refers to a crewman who was lost when he was "swept overboard by a *big sea*" (Hurston 1948, 324; emphasis added). This is an allusion to Hughes, whose autobiography was *The Big Sea* (1940). Hughes's mistaken account of Toomer's failure to introduce the Gurdjieff Work in Harlem in *The Big Sea* is the most-often quoted narrative of esotericism in Harlem in the 1920s, and it served as the authoritative account of Toomer's activities in many scholarly studies of the Harlem Renaissance.

Conceding in a recent biography of Harlem Renaissance novelist Nella Larsen
that Hughes could not have had any insight into the activities of Toomer's
groups, George Hutchinson states that "Hughes's whimsical discussion of
Toomer's meetings, which he did not attend, became the basis of a host of
misrepresentations that unfortunately continue to circulate in the scholarly
literature" (Hutchinson 2006, 541 n. 36). Another dismissal of Hughes takes
place in Melvin B. Tolson's epic poem, *A Gallery of Harlem Portraits*. Tubby
Laughton, a Langston Hughes surrogate, runs into a café where he confronts "a
big-bellied yellow man," a Gurdjieff surrogate. (Gurdjieff's Armenian ethnicity
leant him the "yellow" coloring used by the Harlem writers to refer to him.
After a perceived quarrel between Gurdjieff and A.R. Orage, they remained
loyal to Orage who mentored their writing, thereby creating a group of modernist writers). The Gurdjieff surrogate knocks Laughton unconscious, and the
poem's epigraph admonishes, "Mind yo' business, Black Boy" (Tolson 1982, 144).
Tolson mocks Hughes by making him fat (Tubby / ton) and laughing (Laughton)
at him. Another deflation of Langston Hughes takes place in Rudolph Fisher's
detective novel, *The Conjure Man Dies*, where the Hughes surrogate is a major
character. Hughes is unflatteringly portrayed as Bubber Brown, a rotund, bow-
legged figure whose face is "blank as a door knob" (Fisher 1932, 46). Bubber
Brown's corpulence closely parallels that of Tolson's Tubby Laughton. This sar-
castic treatment of Hughes is noteworthy, for most biographies of Hughes portray him as a handsome man and a lady-killer; Hughes's physical deformity is a
metonymy by which the Harlem Orageans displayed Hughes's psychological
nastiness as physical imperfection. Fisher pairs Bubber Brown with Langston
Hughes when Brown states that he is with "tongue hangin" (Fisher 1932, 11)—as
ang-tongue approximates the sound of Langston. Fisher's novel is written
entirely in the phonetic *cabala* (bi-directional phonetic assonance and resonance), as are most of the texts published by the dozens of New York writers
who followed Orage. The phonetic *cabala*, the code of the alchemists, was
spread by Fulcanelli's *Le Mystère des Cathédrales* (*The Mystery of the Cathedrals*),
written during 1922 and published in Paris during 1926.

Despite Langston Hughes's dismissal of the occult, the occult was as a reasonable interest for the African-American literary and fine artists of the 1920s,
since it was an emancipating reaction to the oppression of America's institu-
tionally racist culture. Simply put, American society was fundamentally constructed around the perception of a hierarchy of fixed types of humanity. Since
these typologies were supported by the science, religion, law, and education of
the day, there was little means to express alternative views. It was a matter of
common sense for oppressed elements of American society to look beyond the
accepted epistemological categories presented by the institutions in power,

and chief among those counter-narratives (along with Marxism, psychoanalysis, women's suffrage, and evolution) was the occult. It is often said that there was an occult revival in the 1920s and that the occult revival was prepared by the popularity of Theosophy, a movement that began in the nineteenth century and that continued to be influential as modern cultural movements began to form. The founder of Theosophy, H.P. Blavatsky, was a prolific author whose books were widely disseminated by the Theosophical Society. Jean Toomer, the central figure in the introduction of esoteric thought into the African American community in the 1920s, had a deep appreciation for Blavatsky's writings, and he used her concepts to originate his revision of racial thought.

Jean Toomer and Occultism

Jean Toomer based his major poem "The Blue Meridian" (1936) a complex treatment of race in America, on Blavatsky's *The Secret Doctrine* (1888), in which Blavatsky gives an exhaustive esoteric cosmological treatment of the evolution of the human "root races." The attraction of Blavatsky for Toomer was the authority with which she explicated the various stages of man's rise from the material to the ethereal over a past that went back two hundred million years and extended into a future that culminated in the twenty-eighth century. In the second volume of *The Secret Doctrine* Blavatsky spoke of a coming race of advanced beings that would accrete over time to replace the present race of man (Blavatsky 1888, 445). This Sixth Root-Race was distinguished by abnormal physical and mental abilities. Toomer identified himself as one of these new supermen, an early arrival; by inserting himself into this vast panorama, he felt that he was correcting and revising the mistaken beliefs and practices of America's institutionalized forms of pseudoscientific eugenics.

Jean Toomer is a highly controversial figure because he introduced the Gurdjieff Work into the Harlem Renaissance, but the Gurdjieff system had no doctrine about race: race was nothing more than one of the many delusions that kept man in a state of "sleep." Orage reduced the concept of sleep to an aphorism that C. Daly King included in *The Oragean Version*: "100. Animals have sleep and waking states. We have sleep but not waking. When awake, we are lightly hypnotized" (King 1951, 218). The effect of the Work (or as the Orageans called it, the Method) was that it awakened its practitioners, and the process could not begin until all of the sources of "sleep"—such as race—had been recognized through *self-observation and non-identification* and done away with. Thus, Toomer used esoteric doctrines to free himself from the internalized psycho-social limitations of being identified as a black American, and he used esoteric concepts as an alternative frame for a reformulation of himself beyond his black racial identity.

Modernism and the Fourth Dimension

In approaching Jean Toomer and the Harlem Renaissance, we are confronted with two topics of considerable scope and difficulty—modern art and modern esotericism. The narrative of Modernism often sites the beginning of modern art and literature in Europe just after 1910 and situates its early movements in the esoteric epistemologies of Theosophy, alchemy, and ritual magic. Two of the major modern esoteric movements were the Gurdjieff-Ouspensky school and the esotericism of C.G. Jung. One of the early introductions of modern esotericism begins in the West with the introduction of P.D. Ouspensky's book *Tertium Organum: the Third Canon of Thought and a Key to the Enigmas of the World* (1922) to the English-speaking world; the volume was originally published in Russia in 1912. Ouspensky was aware of the entire esoteric tradition of the West, and he intended that *Tertium Organum* be the third major philosophical synthesis, the previous being those of Aristotle and Bacon. Though rooted in esotericism, Ouspensky brings up Blavatsky only to correct her doctrines on space and matter, and he also dispenses with fundamental parts of Aristotle. His exposition of modern esotericism is based on the fourth dimension—though *his exposition of the fourth dimension differs from that of modern physics*—and most importantly, Ouspensky discusses the "psychological attempts to investigate the fourth dimension" (Ouspensky 2011, 155). Ouspensky introduces the idea that the fourth dimension is experiential and a part of life. Through the influence of Ouspensky, a reverence for the fourth dimension is encountered repeatedly in the 1910s and 1920s, such as in the hypercube architecture of Claude Bragdon (the architect who translated Ouspensky into English), and in the fourth dimensional writings of Gertrude Stein and Jean Toomer. *Tertium Organum* is an encyclopedic treatment of the possibilities of acquiring cosmic consciousness and super-humanity—though Ouspensky does not supply a method for manifesting this new consciousness.

Despite Ouspensky's rejection of Blavatsky, the Americans who took up *Tertium Organum* treated Ouspensky's book as the culmination of the Theosophical system. *Tertium Organum* was taken to America, where architect Claude Bragdon translated it and published it in a private edition in 1920. Bragdon believed Ouspensky's book to be the "long sought New Testament of the Sixth Race which will justify the meekness of the saint, the vision of the mystic, and create a new heaven and a new earth" (Bragdon 1918,

"Correspondence"). Bragdon's assessment of *Tertium Organum* was highly influential and directly contributed to Jean Toomer's developing beliefs concerning race. While embracing Ouspensky, Toomer also retained an interest in Blavatsky who he interpreted to suit his own psychological and spiritual needs. Toomer was particularly influenced by Blavatsky's presentation of the "higher man," and he used her esoteric historiography to account for his own peculiarities. Blavatsky had described the "sixth subrace of the Aryan root race" (Blavatsky 1888, 262) as emerging in the early twenty-first century, thus Toomer was one hundred years too early to belong to the next, more spiritual, stage of humanity. He rationalized this anachronism by viewing himself as a forerunner to the general coming of the new human. This he justified by the events of his life. According to Blavatsky, the sixth sub-race will possess certain psychic powers, and the mystical experience that Toomer underwent in 1926 convinced him that he had advanced spiritual attributes. Toomer's long poem, "The Blue Meridian" (1936) is a paraphrase of Blavatsky's *The Secret Doctrine* that describes the encounter between the ordinary man and the man of the future. Toomer derived the phrase "blue meridian" from Blavatsky's concept of the "Meridian of Races" in *The Secret Doctrine.* At issue for Blavatsky was the "perfect adjustment of Spirit and Matter" (Blavatsky 1888, Vol. 2, 300–301). In another passage Blavatsky speaks of "azure seats": "The azure seats remain empty. Who of the brown, who of the red, or yet among the black (*races*), can sit in the seats of the blessed, the seats of knowledge and mercy!" (Blavatsky 1888, Vol. 2, 424; emphasis in original). Jean Toomer interpreted this passage to apply to himself—so that he saw himself as a member of the blue race endowed with a fourth dimensional consciousness.

For symbolic emphasis, Toomer places this forerunner of futuristic hyper-consciousness at the top of a New York skyscraper. Toomer's symbolism doubly invokes both modern material culture and the spiritual world. Not only does the modernist technology of the skyscraper elevate man above the material concerns of life, Toomer invokes an even higher ascent through the mooring mast for Zeppelins at the top of the Empire State Building. At the same time, he invokes mystical transcendence through the searchlight on the Palmolive Building—an objective correlative for the Cosmic Ray, which was one of the most important concepts in A.R. Orage's teaching. Since the Cosmic Ray was the descending path of spiritual energy from the Sun Absolute to the Earth, it is telling that Toomer placed himself at its termination, which Orage is at great pains to show is a point of *growth*. The stanza concludes with a sighting of Toomer himself presented as the superman of the future: "Above you will arch a strange universe, / Below you will spread a strange earth, / Beside you will stand a strange man" (Toomer 1988, 69).

Esoteric Groups in New York in Greenwich Village and Harlem

In 1922 A.R. Orage followed Gurdjieff to France and remained at the Institute until the last weeks of 1923. By January 2 of 1924, Orage was in New York laying plans for Gurdjieff and his troupe to visit New York later in the month. Gurdjieff and company arrived on January 13, 1924. The troupe performed on February 2, and Jean Toomer described Gurdjieff as being "like a monk in a tuxedo" (Taylor 2001, 46). Largely through the influence of Orage, Gurdjieff's visit to the United States was successful in attracting a wide following, many of whom followed Gurdjieff to France to study at his Institute for the Harmonious Development of Man. After talking at length with Orage, Jean Toomer decided that he, too, would go to see Gurdjieff in France (Taylor 2001, 62). On arriving at the *Prieuré, Gurdjieff's estate,* Toomer discovered that Gurdjieff had been badly injured in an automobile accident, had closed the Institute, and that he was not wanted. Toomer overcome these initial objections but soon went back to the United States to study with Orage; later he returned to Paris to assist in the editing of Gurdjieff's huge epic, *Beelzebub's Tales.*

Toomer's strongest connection to esotericism was to his teacher, G.I. Gurdjieff: Toomer patterned himself on Gurdjieff, imitating his mannerisms, his many idiosyncrasies of speech, and incorporating Gurdjieff's literary inventions into his own writings, to the point of plagiarizing episodes from *Beelzebub's Tales* in his unpublished novels "Transatlantic" and "The Gallonwerps." The attachment of Jean Toomer to Gurdjieff is important to acknowledge and to evaluate, as it was not the pattern for what followed in the Harlem group. Gurdjieff headed a rather large enterprise that he was determined to continue to expand. In order to draw more money to himself, he in effect franchised Orage, and then Toomer, to found chapters of his Institute, which were then expected to funnel large sums of money back to Paris. Orage sent Toomer from the Greenwich Village headquarters of the New York chapter up to Harlem to organize an African American group. This expansion was a training course that allowed Toomer to establish himself as a teacher of the first (exoteric) level of the Gurdjieff Work. Toomer was not in Harlem on his own, but was often accompanied by Orage or another advanced figure, the academically trained psychologist, C. Daly King. It is difficult to determine to what extent Toomer independently led the Gurdjieff meetings in Harlem, given that the Harlem members were as devoted to Orage and even to King as they were to Jean Toomer; the members of the Harlem group must have had substantial and intense contact with Orage and King. Once Toomer successfully recruited and established a Gurdjieff group in Harlem, he was sent to Chicago in November of 1926, where he had his own groups, and C. Daly King continued to direct the Harlem Gurdjieff group. Since Jean Toomer's revival as a literary artist in the 1960s, his supposed rejection of his black identity has come in for a great deal of analysis and discussion. Jean Toomer's status in esoteric circles was just as controversial as his racial status. In 1926 when Toomer assumed direction of esoteric groups in Chicago, Gorham Munson said, "He play acts as a spiritual leader" (Munson 1926, "Significance"). Toomer's Chicago groups were not made up of African Americans, but included well-to-do businessmen, intellectuals, and writers from the Gold Coast section of Chicago (Kerman 1987, 170).

Jean Toomer's contribution to Orage's Greenwich Village groups was impressionistically presented in Carl Van Vechten's novel, *Firecrackers* (1925), in which the gymnast, Gunnar O'Grady, is partly based on Jean Toomer who studied physical training in college and later taught gymnastics (Kerman 1987, 127). The name Gunnar O'Grady is a phonetically coded composite of George Ivanovich Gurdjieff (G.I.G. / G.O.G.), and A.R. Orage (Gunn-AR O'Grady). Even though there are realistic aspects to Van Vechten's novel, it is a complex work, combining elements of the comic novel with underlying esoteric themes. The *esoteric realism* that Van Vechten pioneered was the model for most of the fiction written by Orage's Harlem followers—Nella Larsen, Zora Neale Hurston, Wallace Thurman, Rudolph Fisher, George Schuyler, Bruce Nugent, Eric Walrond, Harold Jackman, Arna Bontemps, and Dorothy West. Esoteric realism was an allusive, coded, heteroglossic style that departed in several distinguishing ways from the avant garde, fourth dimensional fiction written by Gertrude Stein and Jean Toomer. By contrast, fourth dimensional fiction was characterized by its construction of a continuous present: Toomer's novel, *Cane*, invoked "A universe that joins space and time into a continuous flow of 'now', in which fragments of past and future are revealed in the present moment" (Kerman 1987, 114).

The black esoteric realists who followed A.R. Orage created many of the most significant texts associated with the Harlem Renaissance, and *without the propelling and sustaining influence of esotericism, the Harlem movement would have been bereft of most of its most characteristic and most highly acclaimed literary achievements*. While it has not been previously recognized, the majority of the writers, patrons, and publishers who participated in the Harlem Renaissance were followers of G.I. Gurdjieff and A.R. Orage. In addition, the aesthetics of the Harlem Renaissance have been poorly understood: chiefly, the critical concentration on the controversies surrounding such topics as race, exoticism, and nationalism have obscured the fact that the majority of the prose fiction adhered to what I am calling the style of esoteric realism. Of course, the secrecy practiced by the Oragean Modernists has also contributed in a major way to the problems of reading Harlem Renaissance texts. But the critical underestimation of those texts has played an equal part in misreading them: their manifold complexities have been glossed over or ignored in favor of simplistic racialized reading of the works, such as Stephen Soitos's reading of *The Conjure Man Dies* discussed below.

Becoming the Superman

An argument can be made that modernism in its quest for liberation, power, and individuality was in the final analysis the pursuit of the superman. Like Orage, Jean Toomer was infused with the superman doctrine, though in Toomer's case it was gained through its expression in the Theosophical books that he had read on his own. Once Toomer joined the "art as vision group" in New York in the early 1920s, he was actively engaged in the attainment of cosmic consciousness, the prerequisite for being a superman. If Ouspensky's *Tertium Organum* had initiated the esoteric quest for the superman under Modernism, Ouspensky had himself brought about the next phase of esotericism by bringing Gurdjieff to attention. And it was Gurdjieff's claim that he possessed exactly those esoteric materials required to transform individuals into supermen, and that the form of those materials in his possession was exactly suitable for the spiritual development of modern persons in the most efficient manner.

Though the Gurdjieff Work was heavily dependent on aspects of Theosophy, it departed from Theosophical teachings about the relationship between the role of the followers and "those who know"—as the Gurdjieffians called the conscious circle of humanity. In Theosophy the conscious circle was a group of enlightened spiritual beings who secretly directed the world, hidden and unapproachable masters who sent down the teachings from afar through their intermediaries. But Orage disseminated teachings that admitted the initiates themselves to the inner circle of humanity. Ouspensky stated that "Two hundred conscious people, if they existed and if they find it necessary and legitimate, could change the whole of life on the earth. But either there are not enough of them, or they do not want to, or perhaps the time has not come, or perhaps other people are sleeping too soundly" (Ouspensky 1949, 310). The central tenet of Oragean Modernism was that the time had come for the creation of the two hundred conscious people required to redirect life on earth:

> Some crises can be truly desperate, of such a nature that their final outcome for mankind on this planet remains in genuine doubt even for the

Schools. At such times it is said that the Hidden Learning is disclosed, much as one might hurl lifebelts indiscriminately into the sea among the struggling fugitives from a sinking ship. *Sauve qui peut.* At such times a rigorous selection is no longer possible; some lifebelt may be caught and used, out of many failures there may be a few successes when successes are most terribly needed. It is just this sort of period which we have now encountered in the history of mankind upon this planet. That is the answer given in this Version to those who ask why such information is available at this time in this way.

KING 1951, 37

Orage rejected the disillusionment that was at times a feature of Modernism, and he aroused his followers to a fever pitch of super-effort, so that they wrote in an atmosphere of tremendous excitement and commitment: Orage embraced the Nietzschean side of the work, where Gurdjieff had said, "Only super-efforts count...it is better to die making efforts than to live in sleep" (Ouspensky 1949, 232). Even though the Harlem esotericists esteemed themselves the only hope for the planet, even they were nothing more than *potentialities* and had to work furiously to overcome their negative attributes. In the Oragean version of the Gurdjieff Work all humans belong to the same category—that of not being men: "For us, *who are not yet men*, that responsibility is but the weightier by reason of the words, not yet.... Every man must somehow find how he can become genuinely human; and to discover this, he must first find out what 'human' really means" (King 1951, 222; emphasis added).

Gurdjieff taught that there were seven types of man: Ouspensky stated that "[Y]ou suppose all men are on the same level, but in reality, one man can be more different from another than a sheep is from a cabbage. There are seven different categories of men" (Bennett 1978, 52–53). These seven gradations began at the physical and ascended to the level of the superman, the man with cosmic consciousness. The Theosophical novelist Bulwyer Lytton had addressed some of these themes in his novel *Zanoni*, where the magus Mejnour seeks "to create a 'mighty and numerous race' of superhuman occult adepts, even if this necessitates the sacrifice of thousands of aspirants for the sake of a single success" (Gibbons 1973, 107). Orage and Toomer were obsessed with the idea of the superman long before they encountered Gurdjieff. Orage had been responsible for spreading the superman doctrine through his journal, *The New Age*. In *Nietzsche in Outline and Aphorism* (1907), Orage advocated the rule of the superman as beings capable of *creativity*: "only peculiarly endowed peoples and individuals are capable of creating, that is, lending to things new and high values" (Stone 2002, 75). Nietzsche is usually thought of as a philosopher, but Orage classed him an occultist: "it is probable...that new faculties, new modes of consciousness, will be needed, as the mystics have always declared; and that the differencing element of man and Superman will be the possession of these" (Gibbons 1973, 107). This doctrine made its way to the center of thought in Harlem, so that when Wallace Thurman emphasizes the need for *creativity* in *Infants of the Spring* (1932, 118, 254), we can grasp its Nietzschean context.

The Followers of Orage in Harlem

The only internal historic account of the Harlem Orageans was Melvin B. Tolson's Master's thesis, *The Harlem Group of Negro Writers* (1940). The thesis was not a detailed account, and far more useful information can be extracted from his allusive epic poem, *Harlem Gallery*. The record of the efforts of the African American Oragean Modernists mainly consists of published works of imaginative literature—novels, long poems, plays, and lyric poems. The practice of Orage's other groups was much different, particularly in that some of them published accounts of their group work or disseminated their informal notes. Like the Harlem Orageans, the other Oragean groups published coded novels of esoteric realism and portrayed Gurdjieff in unflattering ways. Gurdjieff is often cast in the novels of esoteric realism as an extremely disagreeable woman. (For instance, in Nella Larsen's *Quicksand* the Gurdjieff character is a man who has murdered his wife; having assumed her identity and wearing her poorly fitting dresses, he works as a political activist and speaker on women's rights.) Orage kept before all of his groups the important distinction between texts that are subjective-accidental and texts that are "objective." Much of what the Orageans hoped to accomplish would be done through their "objective" texts.

As we have seen, the models for the coded novels of the Harlem Orageans were Carl Van Vechten's comic satires. Prior to and during the Harlem Renaissance (1922–1930), Carl Van Vechten published eight best-selling novels. Some of Van Vechten's works are coded and contain esoteric doctrines, ideas from Ouspensky's pre-Gurdjieff writings in the early novels and Gurdjieffian ideas in the later novels. *Van Vechten's occultism and use of code has previously eluded literary critics and scholars.* Van Vechten's novels are now generally dismissed as being quaint and mannered, except for *Nigger Heaven*. The latter novel is usually discussed in harsh terms for its supposed exploitation of Harlem through exotic primitivism and racial stereotypes, thus its supposedly negative influence on the Harlem writers. However, the Harlem group was devoted to Van Vechten, a fact that receives problematic assessments in scholarly accounts of the Harlem Renaissance. Writing alongside of the Harlem writers, C. Daly King, inventor of the "sealed room" mystery sub-genre, published mystery novels in the 1930s that were similarly coded *legominisms* (transmissions of esoteric knowledge). Rudolph Fisher was the only Harlem novelist to adopt King's sun-genre, publishing a "sealed room" detective novel called *The Conjure Man Dies* (1932). Fisher's novel is replete with anomalies ("lawful inexactitudes")—indications to the reader to pay attention: women dressed as men, wrong spellings, mis-numbered lists. Signally, Fisher's novel glaringly violates the conventions of the detective novel genre. The detective does not solve the case, which is solved by two inept buffoons. In *The Blues Detective* Stephen Soitos has a *community* of detectives solve the case (Soitos 1996, 103–104). This device allows Soitos to attempt to rationalize all of the absurd and disparate elements that denote that the text is esoteric and coded. The murder is committed with a *handkerchief* (a conventional Oragean code for Gurdjieff). Rudolph Fisher was an avowed individualist. The supposition that he installed a community as hero in his novel is testimony to the determination of conventional critics to supply Fisher with a set of values that are sanctioned by contemporary Afrocentric thought but have no resonance with the elitism of Oragean Modernism.

Nella Larsen, Zora Neale Hurston, Wallace Thurman, Rudolph Fisher, George Schuyler, and Dorothy West published novels of comic satire, closely adhering to Carl Van Vechten's esoteric realism. Variations from this formula were Hurston's experiments with new forms, basing some of her work on the naturalism of Danish novelist Jens Peter Jacobsen, and her innovative novels that were spiritual allegories—*Eyes* and *Seraph*; Hurston and Arna Bontemps also wrote historical novels, respectively "Herod the Great" and *Black Thunder*. Working in the long poem and the lyric poem Georgia Douglas Johnson, Jean Toomer, Melvin B. Tolson, and Gwendolyn Bennett produced an estimable body of esoteric poetry. While the Harlem writers were producing their coded esoteric texts, so were the white followers of Orage. New York novelists in the Oragean modernist mode besides Carl Van Vechten included Dawn Powell and James Agee. The Rope, a group of American lesbians living in Paris, was in direct contact with Gurdjieff but wrote ciphered texts in the Oragean modernist mode, including Djuna Barnes's canonical novel *Nightwood* (1936).

Van Vechten's esoteric comic novel, *Firecrackers*, is a *roman a clef* that described the founding of a branch of Gurdjieff's Institute in New York. The account calls the organization Pinchon's Prophylactic Plan, but the fictional prospectus that Pinchon (based on Orage's secretary, Muriel Draper) circulates actually mentions Gurdjieff and Ouspensky. What obtained among the Oragean modernists was radically different from what Gurdjieff taught in France: Gurdjieff's demonstrations were performed in public, there was no writing commissioned by Gurdjieff and he took no interest in his students's writings, and never was his code—if there were one—divulged, thought Orage and others searched for the key to his texts.

The theme of esoteric organizations also appears in the writings of the Harlem writers, but it is a minor motif. A far more substantial motif is the importance of Jean Toomer to the Harlem esotericists. Close readings of their texts consistently situate Toomer as a central figure. Characters based on Toomer as a superman appear in several Harlem texts: Jean Toomer is The Curator in Melvin Tolson's *Harlem Gallery*, he is Hurston's Moses (*Moses Man of the Mountain*), Schuyler's Max Fisher (*Black No More*), Larsen's Dr. Anderson (*Quicksand*), Fisher's Dr. John Archer (*CMD*), and in Wallace Thurman's *Infants* the protagonist declares that Jean Toomer is the only Negro with "the elements of greatness" (Thurman 1932, 221). The Harlem group looked on Toomer with high regard due to the profound mystical experience that he underwent in April of 1926. Toomer become fixated on this epiphany and he wrote a detailed account of his transformation that he distributed among his peers. This document, "Birth Above the Body" has since its inception created a controversy as to whether or not it was a mystical experience (see Kerman 1987, 158–159). Frederick L. Rusch states that "not only did Toomer's episode of 1926 give him a feeling of personal wholeness, it also reinforced his antipathy to separateness and rigid classification, and demonstrated the possibility that all human brings could be united in a 'Brilliant Brotherhood'" (Rusch 1993, 31). Looking back on his ecstatic two weeks, he felt they had shown him that it "is possible for the whole of mankind to become one in consciousness," and that this could then be "the real basis of our potential ability to realize the brotherhood of man" (Rusch 1993, 31). Rusch also observes that because Toomer's mystical experience happened within the context of the Gurdjieff Work that "it was probably the years *of conscious* effort that had laid the ground work for his mystical episode" (Rusch 1993, 31). Toomer's epiphany was a rarity, and the written account is a rarity in the Harlem literary corpus, the only comparison being Melvin Tolson's abbreviated and generic account of a mystical experience in his fugitive sonnet "The Wine of Ecstasy": "The opium of custom drugs the clod; / The wine of ecstasy makes man a god!" (Tolson 1938, 153, lns. 13–14). Tolson's sonnet is intricately coded and contains allusions to Kabbalah and to the Gurdjieff Work. Tolson's godlike man is Jean Toomer, and the subtext of Tolson's long poem *The Harlem Gallery* is the actualized superhumanity of Jean Toomer.

A Marxist Masquerade: Occult Psychohistory Versus Dialectical Materialism

In the final analysis, the black Oragean Modernists of the Harlem Renaissance directed all of their efforts to the creation of an "objective" work of art in order to save the planet. Such "objective" works of historical intervention were possible because the Harlem esotericists understood history as a process subject to the Law of Octaves (or Law of Seven): the knowledge of when to apply "artificial shocks" to the intervals in an octave gives "those who know" the ability "to step out of the role of passive spectator" (Ouspensky 1949, 134). Orage taught that the greatest of such "objective" works known to modern esotericists was the drama of Jesus the Christ:

> About us, in the creeds, the sects and the distortions of modern Christianity lay the fragments, of another work of Objective Art, the life of Christ, so it has been said. According to that account the story of the Christ, a messenger of God upon this planet, was and is Objective Drama, played not on a stage but in life by the Essene initiate, Jesus. This play had its origin far earlier, in ancient Egypt, as the drama of the life, death and resurrection of Ausar (Osiris), the God-in-Man; its function was to present ultimate human truths through the medium of consciously acted roles. For centuries, we are told, the later Essene brotherhood, a School itself deriving from Egyptian origins, had held the aim of presenting this drama in life rather than as a prescribed mystery play and for generations had trained its postulants to that end. Eventually the cast of thirteen was complete with Jesus, who had been sent to Egypt for temple training there, cast as the leading actor and Judas, who must play the next most difficult role, that of the betrayer, fully prepared for his part. With the necessary modifications demanded by the local scene and times, the action began.
>
> KING 1951, 163–164

The Harlem Orageans's work of "objective" art was a historical "drama in life" using the Scottsboro Nine and the Communist Party in imitation of the Essene intervention using the messiah, Jesus the Christ. Wallace Thurman transformed Orage's formula into a contemporary course of action: "And if out of a wholesale allegiance to Communism the Negro could develop just a half dozen men who were really and truly outstanding the result would be worth the effort" (*Infants* 1932, 219). Thurman advanced the creation of a group of supermen by planning to use the Communist movement to incubate a small *conscious* elite within the unconscious mass of millions of unconscious "automatons" (Ouspensky 1949, 309). Communism was an attractive site for this activity, since at the time it was part of the counter-culture and was embraced by various avant gardes as well as appealing to workers. Thurman's plan is also found in Melvin Tolson's epic poem, *Harlem Gallery*: "No guinea pig of a spouse / to be cuckolded in a mood indigo," (Tolson 1965, lns. 985–986). Tolson's lines present the strategy of *brood parasitism*, whereby an animal tricks another animal into raising its young. It is common knowledge that the cuckoo of line 986, "to be *cuckolded* in a mood indigo," deposits its eggs in the nests of other birds. To further emphasize that brood parasitism is his topic, Tolson gave the name of yet another bird that is a brood parasite, the *indigo* bird.

One aesthetic effect of the brood parasitism plan was the influence of Egypt on the Harlem Orageans readily evident in Aaron Douglas's murals and in Hurston's novels, though critics mistakenly attribute the Egyptian influence to Douglas's and Hurston's Afrocentricism. Though Hurston only wrote one novel (*Moses*) that treated Egypt directly, close readings of all of her novels show that her Egyptian symbolism, themes, and imagery were derived from an esoteric text, Gerald Massey's *Ancient Egypt: the light of the world* (1907). Also reflective of the concern with historical intervention by the Harlem Orageans was Hurston's unfinished historical novel, "Herod the Great." Since Hurston scholars do not recognized that Hurston was an esotericist, it has been difficult for them to integrate "Herod" into her corpus, as Michael Lackey's review of Deborah Plant's book makes clear: "If Hurston's *Moses* challenges the Old Testament version of the ancient Hebrew leader by suggesting that Moses was actually an Egyptian, Hurston's *Herod* challenges the New Testament version of the baby-murdering tyrant by suggesting that he was actually a forerunner of Christ...Original in thought, she had to be bold in spirit as she created a work that defied history" (Lackey 2011, 142). Missing the Oragean connection, Plant cannot convincingly explain why Herod is "Hurston's ideal individual." Hurston's unfinished novel "Herod" was based on the Oragean belief that two thousand years ago Essene esotericists had intervened in history. Moreover, Gurdjieff and Massey shared the idea that ancient Egypt was the source of Christianity: "In the Appendix to *Ancient Egypt*, Massey listed more than 200 direct parallels between the Jesus legend and the cycle of Osiris/Horus. The earthly Jesus is congruent to Horus; Jesus the Christ corresponds to Osiris, the resurrected god" (Finch 2006).

Aaron Douglas, Melvin Tolson, Arna Bontemps, and Dorothy West are the writers of the Harlem Group who became the most openly associated with leftist politics. Douglas openly associated himself with the Gurdjieffians and attended Muriel Draper's group after Toomer left New York in 1926. Douglas consistently maintained that his artwork was not influenced by esotericism. An examination of Douglas's paintings reveal them to be compilations of esoteric symbols readily found in the books by King and Ouspensky—stars, rays, circles, triangles. In denying any esoteric content, Douglas practiced the Gurdjieffian technique of "experiment"—the adoption of *artificial roles* (King 1951, 119)—in his treatment of the interface between politics and esotericism. Scholarly discussions of Douglas's paintings try to align his artwork with his leftist politics, *though when Douglas became a Communist his style did not change*: "Although the library murals, *Aspects of Negro Life*, might not appear greatly different from the earlier pieces, Douglas asserted that they were drawn from a more radicalized leftist impulse, though he declined to position himself as a proletarian painter..." (Ragar 2008, 141). Marissa Vincenti attempts to account for Douglas's style during his leftist period in these words: "A key to unpacking *Poetry's* complex imagery lies in Douglas' description of the Fisk murals themselves. Instead of employing naturalistic representation, Douglas stated that a 'mere symbol of the idea' was used, adding enigmatically that the cycle's success was due to 'an unexplained means of symbolistic [sic] representation'" (Vincenti 2007, 14). Douglas's explanation paraphrases Ouspensky's discussion of esoteric symbolism and "objective" art: "...*a symbol can never be fully interpreted. It can only be experienced*, in the same way, for instance, as the idea of self-knowledge must be experienced" (Ouspensky 1949, 282; emphasis added).

Aaron Douglas drew a mock-up cover for a leftist journal, *Spark: Organ of the Vanguard*. The inspiration for this journal was *The Vanguard, Organ of the International Left Opposition of Canada*, published in Toronto from 1932–36. It is worth noting, considering what is being said here about the cooption of the Communist Party by the Oragean Modernists that the Canadians who published the *Spark* were a reformist caucus that had been expelled from the Communist Party of Canada (Dowson 1932, "Vanguard"). On Douglas's cover *Spark* reverses to "crap," a device used previously by Wallace Thurman (Woodson 1999, 18), and *Organ* and *Vanguard* refer, respectively, to Orage and to Gurdjieff. Amy Kirschke states that the *Spark* cover "remains a complete mystery" (Kirschke 1995, 90), for Douglas was not otherwise given to directly presenting political content in his artwork. The *Spark* cover shows a picture plane segmented by curved and straight lines. Within the intersections are depictions of a marching column of soldiers, warships at sea, plutocrats in top hats, revolutionaries, a lynched man hanging from a tree, tanks atop raised terrain, and the skyline of a city. A fist wearing a manacle and a broken chain thrusts upward through the foreground (Kirschke 1995, Figure 44).

FIGURE 6.1   *George Schuyler's mock-up cover for Spark: Organ of the Vanguard.*
HTTP://CHAPTERS.AIGA.ORG/CONTENT.CFM/DESIGN-JOURNEYS-AARON-DOUGLAS-2#2

The lines suggest the esoteric figure of the enneagram, the nine-pointed "star" passed down from "pre-sand Egypt" that symbolically expresses Gurdjieff's cosmic teachings.

Two enneagrams can be aligned with sections of the drawing; the numeral 6 in the drawing aligns with the 6 on the enneagram (signifying objective consciousness and a mental body). Thus, Douglas integrated a recognizable esoteric symbol into his design for the cover of a Communist magazine. Though the esotericists stopped short of publishing the journal, as a leftist artist, Douglas became the president of the Harlem Artists Guild, which had a membership of ninety artists by 1935 (Ragar 2008, 147–148).

In the 1930s Melvin Tolson failed to publish a book of Communist-inspired poems, *A Gallery of Harlem Portraits* that contained esoteric ciphers in the table of contents. Tolson's *A Gallery of Harlem Portraits* was posthumously published in 1979. The volume of monologues was influenced by Edgar Lee Masters's *Spoon River Anthology*, though Tolson's characters were alive. Masters's rural, Midwestern setting gave way to Tolson's concern with the

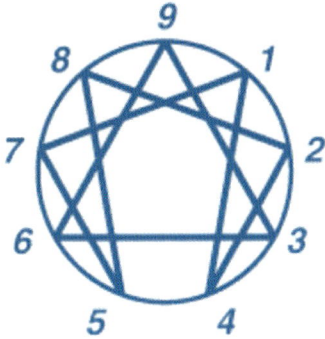

FIGURE 6.2 *G.I. Gurdjieff's enneagram, the universal symbol that unites the"Law of Seven" and the "Law of Three."*

diverse, urban population, reflective of Tolson's time in New York when he encountered the Harlem group during his time at Columbia University in 1931–32. On the surface, Tolson's poems expressed a revolutionary political agenda, which was reputedly the cause of its rejection by commercial publishers. The *Gallery*'s imagist poems did not allow esoteric wordplay. The names of Tolson's characters are similar to those of the European immigrants in the Masters *Anthology*. Tolson's names are loaded with esoteric significance: "Aunt Tommiezene" (aren't commie), "Jesse Seegar" (Gurdjieff), and "Gloomy Dean" (Jean Toomer). Tolson declared himself a Marxist but in contradiction to Marxist aesthetics came to write in a difficult Modernist style; Tolson never identified himself as an esotericist. Crucially, Tolson's epic poem *Harlem Gallery* is a "dramatis personae" in which he names the members of the Harlem group that are not identified in other texts by the Harlem group. He gives the following instructions shown below in italics on using the eyes and ears to read. Here he includes two names using the phonetic *cabala*:

> The West Wing
> is no belt of calms:
> in the midst of its dramatis personae,
> *the listening ear can hear,*
> among the moderns, blue
> tomtoms of Benin;
> *the seeing eye can see fetishes unseen,*
> via
> rue Fromentin and Lenox Avenue.
> lns. 1068–76; emphasis added

Line 1073 above names Louise Thompson [Patterson]; here doubling is a signaling device, and the name is repeated throughout the poem. Patterson—briefly both Thurman's wife and Hurston's secretary—was not a writer but came to the forefront during the 1930s as a leftist cultural organizer. Tolson identifies this important Communist as another Gurdjieffian who assumed the *artificial role* of a Marxist. In the first line of the example above, Tolson also identifies Dorothy West as another Marxist who was a covert Gurdjieffian. Dorothy West not only visited the Soviet Union, she published a left-oriented journal of the arts, *Challenge* (1934–37). Her novel *The Living is Easy* (1948) is coded using the phonetic *cabala* and is replete with the Oragean esoteric vocabulary.

These examples suggest that the Harlem Orageans attempted to intervene in history by means of an "objective" work of art (able to affect all human beings [King 1951, 162–163]) based on the case of the Scottsboro Nine. James Miller states that "The Scottsboro case has been called one of the great defining moments of the twentieth century, providing a vocabulary and constellation of images not only for its own time but for subsequent generations as well—each of which has been compelled to reinterpret and to reappropriate Scottsboro for its own purposes" (Miller 2001,1). To further their aims the Harlem Group established the Harlem Artists Guild and the Vanguard Club through which they disseminated their esoteric teachings while outwardly behaving like Communists. It remains to be determined which other figures of the left in Harlem in the 1930s were Gurdjieffians, though sculptor Augusta Savage, Louise Thompson's closest associate. In their "objective" drama centered on the Scottsboro Nine case, Gurdjieffians George Schuyler and Aaron Douglas prominently took up opposite sides—Schuyler assuming the anti-Communist (Judas) role, while Douglas—along with Louise Thompson, Dorothy West, Augusta Savage and others—advocated the Communist side—or the roles of the "disciples" (Ragar 2008, 138–139 fn. 11). Recently a pastel portrait of two of the Scottsboro Nine by Aaron Douglas in the *Neue Sachlichkeit* (New Objectivity) style has been rediscovered. Douglas reverted to an earlier realist style, creating a poignant modern icon in order to more effectively portray the accused rapists as martyrs. Arna Bontemps published *Black Thunder* in 1936, a novel "inspired and deeply informed by his anguished and brooding response to the Scottsboro case" (Miller 2009, 133). Bontemps established believable credentials as a leftist: "He was active in the pro-Communist South Side Writers Club of Chicago, had trusted Communist friends, signed on with activities sponsored by the League of American Writers, and maintained revolutionary convictions and informal links, though not official ties, to the Party" (Washington 2002).

Scholarly accounts of the Harlem Group list Bontemps as having attended some of Toomer's Gurdjieff meetings in the 1920s, but he is not supposed to have established a serious interest in esotericism. Bontemps's novel of black revolution, *Black Thunder* (1936), is, however, an esoteric text similar to those of the earlier novels by Larsen, Thurman, and Hurston. Bontemps's novel is heavily coded: *Black Thunder*—a poor title for "a story that concluded not with material triumph over racial oppression but with the failure to achieve emancipation" (Leroy-Frazier 2010)—phonetically suggests the words "tac[tical] blunder" as in **Bl**ack **Th**under in keeping with the incompetent nature of the slave rebellion it narrates. Like the other Harlem esoteric novels, the text is laced with intentional errors ("lawful inexactitudes"), such as the spelling of *Pharoah* for Pharaoh (Bontemps 1936, 69); Pharoah, the pumpkin-colored alleged betrayer of the rebellion is the novel's rendering of Gurdjieff, and he is given the name of an enslaver as befits the Oragean tendency to disparage Gurdjieff. Old Ben (10) is the novel's embodiment of P.D. Ouspensky. Bontemps's novel is dense with the names of the Gurdjieffian teachers on every page—e.g., A.R. Orage: "hearing...word...large" (66), "cellar and warm porridge" (141), "mortar trough" (162). *Black Thunder* includes the allegories, concepts, and the vocabulary of Orage's lectures—e.g., intervals, work, shocks, circles, force, observation, and sleep. Aaron Douglas taught at Fisk University from 1939 to 1966; Arna Bontemps was the head librarian at Fisk University from 1943 to 1964. Librarian Arna Bontemps acquired Toomer's papers for Fisk University in Nashville, Tennessee in the 1960s.

Conclusion—the End of Race and Folk

African American culture has primarily been understood as a folk culture, with black folk religion as its organizing principle. Perhaps the major tension in the Harlem Renaissance was the conflict between the metanarrative of folk culture and the metanarrative of black modernity. We may think of esotericism as a totalizing rejection of African American folkways, though often this stance has been overlooked by the interpreters of the Harlem renaissance. Early short stories by Zora Neale Hurston were parodies of texts from the Bible. Hurston situated the novel *Moses Man of the Mountain* in the Exodus event; however, her Moses despaired for the future of the liberated slaves. Her folk play *Mule Bone* dramatized a dispute that divided a town along religious lines, with Methodists set against Baptists. Hurston and her esoteric colleagues interpreted the black folk church as a generator of "sleep," and as such they viewed it with disfavor. It is to be wondered at that their modernizing program consisted of an objective drama that would recreate the passion of Christ using the Scottsboro Nine: whatever else may be said of this program, it is obvious that in no sense does it recapitulate the metanarratives of African American religion. The Orageans's approach to a modernizing salvation of the Earth was equally unsympathetic both to conventional African American religion and to the Communist Party.

The discovery of Black Oragean Modernism and the larger Oragean literary tendency has only just been broached. Other writers will no doubt be added to this movement. It already seems that Ralph Ellison's *Invisible Man* is an esoteric text, where Brother Jack is Gurdjieff. I mention this preliminary finding only to suggest the far-reaching implications of the exploration commenced in this essay, so that other scholars can begin to work in this area. This is not going to be easily done, as scholars are not prepared at this point to do the necessary work: a great deal of knowledge must be mastered before anything useful can be said about the esoteric in Modern American literature. And work with the esoteric has its own pitfalls. I foresee a long period of regretful productions that will rival those excesses produced by the dissemination of cultural and critical theories in place of literary theory since 1965. I doubt that the refusal by literary scholars to engage with the esoteric has been due to their recognition that they simply cannot stand up to the rigors demanded by the esoteric. The Oragean Modernist writers have plunged ahead into the cosmos, and it remains to be seen whether anyone is sufficiently evolved to investigate where they went and what they have brought back.

CHAPTER 7

Mathematical Theology
Numerology in the Religious Thought of Tynnetta Muhammad and Louis Farrakhan

Stephen C. Finley

Introduction

"1930" is more than just the year that the Nation of Islam (NOI) God, Master Fard Muhammad, was said to have appeared in inner-city Detroit to find and rehabilitate the Original People of the earth (Gardell 1996, 50; Marsh 1996, 37). Nineteen (19) and thirty (30) represent two of the most important magical numbers used to divine truth, foretell future events, and interpret human, astrological, and cosmic occurrences in religious terms within the Nation of Islam. This essay explores the meaning, function, sources, and dynamics of numerology in the religious thought of Mother Tynnetta Muhammad and Louis Farrakhan in the NOI. Two of the most important theological thinkers within the NOI, Muhammad's esoteric system based on the number 19 and Farrakhan's number 30 operate in tandem to interpret some of the most important religious events of the NOI, in particular Farrakhan's reported UFO encounter of 1985 (Finley 2012; Finley 2009, 328–388).

Located in the field of African American Religion and the nascent field of Africana Esotericism (AES), more specifically, African American Esotericism in conversation with Western Esotericism, this essay will make three related arguments. First, nineteens and thirties are used to ascribe meaning and coherence to a world of abstractions that enable the NOI to navigate life in existential and epistemological certainty. Second, such a quest for *theosophical empiricism* assures and verifies the persistence of black bodies after "death"—the ostensible cessation of biological functioning of the human body. Finally, both of these ultimate purposes of numerology evince a form of esotericism that Mother Tynnetta and Minister Farrakhan apprehend and authenticate, not by appeal to Europe nor Renaissance or Enlightenment thought (Fairve 2010, 35–36, 53–54; Hanegraaff 1998, 401–405), but rather vis-à-vis the classical African civilization—Egypt—and sources that for them signify black origins.

Mother Tynnetta Muhammad and the Miraculous Number 19

Mother Tynnetta Muhammad has developed an extensive system of knowledge based on the Number 19 that plays an important role in the religious thought of the NOI. While Mattias Gardell calls her "the leading theologian in the Nation" (Gardell 1996, 128) then contradicts himself at another point calling her the "leading female theologian" (Gardell 1996, 123), Mother Tynnetta, as they refer to her affectionately within the NOI, is clearly one of the most prominent theological thinkers in the organization. Previously she had been one of the numerous secretaries of the Honorable Elijah Muhammad (d. 1975) with whom he was engaged in what was interpreted at the time as extramarital relations. Her status over the last four decades, however, has been transformed from one, which was marred by salacious accusations and details of her relationship to Elijah Muhammad, to one in which she is a trusted member of Minister Louis Farrakhan's inner circle, considered a "mother" of the Nation, and one of the "wives" of Elijah Muhammad (Finley 2013). She is an independent and creative generator of secret knowledge that she maintains has its roots in the history and work of the NOI (T. Muhammad 1986, 76–88; 95–102). In fact, she functions as a spiritual interpreter of some of the most consequential events in the NOI and in Minister Farrakhan's life.

For instance, she maintains—in concert with Farrakhan's report of his experience on the Mother Wheel, a UFO, into which he reports being abducted on September 17, 1985—that this event did occur, and she vigorously defends his international travel and political activities in which he engaged after the event. She says, for example:

> Minister Farrakhan was guided in his decision to go to Lybia, by means of a Vision coming to him in much the same way as the Vision came to Moses in the Sacred Valley of Tuwa. She was guided in this Vision through the words of the Honorable Elijah Muhammad speaking to him from inside a Great Plane call [sic] the Mother's Wheel, which is described in Ezekiel's Vision, Chapters one and two. He was told to expose the military plans of President Reagan and his Joints Chiefs of Staff which was to be staged in some part of the globe...
>
> T. MUHAMMAD 1986, 55

Here, she demonstrates that she is a staunch defender of and believer in the mystical experiences of Minister Farrakhan and his UFO abduction narrative, and she believes it to be the fulfillment of biblical prophecy when she concludes, "I read a passage in the Book of Ezekiel, in Chapters [*sic*] 10 and 11 which encompassed detailed aspects of the Minister's Vision on board the space craft or wheel" (T Muhammad 1986, 57). Mother Tynnetta's account of Farrakhan's experience carries weight because of her position as "Mother" and theologian.

On this putative event on a "spacecraft," Farrakhan reports encountering his religious mentor, Elijah Muhammad, and he maintains that God, Master Fard Muhammad, was present as well (Finley 2012, 435, 454, 457). At the same time, Mother Tynnetta establishes her own productive space which she stabilizes not by allusion to her historic relationship to Muhammad or Farrakhan and in particular this UFO narrative but by her own productive religious activities. For example, she says that she has "dreams" and that these dreams are prophetic and insightful, suggesting that even while she alludes to Farrakhan as instructive, her own experiences independently confirm his teaching (T. Muhammad 1986, 84). Most importantly, she develops her own system of secret knowledge that unlocks the mysteries of the cosmos.

Mother Tynnetta argues that the key to divining the deepest and most profound truths of the universe are found in the recognition and strategic deployment of the number 19. Briefly, she maintains that the truths of the world can be divinized by a mathematical Qur'anic code of 19. Knowledge of the cosmic significance of the number 19 can be used to decode the meaning of the Qur'an, the Bible, and historical, meteorological, and geological events. What makes her theory consistent with esoteric religion generally and how she understands the meaning of the NOI particularly is her objective to conflate religion and science and to re-enchant nature as active and certain rather than arbitrary. And Wouter Hanegraaff, in his *New Age Religion and Western Culture: Esotericism in the Mirror of Secular Thought*, concurs, suggesting that, "This concern with synthesizing religion and science has remained characteristic of esotericism right up to the present day, and is the foundation of an ever-present ambiguity" (Hanegraaff 1998, 397). To this end, Mother Tynnetta declares, "This makes science and religion wedded as one" (T. Muhammad, 2003). As a consequence, she aggregates the Mathematical Code, astronomy, numerology, and many of the arts, including musical theory, to erect her own science of interpretation that fashions a space that only she inhabits and which gives her discursive privilege in terms of the events that she interprets and the manner in which she appropriates such knowledge. In this way, the use of the number 19 for purposes of divination becomes her own creative project, particularly her emphasis on aesthetics and meteorology. She explores the numerous applications of the number 19 in her magnum opus, *The Comer By Night 1986*, and in the weekly column "Unveiling the Number 19," published on thefinalcall.com, one of the NOI's websites. He column is given prominent placement in the Final Call newspaper, and, in it, she works out the far-reaching implications of her system of knowledge.

She claims and acknowledges, however, that the discovery of the "Miraculous Mathematical Code of the Holy Qur'an" was Dr. Rashad Khalifa's, "who was martyred on January 31, 1990 at the age of 54. He is [*sic*] also a citizen of Africa and our Brother who was born in Tanta, Egypt" (T. Muhammad 1986, viii; cf. 102). By claiming that Dr. Khalifah was a "citizen of Africa and our Brother," Mother Tynnetta may be attempting to make an epistemological link between the mathematical code of 19 and the truth of the Universe from the perspective of people of indigenous African descent, for which Egypt is the classical African civilization. She also wants to link the code particularly to the NOI. This would seem consistent with her stated future endeavor. In the "Second Preface" to her book, *The Comer by Night 1986*, she contends:

> We will focus on some of the new archeological and astronomical discoveries being uncovered by scientists who have been linked to the ongoing Revelatory Science of the 19-based Mathematical Code. Further evidence will be explored proving that the Honorable Elijah Muhammad brought to the Lost and Found Aboriginal Members of the Nation of Islam, the roots of Universal Knowledge and the Supreme Wisdom originating from the God of the Universe and the lord of all the worlds.
>
> T. MUHAMMAD, 1986, xii

So, while she gives Dr. Khalifah the credit for the discovery of the Code, she locates its origins with the God of the Universe, a black material God, and Elijah Muhammad, the Messenger of God, who was also black, was the instrument through which the knowledge was ultimately and symbolically associated. By locating the origins of this secret knowledge on the continent of Africa, she appears to be establishing Africa and African Americans as the source of the greatest knowledge in the world and to reinforce the idea that esoteric thought has its genesis in Egypt and with "black" people.

Related to this, she is interested in the identity of black people, explaining their true place in the cosmos, interpreting the experience of black people in American vis-à-vis white supremacy, and she desires that their relationship to Allah be finally disclosed. She intimates that this is secret knowledge of the most monumental proportions. It is a gnosis, however, that will have its ultimate "resolution" in the number 19. This is significant in that what was once hidden—God and the secret knowledge of the Universe—can now be absolutely known and expressed rationally through the mathematical and numerological code over which she has mastery, thus reconciling any possible tension between the idea of gnosis—that God is hidden and the universe is a *mystery*—and Elijah Muhammad's idea that God can be known because God was a living, breathing, and fleshly man, who could be known and experienced bodily (E. Muhammad 1965, 1–10). Though Mother Tynnetta fails to define the Code succinctly and sufficiently—exposing its internal logic, which often seems arbitrary—she suggests that the nature of Islamic knowledge, indeed all religious and scientific knowledge, is ultimately mathematical, and she locates her contention in the appearance, teachings, and experiences of Master Fard Muhammad, Elijah Muhammad, and Louis Farrakhan—especially in light of his UFO narrative.

Having (re)located the genesis of the mathematical code of the number 19 with the Original People of the earth, which in NOI mythology refers generally to the world of color, especially Asians, Native Americans, Latinos, and especially African Americans and the Nation of Islam (Finley 2012), she, then, "documents" retrospectively the many instances in which the number 19 was an interpretive factor in the doctrines and practices of the NOI, intimating that the Nation, rather than Rashad Khalifa, is the true originator, caretaker, and purveyor of the secrets that can be unlocked by the magical use of the number 19. She offers a litany of proofs. For instance, she suggests that it is intentional that Sura 74.30 of the Qur'an reads "Over it are nineteen" (T Muhammad 1986, 125–126). That verse 30 is about the number 19 points to Master Fard Muhammad, Allah in person, she contends, who appeared in the year 1930 to find the remnant of the Original People, by which she means African Americans, who were lost in the wilderness of North America (E. Muhammad, 2006, 17). Furthermore, it was in 1975, the year of Elijah Muhammad's "departure," that the code was revealed, thus connecting the code to the ostensible death of the Nation's leader:

> We are going to examine in this second part of my writings the possible reasons why the Qur'anic Code, based on the number 19 was only recently discovered in 1975, in the same year as the departure of the Honorable Elijah Muhammad. We will also explore some of the evidence that proves that the Honorable Elijah Muhammad is alive and in the company of his Lord. Through the unique and scientific language of mathematics, we will offer our proof as we retrace our footsteps and review the dynamic teachings of the Honorable Elijah Muhammad who has revealed the utmost truth about the Reality of God through the unique language mathematics taught to him by the mysterious man, Master W. Fard Muhammad.
>
> T. MUHAMMAD 1986, 80

A few things are noteworthy, here. First, Mother Tynnetta associates the "discovery" of the code 19 as an esoteric and numerological category with the "departure" of Elijah Muhammad in 1975. But it is also significant that she uses the term "discover," which neither implies invention nor development, which, again, she locates symbolically, if not actually, with the NOI. Second, she conflates Muhammad's ostensible "death" and the number 19, thus insinuating that the number 19 is either essential to Muhammad's enduring bodily survival or to proving and understanding it. Third, she also declares that Muhammad is with "his Lord," suggesting that Master Fard also continues to exist bodily. In so doing, she implicates the Mother Wheel, the UFO, in which Minister Farrakhan claimed to have experienced Muhammad, while Fard was also present.

Mother Tynnetta apprehends the number 19 throughout the history of the NOI and in numerous significant events. During the first years after its founding, for example, Master Fard Muhammad created a ritual catechism in which new adherents had to learn 154 Lessons and their answers (T. Muhammad 1986, 87, 104, 112). Speaking, again, in the context of the Mother Wheel and the smaller wheels within it, she says this regarding the 154 Lessons:

> There is a powerful message that can be read in these numbers that connect to the description and the work of the wheels as taught to us by the Honorable Elijah Muhammad. I only wish to lightly touch upon it at this time. First of all, the number [sic] 15 and 4 are numbers written in the code of our Lessons reading 154, which can also be resolved to the number 19 $(15 + 4) = 19$.
>
> T. MUHAMMAD 1986, 87

Mother Tynnetta fails to explicate exactly what that "powerful message" is, and it is unclear what method she uses to determine how the divine mathematics should work for 154 or any number. Why not 1 plus 54, or 6 plus 4, or 1 plus 9?

Notwithstanding the matter of methodology, even in this instance, she implicates Master Fard, Elijah Muhammad, and Louis Farrakhan—the entire history of this particular genealogy of the NOI, in fact, when she divines the number 19 in the example of the Lessons and the allusion to the Wheel.[1] This is most significant, given that after the "death" of Elijah Muhammad in 1975, many movements arose, claiming his legacy and hence, Fard's (Finley 2012, 444

---

1 Note that others, besides Farrakhan, claimed to be heirs to his legacy, including rivals Silis Muhammad, and Royall Jenkins, John Muhammad, the brother of Elijah Muhammad, Wallace Deen Muhammad, Elijah's son, and many others.

8n; Finley 2009, 355 cf. 363; Lieb 1998, 180). The existence of the Mother Plane or Wheel was taught to Muhammad by Fard, and Muhammad bequeathed its secrets to Farrakhan—who claims to have been incorporated into it in a mystical vision in 1985—where, as the legitimate heir to the NOI, he encountered Muhammad and Fard. Ultimately, then, the number 19 discloses the secrets of the Wheel and the persistence of the black physical bodies that inhabit it (T. Muhammad 1986, 85–88).

Louis Farrakhan and the Mysterious Number 30

The number 30 is intricately tied to Farrakhan's experience of the Mother Wheel, the most significant religious event of his life, but it also signals and confirms for him the ultimately divine nature of his experiences, which construct a coherent religious narrative in relationship to the Wheel. For example, Farrakhan—a calypso singer and entertainer—joined the NOI in 1955, and the number 30 appears prominently in his decision to commit fully to the Nation. He explains:

> [Then] the letter came, that all musicians had to get out of show business or get out of the Temple...I don't know who it was who told me...He said, 'Man the Messenger sent a letter and everybody in show business had 30 days to get out of show business or get out of the Temple'.
>
> J. MUHAMMAD 2006, 336

Accordingly, Elijah Muhammad issued an edict requiring that all members who were professional entertainers had to make a choice either to leave show business or resign from the Nation. Note that Farrakhan suggests that they had thirty days to make their decision. To this end, Farrakhan observes, it was on the thirtieth day of that thirty-day deadline in 1955 that he made his choice to follow Islam and leave the realm of entertainment, and on the night of his resolve, he had a vision:

> It was the last day, the 30th day or just about December 26th, or the 27th when I had this engagement in the Nevele Club. Nevele is eleven spelled backwards. It was a Jewish resort. I just said I'm going to get it all out of my system. I sang ballad. I sang some classical. I sang the blues. I played some classical violin. I played jazz violin...I went home to go to sleep. In the night, I saw these two doors. One had *success* written over it and a mound in the floor that came up, maybe as high as this table. It was

almost like a pyramid of diamonds and gold. But the other door had *Islam* over it with a black veil over the door. I was told to choose. And I chose Islam.

J. MUHAMMAD 2006, 336; cf. FINLEY 2009, 342–343

It was on the thirtieth day of the thirty day period in which Farrakhan had to make a major choice about his religious life, and all at once, he suggests, he was going to get all of the musical performance out of his system, enjoying himself at a nightclub, seemingly for the last time. Recounting the vision that appears to symbolize his choice of Islam over worldly riches, he seems tacitly aware of the significance of the number 30 as he reflects on his story in this 2006 interview. In what appears to be part of the same vision of 1955 or an extension of it, he recalls "two men" talking about his membership form. Farrakhan, reports, "There was cursive writing on my form. One said, 'Turn it over, it's not time for him to see this yet.'" The trope of cursive writing would be an important marker thirty years later when he would have yet another vision.

Perhaps the most significant relationship that he sees via the number 30 is the relationship between his vision of 1955 and his visionary UFO abduction narrative of 1985, and he suggests that his vision of the Mother Wheel is the organizing moment that allows him to make sense of the vision of 1955 and, indeed, his entire religious life (Finley 2012; Finley 2009, 346–347 39n). On September 17, 1985, while on a religious excursion to Tepozteco Mountain in Tepotzlan, Mexico, Farrakhan claims to have been carried into the Wheel by a smaller wheel and lead into a room where he heard the voice of Elijah Muhammad, who ostensibly had died in 1975. He reports that Master Fard Muhammad was also present (Farrakhan 1989; cf. J. Muhammad, 1986, 377–388). The details of his encounter are superfluous. What is important is the means by which he connects the UFO abduction of 1985 to his vision of 1955. He does so directly:

> That was 1955 and then 1985, or thirty years later comes and I'm up on the Wheel. Then this thing comes down and there's this cursive writing on it. I leaned forward to read it. Then the Honorable Elijah Muhammad speaks and whatever was on that screen disappears. I never consciously knew that I read it.
>
> J. MUHAMMAD 1986, 339

At this juncture, the trope of cursive writing, which appeared on his membership form in his 1955 vision merges with the cursive writing that he perceived on the screen in his UFO abduction narrative of 1985. Albeit the image of "cursive writing" in the 1985 experience on the Wheel evokes the 1955 vision, causing him to connect the two, the relationship between them is made concrete by the presence of the number 30. Again, Farrakhan points out that they were linked by "thirty years" when no acknowledgment of the temporal duration between events appeared otherwise necessary.

Minister Farrakhan is aware of the presence of the number 30 in many significant religious and historical events of his life in the NOI, though he fails to acknowledge explicitly the correlation between some of the most epic events and the number 30. Yet, he makes regular reference to the number 30, seemingly without obvious relevance to the episode in question. For instance, Elijah Muhammad "died" in 1975—or so it appears—and Farrakhan was positioned to ascend to the leadership of the Nation. He was the putative successor to Muhammad, since he was the National Spokesman for the movement, the number two man in the NOI (J. Muhammad 2006, 328–332; Gardell 1996, 124, 126). In what amounted to a coup, Muhammad's son, Wallace Deen Muhammad, who had defected or was excommunicated from the Nation on no less than a few occasions (Marsh 2000, 102–103, 109, 162; Finley 2009, 267–270), out maneuvered and threatened Farrakhan, as he laid claim to the mantle of command, made available by his father's death. Edward Curtis notes:

> Given this, it is all the more remarkable and even curious that Wallace eventually inherited the mantle of leadership from his father. While Elijah Muhammad never publicly appointed a successor, he seemed to defer quietly to his son's efforts to secure his right to the throne throughout 1974 and early 1975. In New York, Wallace flatly told National Secretary Abass Rassoull and National Spokesman Louis Farrakhan that he would succeed his father and specifically warned Farrakhan not to interfere.
>
> CURTIS 2000, 112

Curtis contends that Wallace was making obvious moves to circumvent Farrakhan's ascendancy prior to the death of his father. In addition, Curtis follows Gardell in suggesting that Wallace Muhammad may have had assistance from the FBI, who considered Wallace more conciliatory and acceptable (Curtis 2000, 112–113; Gardell 1996, 101–102). Farrakhan acquiesced, albeit not without some other strategic moves by Wallace, who had Farrakhan relocated from Harlem to Chicago so that he could maintain closer surveillance of him (Marsh 2000, 105; Gardell 1996, 122–123). Some viewed this as a demotion (Marsh 2000, 105).

Thirty (30) months later, Farrakhan seceded from the movement, simultaneously believing that he had been "excommunicated" (Marsh 2000, 107–108), claiming that Wallace had distorted his father's teachings. But observe how Farrakhan describes his exodus from Wallace's movement to reconstitute the NOI:

> ...Though he [Elijah Muhammad] said many things that would lead me to believe that he wanted me to take his place in his absence. I didn't feel confident. So if the Imam or W.D. Muhammad felt that he could, and knew the direction, then I would help him as I helped his father. Thirty months later, I came to the conclusion that, that was not best for me... Now it was approximately three years. It was actually 30 months. I was up; ready to take on the Herculean task of attempting to rebuild his [Elijah Muhammad's] work.
>
> J. MUHAMMAD 2006, 328–329

It is curious here that Farrakhan corrects himself regarding how long he had been with Wallace D. Muhammad before being helped in his decision to leave in order to reconstitute the Nation of Islam. Why did the initial response of "approximately three years" need clarification and precision to which he asserts "It was actually 30 months?" It seems clear that he is conscious that the number 30 signals, for him, that an event is divine in nature and marks his religious journey as coherent and providential.

Further illustrating this point was his meeting with Betty Shabazz, the widow of the martyred human rights leader, Malcolm X. Amid rumors that Farrakhan was involved in his assassination in 1965 and hostilities between the Shabazz family and him, Minister Farrakhan met with her in 1995 as part of the ongoing conversations of reconciliation—the major theme of the upcoming Million Man March in Washington, D.C. He explains:

> Last week Betty Shabazz and I sat down together after thirty years. I won't say we embraced each other, but we made an initial step at reconciliation. I declare that I, Louis Farrakhan, had nothing to do with the murder of Malcolm X. That's why I'm calling, and we're going to call, as one million men, to the government of America to open up the files, and let us see where the real enemy is...History will judge me, but after thirty years, we can't continue to allow the enemy to keep the wound open by constantly pouring filth in the wound.
>
> FARRAKHAN 1996, 50

Did the number 30 signify to Farrakhan that 1995 was the right time to initiate reconciliation with the family of Malcolm X? It is difficult to think that

it was not a factor. In religious matters of importance, such as this, he apprehends the number 30, or perhaps he constructs events to correspond to the
number 30.

For instance, Tracy Johnson wrote a *Los Angeles Times* article called
"Farrakhan Said to See Quake in Next 30 Days," published on August 17, 1996 in
which he covered a dispute between a property company and a NOI mosque
and western regional headquarters in Inglewood, California, in which the NOI
was evicted due to their inability to comply with an agreement to zoning problems with the city that would have allowed them to buy the building. The minister of the mosque, Tony Muhammad, alleged that more than one hundred
law enforcement officers including FBI and ATF agents aggressively effected
the eviction, to which, he reported, Farrakhan responded with the prediction
of a massive earthquake within thirty days. While the account was merely
attributed to Minister Farrakhan, without any concrete indication that he
actually made the claim, it seems curiously consistent with his deployment of
the number 30.

The Meaning of Numerology in the Nation of Islam

Mother Tynnetta Muhammad and Minister Louis Farrakhan signify on one
another in a way that affirms the presence, the efficacy, and the consonance of
the other's significant number. In what may be his most prominent and important speech, which was his address to the Million Man March called "Toward a
More Perfect Union," Minister Farrakhan affirms Mother Tynnetta's number 19:

> In the background is [*sic*] the Jefferson and Lincoln Memorials, each one
> of those monuments are nineteen feet high. Abraham Lincoln the six-
> teenth president, Thomas Jefferson the third president, and sixteen and
> three make nineteen again. What is so deep about this number nineteen?
> Why are we standing on the Capitol steps today? That number nineteen,
> when you have a nine, you have a womb that is pregnant, and when you
> have a one standing by the nine it means that there is something secret
> that has to be unfolded...slaves used to be brought right here on this mall
> in chains...Right along this mall, going over to the White House our
> fathers were sold into slavery.
>
> FARRAKHAN 1996, 127cf. 139

Farrakhan indicates that the secret that the number 19 reveals is that the trade
of black bodies as commodities occurred on the very ground on which millions

of black men were standing and that this truth is lodged in the history, symbols, and monuments of America, which is to suggest a causal relationship between white supremacy which he mentions in the speech, the foundation of America, and marginalization of black bodies, male bodies in particular. But he also feminizes the number 19 by suggesting that the digit nine refers to a womb (which is a recurring and prominent theme in his work). He is probably alluding to the religious insights of Mother Tynnetta as a woman, whom, I would argue, is empowered and affirmed in the realm of secret and esoteric knowledge in a way that she may not be in the traditionally male-dominated roles of institutional religion that often exclude women in intellectual and powerful positions.

Mother Tynnetta returns the favor, seemingly acknowledging my contention that 30 is an important number for Minister Farrakhan. In the context of a conversation in which she explains Farrakhan's period of silence prior to his "efforts to rebuild the Nation of Islam," (T. Muhammad 1986, vi), she appeals to the biblical book of Revelation for support:

> The eighth chapter of Revelation begins with the opening of the 7th Seal which is followed by a period of silence in heaven about the space of half an hour. This space of half an hour is then followed by the work of the seven angels who had the seven trumpets prepared to sound. If we calculate this **30** minute period of silence to the **30** month period of silence before Minister Farrakhan began to sound his trumpet of Divine Warning, then we are able to recognize why this period of God's Final Judgment of the nations is called the Final Call.
>
> T. MUHAMMAD 1986, vi

Tynnetta Muhammad connects two numbers 30 to Minister Farrakhan, one, a reference from the New Testament, and the other, from Farrakhan's own experience, in her remonstrance that supports his reconstitution of the NOI. By doing this, she indicates that the number 30, in reference to Minister Farrakhan, has religious significance and carries divine weight that authorizes many of his activities.

Mother Tynnetta and Farrakhan both use complimentary numerological systems that allow them to make the abstract concrete and the absurd meaningful. Through strategic usage of the numbers 19 and 30 they are able to give coherence to events that may or may not be connected to these numbers, but that give them a meaningful sense of *terrestrial enchantment* that, while material, consciousness or intention pervades the universe, and this force can be affected and manipulated on behalf of the person who has unlocked its secrets

(Hanegraaff 1998, 373, 394; von Stuckrad 2002). Throughout the history of the African presence in America, we see examples of the ways in which religion—including magical practices—functioned as a means of making sense of the world and of gaining a psychological sense of control over a world that for African Americans was wrought with the absurdity of violence that was directed at black bodies. The need for such a mechanism to mediate the relations between African Americans and whites who maintain an inordinate amount of power to affect their lives in adverse ways was most clearly seen in the experience of slavery, as Yvonne Chireau notes:

> Conjure also may have allowed black people to attain a measure of control over their lives, as bondpersons. The world that the slaves inhabited was unpredictable and uncertain. Anxiety over inevitable violence, separation from loved ones, or the unforeseeable risks of escape must have engendered persistent insecurity for African American slaves. Blacks also endured the ever-present realities of racial subjugation and other forms of affliction such as sickness and destitution.
>
> CHIREAU 2002, 17

The work Anthony Pinn (2003, 69) would suggest that the absurdity and experience of *terror* that Chireau discusses, here, continues to serve as a hallmark of black experiences in America, not vis-à-vis the historic systems of slavery and ritual lynching, but as characterized, in part, by the aggressive and violent policing, surveillance, and abuse of black bodies and a corporatized prison industrial complex as a means of social control (Alexander 2010; Cone 2011, 163–164; Pinn 2003, 69) that are endorsed by an American culture of white supremacy, capitalism, and patriarchy.

As such, practices like numerology, as attempts to gain control over the world and nature, continue expose power relations that are often concealed in American religious mythologies of meritocracy and innocence and may suggest the pervasiveness of relative powerlessness of those whose social location does not confer what are in fact unearned and unmerited advantages of whiteness, maleness, and other privileged subject positions. The uniqueness of the form of knowledge employed by the numerology of Mother Tynnetta and Minister Farrakhan, again, is a *theosophical empiricism*—an apprehension of secret knowledge that is divine in nature and is utilized to confer religious meaning on events that might otherwise be mundane that eschews the supernaturalism inherent in the conjure about which Chireau theorizes. Rather, it is a material perspective that appears influenced by science and rationalism in its quest for certainty.

This certainty has the ultimate purpose of proving the *material perpetuity* of black bodies. This is to suggest that certain black bodies—although all have the potential—endure indefinitely. By *material perpetuity*, I intend contrast with notions of reincarnation, transmigration or metempsychosis, or progressive spiritual evolution (Hanegraaff 1998, 262–263), particularly since the NOI jettisons any notion of the soul or spirit. The world is material, God is material, and the afterlife is a material existence that occurs after the destruction of this present and evil age that is dominated by white supremacy (E. Muhammad 1965, 3–10). Mother Tynnetta and Minister Farrakhan contend that particular black bodies do not die, that is, they do not cease biological functioning even after apparent death. Elijah Muhammad and Master Fard Muhammad are prototypical black bodies in this sense.

For this reason, Farrakhan's UFO experience of 1985 is of immense importance, since it was in this experience that he claims to have communed with both of them on the Mother Wheel, although Elijah Muhammad's presence was the most prominent. It is not coincidence, then, the numbers 19 and 30 appear most prominently in their discourses on the Wheel. Recall Farrakhan's connection of the number 30 with his abduction about, when, after joining the NOI in 1955, he reflected, "thirty years later comes and I'm up on the Wheel." He expounds in the implications in a book written by trusted NOI theologian, Jabril Muhammad, called *Is It Possible That the Honorable Elijah Muhammad Is Still Physically Alive?* (J. Muhammad 2007). In short, Farrakhan answers emphatically, "yes." (see Finley 2009, 359, quote myself). Farrakhan says, "When I considered all of the scriptures, when I considered his direct words to me, and when I considered other things I heard, for the first time during that period, I then became convinced that the Honorable Elijah Muhammad was in fact alive" (J. Muhammad 2007, 31). The Wheel confirmed his belief. Tynnetta Muhammad also sees the Mother Wheel as the most important religious idea in the NOI, which substantiates the *material perpetuity* of black bodies, and she argues that it is connected to the mathematical code of 19. The appearance of the numbers 19 and 30 with respect to the most important religious event for the NOI, Farrakhan's reported UFO abduction, is the central narrative that "proves" for them the prophecy that Elijah Muhammad and Master Fard Muhammad are *alive* bodily.

Finally, Mother Tynnetta and Minister Farrakhan both argue that their esotericism or secret knowledge originates in Egypt and among African Americans, rather than in Europe. The Miraculous Mathematical Qur'anic Code of 19 was only recognized in Egypt by the Sufi, Dr. Rashad Khalifa, and she works diligently to support this claim by connecting it, not simply to Africa, but to all of the important events in NOI history. Likewise, Farrakhan, who has much to say on the matter, sums it up with the observation that the secrets and symbols of Freemasonry that are seen in Washington, the sight of his million man march address are "Egyptian...This whole layout is reminiscent of our great historic past, Egypt"(Farrakhan 1996, 127). The idea of Egypt plays prominently in the mythology of the NOI in which the Original People founded civilizations in the Nile Valley thousands of years ago.

Numerology offered Mother Tynnetta, Minster Farrakhan, and the NOI existential and epistemological certainty, through what I am calling theosophical empiricism, in a world of uncertainties and symbolic and actual violence directed at black bodies, guarantees the material perpetuity of these bodies, and connects esotericism to Egypt, the classical African civilization and to an important moment in NOI mythology and points to origins of black religious thought that are "black" in their genesis. What we gain from the data of numerology and the NOI is the centrality of the body in NOI religious discourses. For African American religion and esotericism, the body is ultimately the carrier of religious meaning, the signifier of black religion, but numerology also functions to support the belief that physical bodies endure after ostensible death, at least certain bodies. Therefore, African American Esotericism should be in dialogue with Religion in America, African American Religion, Theory and Method in the Study of Religion, and Western Esotericism, and Afrofuturism. It is my desire, that given the appropriate platforms, that this work will impact and be impacted in important scholarly ways by these conversations.

Furthermore, what this project calls for is further exploration of the ways in which religious groups, though material in focus, posit a nature of reality that is not fixed and immutable, but can be affected by human consciousness. It was this attention to materiality and the body that made the NOI and esotericism so compelling. Indeed, I came to my interest in the NOI precisely because of the ways in which it subverted the dominant metanarratives that African Americans were most meaningfully Christian, that esotericism was a white and European religious orientation, and because of the importance of the body.

CHAPTER 8

On the Knowledge of Self and Others
Secrecy, Concealment and Revelation in Elijah Muhammad's Nation of Islam (1934–1975)[1]

Justine M. Bakker

Introduction

In November 2011, I first immersed myself in the eclectic, complex, and mesmerizing teachings of the Nation of Islam (NOI), an African American religious movement founded in 1930 by the mysterious peddler Fard Muhammad, who would subsequently be revered by his successor, Elijah Muhammad, as God-in-Person. This was around the same time that I – in a completely unrelated event – completed my first course in the academic field of "Western Esotericism." The content of parts of the NOI's teachings and practices and some of the ideas that I got acquainted with in the course seemed, in some ways, remarkably similar. I was immediately captivated by this seeming resemblance, and I wanted to get to the bottom of it. What struck me, however, was the lack of research on esotericism in the NOI. To be sure, scholars have touched upon the topic (Curtis 2006; Finley 2009, 2012), but only as recent as 2013 a more extensive account was published (Finley 2013).

In this text, a book chapter entitled "Hidden Away," Stephen C. Finley discusses esoteric elements in Elijah Muhammad's NOI (1934–1975), and specifically addresses in what way esotericism in the NOI relates to and, perhaps more importantly, challenges Antoine Faivre's famous definition of Western Esotericism as a "form of thought" with four intrinsic and two additional characteristics (267–268). Finley's text will serve as the starting point of this chapter, in which I will use a history of religions approach – specifically the historiography of the field of Western Esotericism – to further explore and elaborate upon one of his arguments. Finley argues that Muhammad, through a teacher-disciple relationship with God, claimed to have access to secret knowledge regarding the cosmos, God, and race – and his followers through him. This knowledge, Finley indicates furthermore, disclosed the concealed

---

1   This chapter is derived from one of the chapter's of my master's thesis. I would like to take the opportunity to thank my thesis supervisors, Wouter J. Hanegraaff and Stephen C. Finley, for their support, insightful suggestions, and useful criticism.

history of the "black nation," also known as the myth of Yakub (269). What Finley, however, does not seem to recognize – or at least does not make explicit – is that this claim to secret knowledge is part of a broader and more comprehensive *dialectic of secrecy, concealment and revelation*. Identifying and analyzing all components of this dialectic – which, as we shall soon see, not only entailed the dissemination of secret knowledge through the myth of Yakub, but also certain practices of secrecy, and conspiracy theory – is, I contend in this essay, fundamental for understanding secrecy and esotericism in the NOI.

Secrecy, Concealment and Revelation

Secrecy – although according to Antoine Faivre (1999, 172) and Wouter J. Hanegraaff (2006, 33) not a defining characteristic of esotericism – is a recurrent element in various and diverse esoteric currents, traditions, and movements (Stuckrad 2010; Urban 1997, 1998, 2001, 2008, 2012; Bolle 1987; Luhrmann 1989; Wolfson 1999). It is, for the purposes of this chapter, useful to distinguish between two forms of secrecy: a *practice of secrecy*, that is, the active behavior of keeping something, for instance a ritual or text, a secret, and a *rhetoric of secrecy*, which claims that there is a secret, which may or can be unveiled in a specific way. Muhammad, as we shall soon see, employed both forms of secrecy: he claimed to have access to secret knowledge, which he subsequently gradually unveiled to his followers, who were, in turn, forbidden to discuss the content with outsiders.

With respect to both forms of secrecy, most scholars are not interested in "exposing" and analyzing the actual content of secrets, but with secrecy as a "discursive strategy," that is, secrecy as a complex religious tactic of unveiling and/or concealing, employed in different social and political circumstance, and for a wide variety of purposes (Stuckrad 2010; Urban 1998; Dakake 2006; Johnson 2002, 2006). In fact, historian of religion Hugh B. Urban argues that secrecy can only be studied from this perspective, as scholars are restricted by the "double bind" problem of secrecy, which entails "the question of how one can ever know with certainty the true substance of what is hidden, and then, supposing one can, the question of whether one should reveal it publicly" (1998, 214). In an attempt to circumvent this "double bind," Urban proposes that we should shift our attention from studying the content of secrets to a study of the purposes and tactics of secrecy.

Although I can relate to Urban's reservations with regards to exposing the content of religious secrets, the NOI provides us with a case in which we do not have to deal with the "double bind" problem: contrary to the secrets of the movements studied by Urban and others, much, if not all, of the content of Muhammad's secret knowledge – initially solely unveiled in sermons only accessible for followers, later also partly disclosed in newspaper columns and books – has been published by members of the movement in the last two decades. Today, Muhammad's secrets are therefore "out" and widely known. This implies that we can study both the purposes and implications of Muhammad's rhetoric and practice of secrecy as well as the content of Muhammad's secrets. Thirdly, and perhaps most importantly, this gives us the unique opportunity to evaluate the relationship between the actual content of secrets and social strategy of secrecy.

As Muhammad's *practice of secrecy* has already been documented by other scholars (Essien-Udom 1962; Sahib 1995; Allen 1996; Curtis 2006), this chapter will primarily focus on his *rhetoric of secrecy*, thereby discussing three interrelated dimensions: (1) the mode of accessing secret knowledge; (2) the content of the claim; and (3) conspiracy theory. The work of Kocku von Stuckrad may help us to gain valuable insights on how we should approach our first task. In *Locations of Knowledge in Medieval and Modern Europe* (2010) von Stuckrad argues, similar to Urban and Johnson, that secrecy should be discussed in terms of discursive strategies. Von Stuckrad is primarily concerned with strategies of unveiling secret knowledge, and his book specifically calls attention to two different modes: through mediation by gods, angels or other superior entities, or through personal experience (63–64). Muhammad employed a similar "tactic" as he claimed to have access to secret knowledge through a direct teacher-disciple relationship with God. In what follows, I will identify and analyze both mode of accessing and the specific content of Muhammad's esoteric truth claim.

In order to complete our analysis of Muhammad's rhetoric of secrecy, we must, in addition, look at a third element, which is intimately connected to and in fact follows from the first two: conspiracy theory. Because, for the NOI, certain knowledge is not only secret or hidden, but also intentionally concealed from black people by white Americans with the sole purpose of keeping African Americans, in the words of the NOI, "blind, deaf, and dumb" to their true history, present, future and potential. As also stated by Michael Barkun in his classic study on conspiracy theory in the United States, *A Culture of Conspiracy* (2003), conspiracy and secrecy seem "indissolubly linked" (4). Barkun writes that conspiracy theory refers to the belief that "an organization made up of individuals or groups was or is acting covertly to achieve some malevolent end" (3). Conspiracy theories are thus rooted in two interrelated convictions: an organization engages in malicious activities that it, subsequently, tries to hide from the general public. I will demonstrate that Muhammad developed a conspiracy theory about American Freemasonry, which is grounded in and served to legitimize and strengthen both mode and content of his claim to secret knowledge, and is, ultimately, connected to a very real history of racial violence and terror.

Allah and His Last Messenger: A Teacher-Disciple Relationship

The NOI was founded in 1930 in Detroit by a mysterious peddler. The man, who called himself Fard Muhammad, claimed to be a prophet from Mecca, and while selling silk and raincoats, he shared his narrative on African American origins and their alleged "original" religion, Islam, with the residents of Detroit's Paradise Valley (Beynon 1937, 895–897). Detroit was the final destination for many black migrants who participated in the Great Migration (Sernett 1997; Grossman 1989). These migrants sought to escape the destructive forces of white supremacy in the southern former slave states, but the utopian "Promised Land" in the North soon proved to be just that – utopian: the Ku Klux Klan and other radical white supremacist organizations were as prevalent as in the South (Evanzz 1999, 54–55), and most migrants were forced to take underpaid jobs and live in overcrowded, impoverished "ghettos" (Baer 1984, 145). Furthermore, the Black Church, in the nineteenth century the most important force in the rural south, found its power slipping away as it became more middle class-oriented, de-radicalized, and distanced itself from debates on race and racism (Wilmore 1998, 163–195). For many black Americans, Fard's narrative, which scorned Christianity and preached Islam, stressed black Americans' glorious history as founders of early black civilizations, and prophesied the imminent destruction of the white world and destructive forces of white supremacy, offered a plausible explanation for the present, and promising blueprint for the future.

One of the early neophytes of Fard's new movement was Elijah Poole, a Georgia-born immigrant, who quickly became Fard's most important trustee and representative: at Elijah's own account, Fard gave him his "original" surname Muhammad and bestowed upon him the revealing title "Messenger" (Muhammad, 1993A, 3). Following Fard's mysterious departure in 1934 – which caused vicious in-fights and schisms in the movement (Beynon 1937, 903–904) – Muhammad claimed his inheritance on the basis of two claims. Firstly, he reasoned that Fard had revealed to him, and importantly to him alone, his true identity. In *History of the Nation of Islam* (1993A, 1–2), we can read Muhammad's account of his first meeting with Fard, during which he ostensibly immediately recognized the prophet as being a savior, stating bluntly: "You are that one that the Bible prophesied would come at the end of the world under the name Son of Man and under the name The Second Coming of Jesus." Whispering in Elijah's ear, Fard answered, "Yes I am the One, but who knows that but yourself," and told him to "be quiet." In a subsequent, again private, meeting, Fard assured Elijah's theory when he told him, "My name is the Mahdi; I am God" (Muhammad 1974, 23). These statements stand at the basis of Muhammad's later proclamations that Fard was God in person.

Secondly, Muhammad reasoned that Fard had instructed him and him alone for a period of "three years (night and day) on the histories of two people, Black and white" (2002B, 32). In light of Fard's deification, these sessions brought about a teacher-disciple relationship that served as a mode of gaining secret, esoteric knowledge, through mediation (see also Finley 2012, 436). Muhammad's claims to accession are therefore interrelated and, combined, gave him the necessary credentials to become the revelator of secret knowledge and leader of the NOI: arguing that Fard was in fact God himself who had returned to Earth to enlighten Muhammad, and just Muhammad, in the secrets of the universe, Muhammad could claim to be only one with access to secret, divine knowledge. In the forty-plus years that he led the NOI, Muhammad disclosed this secret knowledge to his followers, most notably through the retelling of the myth of Yakub.

The Myth of Yakub: Unveiling the "Secrets of the Universe"

In "Hidden Away," Finley argues that the myth of Yakub is roughly organized around five periods (270). As the myth is rather complex, Finley's strategy of dividing the myth in different periods is, for the sake of clarity, particularly useful, and his approach will therefore be imitated in this chapter. However, in contrast to Finley, I will divide the myth in six rather than five periods. The first period revolves around the self-creation of a black, material God and his subsequent creation of the cosmos. The second entails the division of the moon and the Earth sixty-six trillion years ago. The third part concerns the migration of the Tribe of Shabazz into the "Jungles of East Asia" (Africa) fifty thousand years ago, and the fourth depicts the creation of the white race, six thousand years ago. The fifth period pertains to black presence in America, and starts with the beginning of slavery. In "Hidden Away," Finley does not consider "slavery" a separate period in the myth. However, as I divide the myth according to different events that had a significant effect on – or in fact change the course of – black America, I believe that the period of slavery should be seen as a separate chapter; it is the practice of slavery and accompanying horrors, after all, that caused black Americans to become, as indicated by Muhammad, the "most deprived people on Planet Earth." Finally, the sixth term initiates the epic shutdown: the advent of Allah in person who raises a Last Messenger from the black nation, and instills him with the task to instruct his people in the true, heretofore secret knowledge of "God, Self, and Enemy."

The epic saga starts roughly seventy-six trillion years ago, when Allah created himself out of an atom produced by an all-black material universe (Muhammad 2002B, 6–10; 2006, 92–97). Allah was naturally black, because there was only darkness when he was self-created, and naturally material, because created in and from a material universe. In fact, the NOI's God is so material that it is even possible for him to die: according to Muhammad, every twenty-five thousand years a new God is born who has the chance to show forth his wisdom. Each God expires after one or two centuries, but his wisdom directs the course of the entire twenty-five thousand year cycle (2002B, 49; 2005, 5). The birth of a new God is accompanied by the writing of a new "future history": at the start of every new cycle, a council of twenty-four scientists – the Supreme God and twenty-three writers – comes together and, through telepathic clairvoyance, look into the future and document all events that will occur in the next twenty-five thousand years (Malcolm X 1971, 50). When these "future histories" expire, they are hidden in a vault in Mecca. The scientists are prohibited to reveal their secret content until a God will be born whose wisdom will surpass the wisdom of the Creator. The birth of this God will initiate the end of time, during which the secrets of the universe will be revealed (Muhammad 2002B, 3; 2012, 29). As will become evident, this God was in fact Fard Muhammad, who revealed the secrets of the universe to his "Last Messenger" Elijah, and whose coming initiated the imminent destruction of the white world.

Following his self-creation, Allah created the cosmos, an elaborate cosmology that included the Sun, stars, nine planets, and the other "gods," the original black people (Muhammad 2012, 6; 2002B, 8). Seven of the planets – Muhammad explicitly mentions Mars – were inhabited with black life, but those black people who lived on Planet Earth were the most significant. They ruled from the continent "Asia," which, back then, was the only continent; as such, Muhammad reasons, all black people should be perceived as descendants from an "Original Asiatic Blackman" (2012, 4; 1974, 93; 2008A, 13–14). The "Great Asiatic Nation" was organized in thirteen tribes, which were different but, in the words of Claude Andrew Clegg III (1997, 42), "formed a Nation united by skin color (black), religion (Islam), and natural disposition (righteousness)."

The legend continues ten trillion years after the self-creation of the black, material God, when a renegade black Muslim god-scientist "in his frenzy to try to force all people to believe as he believed and to speak the same language with no difference in dialect," attempted to destroy the black nation by filling the Earth with powerful dynamite (Muhammad 2002A, 10–11; Finley 2009, 100–101). The subsequent explosion failed its destructive purposes, but did result in the "deportation" of the moon from planet Earth. One of the tribes was killed in this attack; the other twelve continued to live on planet Earth. The Tribe of Shabazz, of which black Americans are descendants, was the strongest and only "scientific tribe" that survived the explosion and went to start civilizations in the Nile Valley in Egypt and Mecca in Arabia (Muhammad 1965, 31).

Unfortunately, the myth of Yakub does not explicate what happened during the trillions of years between the foundation of civilizations in the Nile Valley and Mecca, and an event that happened fifty thousand years ago, when a second dissatisfied black scientist, Shabazz, entered the saga. According to Muhammad, Shabazz encouraged other members of the Tribe of Shabazz to resettle in the "jungles of East Asia," i.e. Africa. The purpose of this migration was, according to Muhammad (1965, 31), to make "all of us tough and hard in order to endure the life of the jungles of East Asia (Africa) and to overcome the beasts there." In fact, Muhammad (2012, 2) indicates that Shabazz wanted to create a new black people that "would be undefeatable." The others disagreed, but gave Shabazz permission to make his "new man," upon which Shabazz took part of his tribe and relocated in the jungle. According to the saga, this migration changed, and more importantly weakened, the physiology of black people. Prior to living in the jungle, black people were "soft and delicate" and had "straight hair" (Malcolm X: 48). Living in Africa resulted in "kinky hair," thickening of the lips, and broadening of the nose (Muhammad 1965, 31). Moreover, fifty thousand years in the jungle resulted in a loss of cultural refinement and civilization, summarized by Muhammad (1965, 107) in a rather strong statement pertaining the course of the black nation: "[f]ifty thousand years ago he [the black nation] had his complete fall" and allowed their "weaker side" to rule.

The fall of the black nation reached a pinnacle with the birth of Yakub, sixty-six hundred years ago. Known as the "big head scientist" for his unusually large head and profound knowledge and wisdom, Yakub developed an evil plan to destroy the black nation. The particularities of his plan first dawned upon him when he was playing with two pieces of steel, and "discovered what is known as the law of magnetism: that unalike attracts and like repels" (Malcolm X 1971, 51). This finding offered Yakub a first clue in his quest for world-domination: to be able to create a people that would be capable of ruling the black nation, he had to make a new people that was completely "unalike" the original people, for the simple reason that "unalike" attracts "like" – the original people would love the new people; the unalike could rule and manipulate the like (Muhammad 2002B, 65; Muhammad 1973, 175). In high school, Yakub further developed his plan when he discovered that black people consisted of two germs [read: chromosomes]: a strong black germ and a weak brown germ. Yakub realized that by the process of "grafting" [read: genetics or genetic engineering], he could separate the two germs and, out of the weaker brown germ, make a new, completely "unalike" people (Muhammad 2002B, 39; 1965, 11–13; Finley 2009, 106–108).

On the Island of Pelan (Patmos in the Bible), Yakub executed his destructive plan with the help of 59,999 followers. During a period of six hundred years, they grafted the white race, a new, distinct, and completely unalike people: "He's a new man to very one of us, a new race of people with a nature and wisdom that is absolutely new and contrary to the aboriginal, the black man" (Muhammad 2002A, 42). According to Muhammad, Yakub's grafting process explained both the physiological and psychological nature of the white race: whites were evil and devilish by nature because they were made by a black man with the sole purpose of destroying black people (2008A, 59; 1993A, 12) and physiological weaker, as they have fragile bones, thin blood, and inferior in mental capacity, due to the fact that their brains weigh less than the brains of black people (Clegg 1997, 51).

This newly created race caused division and bloodshed since their materialization, but their attempt to destroy the black nation came to a crescendo with slavery – the advent of which marks the fifth period of the myth of Yakub. The genesis is located in the year 1555, when the English slave trader John Hawkins transported the first African slaves to Jamestown, Virginia, in a slave ship that carried the elusive name "Good Ship Jesus" (Muhammad 2012, 17–19). In Jamestown, during a period of sixty-four years – from 1555 to 1619 – white Americans transformed the "Original Asiatic Blackman" into a slave race, the "so-called Negro" (Muhammad 2002C, 2, 100). According to Muhammad (2012, 18), slavery robbed the black nation from the real knowledge of God – a material as opposed to spiritual being –, Self – their own language, name, religion, and culture – and Enemy – the real nature and purpose of the white race. Moreover, the destructive forces of white supremacy tricked them into believing that they were inferior. Chief responsible was the religion of Christianity: by the use of "tricknology," white Christians created a false reality based on illusion and lies such as a false concept of God, heaven and hell. According to Muhammad, heaven and hell are possible conditions on earth – hell is the current state of black America, heaven may be achieved – not spiritual places that one would go to after one passes away (Muhammad 2002C, 6; 1965, 2, 9; 1997, 4–6).

As previously stated, the relocation of the Tribe of Shabazz in Africa, which resulted in a loss of knowledge and civilization and allowed the "weaker side" of the black man to rule, initiated a first phase in the "fall" of the black Nation. As Muhammad (1965, 108) argues that every fifty-thousand years, the universe will be completely renewed, the creation of the white race and slavery were, in my understanding of the myth of Yakub, perceived as a "necessary" second and third phase in the "fall" of the black nation: only when a complete "fall" had occurred, a God could manifest on Earth in order to instruct black Americans in their true, hitherto hidden and concealed knowledge and, as such, resurrect them in a new, righteous, "god-like" and ultimately perfect people.

This God came to the United States in 1930, in the person of Fard Muhammad. Fard was born in Mecca in 1877, as the son of a black father and white mother. According to Muhammad, Fard had to be made from "both grafted and ungrafted people" in order to fulfill his predestined job: only when he was "half-half," he could navigate between black and white during the times of Jim Crow, and hide until the time was right to make himself known (1993A, 3–4; 1993C, 75). As previously stated, Fard only stayed with the black nation for a short period, leaving the bulk of the work to his Messenger. Once Elijah Muhammad had "awakened" enough black Americans from their "spiritually-dead" mental state, Allah would initiate the Day of Judgment. The final War of Armageddon will be settled with a "great decisive battle in the sky": a God-designed, human-made technologically advanced military weapon, known as the Mother Plane, would carry out the destruction of the white world (Muhammad 1993C, 83–90; 1973, 236–242; 1965, 290–294; 2008B).

Those black Americans that had heard "the call of Islam" and were followers of the NOI would survive this attack. Muhammad's contemplations on the hereafter are rather vague and sketchy, but it is clear that people would have been raised up, resurrected "into the knowledge of the white race as being devils, the enemies of Allah, and the black nation" (Muhammad 2002B, 67). Accordingly, black Americans' inherent natural disposition as righteousness will be restored: the wicked (brown) germ will be removed, and, therefore, black people in the hereafter would be incapable to sin (Muhammad 1965, 108). Furthermore, the wisdom of Fard is infinite and it seems as if he will be the last God (Muhammad 2012, 13; 2005: 9). The myth of Yakub therefore concludes as it began: a black utopia, in which the intimate relationship between God and his Creation will be restored, in which righteousness, blackness, and Islam will unite the black nation, and in which black Americans will ascend to their predestined role as rulers of the world and finally become the "gods" that they were when they were created.

Cloaked in the Symbols of American Freemasonry: Conspiracy Theory

Through the dissemination of the "secrets of the universe," i.e. the myth of Yakub, Muhammad claimed to put forth a vision of the truth that is superior to all other interpretations of God, the cosmos, and the origins, present, and future of black people; a vision of the truth that is superior to existing narratives in both science and religion. At the same time, for the NOI, this knowledge was not only *secret* or *hidden*, but also intentionally *concealed from* the black nation, as white American Freemasons knew, but intentionally obscured some parts of the myth of Yakub using ritual and symbolism. As will become evident, Muhammad developed a conspiracy theory about American Freemasonry that is grounded in and serves to legitimate and strengthen the myth of Yakub; a conspiracy theory that is, for that reason, quite different from "mainstream" conspiracy theories about Freemasonry (see, for instance, Davis 1972; Barkun 2003, 126–140; Lee 2011, 19–42).

Acknowledging that he was once a mason himself, Muhammad (1994, 16, 24) reasons that white masons refuse to teach black masons the real truth behind, or the "theology inside," Masonic symbolism and ritual. Fully immersed in the secrets of the universe by God himself, Muhammad realized that Masonic symbolism and ritual in reality point to black people. More specifically, white American Freemasons have deliberately cloaked the truths of the myth of Yakub in their rituals and symbols, so that black people could not know the truth about their superior nature and divine origins, and the inferior and evil nature of whites (see also Finley 2009, 178–179). Thus, Muhammad employed a specific strategy of unveiling secret knowledge, which reveals that a secret society intentionally obscured this secret knowledge; in a complex dialectic of secrecy, concealment, and revelation, emerges a conspiracy theory *about* a secret, esoteric society *within* Muhammad's own claim to secret knowledge. In what follows, I will briefly discuss two instances in which Muhammad explains the "theology inside" Masonic symbolism and ritual.

Firstly, the NOI maintains that the symbolism behind the white leather aprons that newly initiated candidate's wear during rituals in reality points to the inferior and evil nature of whites (Malcolm X, 61; T. Muhammad 2010). The myth of Yakub explains that the white race, after their creation of Pelan, returned to Mecca in a first attempt to destroy the black nation. However, the

King of Mecca stripped them of their knowledge, literature and clothing, gave them "an apron...to hide their nakedness" and exiled them to "West Asia" [Europe], where they lived as savages for a period of two thousand years (Muhammad 2002B, 57; 1973, 69). For the NOI, the white leather apron thus symbolizes the degradation of the white race and their inherently evil nature. Moreover, the fact that Masons wear the apron proofs that they are aware of their inherent inferior nature, but deliberately cloaked this truth in the symbolism of the white leather apron.

Secondly, Muhammad explains the "theology inside" the initiation ritual into the third degree, the degree of Master Mason. In this ritual, initiates are identified with Hiram Abif, the architect and master builder of the Temple of Solomon. The initiation ritual begins with the question of what the future Master Mason is going to do in the West, to which the blindfolded initiate replies that he is going to, "seek for that which was lost and is now found" – the initiate will seek the Master's word. According to the legend, Hiram entered the Temple around noon, when three Fellow Crafts surrounded the Temple and trapped him inside. They demanded that he would give them the "Master Word," but Hiram refused, arguing that they would receive it once the time was right. Unpleased with Hiram's turndown, each of them gave the master builder a blow with a working tool – the third and final blow resulting in Hiram's death. The three craftsmen carried his body out of the temple, dug a grave, and buried him. Hiram's sudden absence was however noted the same day, and King Solomon ordered fifteen other craftsmen to go find him. Once they had found Hiram's grave, Solomon ordered that they had to dig up Hiram's body and bury him decently, in the Temple (Bogdan 2007, 85–89).

According to Muhammad, the history of Hiram Abif symbolizes the present-day situation of the black community: "He [the black man] must be restored; he must be taken back in the Temple of his own. The Temple of which he was the architect...You are Hiram Abif yourself" (1996, 37). The figure of Hiram thus symbolizes the black man, who was struck on the head, causing him to be "mentally-dead" until a savior from the East, i.e. Fard, came to resurrect him in the West. England, France, and the United States are personified as the three men who killed Hiram Abif, and the savior of the architect, Solomon, is symbolized as Fard Muhammad, the savior of the black man (Muhammad 2008D, 34–38, 42–43). The symbolism in the Masonic ritual into the third degree thus points to black people: the "theology" inside this third degree initiation ritual is that it actually refers to the coming of Fard. White masons have been fully aware of this, and, according to the NOI, have intentionally obscured it using Masonic symbolism. This ritual, Muhammad argues furthermore, is also proof of the evil nature of white Masons, as he reasons that, since the

Masonic ritual of the death and resurrection of Hiram Abif has no record in the Bible, it is the symbolic reminder of the deviltry carried out by whites (Muhammad 1993C, 42–44).

In sum, the symbolism in these Masonic rituals point to different truths in the myth of Yakub: whites are made-people and therefore evil, unrighteous and inferior by nature, whereas black people are created by God, and therefore superior, divine, and predestined to reclaim their position as world rulers. By arguing that American Freemasons know but intentionally obscured black America's secret history and glorious future in their ritual and symbolism, Muhammad's conspiracy theory legitimized the esoteric truths of the myth of Yakub. Put differently, claiming that parts of the myth of Yakub are cloaked in Masonic symbolism and ritual proofs, for the NOI, that the myth of Yakub is in fact true. This theory therefore further inverts the power relationship between black and white: whereas initially only whites (more specifically, white Freemasons) were aware of the secrets regarding black people's divine nature and potential, black people have now been immersed in the truth as well, and are, moreover, conscious of the fact that white people knew this truth and tried to obscure it, precisely because it proofs that black people are superior. Muhammad's conspiracy theory on American Freemasonry is therefore essential for his rhetoric of secrecy.

Conclusion

In the foregoing sections, I have explored several elements of Muhammad's dialectic of secrecy, concealment and revelation, thereby specifically concentrating on his strategy of unveiling secret knowledge, the content of his claim, and conspiracy theory. In contrast to most studies on the NOI, this essay has, therefore, not addressed his practice of secrecy, but predominantly his rhetoric of secrecy. Central to this rhetoric is, as should be evident, the myth of Yakub, the truths of which were according to the NOI on the one hand concealed by American Freemasons, and, on the other hand, unveiled by Elijah Muhammad. By way of conclusion, I will specifically address in this section the social purposes and implications of secrets and secrecy in Elijah Muhammad's NOI, and assess the relationship between the content of Muhammad's secrets and his rhetoric of secrecy.

First of all, the quest for secret knowledge functions as a backbone for and legitimates the authority of Elijah Muhammad. Let me explain. When Fard suddenly disappeared in 1934, he left his fledging movement in a state of despair, as various members vied for control over the NOI. Eventually, it was

Muhammad who acquired the mantle of leadership, on the basis of two claims: Fard had revealed to him that he was God-in-Person, and had instructed him on the secret knowledge of "God, Self, and Enemy." The claim to possess secret knowledge is thus part of Muhammad's claim to inheritance of Fard's legacy. Put more strongly, the fact that Muhammad could claim to possess secret knowledge that God had transmitted to him – and thus that he was the only one with access to this knowledge –permitted him – and only him – to become the leader of the NOI, and thus the savior (or so the NOI believes) of black America: after all, in the subsequent forty-plus years that he led the NOI, Muhammad's most important task was the revelation of this secret knowledge.

Secondly, examining the actual content of his secret knowledge reveals the importance of the myth of Yakub for black America: the saga, we may now conclude, rewrites African American history, and by extension concepts of race and identity. In fact, it is a discourse that is rooted in and a response to the particularities of the African American religious experience. In a way, the myth of Yakub, which offers a critique of religion, reason, science, racism, colonialism, and imperialism, should be seen as a response to what Anthony Pinn has termed the struggle for "complex subjectivity." Theorizing distinctively about black religion, Pinn maintains in his phenomenal *Terror and Triumph: The Nature of Black Religion* (2003), that black religion is "the quest for complex subjectivity," which he explains as "a desired movement from being a corporeal object controlled by oppressive and essentializing forces to becoming a complex conveyer of cultural meaning, with a complex and creative identity" (158). All black religions share the attempt to counter the processes of dehumanization and objectification thereby offering different responses to the struggle for complex subjectivity: the search for fullness, for increased agency, and the battle against the terror of fixed identity – a black identity that was fixed in historical time and space, defined as an inferior, insignificant, will-less object of history (157–175). The myth of Yakub, which effectively revised the established Caucasian American notions on the ontological nature of black and white, challenged the idea of African Americans as having "no culture, no civilization, no 'long historical past'" (Fanon 1964, cited in Pinn 2003, 20), and offered tools to combat feelings of subjugation and objectification. As such, the heretofore secret knowledge offers black America the tools to transcend the perceived terror and horror of the status quo, and offered a very tangible, scientific, and earthbound theological and cosmological explanation. Perhaps most importantly, this narrative re-envisions black humanity: if and once they will be immersed in the secrets of the myth of Yakub, black people will partake in God's divinity, and become, indeed "the Gods [they] once were."

Thirdly and finally, arguing that the knowledge Muhammad – and subsequently his followers – possessed was secret, not only elevated the direct recipients of this knowledge but also the specific content of the claim: it implies that, after all, it is God himself who is the ultimate source of this knowledge. This suggests that God has specifically chosen black America to share the "secrets of the universe" with. Designating the myth of Yakub as secret knowledge therefore did not only have a practical significance – Muhammad could claim authority – but also a doctrinal significance: it strengthened the statement that the followers of the NOI were superior, god-like beings.

The presented analysis attempts to fill some of the lacunae in research on the esoteric in the NOI, but in order to fully grasp the range and depth of the esoteric in the NOI, we need more research: the analyses of the esoteric in the NOI included in this anthology are just the metaphorical tip of the iceberg. Future research may, for example, focus on the esoteric roots of the myth of Yakub: different parts of the myth incorporate esoteric ideas and practices hitherto predominantly found in New Thought, Theosophy and Spiritualism. Furthermore, scholars should identify and discuss the esoteric in Louis Farrakhan's NOI – as will be done to some extent by Stephen C. Finley in this anthology – or offer a historical and comparative analysis of the esoteric in the entire history of the NOI. What we need most of all, however, is a sound theoretical and methodological basis from which we can start and in which we can situate our discussions; research that, therefore, challenges some of the persistent paradigms in the fields of African American Religion – such as the emphasis on the Black Church – and Western Esotericism – such as the burdened denominator "western." Hopefully, this anthology is the first of many texts, as, undoubtedly, more cases of African American esotericism, gnosticism, and mysticism wait to be revealed.

CHAPTER 9

Post-Imperial Appropriation of Text, Tradition, and Ritual in the Pseudonymous Writings of Henri Gamache[1]

Hugh R. Page, Jr.

Introduction

Five short monographs originally published in the 1940s, and purportedly authored by Henri Gamache: *The Master Book of Candle Burning* (1998); *Mystery of the 8th, 9th, and 10th Books of Moses* (1993); *The Master Key to Occult Secrets* (1983); *Terrors of the Evil Eye Exposed* (2010); and *The Magic of Herbs Throughout the Ages* (1942) have long been popular among practitioners of Black Diasporan conjure.[2] One of the distinguishing traits of these works is that they democratize access to the *numinous* through the abrogation of power typically vested in institutional hierocracies.[3] By making readily available biblical texts, Judeo-Christian hermeneutical traditions, and selected data on indigenous religious rituals from around the world, these books provide non-specialists with the practical knowledge and expertise to create personal liturgies for healing and canons for appropriating the Bible that resist hegemony and promote individual and communal self-empowerment. Interestingly, all appear to be, in fact, pseudonymous works. Such is a *datum* whose implications need fully to be explored in a treatment beyond the scope of the current study.

This essay will present an overview and selective reading of the Gamache *corpus*, with particular attention being given to its constitutive genres and

---

1   An earlier version of this article was given in 2005 as a paper at the Annual Meetings of the American Academy of Religion (AAR) and Society of Biblical Literature (SBL). It was presented in one of the sessions sponsored by the African American Biblical Hermeneutics Section of SBL. The author expresses gratitude to the organizers of that session as well as to those whose queries and comments enabled subsequent expansion and improvement of that original essay.

2   See Long (2001: 124–125) and Anderson (2005: 120–121).

3   Other works attributed to him, such as *Doorway to Your Success* and *Your Key to Power*, are listed in the prefatory section of The Master Key to Occult Secrets (1983) but difficult to locate.

engagement of the Bible. The history of reception (and interpretation) is an essential part of the field of Biblical Studies. Among those with a particular interest in how the Bible has been received and interpreted within the larger *Africana milieu*, more attention has been paid to ecclesial, political, and artistic *loci* of engagement than to those that are decidedly non-mainstream. Analysis of esoteric appropriations of the Bible in the Black Atlantic World is in its infancy. My own interest in this area grows out of a deepening appreciation of the extent to which within the *Africana* world—particularly in certain parts of West Africa, the Americas, and the Caribbean—there may be said to exist a *poetics of secrecy* infusing daily life. According to such, one engages with others, *makes* community, and negotiates meaning by becoming well *versed* in one or more localized grammars, the cultural *phonemes* (sacred sounds) and *morphemes* (words of power) of which articulate a *syntax* for navigating a cosmic topography with seen and—most importantly—unseen dimensions. The language world and *lexicon* informing this *poetics* can be understood only in part through social scientific and humanistic inquiry. The *veil* concealing a number of its more important aspects can only be lifted through direct encounter with an ontological experience incapable of being fully described in scholarly terms. To know and understand, one must cease being a researcher and become—as it were—an *initiate*. I write, in a sense, as one traversing in both directions that disorienting *threshold* separating the academy and its *etic* taxonomies from the world of the *Africana* Diaspora in North America and its *emic* classifications of esoteric phenomena. I do so as one grafted onto that branch of women and men whose *koine* expresses this *poetics of secrecy* through a Blues aesthetic. My perspective, therefore, is that of scholar poet, musician, and *devotee*.

Gamache—The Author

At this point, it is perhaps most reasonable to assume, *apud* Yronwode (2013: 8), that Henri Gamache was the *nom de guerre* of either Joseph W. Kay, also known as Joseph Spitalnick (1889–1967), or an unnamed woman who served as *amanuensis* for Kay/Spitalnic. She notes that Kay was a Jewish jazz musician, independent publisher, and distributor of esoteric paraphernalia.[4] However, the suggestion that a rather shadowy figure known only as Mr. Young is in fact the source for all of the Gamache works is also feasible (see Long 2001: 125; and

---

4 See also Ironweed's online profile (1995–2003).

Davies 2009: 241). Interesting questions arise from this assumption. One has to
do with the overarching intent of this *oeuvre*. Was it to chronicle indigenous
Africana practices for purposes of preservation, sharing, and community
empowerment as Yronwode contends (2013: 8)? Was it to create commodities
capable of being sold for profit? Was it to use pseudonymous attribution to
legitimize new and emerging versions of *Africana* conjure? A reading of the
corpus indicates that the author is: familiar with academic research on global
folklore such as that of W. Robertson Smith and Zora Neale Hurston; knowledgeable of the Kabbalistic practice of Psalm-based prayer—i.e., using psalms
therapeutically for healing and protection; and well-versed in Black Diasporan
midrash concerning Moses.

Of comparable interest is the identity of Gamache implied in these works,
an element through which their authority is indirectly asserted. In some works
he is cast as an urbane *curator* of odd customs and lore: one who gathers and
assembles bits and pieces of useful information from around the world.[5] In
others, he takes on various roles: e.g., biographer,[6] apologist for the "Philosophy
of Fire,"[7] and advocate for reasoned deconstruction of superstitious beliefs
that have outlived their usefulness.[8] He is not bound by scholarly conventions
such as the need to provide complete citations to secondary sources (e.g., publishers, publication dates, etc.) or assiduously to enumerate pages in every
manuscript bearing his name.[9] He is, however, committed to making accessible stories, rituals, images, and formulas / recipes whose efficacy is acknowledged by those from whom they have been gathered. On the whole, the
Gamache one encounters in this body of work is a *bricoleur* whose *amalgam* is
made up of Jewish, Christian, and other artifacts of power, one of which is the
Bible. His is a multi-layered and, in some respects, unconventional engagement of the latter: at once critical, theoretical, creative, and constructive from
a theological standpoint. He situates biblical literature within a rather vast universe of cultural lore, a substantial amount of which is from various parts of
the *Africana* world. His vision is inclusive and universal. It appreciates the
value of those things traditionally hidden and selectively revealed.

---

5   Such is the picture one finds very clearly expressed in the prefatory remarks of *The Master
    Key to Occult Secrets* (1983: 3) and *The Magic of Herbs Throughout the Ages* (1942: 3–7).
6   See the "Introduction" to *The Mystery of the Long Lost 8th, 9th, and 10th Books of Moses* (1993).
7   See *The Master Book of Candle Burning* (1998: "Preface" and 1).
8   This is the sense one gets from *Terrors of the Evil Eye Exposed* (2010: 3–4).
9   It must be acknowledged that the problem with the enumeration of pages may attributable
    to publishers responsible for producing reprints of these works without having proper qual-
    ity controls in place.

The Sources

The Master Key to Occult Secrets, subtitled *A Study of the Survival of Primitive Customs in a Modern World With Sources and Origins,* is a collection of what the author terms, "customs, rituals, and nostrums" (1983: 3) arranged by the author in a series of 100 "treatises." Included are cultural practices of African, Jamaican, Medieval European, American, Jewish, Christian, Western Esoteric, Hindu, and Greek origin. Some of the rituals are derived from or utilize texts found within the Hebrew Bible and New Testament: e.g., Genesis 19:1; 33:3; 37:29, 34; 43:26; 52:6; Numbers 14:6; Joel 2:13; Ezra 9:3; Psalm 47; Job 1:20; Matthew 26:65; and Acts 14:14. The author acknowledges that the coupling of popular embrace and demonstrable efficacy of these practices will likely continue to fuel confidence in the miraculous (1983: 3). *The Magic of Herbs Throughout the Ages* (1942) is at once an overview of herbal lore and a selective repertory of *material medica.* The historical and cultural sweep of the book are inclusive of remote antiquity, ancient Israel, India, England, and both the Greco—Roman and European worlds. The core of the book is a profile of fifty plants. From a biblical perspective, perhaps one of the work's most interesting dimensions is the author's assertion that Moses was one of humanity's earliest herbalists (1942: 9). *Terrors of the Evil Eye Exposed* (2010) offers a brief survey of Jewish, Christian, Muslim, Hindu, African, European, and other traditions associated with the supernatural power of the malicious gaze, as well as a compendium of apotropaic measures for dealing with this phenomenon. In it, biblical references to both the power of the human eye and the "evil eye" itself are cited: e.g., Leviticus 19:31; 20:6; Deuteronomy 15:9; Amos 9:4; Matthew 6:22. One text (Judges 9:45) is also used as a proof text for one of several preventive measures (salt). A host of other protective and curative measures from around the world is listed as well. Such include shoes, lemons, and assorted symbols (e.g., hands, feet, eyes, crosses, dots, etc.). The author acknowledges the pervasiveness of belief in the "evil eye" in his day and appears to be an advocate for the superiority of "science" and "reason" (2010: 3–4) over the ancient and popular beliefs he enumerates. As intriguing as the aforementioned works are, by far the two most interesting books in the Gamache *oeuvre* are *The Master Book of Candle Burning* (1998) and the *Mystery of the Long Lost Books of Moses* (1993).

    The Master Book of Candle Burning is an introduction to what the author terms "the Philosophy of Fire" or "Fire Worship." It is of modest length (106 pages) and consists of ten chapters that cover the history, principles, practices, and biblical texts central to this system of intercessory prayer. The author claims to have gathered his data from, among others, "mediums, spiritual advisors, evangelists, religious interpreters, neologistics, and others who should be in a position to know" (iii). His aim is to orient readers to a set of symbols and practices that can be adapted for personal use by those who wish to use candle burning as a spiritual exercise.

The book begins with an overview that traces the veneration of fire to the earliest epoch of human history. It then moves on to examine the biblical allusions to the veneration of fire. The author notes several references in the Torah, Prophets, and Writings in support of the notion that fire played an important role in religious worship and as a trope for the Divine presence in early Israel. These include Genesis 3.24; 15.17; Deuteronomy 4.24; Exodus 3.2; 1 Kings 18; 2 Chronicles 7; Habakkuk 3.3–5; Leviticus 23.1–13; 24.1–7; and John 1.1–10. The author recommends that the reading of the passages in Habakkuk, Leviticus, and John be combined with prayer and the burning of candles for the purposes of healing, worship, and enlightenment respectively. In this opening section and in Chapter 5 of the book, the author also calls attention to four types of candles that can be used: (1) those of a specific color; (2) seven day candles; (3) cruciform candles; and (4) figural candles of representational images.

The remaining chapters of the book introduce readers to the symbolism of colors (Chapter 2), the sub-canon of biblical texts used in candle burning rituals, and the manual acts central to candle burning rituals. The author devotes two chapters to the practical and religious foundations of candle burning (Chapters 7 and 9). Specific instructions are given for setting up an altar (Chapter 3), dressing or anointing candles with oil (Chapter 4), and for burning candles for solace from the trials of war (Chapter 6). The author describes, but does not endorse, candle-burning procedures used for malevolent purposes (Chapter 8) and devotes the final chapter (10) of the book to thirty-seven exercises—his designation for complete candle-burning liturgies—that can be used to address a variety of life circumstances. These include overcoming household problems, protection from enemies, alleviation of financial difficulties, finding love and companionship, overcoming anxiety, protection against evil, securing domestic tranquility, obtaining spiritual guidance, realization of personal aspirations, handling lawsuits, and healing depression.

The author's system of candle burning is decidedly Christian in orientation. Adherents are instructed to set up an altar on which a Bible, an incense burner, and two cruciform candles are placed as permanent fixtures. Candles in various colors are also placed on the altar and burned as part of rituals for healing and other purposes. Some of these candles are resonant with astrological symbolism while others are selected because of their sympathetic correspondence to conditions that the operator hopes to eliminate or realities she/he hopes to manifest. Prescribed rituals include two fundamental components: (1) the dressing, strategic placement, lighting, and symbolic movement of candles on the altar and (2) the prayerful reading of specific passages from the Bible for a specific amount of time over a series of days. Virtually all of the texts prescribed come from the Psalter. Three are taken from the Song of Songs (Chapters 1, 2, 3, and 8).

The Master Book of Candle Burning is a prayer book or sacramentary of sorts for those wishing to become devotees of his "Philosophy of Fire." However, he notes that it is not to be followed slavishly. He sees mastery of the principles he teaches as the starting point from which enterprising practitioners may develop their own rituals. He says:

> By adhering to these basic fundamentals, the more progressive individual may create his own particular symbolism, rituals and exercises to satiate his own thirst for spiritual development and satisfaction.
>
> 1998: 55

Thus, if one understands that the altar is a symbolic representation of cosmic reality, that candles represent individuals and life circumstances, and that candle movement is symbolic of tangible changes that will take place on the physical plane, then one is free to develop—according to one's leanings and proficiencies—individual candle burning rituals that are both meaningful and effective.

From the standpoint of *genre*, Gamache's *Mystery of the 8th, 9th, and 10th Books of Moses* is a difficult book to classify. The author subdivides its thirteen chapters into three distinct sections. The first contains a biographical *midrash* focused on Moses that fills in certain gaps omitted in the biblical record. By and large, its aim is to establish that Moses was the recipient of a secret tradition not retained in Scripture. The second section is a critical examination of the compositional history of the Old Testament that seeks to account for the selective inclusion of traditions about Moses. The third section consists of two brief perorations that cast Moses as the biblical source of *Africana* esoteric spiritualities and as the mediator of the traditions that would become the core of 13th century Kabbalistic lore. These assertions are neither surprising nor unprecedented. However, their juxtaposition—which makes Moses in a sense the exemplar of the Black Diasporan *shaman* in the new world—is remarkable. The Moses Gamache presents to readers is in many respects the embodiment of the early to mid-20th century *conjure* practitioner—i.e., a person fluent in the idiom of Jewish mystical theory and praxis, Diasporan root work, and evocative rituals of power. Of Moses import, the author says:

> All through the West Indies and across America, too, there have been stories of the Power of Moses. He is the fountainhead of mystic powers.

Countless people place their faith in the power of amulets and seals which are replicas of those said to have been used by Moses and the Prophets and their contemporaries. Many are the fetishes, amulets, and charms in use today which, when they are put under close scrutiny, bear a striking resemblance or at least sympathetic symbolism to customs which date back to the time of Moses.

> 1993: 67

The remainder of the third section of the book is an anthology of prayers, formulas, amulets, and seals that provide access to what Gamache terms "'Universal Power'" (1993: 77). They come from a variety of sources and their compilation is a result of the author's culling of existing occult and other source materials.[10] Gamache, the literary and scholarly detective, creates an explanatory meta-narrative in which Moses is cast as mediator of a universal gnosis with reflexes in Africa, the African Diaspora, and the Near East. The life experiences and revelatory encounters of Moses initiate him into a body of secret tradition that he, in turn, mediates to subsequent generations. However, oral accounts and sporadically recorded literary fragments of this tradition are all that remain. This final section of the book concludes with a list of 73 texts— 52 of which hail from the First Testament—in which significant "revelations" are given to individual women and men. Of this canon within a canon, he says the following:

In all of these revelations does the true path emerge, finally, into the light of understanding. It is true that much of the ancient lore has been left out, many things have been hidden and obscured – but on the whole, it conveys a message which manifests the Divine Spark on every page. No wonder that so many of God's creatures find the Bible a consolation and an inspiration.

> 1993: 103

In sum, the book is an odd compendium of empirical research, biblical interpretation, and advice on how to harness both in accessing power to transform reality.

From an inter-textual point of view, Gamache is in conversation with traditions from several universes of discourse. All of the works attributed to him— *The Master Book of Candle Burning* and *Mystery of the 8th, 9th, and 10th Books of*

---

10   See for example Ironweed's description of the book—www.luckymojo.com/8th9th10thmoses.html — accessed 18 January 2014.

Moses in particular—are transgressive works that subvert ecclesial and political hegemonies. They offer readers a means to access the Bible as a source of inspiration and strength. Moreover, they do so by empowering readers to retain individual agency in matters spiritual. There is need for neither priest nor parish. The personal *oratory*, altar, Bible, library, and storehouse of spiritual supplies maintained in the home become the means through which each person is enabled to seek the divine and secure the assistance needed to overcome life's day-to-day challenges, both small and great. Insofar as all of these monographs are commodities that themselves suggest the necessity of obtaining other commodities (e.g., candles, oils, incense, and additional ritual paraphernalia), it could be argued that they were originally intended to create consumers dependent on a particular line of spiritual products. This is a matter to which Carolyn Long has already called attention to in *Spiritual Merchants: Religion, Magic, and Commerce* (2001: 248–249) and concluded that there is in fact a complex relationship between spiritual suppliers and the African American communities for which they developed and sold products beginning in the 1930s. These entrepreneurs—Black, White, and Jewish—were suppliers and innovators. In some sense, they were an integral part of the conversation that resulted in the evolution of Africana esotericisms in the North American Diaspora as well as the evolution of what has come to be known as *hoodoo* or *conjure*.

Conclusion

Based on content and production values, Davies places the Gamache *corpus* within the "pulp magic" category of American *grimoire* (2009: 241–242). However, this too narrowly confines them to a subgenre that in his words consists of, "worthless, pappy throwaway literature fit only for those too intellectually limited to digest more serious fare" (2009: 233). Building on his proposed derivation of the word *grimoire* from the French noun *grammaire* (2009:1), it is perhaps better to see the entirety of the Gamache corpus as a *grammar* whose phonemic, lexemic, and syntactic potentialities served as the basis for one of many *prosodies of liberation* growing out of the *poetics of secrecy* in the African American Diaspora. The Gamache *oeuvre*, like the Bible, can be understood therefore as a meta-language, familiarity with which provides access to freedom.

From an ecclesial perspective, these books are part of an underground intellectual current, officially taboo within the orthodox Christian mainstream. However, the fact that most of them are still in print and readily available suggests that there is a viable audience interested in purchasing and reading them. Moreover, one could argue that part of their attractiveness can be traced to an unresolved ambiguity within denominational Christianity revolving around the idea of the *priesthood of all believers*. Works like those of Gamache, Strabo (2006), John George Holman (for which, see the recent critical edition—Harms 2012), and others—all of which are part of this esoteric tributary—build on the idea that individual people of faith have the capacity to care for their own spiritual needs, commune with God, and access the *numinous* directly.[11] They are empowering and hopeful works that allow individuals to assume, if they so choose, a greater degree of personal control over their spiritual wellbeing. In some respects, they stand as well in the tradition of popular breviaries, missals, hymnals, rosaries, and chaplets—all of which enable personal management of spiritual matters without the intervention of clergy or judicatory authorities. One is also reminded of John Wesley's small 18th century monograph *Primitive Physic* (1993), which functioned as a *repertory* and *materia medica* for early Methodists.

As greater attention is focused on the construction of spiritualities of resistance in the Black Diaspora, a closer examination of works like those of Gamache and others that are part of the esoteric underground is merited. While it is clear that earlier exemplars of such work were not authored by people of African descent, they are important nonetheless because they have assumed authoritative status within reading communities that are Black. Moreover, one suspects that growing dissatisfaction with institutional Christianity—within and outside of *Africana* communities—and a desire to reclaim some of the innovative spiritual practices developed by African Americans beginning in the 17th and 18th centuries, may result in the creation of an even wider reading audience for these and comparable works.

One can already see evidence of this development in the evangelical Christian community today—e.g., the emphasis on "seed-sowing" and the belief in the efficacy of the spoken word in prayer. The recent work of popular authors like Joyce Meyer, Bruce Wilkinson—*The Prayer of Jibes: Breaking Through to the Blessed Life* (2000); *The Secret Power of Speaking God's Word* (2004), Ann Spangler—*Praying the Names of God* (2004), David Wilkerson—

---

11   Harms classifies Holman's work under the *genre* of *Hausvaterliteratur*, whose targeted reader was the "independent land-owner of little means who might have had crops, livestock, and possibly a servant or two, but with a shortage of free cash and little access to medical services for either animals or humans" (2012: 3). Some of the circumstances giving rise to this type of literature have been and remain prevalent within certain sectors of the *Africana* community in North America.

Knowing God by Name (2003), and Mark Batterson—*The Circle Maker: Praying Circles Around Your Biggest Dreams and Greatest Fears* (2012) show surprising evidence of a theology, at once evangelical *and* esoteric, holding that power inheres within specific words, sacred names, and ritual actions. Not only does this show the continuing prevalence of an esoterically oriented world view in American religious life, it also shows that some of the same institutional religious tensions within the *Africana* Diaspora are prevalent outside of it as well. Esoteric discourse, whether in the form of *conjure* or a *logocentric* and evangelical spirituality, is often a site of social and other forms of resistance.

It is important to remember that *Africana* spiritual *praxis* is not narrow in its engagement of the Judeo-Christian tradition. It is and must remain a transgressive site of struggle and identity negotiation in which political, religious, and ecclesial hegemonies are challenged. As new *imperialisms* are being re-inscribed by social organizations, political authorities, and ecclesial structures that disempower ordinary readers, it is important that we focus more attention on works like those of Gamache that provide a means to spiritual self-actualization that is unmediated and unfettered.

CHAPTER 10

Mystery Matters
Embodiment and African American Mystics

Chad Pevateaux

Introduction

If esotericism as a concept shifts meanings over time and involves dynamics of construction and personal projection (and which of our concepts do not?), we nevertheless use this term, at least in part, to mark modes of knowing and experiencing that have been rejected by dominant traditions. And we may certainly deem African American mysticisms as modern mysticism's rejected, or nearly completely unattended, other. "If the first three-quarters of the twentieth-century discourse on mysticism," writes Jeffrey J. Kripal, "was dominated by perennialist language and the last quarter by epistemological questions and constructivist (essentially Kantian) commitments," then perhaps, he suggests, what we require is a third turn, "...this one to the mystical body as a real body, indeed as a variable set of bodies." This turn would involve studying "real suffering, real desires, real skin...as some of the deepest structuring principles of mystical literature and their interpretation" (Kripal 2003, 596). With rich and varied examinations of power and gender, many scholars have moved in just these directions (e.g. Jantzen 1996, Hollywood 2002, and Boesel and Keller 2009). Yet, African American embodied mysticisms remain understudied.

"Scholars have neglected," Alton B. Pollard points out, "the mystical flowering of the African Diaspora" (Pollard 2009, 3). As a working definition of mysticism, Pollard helpfully offers the following: "*Mysticism is a generic term for intimate discourse and practices that speak to what it means to be human in relationship to the transcendent and the mundane*" (Pollard 2009, 4). Along these lines, this essay seeks to correct the neglect of African American mysticisms through comparing those of Howard Thurman and Langston Hughes, the former more exoteric and transcendent focused, the latter more esoteric and mundane. For Thurman, the mystery of life involves a mystical relation with the transcendent as found in the spirituals, whereas for Hughes it roots us more in the earthiness of the blues. Both, however, suggest that the study of Africana mystics requires an emphasis on embodiment. Embodied and visceral, yet preceding and exceeding bodily limitation, a mystery exists between Thurman's Spirituals and Hughes's Blues that reveals a both/and, neither/nor,

© KONINKLIJKE BRILL NV, LEIDEN, 2015 | DOI 10.1163/9789004283428_012

a/theistic aspect to much African American religious experience. Moreover, our analysis of embodied African American mysticisms will illuminate the (in) capacities we share with nonliving matter, and how this matters.

In putting the mystical in relation to the poet Langston Hughes, I do not mean that he deemed himself to have experienced the salvific power of the Christian God, or any God, per say. Rather, I simultaneously seek, on the one hand, to extend the term beyond its usual evocations of a sense of a presence of something transcendent in order to show its usefulness for understanding mundane material as well, and, on the other hand, to problematize any ultimately neat or final distinctions between the transcendent and the immanent. As with any such duality, the very thought of one activates the other. What is interesting for our purposes is the way the interplay between mystical and mundane may generate a "more" regardless of any final theistic or atheistic import.

By invoking the *more* here I mean less to conjure the ghost of William James than to place us in the context of African American religion according to Anthony B. Pinn, who argues that, "black religion at its core is the quest for complex subjectivity, a desire or feeling for more life meaning." Explaining religion as a response to identity crisis, Pinn says, "In some ways, this may be described as a form of mystical experience, a type of transforming experience that speaks to a deeper reality, guided perhaps by a form of esoteric knowledge," but the most important defining feature is "this yearning for complex subjectivity" (Pinn 2003, 173). I first began reading Thurman and Hughes as supplements for each other nearly twenty years ago when I was doing youth ministry in an Episcopal church in Texas then attended by Karl Rove. Concerned about how so many congregants could take comfort in a Heavenly salvation yet remain apolitical and unconcerned about the suffering of the oppressed, I worried about how an emphasis on a transcendent hereafter anesthetized efforts at transformation in the here and now (very good).

Thus, I listened when James Cone said, "If whites were really serious about their radicalism in regard to the black revolution and its theological implications in America, they would keep silent and take instructions from blacks" (Cone 1986, 62). One has only to read the essays at the end of the twentieth anniversary edition of *A Black Theology of Liberation*, however, to know that Cone himself gains from listening to others. I thus began cultivating the discipline, which still informs my scholarship today, of listening for and to others: listening *for* others means striving to hear what or who may have been missed or marginalized, while listening *to* others means giving power and authority to those marginalized voices and allowing them to transform prior misconceptions. As much as possible, then, I would read Thurman to the youth, but also supplement his Christian theology with Hughes and others from outside of orthodoxy.

The yearning for complex subjectivity as it gets embodied in the spirituals and the blues, I will show, can also be subject to the emergent complexity of the cosmos. Thus, with an emphasis on embodiment comes the importance of relations of time and space. In this, we also follow Pinn in examining "p(l)ace" as "the setting of parameters and boundaries of focus around time and space so as to mark off opportunities to wrestle with fundamental questions of life" (Pinn 2012, 16). What I hope to suggest, however, is that the parameters of the possible may shift along with our categories for it. Realizing that the possibility of error is as common to all humans as our fundamental dignity, we can traverse complex questions through the common ground of admitting our shared ignorance. Even the most ardent atheists and fervent fideists may admit that mystery matters. As Pinn argues, the quest for complex subjectivity is ongoing. As a philosopher of religion, I employ the method of exploring possibility. Thus, I argue that the mystery, which may be interpreted as mystical or mundane, may always be more than our attempts to circumscribe it—or ourselves.

Mystical Mystery: Thurman's Pulse of Infinite Worth

"When I identify with a man," Howard Thurman says in his book *The Luminous Darkness*, "I become one with him and in him I see myself" (Thurman 1965, 110). For Thurman, seeing oneself in another involves recognizing *"the equality of infinite worth"* as "the truest experience of myself" (Thurman 1998, 270, emphasis in original). Thus, "the statement 'know thyself'," Thurman says of the ancient aphorism, "has been taken more mystically from the statement 'thou has seen thy brother, thou hast seen thy God'" (Thurman 1965, 111). We may see similar wisdom contained in the Hermetic Nag Hammadi text, *Discourse on the 8th and the 9th*, which also records a mystical vision seen with/in another: "Father Trismegistus! What shall I say? We have received this light. And I myself see this same vision in you.... I see myself!" (NHC VI 59, 24–29 and 60, 31–61, 1). Whereas the ancient Egyptian insight may be interpreted to involve ascent out of messy materiality, Thurman inflects his experience of infinite worth, which he sees as the core of the religious impulse, with an enlivening sense of embodiment that entails engagement with social justice. Whereas hermetic mystical vision climaxes in silence, Thurman's mystical experience bodies forth in preaching, singing, and social action.

We may give Thurman's mystical vision flesh through listening to what he has to say in his 1947 essay, "The Negro Spiritual Speaks of Life and Death." Thurman delivered it as Harvard Divinity School's prestigious Ingersoll Lecture on the Immortality of Man, having been preceded in this honor by the likes of William James, Josiah Royce, and Alfred North Whitehead. Though he had for a long time been reticent to speak on African-American practices before white audiences lest he encourage the notion that "black scholars were incapable of reflecting creatively on any matters other than those that bore directly on their own struggle," Thurman chose to make an exception in this case because he hoped that by sharing the survival strategies and creative thinking of the slaves he might "deliver those in another kind of bondage into a new freedom" (Thurman 1998, 55).

"Oh Freedom! Oh Freedom!" Thurman quotes from a spiritual. *"Oh Freedom, I love thee! And before I'll be a slave, I'll be buried in my grave, And go home to my Lord and be free."* With this Thurman says it is "obvious indeed...that death is not regarded as life's worst offering. There are some things in life that are worse than death" (Thurman 1998, 58). What the spirituals say about death is that it is neither ultimately definitive nor final. The slaves' songs testify to "the sense of alternative in human experience, upon which, in the last analysis, all notions of freedom finally rest," Thurman writes. While acknowledging death's inevitability, the spirituals also reduce death to a moment in time from the perspective of an immortal soul, thus bringing it under a measure of control and choice, at least in regard to how one spiritually participates in it. "The significant revelation," says Thurman, "is in the fact that death, as an event, is spatial, time encompassed, if not actually time bound, and therefore partakes of the character of the episodic." In their power to attain a more ascendant perspective of detachment in regards to death through a view of the afterlife, humans, Thurman argues, demote death to "an experience *in* life." Thurman explains, "the logic here is that man is both a space binder and a time binder" (Thurman 1998, 59). Slaves, transcended death and their daily suffering through the theology carried in their songs. Their lives were infinitely more than bodily existence and death.

Faced with harsh realities, the slaves found strategies of spirit to survive, even in the face of suffering and death. Contrary to the sanitized social space that largely removes sickness and death from sight with hospitals and mortuaries, the slaves' sense of space was entwined with death. For us moderns, "our sense of personal loss may be great but our primary relationship with death under normal circumstances tends to be impersonal and detached," says Thurman. "This was not," he says, "the situation with the creators of the Spirituals" (Thurman 1998, 60). Through all the processes of dying and death, the body remained in the homes of the slaves and its passing was experienced by all those who "kept watch" with the sick and the dead. As Thurman describes: "the 'death rattle' in the throat, the spasm of tense vibration in the body as the struggle for air increased in intensity, the sheer physical panic sometimes manifest—all these were a familiar part of the commonplace pattern of daily experience. Out of a full, rich knowledge of fact such a song as this was born: *I want to die easy when I die. I want to die easy when I die. Shout salvation as I fly. I want to die easy when I die.*"

Rather than resignation, this hope of salvation when faced intimately with death gave the slaves a reinvigorated power for living. Far from paralyzing action, singing of salvation "gave the mind a new dimension of resourcefulness." "I had a college classmate," continues Thurman,

> who cleared his throat just before responding to the question of his teacher. The clearing of the throat broke the impasse between his mind and his immediate environment so that he could have a sense of ascendency in his situation. It was in some such fashion as this that these religious songs functioned. (Of course, they did much more than this.) Once the impasse was broken, many things became possible to them. They could make their religion vehicular in terms of the particular urgencies of the moment. 'Steal away to Jesus' became an important call to those who had ears to hear.
>
> THURMAN 1998, 72

Like the spacing of his friend's throat clearing, so clearly connected to throat rattle of dying, the rhythms of the spirituals punctuated the lives of the slaves providing a sense of ascendency that put them, if ever so fleetingly, on a heavenly high ground above the present soil of suffering.

"For these early singers," says Thurman, "Heaven was a place—it was not merely an idea in the mind." "This must be held in mind," he continues, "constantly. The thinking about it is spatial." Hence the words of a spiritual: "*In bright mansions above, In bright mansions above, Lord, I want to live up yonder; In bright mansions above.*" "Such an aspiration," says Thurman, "was in sharp contrast to the dimly lighted cabins with which they were familiar." In the spirituals, Thurman says,

> The idea at the core of the literal truth in the concept of heaven is this— life is totally right, structurally dependable, good essentially as contrasted with the moral concepts of good and evil. ...The profoundest desires of man are of God, and therefore they cannot be denied ultimately. ...The

human spirit participates in both past and future in what it regards as the *present* but it is independent of both. ...And this is the miracle of [these slave singers'] achievement causing them to take their place alongside the great creative religious thinkers of the human race. They made a worthless life, the life of chattel property, a mere thing, a body, *worth living!*...To them this quality of life was insistent fact because of that which deep within them, they discovered of God, and his far-flung purposes. God was not through with them. And He was not, nor could He be, exhausted by any single experience or any series of experiences. ...Men in all ages and climes, slave or free, trained or untutored, who have sensed the same values, are their fellow-pilgrims who journey together with them in increasing self-realization in the quest for the city that hath foundations, whose Builder and Maker is God.

THURMAN 1998, 79

With such a motion and call to all to be fellow pilgrims journeying towards an ever greater realization of the infinite worth of life, Thurman reconstitutes embodiment more expansively than an objectifiable thing. "They made a worthless life," he says, "a mere thing, a body, *worth living!*"

We might better understand Thurman's thoughts on embodiment by drawing on Edmund Husserl's distinction between *Körper* and *Leib*, "physical body" and "lived body," or body and flesh. The contemporary French phenomenologist and Christian theologian Jean-Luc Marion further develops this distinction by arguing, contra the Cartesian dichotomy of mind and body, that "flesh...gives the *ego* itself" (Marion 2002, 100). As Marion's translator Robyn Horner notes: "What individualizes is not thought or bodily extension but the tension between them that is played out in flesh" (Marion 2002, xvii). A body, then, is that which can become objectified and viewed as "a mere thing," as Thurman says, whereas flesh is that which feels and is capable of suffering. Before any object in the world, I am given to myself in feeling myself through touch and pain. "It is no accident," Thurman wrote elsewhere, "that the New Testament Greek word for slave is *soma*, which means body, a thing" (Thurman 1998, 281). As opposed to such an idea of subjectivity aligned with body, objectification, thing-ness, and slavery, then, Thurman preaches an idea of self experienced as flesh that precedes and exceeds time-space bounded bodies.

When faced with life's suffering and inherent inequality, Thurman feels "that I am stripped to what seems to me to be the literal essence of my own pulse beat in which the sense of equality is grounded—that is the sense of my own self...My own self as distinguished from your self. My own self, of infinite worth and significance. This may be, perhaps, the only authentic equality that there is" (Thurman 1998, 269–270). This sense of "my own self" as an equality of infinite worth involves a differentiation from others and owning of one's value while also entailing the value of "your own self" and the infinite worth of others.

In the struggle to affirm one's own worth, however, we all too easily ignore or marginalize the worth of others, yet Thurman's "equality of infinite worth" demands inter-subjective recognition. Hence Thurman's most enduring metaphor of "those whose backs are against the wall" from his book, *Jesus and the Disinherited.* "The masses of men live with their backs constantly against the wall. They are the poor, the disinherited, the dispossessed. What does our religion say to them?" Thurman asks as his guiding question (Thurman 1976, 13). He answers by saying that the God of Jesus identifies with those who suffer and transforms death into life.

Though Thurman's language in terms of gender is clearly outdated, his call to attend to the poor, the disinherited, and the dispossessed, a disproportionate amount of who are indeed women, still resonates today. And his theology of flesh, with flesh as that which feels and is capable of suffering, carries to all who suffer, crossing race, class, and gender barriers, and, even species barriers. For nonhuman animals clearly are capable of great suffering as well. To all, Thurman's infinite worth speaks of the transcendence of suffering and death. Thurman's theistic vision, then, is embodied as the universal motion of hope in a hereafter that turns suffering to joy and death to life. For Langston Hughes, to whom we now turn, Thurman's heavenly hope beyond death was, however true, nevertheless insufficient to honor all of life's mysteries.

Mundane Mystery: Hughes's Beat of the Earth

Though Langston Hughes, who travelled in some of the same esoteric circles of Harlem Renaissance writers and artists as Jean Toomer did, loved the spirituals and wove their rhythms into his poetry and prose, he felt more drawn to the blues, which honored the earthiness of life and love and pain and sorrow in a way that the spirituals lacked.[1] "There's great beauty in the mysticism of much religious writing," said Hughes once in an interview, "and great help there, but I also think that we live in a world...of solid earth and vegetables and a need for

---

1 For more on Toomey, see, "The Harlem Renaissance as Esotericism: Black Oragean Modernism," by Jon Woodson in this volume. See also Hughes's 1926 essay, "The Negro Artist and the Racial Mountain," in which he discusses Toomer's novel *Cain.*

jobs...and housing" (Emanuel 1993, 175). For Hughes, the spirituals need the blues.

As to his own personal belief, whether theistic or actually atheistic, Hughes kept it secret. In his poem titled, "Personal," Hughes writes:

> In an envelope marked:
> *Personal*
> God addressed me a letter.
> In an envelope marked:
> *Personal*
> I have given my answer.

Recent scholars have remarked that Hughes's ultimate personal secret could well have been homosexuality, which definitely could be a reason Hughes never felt fully comfortable singing the spirituals, which show a curious lack of sexuality, as a believer, despite his sympathy for their sentiments (Tidwell and Ragar 2007; Jones 2004). "I was saved from sin," Hughes writes in his autobiography, "when I was going on thirteen...But not really saved" (Hughes 1940, 18). At a big tent revival, he had been forced to repent, and had expected to see the light and meet Jesus, but, he writes, "That night...I cried. ...I hadn't seen Jesus" (Hughes 1940, 21). Yet as a mature writer, Hughes produces the powerful short story, "Big Meeting" that displays intimate knowledge of the enlightening power of camp meeting spirituality, while at the same time identifying with those left out in the dark.

The narrator of "Big Meeting" is a black, teenage boy sitting outside a night-time tent meeting looking in (Hughes 1958, 66–76). Eventually two white people pull up in a car to watch as well. Inside the tent, the community of believers passionately performs a reenactment of the crucifixion such that Jesus becomes identified with those under the tent, particularly in their suffering and pain. At the climax of the story, in a swell of cries of joy and pain from the crowd, the preacher proclaims, "*they lynched Him on the cross."*

"In song I heard my mother's voice cry," says the narrator, "*Were you there when they crucified my Lord? Were you there when they nailed Him to the tree?"*...

The answer, of course, is that, yes, they were there, because they just saw it happen in front of them through communal, embodied performance. The story continues:

> "Let's go," said the white woman in the car behind us. "This is too much for me!" They started the motor and drove noisily away in a swirl of dust.

"Don't go," I cried from where I was sitting at the root of the tree. "Don't go," I shouted, jumping up. "They're about to call for sinners to come to the mourners' bench. Don't go!" But their car was already out of earshot.

And the story ends with the narrator saying, "I didn't realize I was crying until I tasted my tears in my mouth."

Hughes leaves us tasting tears while outside the tent yet hoping to participate in the transformative motion of liberation from oppression and in the reconciliation of the races. Though he could not share Thurman's hope in a transcendent savior, Hughes's short story shows he did have his own kind of embodied hope that cried out in the dark, and that through this shout could lift the body and soul.

Hughes again encodes his own failed conversion experience from youth in a poem he calls "Mystery"(Hughes 1994, 416). Except, here the teenager is a girl. The first stanza sets up his ironic religious vision:

> When a chile gets to be thirteen
> And isn't seen Christ yet,
> She needs to set on de moaner's bench
> Night and day.

Then, after interspersing verses from the spirituals with his poetic verse, Hughes ends with a stanza that we might see as almost his personal theme song evoking the following:

> *The mystery*
> *and the darkness*
> *and the song*
> *and me.*

There is a mystery to life, Hughes intones, in the meaningless suffering and the unspeakable joy of knowing the flesh of another. There is a darkness in the skin of his people and in the hearts of those who lynch them. There is a song that cries in despair and in hope. And, there is perhaps the greatest mystery of all—*me*, in the midst of all of this. In the midst of mystery, the voice embodied in this poem speaks of being caught up in all that is—the joy and the pain—and not overcome. There is something there, something more, something that only the wail of a blues note held long can capture. Longing for more in face of life's mystery, it cannot be held for long. It can only cry—in mystery.

Hughes does not disdain the heavenly hope, he just worries it leaves important realities of life out in the dark. "Working all day all their lives for white folks, they *had* to believe there was a 'Hallaluian Side'," Hughes writes in his short story (Hughes 1958, 71). And yet there is also an earthiness unilluminated by the light of the spirituals. The blues speak of sex, and death, and despair more truly than any Jesus song Hughes heard howled in the tent meetings of his youth. Giving voice to the enfleshed feeling of sorrow and taste of tears in the mouth is what I think Hughes thinks the spirituals and the blues could perhaps together accomplish. It is not as if one merely rounds out the other; rather, it is in the spacing between the spirituals and the blues and a rhythmic interchange between them, with jazz-like meanderings and interweavings, that they together communicate the deep mystery.

For all the emphasis on a transcendent and ultimately inclusive community that Thurman sees in the spirituals, Hughes feels the need for the blues to honor the solitary soul of the city dweller. Much as Anthony B. Pinn suggests that scholars should unsettle the dominant meta-narrative of African American religion as theistic and Christian through studying nontheistic humanist religious practices, so do I think Hughes seeks to honor the blues as a way to give voice to those outside the glow of the identifiable Christian tent. In his essay, "Songs Called the Blues," Hughes writes:

> The blues and the Spirituals are two great Negro gifts to American music. The Spirituals are group songs, but the Blues are songs you sing alone. The Spirituals are religious songs, born in camp meetings and remote plantation districts. But the Blues are *city* songs rising from the crowded streets of big towns, or beating against the lonely walls of hall bed-rooms where you can't sleep at night. The Spirituals are escape songs, looking toward heaven, tomorrow, and God. But the Blues are *today* songs, here and now, broke and broken-hearted, when you're troubled in mind and don't know what to do, and nobody cares.
>
> HUGHES 1958, 159

Scholar Stephen Tracy maintains that "despite the differences between spirituals and blues that Hughes enumerated in 'Song Called the Blues', he saw a greater inherent bond that transcended what he saw as the superficial discordances between the blues and spiritual and gospel music" (Tracy 1995, 56). I wish to suggest that this bond between the spirituals and the blues was not some higher synthesis that Hughes realized in his writing, but rather the very spacing between the spirituals, with their emphasis on the heavenly hereafter that could yield such hope and strength for the journey, and the blues, with their emphasis on the here and now and its very real suffering and pain that seems to have no possible sublation. The blues, says Hughes, "are sad songs, with a kind of triumphant sadness, a vital earthiness about them from which life itself springs" (Hughes 2002, 200). The vital earthiness of life itself springs forth as humans sing the blues in the face of sadness and death.

Whereas Thurman articulates the strategy for living by which the singers of the spirituals dealt with death by relocating themselves in a Heavenly hope, Hughes voices a different view of death, seen perhaps most poignantly in his poem, "The Weary Blues." For Hughes, even if individual bodily death is really the end, the rhythm of life nevertheless runs forward through the blues. The bodily heart might stop but the song beats on.

> Thump, thump, thump, went his foot on the floor.
> He played a few chords then he sang some more—
>   "I got the Weary Blues
>   And I can't be satisfied.
>   Got the Weary Blues
>   And I can't be satisfied—
>   I isn't happy no mo'
>   And I wish that I had died."
> And far into the night he crooned that tune.
> The stars went out and so did the moon.
> The singer stopped playing and went to bed.
> While the Weary Blues echoed through his head.
> He slept like a rock or a man that's dead.
>   HUGHES 1994, 50

Even with the ambiguous ending where the player may be dead or sleeping as a thing, even if there is a cosmic collapse with the extinguishing of star and moonlight, still the song has been sung. Sorrow has been shared and lifted with the notes in the air. Though the body dies, the blues may rise.

Whereas Thurman affirms infinite worth, Hughes values the finite. Hughes affirms the body in the here and now—without even a hope of the transcendent. As Pinn argues, "some enslaved Africans sang spirituals celebrating the ontological and existential synergy between the divine and the human, best represented through the immanence of the divine in Christ; others signified this perspective and gave their full attention to humanity through the language of the blues, in which metaphysical assertions are met with suspicion and immanence is of primary concern" (Pinn 2012, 150). Song and poetry, though, generate their own transcending movement whether or not there is a God.

Thus, "in terms of textual effects," writes Kevin Hart, "it little matters whether one is responding to the transcendent or the transcendental" (Hart 2003, 199). What Hughes reminds us, however, is that these effects go right to the bone. Words matter, both in the sense of worth and in the causing of material effects. Whether or not there is a God or anyone to hear, there is still the mystery of the blues that beats on through Hughes's texts. And this mystery matters. Just reading the writing, we in a sense taste the tears in our mouths. Hoping beyond hope, the blues cry even if no one is listening. And, for Hughes, I maintain, that somehow transforms today's pain.

Mystery Matters

"The language used by the oppressed in developing their stories," argues Pinn, "has a materiality of its own that renders the gods true." For Thurman, the transcendent is signaled through the fleshly hope in a heavenly hereafter; for Hughes, the transcendental effects of song and poem affect our embodied existence so as to transform the here and now. The foregoing p(l)acing of Thurman and Hughes, and the spirituals and the blues, suggests that the materiality of embodied life involves us in undecidable mystery in regards to the immanent and transcendent and the effects that affect us. The capacity to hope in heaven creates real ascendancy in regards to the suffering of flesh, and the power to be affected by text and song generates real transformation right down to the bone. In a sense, the ultimate ontological status of the Ultimate Mystery is suspended at the level of embodied life.

What matters, Pinn says, is that the words and actions portrayed by African American religion "point to modes of consciousness that imply *more*—more possibilities, more complexity, more vitality" (Pinn 2003, 179). Defining the life of the human being in contrast to the materiality of stones or the transcendence of gods, even of our own creation, establishes a hierarchy that may have negative effects. The desire for more may also devolve into the base urges that fuel capitalistic consumerism. How might we see the worth of the human without securing a definitive more, which is so easily converted to dogmatism and violence, or requiring a less, which is disparaged?

"Such a sense of worth," says Thurman near the end of *The Luminous Darkness*, "is not confined by narrow limits of the self so that worth may be determined by contrast with something or someone of less worth. ...Such a sense of worth is rooted in one's own consciousness which expands and expands until there is involved the totality of life itself." According to Thurman, the know thyself of humanity "is to feel life moving through one and claiming one as a part of it" (Thurman 1965, 98). When claimed by fleshly life, however, we are caught up in a mo(ve)ment of more that may have no end.

Perhaps now we might see that a mystery remains—the spirituals do not actually fully exit the immanent to attain the transcendent, nor do the blues avoid the transcendent in the midst of their immanence. Both are sung by people who are at once passively formed by outward socio-historical processes and simultaneously actively forming those very processes. This very process generates something "more."

Thus, differing interpretations of the mystery of embodied life are possible: mystical and mundane. Between the two a mystery remains that moves us. Perhaps the very categories through which we know reality—perceptual and conceptual—might change, grow, and expand themselves. If we live differently, with different interests, we might discover different realities. Granted, the givenness of reality exerts causal pressures that we must negotiate, but our modes of engagement with these may evolve. If the very categories through which we engage the world might be transformed, we might move toward more and more expansive and different views. The mysterious mo(ve)ment of more makes us keep on going.

As Hughes said of the singers of the spirituals and the blues, whether happy or sad, "you kept on living and you kept on going. Their songs had the pulse and the beat of people who keep on going" (Hughes 2002, 7). Thus, I would say that there are at least two mo(ve)ments in which scholars might open to the mystery of "More"—the phenomenal and the transcendental. What appears may be more than we have previously thought or imagined, and the very modes of appearing and perceiving may undergo transformation such as to open onto more realities to come.

Further Study

The suspension of the ultimate ontological status of the transcendent that I argue the spacing between the spiritual and the blues embodies mirrors the question of the existence of the "hidden continent" that Wouter Hanegraaff identifies between the alternatives of *sui generis* and constructivist approaches in the study of esotericism. "At bottom," Hanegraaff writes in the conclusion to his *Esotericism and the Academy: Rejected Knowledge in Western Culture*, "this is the old dilemma of realism versus nominalism, and scholars tend to suggest that they are mutually exclusive: thus, one either sets out to write the history of 'the Western Esoteric Traditions', or one sees 'esotericism' as no more than a social construct reflective of more fundamental discursive processes" (Hanegraaff 2012, 368). I suggest that the incorporation of formerly rejected material like African American mysticism and the dynamics of the spirituals and the blues between Thurman and Hughes means that the resolution of this divide, if indeed ultimately there is one, lies through a more thoroughgoing study of embodiment.

"[A]t least at the bottom of all our mystical states there are techniques of the body which we have not studied," Marcel Mauss argues. "This socio-psycho-biological study should be made. I think that there are necessarily biological means of entering into 'communication with God'" (Mauss 2006, 93). Commenting on this passage, Talal Asad says, "thus, the possibility is opened up of inquiring into the ways in which embodied practices (including language in use) form a precondition for varieties of religious experience. The inability to enter into communion with God becomes a function of untaught bodies." According to Asad, then, "'Consciousness' becomes a dependent concept" (Asad 1993, 76–77; cf. Hollywood 2004). Following Foucault, many interpret such an entwinement of consciousness and practice as trapping us in discourse, merely skimming the surface of reality in the hall of mirrors created by cultural construction (such as Russell McCutcheon's position in a recent exchange with Ann Taves over the status of "religious experience"—McCutcheon 2012). As Cornel West argues in regards to the question of human subjectivity,

> Foucault's answer—anonymous and autonomous discourses, disciplines, and techniques—is but the latest addition to the older ones: the dialectical development of modes of production (vulgar Marxisms); workings of the *Weltgeist* (crude Hegelians); or activities of transcendental subjects (academic Kantians). All such answers shun the centrality of dynamic social practices structured and unstructured over time and space.
>
> WEST 1989, 225

I would argue that part of what is needed here is a more thorough thinking through of what Asad notes parenthetically—the way language is an embodied practice that matters, meaning discourse is not only important but also always already material. Consciousness as dependent then means not that we are trapped in a surface linguisticism, but rather that language fuses mysteriously with materiality such that words do things as things are done to them by differing social practices. Moreover, discourse, concepts, and consciousness are so entwined with all that is such that differing movements of culture, history, and consciousness can create entirely different realities, not merely differently interpreted realities.

What we need, dare I say, is a more Derridean reading of Foucault. "Is it a dumb reading of Michel Foucault, for example," asks the deconstructionist, feminist theorist Vicki Kirby, "to consider that if discourse constitutes its object, then matter is constantly rewritten and transformed?" (Kirby 1997, 4). It is not dumb—neither stupid nor silent—for, even in reading language we create material effects, even as the material text affects us. Though little read this way, Jacques Derrida always proposed understanding discourse in such expansive, enmeshed, world shaping and shaped ways. "The paradox," Derrida says, "is that even though I proposed to deconstruct the hegemony of linguistics, my work is often presented as a linguisticism" (Derrida 2001, 77). As he says in the interview, "Eating Well,"

> If one defines language in such a way that it is reserved for what we call man, what is there to say? But if one re-inscribes language in a network of possibilities that do not merely encompass it but mark it irreducibly from the inside, everything changes. I am thinking in particular of the mark in general, of the trace, of iterability, of differance. These possibilities or necessities, without which there would be no language, *are themselves not only human.*
>
> DERRIDA 1995, 284–85

What Derrida suggests is thus not only that Cartesian subjectivity that would know itself in talking to itself—"I think, therefore I am"—is displaced through the prior feeling of flesh (Marion), but also that our feeling ourselves follows after an irrecoverable mystery opened in the p(l)acing between the material and immaterial, which may never be purely divisible. I follow (*je suis*) mystery, therefore I am (*je suis*).

In regards to the question of subjectivity, then, Derrida argues, "nothing should be excluded" (Derrida 1995, 269). Following Derrida more than Foucault then means that the "unknow thyself" of humanity entails daring to know ourselves and others through participation in a mystery beyond clear cut divisions—immanent and transcendent, material and immaterial, living and nonliving, human and other. Though it is beyond the scope of this paper to say more, I maintain that listening to Derrida, the African-born, self-described "little black and very Arab Jew," might help us, among other things, to better understand theurgy and other practices arising from the "cosmotheism" that Hanegraaff identifies as a major current of western esotericism (Derrida 1993, 58; Hanegraaff 2012). Seeing the vision of this vibrant deconstructive universe exceeds description, and structurally so, because we *are* it, though we are not who we think we are. There is a mystery that we embody, which means so long as we live there is evermore mystery to come. Complex subjectivity indeed.

CHAPTER 11

Show and Prove

Five Percenters and the Study of African American Esotericism

Biko Mandela Gray

Introduction

Most intellects do not believe in God/But they fear us just the same...On and on/and on and on/My cipher keeps moving like a rolling stone.
ERYKAH BADU, 1997

Erykah Badu's words above point to a group of primarily African American men and women called the Five Percenters or the Nation of Gods and Earths (NGE). The Five Percenters follow the teachings of Clarence 13X "Allah," a man who claimed that each Black man was a God. Musicologist Felicia Miyakawa and investigators Michael Muhammad Knight and Yusef Nuruddin have pointed out that there are esoteric elements in the Five Percenter way of life. However, to my knowledge, there has yet to be a scholarly investigation of the Five Percenters *primarily* concerned with the esoteric nature of this organization. Miyakawa, for example, focuses on the musical production and gender dynamics in the NGE; Knight offers a more general overview of the emergence and development of this group; and Nuruddin offers a social-scientific analysis of the Five Percenters, connecting it to the broader context of African American Islamic groups (Miyakawa 2005, 2010; Knight 2007; Nuruddin 1994).

This chapter is my contribution to the conversation regarding the esoteric nature of the NGE way of life. In this chapter, I will argue that the esotericism of the Five Percenters can be understood in terms of what I call a *demonstrative* phenomenological disposition—a mode of being grounded in the *inseparability* of what is traditionally understood as ontology and epistemology.

I'll begin with a brief exposition of the Five Percenters, discussing the emergence and development of the contours of their way of life. In the second section, I place Five Percenter culture in conversation with some of the more dominant approaches to Western Esotericism, especially that of Antoine Faivre, an influential and founding scholar of the field. In the last section, I will use a phenomenological analysis to discuss what appears to be the nature of the esotericism of the Five Percenters.

© KONINKLIJKE BRILL NV, LEIDEN, 2015 | DOI 10.1163/9789004283428_013

Arise, You who are Gods![1] The Emergence, Development, and Basic Contours of NGE Thought

In 1964, a man in New York named Clarence 13X separated from the Nation of Islam. Many reasons are given for this separation, some of which concern 13X's violation of the NOI codes of conduct due to his gambling habits and drug use, but one thing is for sure: during his involvement with the NOI, Clarence 13X had begun to rethink some of the Nation's core doctrines. Instead of affirming that Allah was fully incarnate in the man of W. Fard Muhammad, Clarence 13X claimed that *each* Black man, in the very nature of his being, is a God in his own right. He supported this claim with the NOI's student enrollment lessons, wherein a member is taught the identity of the black man: "1. Who is the Original Man? The Original Man is the Asiatic Black Man, the Maker, the Owner, the Cream of the Planet Earth, the Father of Civilization, and *God of the Universe*" (Nuruddin, 1994, 116, my emphasis). Clarence 13X took this statement literally. He laid claim to his status as a God, and began calling himself "Allah." He suggested that Black men's lives would only be better if they would realize who and what they *are*—that is, "*God[s]* of the Universe." Allah called the realization of one's own divinity "coming into knowledge of self," and began sharing this knowledge with other men about who and what they are.

Primarily concerned with future generations, Allah directed his focus specifically toward the young Black men in New York where he lived. He taught them that, as Gods, they had complete autonomy over their lives. Allah turned the meaning of the term "Islam" into an acronym for "I Self Lord And Master," pointing to who the Black men are and what they are capable of, instead of the description of a religious institution. He also understood the term "Allah" as the acronym "Arm-Leg-Leg-Arm-Head,"[2] describing the God's body. Because each man is a God, he is able to live his life however he pleases; there is no agreed upon ethical code or established set of norms to which each God should submit. A God's way of living is completely up to him, producing considerable fluidity and flexibility within the Five Percent Nation. Michael Muhammad Knight recalled an experience where he heard one God denounce marijuana, only to be followed up by another God who endorsed its use. Gods are free to wholly determine how they will live.

In a social climate marked by repeated legal and extralegal attempts at reinforcing white supremacy, Allah's message that Black men are Gods turned

---

1   I am indebted to Felicia Miyakawa for this subject heading. See Miyakawa 2005, 15.

2   I borrow this stylized way of typing these terms from Felicia Miyakawa. See Miyakawa 2010, 32.

arguments for black inferiority on their head. For young victims of repeated police brutality and harassment from whites, realizing that one was a God provided solace and re-orientation; instead of concerning themselves with enacting retributive violence against whites, the new young Gods of Allah's Five Percent Nation committed themselves to spreading the powerful and attractive message of inherent black divinity (Allah, 2009; Knight, 2007).

Realizing one's inherent divinity—that is, coming into "knowledge of self"—was not simply the acknowledgement of one's own autonomy, however. Although his fundamental claim was about the existence and identity of God, Allah vehemently denied that what he had developed was a religion. Rather, it was a *science*. Allah claimed that Black men could—and had to—show and prove their existence as God by scientifically analyzing different aspects of their lives, and then subsequently living in light of the knowledge they found through these scientific analyses. He based his scientific method on a set of 120 foundational lessons (called the "120"). Upon being equipped with these lessons, Gods would be able to "show and prove" their inherent divinity by "sciencing out" or finding deeper meanings within the world through their use of the 120 (The Supreme Mathematics and Supreme Alphabet—the numerological and alphabetical systems included in the 120—are listed in the appendix).

Having become a member of the Nation of Islam's security force (called the Fruit of Islam [FOI]) while still with the NOI, Allah brought the FOI's emphasis on rote memorization and verbal mastery to the streets. In order to be part of the FOI, one had to memorize—and then verbally recite *with perfection*—the initiatory lessons of the NOI. Allah required his young Gods to do the same with the 120, claiming that they had not fully realized who they were until they were able to perfectly recite—and then subsequently use—the foundational 120 lessons (Allah 2009, 135). Allah gave his lessons orally; there were no *written* lessons to memorize. As such, the 120 are not reproduced textually in their totality: the only way to gain access to the 120 in full is to have an enlightener—that is, a God or an Earth who will disseminate the 120 as they were given to him or her. Five Percenter investigator Michael Muhammad Knight elaborates: "the 120 gives up its heart when translated to hypertext. Shared on a playground or a prison yard, the degrees become living things" (Knight 2007, 204). The 120 are meant to be transmitted orally.

Allah also provided the rationale for why this group has been called the "Five Percenters." Using the NOI's "Lost-Found Muslim Lesson No. 2," Allah taught his young followers that a person is a member of one of three different groups: the "ignorant 85 percent," the masses of people who are deceived because they believe in a "mystery God" (that is, a transcendent and supernatural Divine entity concerned with our well-being) and do not have knowledge of self; the 10 percent, the small elite who do have knowledge, yet use this knowledge to deceive the 85 percent; and the remaining 5 percent, the "poor righteous teachers" who have knowledge of themselves and are thus supposed to dedicate their lives to sharing this knowledge of self with others (Allah 2009, 121–122; Nuruddin 1994, 116–117).

Allah's teachings spread by word of mouth, and more and more men began realizing who they were. His Five Percent Nation grew in status and influence. It eventually fell under local and federal scrutiny. Newspapers called the Five Percenters a hate group; the mayor of New York had them investigated for criminal activity; J. Edgar Hoover's FBI kept them under continuous surveillance; and, ostensibly for calling himself a God, Clarence 13X was sent to the Matteawan mental institution for the criminally insane (Allah 2009, 165). In Matteawan, Father Allah continued to teach young men in the institution with him, as well as those who came to visit him. In turn, they shared the knowledge of self with others, and the Five Percent Nation continued to grow despite Allah's institutionalization. Clarence 13X was released from Matteawan in 1967, and continued teaching (Allah, 2009, 178–179; Knight, 2007, 210).

Until his release from Matteawan, women were not present in any formal way in the Five Percent Nation. The reason for this largely had to do with Allah's patriarchal stance toward women: "Allah's own concepts of gender roles grew simultaneously from Nation of Islam teachings and the natural patriarchy of life on hard streets where physical might made right and...prostitution [was] a mere footnote to survival" (Knight 2007, 209). In the beginning, the women who were present were those who were the girlfriends or frequent sexual partners of the young Gods who shared Allah's teachings with them. As the movement grew, however, Allah acknowledged the presence of the women, calling them "Earths," the physical and epistemological "soil" within which the Gods plant their physical and epistemological seeds. Often understood in a twofold fashion, the term "seed" refers to both the man's semen as well as his understanding of the 120. Earths are the "[mothers] of civilization...Queen[s] at the side of Allah" (Allah 2009, 125).

On the basis of the female's ability to carry a child in her womb, the ideal role for an Earth is domestic, taking care of children and making sure the home is maintained. Musicologist Felicia Miyakawa explains: "While Gods are free to choose their own paths in life, the role of Earths is somewhat more restricted... The main goal for an Earth is reproduction because through reproduction a woman symbolizes the life-giving forces of the earth" (Miyakawa 2005, 34). Earths occupy a role that has often been understood as "secondary but absolutely necessary," and this has raised questions concerning the NGE's treatment of its female members (Black 2007, 41). Miyakawa has argued that the women do not "consider themselves oppressed or restricted. Instead, they embrace their roles with joy...these women feel beloved, protected, and respected" (Miyakawa 2010, 48). While I am sure that the Earths Miyakawa interviewed feel this way, from my perspective, it still remains a question as to whether the role assigned to Earths affords them the same mobility and freedom as the Gods. For example, the Gods are afforded the opportunity to have multiple Earths, while the Earths are usually encouraged to remain loyal to one God (Knight 2007 208–213; Miyakawa 2005, 34–35). Such inequity, due largely to the ontological claims regarding the men and women, continues to raise questions concerning the women in the movement. Responding to these issues in more detail, however, is beyond the scope of this essay.

Allah was assassinated in 1969, but his death did not mark the end of his movement (Allah, 2009, 119–120; Knight, 2007, 242–246). His teachings continued to spread throughout New York in the form of oral lessons shared on basketball courts, in basements, and on prison yards, just to name a few examples (Knight, 2007, 187–207). Having provided a brief narrative as well as some of the basic contours of Five Percenter thought and life, I will now focus on the esoteric nature of this group.

"Knowing the Ledge": The Five Percenters as an Esoteric Current

In this section, I explicitly discuss the esotericism of the NGE by placing their way of life in conversation with the work of the influential Western Esotericism scholar Antoine Faivre. I primarily concern myself with Faivre's work because he has been influential in the field, heavily contributing to the development and expansion of Western Esotericism studies.

Faivre developed a useful set of criteria for identifying esoteric groups in the West. He suggested that Western esoteric groups share a "form of thought"— that is a structure of knowing—that has six fundamental characteristics. Four of these are intrinsic; per Faivre, these four characteristics are present in all Western esoteric currents Faivre has investigated throughout his career.[3] The intrinsic characteristics are *correspondences, living nature, imagination and mediations,* and *transmutation.* The other two are non-intrinsic in that they show up frequently, but are not always present; they are *concordances* and

---

3 It is important to note that Faivre extensively combed the historical records in order to come to this conclusion. Though no one would make a claim to an exhaustive knowledge of any subject, the breadth and depth of Faivre's scholarship should not be overlooked in his formulation of these criteria.

transmission. Although other scholars have critiqued Faivre's criteria, such criticisms have often been *expansions,* not *revisions,* of Faivre's thought, suggesting that Faivre's work is useful as a fruitful starting point for esoteric investigation (Bogdan 2007, 25–26). Below, I will show that the thought of the Five Percenters exhibits all four of the intrinsic components.

Firstly, Faivre suggests esoteric currents always understand the universe in terms of symbolic and real *correspondences.* Whatever occurs here within human individual and social life has a direct correspondence in the broader cosmological context (Faivre 1994, 10–11). Five Percenters establish natural correspondences; for example, there is a natural correspondence between their own bodies and the world around them. Historian and Five Percenter Wakeel Allah makes clear how the NGE draws correspondences between black men and women and the world and universe, in both symbolic and physical terms. Regarding black men, he claims that in physics, existence comes in three forms, "liquids, gases or solids. God therefore is the apt title given to the highest form of mental, spiritual, and physical existence—the Black Man" (Allah, 2009, 124–125). As with the physical universe, the Black Man exists in three forms, physically, mentally, and spiritually. A correspondence between Black men and the laws of physics has been established, per Five Percenter thought.

Natural correspondences are also found between the bodies of black women and other natural bodies, particularly the earth. Indeed, the reason *why* black female Five Percenters are called "Earths" is because they, like the earth, give life:

> As the earth produces life, so does the Black woman produce life and she "is the field from which the Black Nation is produced." Another striking similarity was that three-fourths of the surface of the Planet Earth is covered under water. So in parallel, the Black woman in Isla must cover ¾ of her body with clothing for "protection from the devil's civilization" and out of "respect for her God".
>
> ALLAH 2009, 125

Each of these examples—earthly similarities, parallels in physics—show that the Five Percenter worldview is filled with natural correspondences. In terms of the first fundamental characteristic in Faivre's criteria, the Five Percenters fit the bill quite closely.

Faivre's second characteristic, *living nature,* is the idea that nature itself either is alive or has a "light or hidden fire circulating through it." Because nature is alive, it can be "read like a book," understood and deciphered in its essential elements; ultimately, understanding nature in this way can lead to a better life. One of the goals of an esoteric adherent is therefore to be able to "read" Nature by deciphering its "sympathies and antipathies," thus producing the knowledge that ultimately results in a better existence (Faivre 1994, 11).

Turning our attention to the Five Percenters, Allah reminded his followers that the NGE way of life is a *science,* not a religion. His foundational 120 Lessons are thus meant to decipher and uncover the essential aspects of whatever one comes in contact with, *especially* nature. For example, included in the 120 are the Actual Facts and Solar Facts, lists of natural measurements, ranging from the circumference of the earth to the distance between different planetary bodies (they are listed in the appendix). In order to "show and prove" one's authenticity as a God or an Earth, one must first memorize and then adeptly handle the Actual Facts and Solar Facts (among other lessons), interpreting them on the basis of the Supreme Mathematics to gain deeper knowledge about anything from current events to the nature of the universe. Islamic scholar Yusuf Nuruddin interviewed a Five Percenter named Sincere Allah, who showed and proved his divinity by interpreting the measurement of the earth's surface with the science of Supreme Mathematics. His breakdown is quoted in full:

> The area in square miles of the planet earth is 196,940,000 square miles... In the 196,940,000 square miles, you've got the year 1960 in there; you've got the year 1964 and 1969. Now, the way I see it is when Allah (Clarence 13X)—Knowledge was born by equality, born back to the culture, to the cipher, only showing and proving that year 1964 when Almighty God Allah (Clarence 13X) when he left the temple you know, in 1964 he showed and proved that the black man was God. Then, in 1969, that's when Mayor Lindsay offered him a lot of money and a certain amount of cars, you know, to stop teaching the babies; stop teaching it. So, he said "No. God can't be bought or sold." So they took him out of here. They figured they would kill him and his whole teachings would be stopped. See, they only killed his body. See, his body didn't manifest itself to the kids. It was his intelligence.
>
> NURUDDIN 1994, 127

Sincere Allah narrates Clarence 13X Allah's emergence and assassination by synthesizing one of the Actual Facts with the Supreme Mathematics. For Five Percenters, the light of nature shines in such a way that allows one to gain new knowledge, like connections between certain significant historical events, as Sincere Allah showed us above. The Five Percenters fulfill Faivre's second criterion.

Faivre's third fundamental criterion is a combination of *imagination* and *mediations*, two complementary elements. The esoteric imagination is the pre-understanding of the world as a context of esoteric significance. In other words, imagination is that condition of possibility for esoteric perception *in general*. Faivre claims, "It is the imagination that allows...[one] to penetrate the hieroglyphs of Nature, to put the theory of correspondences into active practice and to uncover, to see, and to know the mediating entities between Nature and the divine world" (Faivre 1994, 12–13).

Faivre's concept of imagination is complemented by his concept of mediations. Mediations are those symbols or beings—human and otherwise—that provide foundational esoteric information. One example of mediations is initiators; those who initiate one into an esoteric current convey esoteric knowledge to the aspiring member (Faivre 1994, 12–13). Another example of mediations is those symbols and symbolic clusters that provide the basis of an esoteric hermeneutic of the world. Imagination and mediations work together to produce a shift in perspective—or, more precisely, *perception*—resulting in a new way of interacting with the world and others in it.

The NGE imagination—that is, the condition for the possibility of esoteric knowledge within the Five Percent Nation—is grounded in *science*. Gods and Earths are *scientists*; they structure their perception of the world around "showing and proving" the inner-workings of the world on indubitable or, in Husserlian terms, *apodictic*, evidence. The Five Percenters are able to interpret the deeper meaning of anything, from something as simple as how one should dress to, as we saw above, something as complex as the reasons why Father Allah was killed. In the examples above, we've seen Wakeel Allah use theoretical physics and basic geology to establish the divinity of the Black Man as well as how women should dress. We've also seen Sincere Allah provide a cause for Clarence 13X's death using the science of the Supreme Mathematics to interpret one of the Actual Facts. Anything in the world—indeed the world itself—can be broken down and deciphered scientifically.

Mediations also abound in Five Percenter culture. From the foundational 120 to the Gods and Earths themselves, NGE culture is saturated with people and symbol systems that mediate deeper forms of knowledge. The scientific imagination is a structure of perception, aided by the hermeneutical tools of the 120 and the dissemination of knowledge by the Gods and Earths themselves. There is no shortage of imagination or mediation within NGE culture.

The last of the four fundamental characteristics is what Faivre calls *transmutation*. For esoteric currents, a successful initiate is not solely transformed intellectually, for intellectual transformation, or the "renewing of one's mind," would not result in esoteric thought. Rather, the initiate has to be modified "in its very nature"; he or she must undergo a total ontological shift in inner and external experience and knowledge. Instead of thinking these two separate, one now thinks of them as two sides of the same coin. In Five Percenter thought and life, this is best expressed through the practice of "showing and proving" one's existence as a God or an Earth. By displaying a facility and adeptness with elements like the Supreme Mathematics and Supreme Alphabet, one lays claim to the legitimacy of his or her status as God or Earth.

Furthermore, this initiation is understood as a "second birth." Initiates are understood to have died to the old person, and become a totally new being (Faivre 1994, 13–14). Due to the fact that each prospective God or Earth has his or her own enlightener, and thus may come into the knowledge of self in different ways, it is difficult to ascertain if there is a structure to the initiation process. However, on the basis of the rationale for their being called "Five Percenters," one can at least infer that Gods and Earths no longer understand themselves as member of the "85 percent"—that is, the ignorant masses who are easily deceived by mystery gods. All Gods and Earths understand themselves as people who no longer live in ignorance of who and what they are, leading new lives in the knowledge of self that they have acquired and continue to cultivate. They are "new beings" in the sense that they have realized who they truly were all along. Five Percenters exhibit the fourth and final element of Faivre's intrinsic criteria.

The specifics of Faivre's thought—the characteristics he singles out as constituting esotericism in the West—have been quite useful here in identifying the Five Percenters as an Esoteric current. And while Faivre's work has been influential in the field, he has not stood alone. There have been criticisms regarding his conception of Esotericism (Bogdan 2007, 13). Indeed, the field of Western Esotericism is a very diverse field regarding the specific conceptual frameworks different scholars use to handle what they understand as esoteric currents in the West. And in each case, it is plausible to understand the Five Percenters as an esoteric current.

Wouter Hanegraaff, for example, suggests that Esotericism be understood in terms of *gnosis*: "It is indeed hard to deny that an emphasis on *gnosis*...is quite typical of the currents and personalities usually considered as falling under the heading of 'Western Esotericism'" (Hanegraaff 2004, 510). Henrik Bogdan elaborates on this definition, claiming that *gnosis* is a "strategy of knowledge" along the lines of faith and reason, but not reducible to the two. *Gnosis* here is a kind of revelatory knowledge that puts one in direct contact with the divine. (Bogdan 2007, 15) With regard to the Five Percenters, for men, the knowledge of the divine *is* knowledge of self *as divine*. For women, it is the direct understanding of the man as divine. Both of these come through a full internalization of the 120. This understanding of esotericism also fits the Five Percenters.

Arthur Versluis, the founding president of the Association for the Study of Esotericism, has also offered a conception of Western Esotericism. He suggests two (very general) characteristics constitute esotericism in the West: (1) Gnosis or gnostic insight, i.e., knowledge of hidden or invisible realms or aspects of existence (including both cosmological and metaphysical gnosis) and (2) Esotericism, meaning that this hidden knowledge is either explicitly restricted to a relatively small group of people, or implicitly self-restricted by virtue of its complexity or subtlety (Versluis 2007, 2).

Again, the Five Percenters could fit this bill: the 120 are not widely available, and they are used to decipher deeper meanings about the universe. Furthermore, the Five Percenters *are* a relatively small group of people, located largely in New York. Given that they do understand themselves as the enlightened "Five Percent," Gods and Earths are not surprised by their relatively small numbers. One way of demonstrating this is through the NGE's relationship with hip-hop. Although many popular rappers during the nineties—from all the members of the Wu Tang Clan to Rakim Allah—were Five Percenters, these same rappers acknowledge that the knowledge they share in their lyrics are often misunderstood. "The dumb are mostly intrigued by the drum," says the GZA, a Five Percenter and member of the Wu-Tang clan (Knight 2011, locations 59–61). The Five Percenters could certainly be understood as esoteric, according to Versluis' standards.

It is clear that there are diverse approaches in the study of Western Esotericism. However, from my perspective, the fact that it is possible—and plausible—to build a case for understanding the NGE as esoteric from within each of these frameworks suggests that there are points of convergence in the work of Western Esotericism scholars. One of the similarities I perceive is in terms of *knowledge* or *cognition*. Per the approaches I outlined above, the concept of esotericism appears to revolve around a system of gnostic knowledge or a structure of thinking. One of the primary reasons that it *is* possible to build a case for thinking about the NGE in esoteric terms is because of the cryptic nature of their 120: along with the fact that the 120 are not readily available in their totality for everyone to access, the Supreme Mathematics and Supreme Alphabet also bear striking similarities to other esoteric systems of knowledge (Nuruddin 1994, 124–125; Knight 2007, 51). This system of knowledge is what can be highlighted in all three of these frameworks as constituting the ground through which we would investigate the Five Percenters as an esoteric group. I call this foundation an *epistemological foundation*.

With regard to the epistemological foundation of the conceptions of esotericism I have discussed above, it is safe to say that the Five Percenters have
epistemology as one of the foundational aspects of their way of life, and therefore could certainly be understood as esoteric per the approaches I've outlined
above. As we have seen, much of their esotericism is largely rooted in the
acquisition and application of the 120; this adoption and application can be
understood in epistemological terms as an engagement with a structure of
cognition premised upon the acquisition of specific forms of knowledge
("showing and proving" *could*—and here I stress the "could"—be interpreted
as little more than the dissemination of certain forms of knowledge).

However, I would suggest that there is more to their esotericism. Consider,
for example, the words of musicologist Felicia Miyakawa: "much of Five
Percent doctrine *hinges* on the identity of god, or Allah" (Miyakawa 2005, 31,
my emphasis). In Faivre's last characteristic of transmutation, we got a glimpse
of the ontological aspect of esotericism, even as it was subordinated to epistemology. And as I showed in the first section, Clarence 13X developed his way of
life in light of his fundamental assertion concerning who and what he was—
namely, that he was Allah. In the Five Percenters, we do not encounter a group
whose way of life revolves *solely* around an epistemological framework. Rather,
this group appears to demonstrate a relationship between epistemology and
ontology, that is, it is concerned with both the acquisition of knowledge as well
as the *being* of its members. In other words, accompanying the epistemological
framework of the 120 is an *ontological framework* concerning the nature or
essence of the men and women. In the next section, by way of a phenomenological analysis, I discuss the conditions that make possible this kind of
relationship.

A Phenomenological Analysis of Five Percenter Esotericism

I have suggested above that the esotericism of the Five Percenters is based on
a relationship between epistemology and ontology. In this I hope to get a better
grasp of this relationship through philosophical phenomenology. I turn to
philosophical phenomenology for two reasons. First, phenomenological analysis is based upon *description*. Edmund Husserl's maxim "to the things themselves!" was aimed at turning philosophy away from its dependence on
axiomatic principles or *a priori* presuppositions. Instead, Husserl sought to
turn to *experience itself* to make sense of our life. Husserl's phenomenology
included two methodological moments: first, he bracketed the question of
"reality," seeking to simply examine our experiences for what they were, and

not on the basis of whether they were real or not (both a schizophrenic hallucination and a "normal" experience have the same philosophical importance in this method). Second, Husserl was concerned with handling the conditions that made our experiences *possible*. In this regard, phenomenology is a transcendental philosophy, in the sense that it is aimed at uncovering the conditions of possibility for any experience at all. For Husserl, therefore, phenomenology was necessary *before* one engaged in metaphysics, epistemology, ethics, or ontology, as these disciplines have already presupposed a framework that was firmly in place. I therefore turn to phenomenology to help me to discuss what appear to be the conditions that make the Five Percenters' brand of esotericism possible.

Second, phenomenology is useful here because it emerged in large part as a response to the dualism pervading Western philosophy. Descartes' famous methodical doubt shifted first philosophy away from metaphysics into epistemology, and his epistemological findings made a sharp distinction between the world of ideas and the world of materials. Descartes privileged the world of ideas, suggesting that it was the "more real" reality, and thinkers followed him—most notably Hegel, and to a lesser extent, Kant. Despite the diversity of their thought, phenomenologists like Martin Heidegger, Jean-Paul Sartre, and Maurice Merleau-Ponty, suggested that our experiences, as well as their conditions of possibility, cannot be understood in terms of metaphysical dualism—and thus are not fully grasped by epistemological analyses alone. We do not live solely—or even primarily—in worlds of ideas and concepts. Rather, our experiences—even the experiences of members in esoteric groups—are best understood as a mélange of conceptual and embodied perceptions of and engagements with our cultural and physical surroundings. In this regard, phenomenology is useful for tracing the connections between Five Percenter epistemology and other aspects of Five Percenter life by describing the situations and horizons that condition their way of living. Here I am primarily concerned with the relationship between epistemology and ontology in the NGE.

I will thus begin my analysis by describing the phenomenological *situation* out of which the esotericism of the NGE emerges. My understanding of "situation" is based on what Martin Heidegger meant by the term—namely, the context of *meaning* or *significance* out of which any kind of experience happens or occurs (Heidegger 2004, 63–64). Descriptions of phenomenological situations can include historical analysis; in the first section, I provided some sense of the historical context out of which the Five Percenters emerged. However, in light of the phenomenological method I am employing here, I am concerned here with the *meaning* content or significance to which these historical materials and narratives point. In that regard, I only provide more historical data here to give more details.

Because the movement is founded upon the divinity of the Black man, I focus on what appear to be two of the more prominent aspects of this phenomenological situation: the first is racial; the second I will call "religious." Here "religious" means relating to a particular religious tradition: for the NGE, this tradition is the Nation of Islam. However, I must be clear that a phenomenological situation is not the conglomerate or aggregate of different pieces, characteristics, or aspects; to think in these terms "would already be a deforming, a slide into epistemology" (Heidegger 2004, 9). My goal here is to describe the situation as it presents itself in its complexity. Therefore, although I focus on each of these aspects individually, this should not be taken as an acknowledgement that these aspects are in any way separable. I will ultimately show that neither the Five Percenter situation nor their *response* to this situation is simply a combination of these two aspects, as if these aspects can stand on their own. I will now turn my attention to the racial aspect of this situation. I'll begin by giving a few more historical details.

In the first section, I suggested that the historical context out of which the Five Percenters emerged was tumultuous. Policemen repeatedly provoked, beat, harassed, and abused young and old black men and women under the guise of "criminal investigations." In 1964, young black men had become fed up with the sustained attention from and oppression by the white legal authorities. They reacted violently, from provoking fights to looting white stores in an attempt to feed poor black families. Yet, as I also pointed out, 1964 was also the year in which Clarence 13X separated from the Nation of Islam and began hitting the streets with his teachings. He taught these young men about who they were, and, in many ways, contributed to the cessation of some of the violence through his teachings and actions (Allah 2009, 94–136). But due to the fact that the FBI was largely concerned with preventing "the low range growth of militant Black organizations, especially among the youth," Allah's early teaching sessions to young men on the streets and playgrounds of Harlem placed his young Five Percent Nation under constant government surveillance (Allah 2009, 153). Furthermore, as I said earlier, Allah was sent to a mental institution, allegedly because he called himself God.

Police brutality, criminal investigations, continued surveillance, constant provocation, all directed toward blacks; each of these historical data point to an existential phenomenon philosopher Lewis Gordon described as "antiblack racism," that is, a concerted effort to subjugate those people who have been deemed "black" through the course of history precisely on the basis of their "blackness"[4] (Gordon 1999). Gordon asserts that antiblack racism is ultimately a form of Sartrean bad faith. Bad faith is, in effect, lying to myself about who I am in an attempt to escape my responsibility for others.

Bad faith is an ontological doctrine. In the case of antiblack racism, the ontological claim is situated in the attempt to reduce Blacks to causally *determined* objects with little to no freedom, as well as reduce whites to acausally *determining* subjects with seemingly absolute freedom. However, human beings are both object *and* subject (or maybe *neither* object *nor* subject—Heidegger would suggest these constructions completely miss who and what we are), and our ability to make decisions is limited by our "facility," that is, the fact that we cannot be everywhere and everything at once. We are subject to "natural laws"; we are embodied; we get sick and hungry; we are unable to be in multiple places at once; and, lastly, we *share* this world with other beings upon which we rely— animal, plant, *and* human—and all of which require our responsibility to them. To dismiss our facility is to dismiss the cognitive and reflective capacities of other human beings, reducing them to objects unable to be, as W.E.B. Du Bois put it, co-workers in the "kingdom of culture" (Du Bois 1994, 3).

The racial aspect of the Five Percenter existential situation is thus one that is *ontologically hostile*; it is characterized by repeated attempts to turn Black being into what Heidegger called the "present-at-hand," that is, objects that have lost their ability to function properly, becoming "conspicuous" in their dysfunction, and thus must be handled by either fixing them, discarding them, or removing them from the current context. Blacks are reduced to their utility; and when that utility is no longer present, it seems that Black life becomes a problem. Racially, for a Black American in an antiblack world, the world *appears*—that is, it is phenomenologically constituted—as an *ontologically hostile* context (Gordon 1999).

The racial aspect of the Five Percenters, however, is general; it could be argued that *all* Black Americans live in an antiblack world marked and marred by white supremacy. Thus, although this racial aspect provides some clarity regarding the situation that produces the emergence of the Five Percenters, it is not enough. There is another aspect of the Five Percenter existential situation—the "religious" aspect.

---

4   On the first page of *Bad Faith and Antiblack Racism,* Gordon points out that the color significa-
    tion of "blackness" is indeed a phenomenological distortion; there are no *white* or *black*
    bodies, only lighter and darker ones. These color symbols carry with them phenomenological
    weight, and have become, in and of themselves, meaning structures within which we under-
    stand our world. See Gordon 1999, 1.

Here, I must be careful, as the Five Percenters vehemently deny that their way of life is a religion. However, their emergence—and even their continued presence—has its phenomenological origins in a religious orientation, namely the Nation of Islam. To respect the Five Percenters, I will put the terms "religion" or "religious" in quotes to remind the reader of their fundamental rejection of this term as descriptive of their way of life.

Ironically, this voracious denial of religion points to the "religious" aspect of the Five Percenter phenomenological situation. This denial is situated within the conception of God's existence, a conception that has its roots in an (onto)theological distinction between Five Percenters and the NOI. Philosophically, the question of existence has traditionally been broken up into two different parts: what Heidegger has called *that*-being (the mere existence or presence of something) or *what*-being (quiddity, the qualities or attributes that determine the specific mode of existence of an object, thing, or state of affairs). (Heidegger 1982, 18) Both the Five Percenters and the NOI agree on the *that*-being of God—they both argue that God exists. The distinction here concerns the *what*-being—the who and what of God. As I noted above, the Five Percenters locate the *what*-being of God in the bodies of *each* black man, and not in the bodily existence of one man or the "collective" black man. For Five Percenters, "religion" indicates a submission to Allah or God (this is, too, derived from the NOI's understanding of religion). But, since Black men are Gods, they are not required to submit to anyone or anything, and thus are not religious. I've already pointed out one significant effect of this claim; because each and every black man is a God within the context of Five Percenter thought and life, there is no agreed upon code of conduct.

Women on the other hand, *can* be "religious": "While black men do not practice the religion of *Islam* (submission) since 'God can't submit to God,' Earths are often considered to be Muslim because they *do* submit to Allah—in the form of the black man" (Knight 2007, 215). For example, though there is not a dress code for men in the movement, "the Black woman in Islam must cover ¾ of her body with clothing [for] protection from the devil's civilization and out of respect for her God" (Allah 2009, 125). The ontological status of the men and women dictate their relationship to "religion" and "religious" practices.

Furthermore, because each man is God, he also can interpret the 120 however he pleases. (I showed some of this above with the lengthy quote from Sincere Allah.) Some Gods have "plus-lessons" that may be external to the original 120 but foundational to their thought, and the Supreme Alphabet has underwent transformations over time (Nuruddin 1994, 127). Every God has the ability—and the duty—to use the 120 in light of their own personal challenges and issues. The Gods—and the Earths—"build" with the knowledge they've gained, "moving the cipher" of Five Percenter knowledge "like a rolling stone."

With regard to Five Percenter knowledge, something interesting emerges concerning the "religious" aspect of this situation. Despite their passionate denials of religiosity, Five Percenters recognize that much of their stock of foundational knowledge is derived from NOI doctrines. Wakeel Allah provides some support for this claim: "Allah and the Elders [Allah's comrades who were with him when he left the NOI] invented the beginnings of the system called the 'Supreme Mathematics' and 'Supreme Alphabets'. They introduced this system along with *the Nation of Islam Lessons* (also known as '120 degrees') to a group of Black Youth" (Allah 2009, 118, my emphasis). The 120 have their basis in the NOI, and the Five Percenters have made use of them. It appears that they make a distinction between the utility of NOI *thought* and the restrictedness of NOI *religion*.

The empirical details I pointed out above indicate the phenomenon of *restriction*. Religion is experienced as a *restriction* on the Black man's being, an onto(theo)logical straightjacket that hinders the Black man from having full capacity to determine how he should live his life as a God. Furthermore, women *can* be religious, because they are *Earths, not Gods.* Their being is not impinged upon nor restricted in being religious. If the racial aspect of the Five Percenter situation constituted the world as ontologically *hostile,* the "religious" aspect of this situation reveals the world as ontologically *restrictive.*

The phenomenological situation of the Five Percenters, then, can be viewed from at least two aspects. First, it can be viewed in terms of the *ontological hostility* of an antiblack racist world; second, it can be viewed in terms of the *ontological restriction* of religion defined as submission to an external deity. Yet, I noted above that a phenomenological situation is not ascertained through the mere aggregation of its aspects. Rather, these aspects point to a deeper phenomenon, which is the more fundamental experiential structure of the phenomenological situation. With regard to the NGE's phenomenological situation, the racial and "religious" aspects point to the more fundamental experiential structure of *ontological concealment.* The NGE situation is characterized by an initial inability to perceive who and what one is in one's very *nature.* Racially, this concealment manifests itself through repeated attempts to render one inferior on the basis of one's race; there are attempts to make a person out to be something that they are not. "Religiously," concealment manifests itself through restrictive codes of conduct and modes of submission that hinder one's ability to autonomously determine one's own destiny; submission to these codes would be a truncation of the Black man's being, and a woman's resistance to the codes set by her God would be a truncation of her being. "Coming into knowledge of self," that is, realizing one's true ontological nature is the NGE response to this ontological concealment.

Ontological concealment is given in the phenomenological situation of the Five Percenters, and they have responded in large part with epistemology. However, because the situation of concealment *and* the NGE's response are *ontological* in their orientation, the 120 point back to the *being* of the NGE's members. It is thus more useful to think of the NGE phrase "knowledge of self" as one word: knowledge-of-self. The 120 cannot be divorced from the ontological shift for which they are the catalyst. Coming into knowledge-of-self is a response to the phenomenological situation of ontological concealment.

The nature of a phenomenological situation is that it leaps ahead of us, rarely revealing itself in its clarity. With regard to the situation of ontological concealment, it is important to note that *this phenomenological situation manifests itself only once one has already begun the process of coming into knowledge-of-self.* To put this more concretely in Five Percenter terms: the "85 percent" do not know they're being deceived, so it makes little to no sense for a member of the 85 percent to *want* to come into knowledge-of-self. This is why enlighteners are necessary; they first reveal to the potential God or Earth this phenomenological situation. Coming into knowledge-of-self first involves recognition of this ontological concealment, and then it involves clearing away this concealment (primarily with the 120) to perceive and then live into one's true nature. This "living-into-one's true-nature" has the character of what Heidegger called in his early work the "enactment" of experience—that is, the *disposition* one adopts in his or her practical engagement with the world. For example, I could phenomenologically analyze the experience of watching television in terms of *what* I'm experiencing (namely, the television), *how* I'm experiencing it (watching it), and my *enactment* of the "how"—namely the disposition I take ("television-watcher") that conditions my actions regarding this experience (turning the channel, setting the volume to an appropriate level, etc.).

Based on the NGE phrase "show and prove," I call the "living-into-one's-true-nature" of the Five Percenters the disposition of *demonstration*. *Demonstration* carries with it the connotation of both "showing" and "proving"; Merriam Webster's dictionary defines the term "demonstrate" as either "to show clearly" or "to prove or make clear through reasoning or evidence." (Merriam Webster Online Dictionary) This demonstrative disposition is not limited to any particular activity; rather, it indicates a perpetual readiness to express and articulate one's knowledge-of-self. From within this disposition, everything from food choices to a recording session in a studio are opportunities to express one's knowledge-of-self and share it with others.

This demonstrative disposition is the phenomenological condition for the possibility of Five Percenter esotericism.

The demonstrative disposition of the Five Percenters stresses the inseparability of epistemology and ontology in their way of life. Showing and proving is situated within the nexus between Five Percenter knowledge and Five Percenter *being*; to show and prove often means displaying one's stock of knowledge, but it is always done with from within the context of one's self-understanding about who and what he or she is. Knowledge and being are intertwined with one another in large part due to the phenomenological situation of ontological concealment to which the Five Percenters respond.

Furthermore, because of the demonstrative disposition of the Five Percenters, they are able to constantly show and prove who they are *through* the development of new knowledge. In fact, each new day provides a space to show and prove: Five Percenters will often ask each other "What's today's Mathematics?" In response to this question, a Five Percenter will use the Supreme Mathematics to "science out" the meaning of today's date, discovering a deeper meaning for the day, and ultimately showing and proving who he or she is. The cipher of Five Percenter knowledge is perpetually growing and changing, and it grows because of this intertwined relationship between their epistemological structure and their ontological claims.

Conclusion

To be clear, although my claim is that these aspects are inseparable in the Five Percenter way of life, it nevertheless is possible to isolate either ontology or epistemology in this group on an analytical level. I did this in Section 2, hoping to show that while this approach to the esotericism of the Five Percenters is quite useful, it makes it possible to ignore or at least downplay the ontological foundations of the NGE way of life. The works of Western Esotericism scholars such as Faivre, Hanegraaff and others do not preclude the kind of conclusions I have drawn in this chapter regarding this epistemological-ontological relationship; however, they do make it possible to primarily focus on epistemological concerns while not attending to some of the complexities present in esoteric groups like the NGE. My phenomenological approach here situates the epistemological foundations of Five Percenter esotericism within an existential-phenomenological context wherein a group of African American men and women struggle against certain constraints and push for what theologian Anthony Pinn has called the "quest for complex subjectivity," or deeper life meaning premised upon producing a self-understanding that resists certain ontological restrictions and constraints (Pinn 2003). Such an analysis can be—and certainly is—attentive to the context out of which particular forms of gnostic knowledge emerge as well as the interconnectedness of these epistemological frameworks with the existential issues and constraints that often prompt the emergence and development of such groups.

A phenomenological analysis—such as the one I put forth here—provides an opening for asking more questions concerning the nature of NGE life, and possibly Africana and Western esotericism more generally. For example, how does the study of NGE esotericism as an epistemological-ontological orientation affect the broader study of African American religion (especially given the fact that the NGE denies being a religion)? Is this epistemological-ontological foundation present in other Africana esoteric groups? Does attention to the existential-phenomenological situation of esoteric groups in both the Africana context and the West more generally provide new insights for the study of esotericism? Such questions are outside the scope of this essay, but it is my hope that the analysis and method I employed in this chapter will open up new ways to respond to these questions.

To this end, the NGE—like many other esoteric groups in the West—is a dynamic and complex current of Africana esotericism. The esotericism of the Five Percenters stretches us beyond our conceptual boundaries, and pushes us to think about the nature of esotericism as a complex human response to existential exigencies. And, given the diversity and complexity of the Africana esoteric context, I suspect that they are not alone.

Appendix 1: The Supreme Mathematics and the Supreme Alphabet

Supreme Mathematics

1 = Knowledge

2 = Wisdom

3 =Understanding

4 = Culture, Freedom

5 = Power, Refinement

6 = Equality

7 = God

8 = Build-Destroy

9 = Born

0 = Cipher

Supreme Mathematics

A = Allah	B = Be or Born
C = Cee	D = Divine
E = Equality	F = Father
G = God	H = He or Her
I = I or Islam	J = Justice
K = King or Kingdom	L = Love, Hell or Right
M = Master	N = Now, Nation, or End
O = Cipher	P = Power
Q = Queen	R = Ruler
S = Self or Savior	T = Truth or Square
U = You or Universe	V = Victory
W = Wise or Wisdom	X = Unknown
Y = Why	Z = Zig-Zag-Zig (Miyakawa, 2005)

Appendix 2: The Actual Facts and The Solar Facts

Actual Facts

1. The total area of the land and water of the planet Earth is 196,940,000 square miles.

2. The circumference of the planet Earth is 24,896 miles.

3. The diameter of the Earth is 7,926 miles.

4.   The area of the Land is 57,255,000 square miles

5.   The area of the Water is 139,685,000 square miles.

6.   The Pacific Ocean covers 68, 634,000 square miles.

7.   The Atlantic Ocean covers 41, 321,000 square miles.

8.   The Indian Ocean covers 29,430,000 square miles.

9.   The Lakes and Rivers cover 1,000,000 square miles.

10. The Hills and Mountains cover 14,000,000 square miles.

11. The Islands are 1,910,000 square miles.

12. The Deserts are 4,861,000 square miles.

13. Mount Everest is 29,141 feet high.

14. The Producing Land (fertile earth) is 29,000,000 square miles.

15. The Earth weighs six sextillion tons (a unit followed by 21 ciphers [that is, zeroes])

16. The Earth is 93,000,000 miles from the Sun.

17. The Earth travels at the rate of 1,037 1/3 miles per hour.

18. Light travels at the rate of 186,000 miles per second.

19. Sound travels at the rate of 1,120 feet per second.

20. The diameter of the Sun is 853,000 miles (Miyakawa 2003, 229, 239–240).

Solar Facts

Mercury is 36,000,000 miles from the Sun.

Venus is 67,000,000 miles from the Sun.

Earth is 93,000,000 miles from the Sun.

Mars is 142,000,000 miles from the Sun.

Jupiter is 483,000,000 miles from the Sun.

Saturn is 886,000,000 miles from the Sun.

Uranus is 1,783,000,000 miles from the Sun.

Neptune is 2,793,000,000 miles from the Sun.

Pluto (Platoon) is 3,680,000,000 miles from the Sun (Miyakawa 2005, 27).

CHAPTER 12

The "Nu" Nation

An Analysis of Malachi Z. York's Nuwaubians

Paul Easterling

Alien can blend
Right on in
With your kin.
Look again
'cuz I swear I spot one every now and then.[1]
ANDRE 3000

Introduction

During the late 1960s, amidst the social and political turmoil in the United States, various religious groups sparked new understandings of what it meant to be human in the world. Particular groups focused on particular factions or demographics of the world population. One such group is the Nuwaubian Nation founded by Malachi Z. York (born Dwight York) in 1967. This movement was started in Brooklyn, New York, but moved its headquarters to Georgia in the 1990s. It centered on themes of the Christian New Thought religion, Islam, Ancient Egyptian based belief systems, and Ufology. Further, the Nuwaubians' belief system is centered on the understanding that they are an ancient people who are not originally from planet earth.

The purpose of this chapter will be to unlock some of the mysteries of the Nuwaubian belief system. The focus will be on York's teachings and writings which have centered on establishing a different identity for African Americans in the United States. York has a deep reservoir of texts, which have become popular amongst African American urban youth. York's group is similar to other African American religious groups, such as the Moorish Science Temple of America, the Nation of Islam, the Nation of Gods and Earths and the Hebrew Israelites, however, the Nuwaubian Nation has its own unique understandings of what it means to be of African descent in a world dominated by white supremacy.

---

1 Outkast. *Aquemini.* (Aquemini: 1998).

Guiding Method

The primary method of this work will be qualitative in nature. It will make use of primary writings, video and audio recordings of Malachi Z. York. This chapter also employs the secondary information of his proponents and opponents. The reason for this is because of the large amount of attention he and his group received from media personalities, newspaper reporters and writers. It is hard to determine why the group has received the attention it has, because despite the charges York was convicted of, it has not all been negative. Nevertheless, due to this attention and York's expansive publications there is wealth of material from which to pull.

In this investigation, I will focus on York's writings/lectures/talks that center on the history and origin of the Nuwaubian Nation as well as their understanding of the very shaping of their belief system. Who is York to the Nuwaubian Nation? Who are they in the world/universe? Who are they to themselves? Who are they to the world? These are the questions that make-up the basis for this chapter. Answers to these questions are meant to shed light on some of the more "obscure" religious traditions like the Nuwaubian Nation.

Situating the Nation: Ancestry and Organizational Violations

African American religion has taken on an innumerable type of expressions since the first African touched the shores of this nation. A great number of these expressions have looked to the past for both inspiration and information to shape the mind, body and spirit of their belief system. For instance, there are still many African Americans who practice African Traditional Religions (ATR) such as Yoruba and Vodun. As well, many African Americans have put their faith in belief systems which are an amalgam of ATRs and "New World" religions such as Christianity. Santeria is one such example, as it combines the texture and tone of an ATR while making use of the motif and characteristics of Catholic saints. And still other traditions, redefine the parameters of "New World" religions as well as create new understandings of the past (both a historical and mythological past) in order to redefine their present and (re)shape their future.

Over the past century, there has been a different type of redefinition of self that has taken place within various traditions of African American religion. These traditions have adopted the motif of the three "great" monotheistic religions while also making use of a theorized African past in an attempt to provide answers and insight into the triumphs and tribulations of Black people throughout the world. Examples of these traditions can be witnessed in the Hebrew Israelite, African American Islamic groups,[2] and Black Christian Nationalist traditions.[3] The Nuwaubian movement can be situated in the midst of these traditions (but not concretely in any) because they seem to combine information from all of them to make up their own unique belief system. For example, York has writings on a great myriad of religious topics including, Jesus Christ (Who Was Jesus Father' n.d.), the Anti-Christ (Be Prepared for the Anti-Christ n.d.), the Moors, the Koran, W.D. Fard, the Egyptian Book of the Dead, Freemasonry, Elijah Muhammad, and UFOs.[4] All of these books are organized as a series of book and/or scrolls meant to serve as teaching tools for his congregation.

Human ancestry is a very important issue for the Nuwaubian Nation. For them, a person or a people's ancestry speaks to their divine or evil nature as a human (or hybrid human)[5] on planet Earth. When discussing the origin of Caucasian people York states: "The Celtics Race is all Caucasians no matter whether these days they live under religious names such as Jewish, Christians, Muslims, Satanists, Wicca, Druids, or Frats, Knights of Columbus, Alhambra, Masonic, Shriners, Rosicrucians, Odd Fellows, Sufi Orders, Knights Templar, Kabbalists and so many others they use to shield their evil 6-Ether practices" (Actual Fact #5: The Celtics n.d., 1).

The Nuwaubians believe that the ancestry of the human race is an integral subject, particularly because the matter receives a lot of attention in the Bible. For them the story of Ham was not a story about Black people or people with pigmented skin tone but a story of people without melanin. According to them,

---

2   In this particular essay I am defining the African American Islamic tradition as the groups within the historical trajectory beginning with the Moorish Science Temple of America then continuing with its off-shoot movement after the death of Noble Drew Ali, including the Nation of Islam, Nation of Gods and Earth...This is different from the African American al-Islamic tradition which would include African Americans Sufis, Sunnis and Shi'a.

3   Black Christian traditions in this instance will included the Shrine of the Black Madonna, Sweet Daddy Grace, the Spiritualist Traditions, Father Devine...

4   See the following works: *Man From Planet Rizq.* (Eatonton, Georgia: The Holy Tabernacle Ministries). *Science of Creation.* (Eatonton, Georgia: The Holy Tabernacle Ministries). *Mission Earth.* (Eatonton, Georgia: The Holy Tabernacle Ministries). *Who Lived Before The Adam and Eve Story.* (Eatonton, Georgia: The Holy Tabernacle Ministries). *Shamballah And Aghaarta.* (Eatonton, Georgia: The Holy Tabernacle Ministries). *Cities Within The Earth.* (Eatonton, Georgia: The Holy Tabernacle Ministries). *Are there (UFO's) Extraterrestrials In Your Midst?* (Eatonton, Georgia: The Holy Tabernacle Ministries).

5   The Nuwaubians believe some human beings have a mixed ancestry with extraterrestrial beings who are not originally from this planet.

the union of Ham and Haliyma resulted in the birth of a child named Canaan, who bored the sign of God's curse, his skin color. Canaan was not dark as the other sons from the progeny of Noah; he was very light skinned, translucent as described by York, which was evidence that he had been struck with leprosy. Another term used to describe white skinned humans for the Nuwaubians is albino, which they define as a skin disease that is symptomatic of leprosy.

For the Nuwaubian Nation, then, the ancestry of the White race begins with Canaan. According to their belief system, Canaan could not stay with his family because his skin color set him apart and caused him to be shunned and ridiculed. Furthermore, Canaan, whose skin and eyes could not stand direct sunlight for an extended period of time, had to flee from his home to find an environment more suitable for his condition. Canaan eventually settled in the Caucasus Mountains of Western Asia where the cooler temperatures and low sunlight would allow him and his progeny to live in relative comfort. According to York, this is the origin of the term "Caucasian." Canaan was a person of Asiatic (Asian) descent who settled in the Caucasus Mountains; therefore he was a Caucus-Asian or Caucasian. York explains: "Canaan had to leave from living amongst his family because he was scabby and white and everyone else was dark brown and smooth, people shunned and persecuted him, so he fled to the Caucasus Mountains (Caucasians or Caucus-Asians means 'deteriorating Asians')" (Actual Fact #5: The Celtics n.d., 14). Leprosy is not the only disease that has resulted from the curse God put on Canaan. Other disorders or disease include: "psoriasis, gonorrhea, syphilis, arthritis, rheumatism, seborrhea, dermatitis (dandruff), eczema, ringworms, chicken pox, impetigo, nasal disorders, bone disorders, etc., and more recently AIDS, herpes, and lyme disease" (Actual Fact #5: The Celtics n.d., 14).

It is interesting that the white race are the descendants of Canaan, son of Ham because the Moorish Science Temple of American (MSTA) was at one time named the Holy Canaanite Temple (Gomez 2005, 206). It is interesting because the Nuwaubians hold the Moors and the MSTA in high esteem. Granted, the Holy Canaanite Temple was one of the MSTA's original names, however, according to Peter Wilson in the text *Sacred Drift: Essays on the Margins of Islam*, the Moorish focus on the nations of Moab and Canaan was a bold statement, which spoke against the assumed benevolence of Israel (Wilson 1993, 17–18). These are diametrical viewpoints of the purpose and state of the Canaanite nation. On the one hand, it is evidence of the curse that God put on white people, while on the other hand this nation (Elihu Pleasant-Bey 2004, 50–51) is one of the sovereign nations of the lineage of Hagar.

Unlike their understanding of the Canaanite nation, the Nuwaubian and Moorish nations hold Egypt in high esteem. "We are descendants of the pure

Egyptian here in the West and will build the Golden City Waianae in the West"
(Actual Fact #5: The Celtics n.d., 22). This perspective is very similar to the
Moorish claim of Egyptian heritage. In their view, Egypt or Kamet is a product
of Moorish science and cultural ingenuity. For the Nuwaubians, Egypt is the
place where human culture intertwined with ancient esoteric and extraterres-
trial knowledge. As a matter of fact this lineage is discussed on one of York's
writings entitled *Actual Fact # 5: Celtics*. York argues that the pure Islam of
Muhammad was given to his family that was "Negroid" or of African descent.
From this lineage came the "Sunni and Shi'ite sects from the Ahmadiyya sect in
India, the Moorish-American in American then to the Nation of Islam in
American to a sub-group called 5%ers" (Actual Fact #5: The Celtics n.d., 22).
These groups are in the same Holy lineage as the Nuwaubians and each of the
groups takes "on their own brand of teaching but rooted back to the same force
of belief, the same use of name Allah" (Actual Fact #5: The Celtics n.d., 22).

Despite the incongruence with how the lineage of Canaan is perceived, the
Nuwaubians argue that this lineage is a reptilian in nature. This reptilian lineage is described literally as a group of humanoid beings that are descendents
of extraterrestrials. These extraterrestrials are reptile instead of mammal and
come from the Orion constellation. York states, "There are many kinds of estra-
terrestrials in your midst. They live in the waters of the oceans and on the surface of the earth and inside the earth. One type you should be aware of is the
reptilian that humans should feel threatened by. They have been breeding with
you and living amongst you for centuries. They are humanoid in shape and
reptilian in heritage" (Are there UFO's Extraterrestrials in Your Midst n.d., 58).
According to the Nuwaubian belief system, this group of humanoids have been
living amongst human beings for thousands of years and have blended into
the normal populations so well that the only way to differentiate them from
Earth-born humans is to closely examine both their family lineage and their
medical history.[6]

The interest of this issue of lineage is significant to York and the Nuwaubians
because it reveals a pattern of associations that have been problematic for
humans on this planet. To put it another way, for the Nuwaubians, the reptilian
or extraterrestrial phenomena has been an issue which has caused serious
conflict on the planet before. For instance, York theorized about the significance of the space program in the 20th century not of the United States but of
Germany. According to York, the Nazi government was connected and in
cahoots with extraterrestrial forces who wanted to subdue and control the

---

6 Investigation into a human's medical history will reveal if there is a pattern of diseases that
   are symptomatic to crossbreeding with the reptilian species.

human race. York states, "The designs for the flying discs began in 1941 A.D. During the years 1945–47 A.D. three German experts Shriver, Habermohl and Meithe and and Italian A. Bellonzo were involved in researching and developing a saucer-shaped craft" (Are there UFO's Extraterrestrials in Your Midst n.d., 21). York also argues that Adolf Hitler had personal contact with an extraterrestrial being who helped him develop technology and science that would give the Nazi army a technological and strategic advantage over the rest of the world. He argues, "Hitler was in contact with 2 witches who were also psychics named Maria Austish and Zigrum who were contacted by beings from Aldebaran, who chose Hitler as their Man on Earth" (Are there UFO's Extraterrestrials in Your Midst n.d., 22).

The efforts of Hitler and his extraterrestrial contact clearly did not fully succeed, but this is an issue that affected Germany as well as the United States. To this point York states, "In 1952 crafts were logged as being seen over the White House in Washington D.C. There was a meeting held and Ashtar Command[7] me with the late President Dwight David Eisenhower, (34th), at which time American was asked 'to lay down their arms' just as the last president Harry S. Truman had done" (Are there UFO's Extraterrestrials in Your Midst n.d., 22–23). For York, the space program of the United States is an extension of the encounter of extraterrestrials and the United States government. Further, these encounters have been allegorized in American popular media through movies (i.e., *Star Wars*), TV show (i.e., *Star Trek*) and books (i.e., *War of the Worlds*).

In addition to ancestry, the Nuwaubians' belief system contains within it a code of ethics, which is to be followed by believers. This series of violations as they are called outline the manner in which members are to understand the dynamics of the Nuwaubian belief system. Prayer (who to pray to) and worship (to ensure guidance and protection) are the overall crux of the nine violations York discusses in his text. Each of the violations is numbered according to their order in Arabic. The first is called "El Way" and states: "Praying and asking help for wealth, or offering them blood, animal or human sacrifices are all form of what Muslims, Christians and Jews do, and then call other pagans for doing it" (El Maura n.d., 101). For the Nuwaubians, one of the major problems with religions in the world is that they call (or have a history of calling) for a blood sacrifice to be made on the behalf of their respective deity. This is problematic

---

7 According to York Attar Command is a group of entities or extraterrestrials from the Pleiades and the Aldebaran Constellations. Further, they "are among entities that come to Earth and have been circling above the Earth for the most part invisible to the naked eye since the early 1950s A.D. They both were humanoid and have less water in their bodies and are 'pasty' in appearance."

because there is no need for human or animal blood to be spilled for God. This is a violation against human life itself. York deals with this issue in more detail when he relates some of the religious rituals to the appetites of the Gods. He states, that in the Old Testament of the Bible "entities who were portrayed as 'Gods' were in fact extraterrestrials. Some of the 'Gods' asked for sacrifices of a human nature." In regard to the New Testament, the Nuwaubians' understanding of ancient Judeo-Christian rituals such as Eucharist are a:

> reflection of earlier rituals where extraterrestrials were eating off the bodies of humans or feeding off their energies. The phrases 'food for the Gods' takes on a new meaning when these factors are overstood. The true 'nectar of the Gods' which the extraterrestrials involved seem to prize most is a substance that is taken from freshly killed humans. The substance which is generated is taken at the moment of death and is the strong surge of adrenaline. This surge of adrenaline through the body accumulates at the base of the brain (the brain stem) and some extraterrestrials thrive on this substance as though it were some kind of ultimate drug for their particular species. This substance is most potent in human children.
>
> Are there UFO's Extraterrestrials in Your Midst n.d., 40–41

For the Nuwaubians, the crucifixion of Jesus is another example of human sacrifice, because his (Jesus) blood had to be spill for the sake of humanity. In other words, it was a ritual to appease the "Gods." Furthermore, these so-called "Gods" are not deities at all, but merely beings posing as supernatural entities in order to control and manipulate humans.

This issue leads to the second violation, called "El Tanah," which states the "setting and worshipping spook Gods intermediaries between oneself and Anu, unseen, unheard, unfelt, making supplications to them, asking them intercession with Anu, and placing one's trust in them is spookism, unconfirmed is wrong" (El Maura n.d., 101). Not only are humans not to pray to or worship beings that may be extraterrestrial, but also they are not to believe in Gods or intermediaries of God that cannot be seen, felt, or heard. Such an act for the Nuwaubians is idol worship and will only lead humans away from the truth of their existence. For them the deity Anu is the only one to be worshipped although it is not clear what this being looks like or where, or even how he/she appears. This is a pattern with certain religions that take issue with an unseen God but themselves cannot produce evidence of their God (Actual Fact #21 n.d., 35). For instance, the Nation of Islam also speaks against spookism, yet they believe that Fard Muhammad is Allah who came to the Earth as a human to lead his people. The problem with this is the great amount of mystery surrounding Muhammad. Meaning it is not clear, if this person ever existed, as the evidence of his existence is quite circumstantial, however, the NOI believe he is God incarnate. This reads as a type of spookism, yet the NOI speak against believing in unseen Gods. The same goes for Anu, there is no evidence of this being's existence, yet the Nuwaubians assert that Anu is the all powerful deity of ancient Egypt, who is meant to be worshipped.

The third violation, El Talah states, "anyone who point the finger at others, saying they are liars, or they are wrong for what they believe are themselves not to be trusted, unless they can prove their accusations" (El Maura n.d., 101). This is a curious violation because throughout York's writings it seems as if he is saying certain religions are wrong for what they believe in; however, the evidence he provides of the incorrectness of their belief is circumstantial. For instance, according to the information concerning human sacrifice, there is no concrete evidence that human sacrifice is a key part of Judeo-Christian belief. It is something that can be proven through interpretation but this is a matter of perspective rather than hard evidence or fact.

"El Raba" or the fourth violation deals with "anyone who believes any guidance other than the Anunnaqi's guidance to be more perfect, or a decision other than the Anunnaqi's decision to be better, is entitled to their belief" (El Maura n.d., 102). The Anunnaqi are also a group of extraterrestrials but this group unlike the reptilian race came to the planet to help human being evolve and progress. York states, "the RIZQIYIAN, ANUNNAQI came to the planet Earth and set up the Nubian culture or what you call the Egyptian culture" (Are there UFO's Extraterrestrials in Your Midst n.d., 74). They are the group of extraterrestrials whose descendants are the Nuwaubians themselves. They are here to help humans fight evil extraterrestrial forces and help usher in a new heavenly state of being for the planet Earth.

To bring this back to the subject of spookism, it is a wonder how belief in the Anunnaqi does not violate the violation of spookism. These beings cannot be seen, felt or heard, so how would this not qualify as spookism? Again, this is a consistent problem for those who take issue with an unseen God or even visible entities posing as God. Nevertheless, York describes the Anunnaqi in detail: "The Anunnaqi are a supreme race of beings from Illyuwn. They are dark reddish brown in complexion with large slanted dark eyes...Their eyes are much larger than that of humans. The average Nubians are starting to be born looking like these Eloheem, Anunnaqi. They also have very 'kinky' or 'wooly' hair. These Annunaqi are the 'Gods' or 'Angels' that your Torah, New Testament and Koran refers to and these are the same deities of the Sumerian Doctrine" (El Maura n.d., 101).

The sixth and eighth violations are related to the fourth dealing with the guidance of the Annunaqi. They called the El Satan and El Tomah respectively and state: "Anyone who ridicules any aspect of the rites of the Annunaqi, becomes one not to be trusted"; and "anyone who believes that some people are permitted to deviate from The Law of Our Guides is not to be trusted" (El Maura n.d., 102–103). The crux of these violations is respecting the word and rites of the Annunaqi and to respect their guidance as the divine progenitors and protectors of human life.

These extraterrestrials, according to York, are benevolent as opposed to the malevolent reptilians and grays.[8] They phenotypically look of African descent, with dark skin and coiled hair. More importantly these beings are the Gods that have been reference in Biblical, Judaic and Quran scriptures. When anyone of the scriptures claimed to have conversed or had interaction with an Angel they were more that likely dealing with the Annunaqi. Moreover, the beings that people of African descent are descended from whereas white people are descended from the malevolent reptilians.

For the fifth violation, the importance of the "Holy Tablets" of the Nuwaubians is the primary concern. In the "El Khasah" (the fifth) it states: "Anyone hates any part of what the Most High has given us from the holy tablets declared to be lawful has nullified his way of life, Nuwaubian, even though he may act in accordance with it" (El Maura n.d., 102). The tablets according to the Nuwaubians are the divinely inspired writings that have been sent by the Most High to correct what was not clearly demonstrated in the Judeo-Christian-Islamic writings.

For the Nuwaubians, the Holy Tablets were designed specifically for them. The Holy Tablets' website states: "The Koran Has not changed the World, nor Has the Torah or the New Testament. They have Done Nothing for us the Nubians but were Used to Enslave Us, So the Most High and His Heavenly Hosts Have Decided that It Was Time to Renew the Nubian History. It is Time for the Nubians to have their Own Scripture for their Spiritual Upliftment and Guidance" (The Holy Tablets n.d.). Furthermore, there is a certain way the tablets are to be read. For instance, it is suggested that readers of the tablets should not eat or do anything that may hinder one's "overstanding" while reading the scriptures.[9] Also, the tablets should be read with a clear mind and heart.

---

8   The grays according to York are a group of hybrid extraterrestrials that humans are most familiar with. They have small bodies, large head and large black eyes. Furthermore, this group is said to have been engineered by the reptilian as a slave race that can do their bidding on earth.

9   "Overstanding" is a word that is used in juxtaposition to the word "understanding" as a way to signify the Nuwaubians have a better grasp the divine and worldly knowledge.

For example, York demands that the readers of the holy tablets "do Not Read the Holy Tablets while Angry, for the Information that is Within the Confines of its Pages are Given to You in Order to Break this Evil Hypnotic Spell of Spiritual Ignorance and Racial Blindness!!!" (The Holy Tablets n.d.). For them, in order to break the spell of hatred and ignorance every person must come to the information with a pure and loving heart. The holy tablets are to be read daily (if possible) and with family so that understanding can be acquired collectively (The Holy Tablets n.d.).

The seventh violation of the Nuwaubians, called "El Sabah" deals with one of the more problematic aspects of world religion in that it has a tendency to produce conflict between diverging belief systems. The violation states: "Supporting and aiding people who are causing religious wars, and hate between those of different beliefs or racist, is an evil act" (El Maura n.d., 103). It seems that for the Nuwaubians inter-religious conflict is extremely problematic and can only lead to bloodshed. This violation is interesting because the logical conclusion to the belief that people of African descent are descended from benevolent extraterrestrials while white people are descended from malevolent ones who are instigators of conflict.

The last violation, El Tasha has to do with bearing false witness with or against Nuwaubians. It states, it is a violation "to turn completely away from the rites of Anu and call yourself a Nuwaubian or, neither learning its precepts nor acting upon it" (El Maura n.d., 103). One cannot rightly call themselves a Nuwaubian if they do not take the beliefs of the Nuwaubians seriously. Furthermore, since the Anu or Annunuqi are the divine harbingers of the Nuwaubians, their words must be observed as law.

Conclusion

This chapter represents an attempt to present some of the core elements characterizing the belief system of the Nuwaubian nation. There is much more to be said about the Nuwaubians. As mentioned, the amount of primary and secondary information presented in this chapter will allow researchers to conduct scholarly conversations about this religious group. Specifically, Nuwaubians have been underappreciated in religious studies in general and African American religious studies in particular. Ethnographic studies provide essential information about this group. Such a methodological approach, will afford a more intimate view of the group's innerworkings.

Appendix: Nuwaubian Facts

Introduction to All: 9 Reasons to be Nuwaubian Not Them (Actual Facts Series n.d., i–ix)[10]

1. "The Invitability of Fact: Everyone seeks facts, truth, confirmation. No one can really endure on blind faith or hopes. The stress and cares of life without facts about something, like not knowing the exact phone number of an important call; or the address of a place you must be at, at a certain time. To not have facts, to feel pain fear, danger, but not know why or where to go to have it aken care of; that's blind faith, not a life to death that cannot ultimately be proven."

2. "The use and mis-use of Sciences: There are not limitations in finding facts when you compare religion to the Scientific method of 'prove it'. The process defined by that which is measurable and repeatable. It speaks to issues and their ultimate origin as well as people, places, and things."

3. "The Problems of Creation vs. Evolution: The first fact is you yourself, your parents, their parents and so on. You reading this, confirms your existence. Next step back is where did you come from, your parents, who came from theirs? That is how it's done with plants, animals, humans and the universe. Nothing new even if a test tube is used it still has the same root seeds for reproduction."

4. "The Devil and Evil: Who has the most to profit from a Good God created us and all things more than a Devil or Devils? It gives him a purpose. It brings him into existence as well. For why would you need a Good if there was no Evil?"

5. "The Bible, Quraan and God Story: On first reading the opening words of the Old Testament in Hebrew as Tanakh 'Torah' or English which birthed the New Testament many other Agnostic text of Nag Hammadi, scrolls found in Egypt in 1945 A.D. and the Qumran Scrolls called Dead Sea Scrolls found outside of Jerusalem in 1947 A.D. which birthed the Quraan of the Muslim's Islamic religious in 610–632 A.D. in Arabia and their religions for each base their belief in a Divine on this first book of Genesis in what they call the Bible."

6. "The name of a religion or God doesn't make it real: People who claim names today like Jews, Christians, Muslims or Judaism, Christianity and Islam and their many sub-divisions, sects and denominations. The fact that there are millions who believe the fictions of their Holy Books, the fictions of the beings of people in their own stories, the fact that there is a place called a Jerusalem or The Vatican in Rome or Mecca in Arabia, none of the above mentions or confirms the facts needed. It's only beliefs and are not argument of their God's existence. A God

---

10   The contents of this appendix are drawn from this source.

each claims is partial to their rituals and them as the chosen ones and that their God would not protect other children of the world unless they all convert to their races, religious beliefs."

7.   "The Personification of God, Angels, Spirits: Many religions claim to worship their God in Spirit or as an unseen Spirit that God is not a Human being. That Angels have wings and are also Holy Ghost or Spirits yet human being; because we as human being know we have all kinds of weaknesses and needs from outside sources. We need to clean ourselves inside as well as outside. We start off as babies weak and dependent. And as we age, we loose our sight, our hearing and receive all other kinds of sickness as we need to eat, we need to drink water, and we have other needs we go crazy or lose our minds."

8.   "The evidence of greatness and miracles: All you have to do is look at Africa and Africans, the Great empires we built. Look at Timbuktu in Mali, look at Egypt, Sudan and South Africa, look at our records, our arts, the first to write a script, and the first doctors in the Holy books."

9.   "The God who doesn't know and lies: In their holy books their God asks questions like: 'Where art thou?' as Adam hides from him as he walked on Earth in the Garden...Then does this God have fears? Yes he said, 'Behold the man is become as one of us to know good and evil and now lest he put forth his hand and take also of the tree of life an eat and live forever'."

CHAPTER 13

Sacred Not Secret

Esoteric Knowledge in the United Nuwaubian Nation of Moors

Julius H. Bailey

Introduction

Few events have altered the study of new religions in America in the late twentieth century more than Jonestown (1978), the Branch Davidians at Waco
(1993), and Heaven's Gate (1997). The legacies of these tragic events frame the
reception and depiction of emergent religious communities, which popular
culture labels as "cults" and assigns all the stereotypical elements associated
with such groups: "brainwashing," a controlling charismatic leader, manipulation, recruiting practices that prey on the susceptible, and so on. Race, rarely
invoked regarding predominately white communities, features prominently in
the coverage of African American communities as exemplified by *Time* magazine's February 28, 1994 cover declaring Louis Farrakhan and the Nation of
Islam a "Ministry of Rage." With a few notable exceptions, scholarship has
done little to alter this perception, positing the quest for racial pride and identity as the central, and in some cases, and only motivating factor for members
of African American alternative religious communities. While race is an important consideration, by focusing almost exclusively on black nationalism to
explain the attraction to these movements, rather than the range of beliefs and
practices embraced by the communities, studies, perhaps unintentionally,
reaffirm the monolithic portrayals that they originally sought to nuance (Van
Deburg 1996; Essien-Udom 1995). This overemphasis on race masks the complex and myriad ways black new religious movements have sought to at once
preserve the sacredness of their esoteric knowledge and offer it as a solution to
contemporary issues facing African Americans.

Given this history, the writings of black new religious movements are often
met with skepticism by outsiders. Although asserting a claim to ancientness
like other "mainstream" eastern and western religions, emergent African
American communities face the dual challenges of racial and religious prejudice. By extension, their sacred narratives are almost compelled to account for
not only religious but also racial difference and explain a complex history that
includes slavery, segregation, and the oppression of a people based in many
ways on their physiogamy. More recent black traditions tend to situate
themselves within the context of those communities that came before them as

well as assert a distinctiveness about their own glorious, but previously hidden past that lends assurances of a brighter future still to come. This chapter, taking seriously the writings of the United Nuwaubian Nation of Moors (UNMM), provides an historical examination of their sacred texts such as the Holy Tablets and the context from which they emerged, as a window onto the creative process of signification, asserting authority, and maintaining the secrecy of esoteric knowledge within a crowded marketplace of black new religious movements that all make claims to a sacred, hidden, and glorious past that portends a brighter future for the African American race.

The UNNM has a diverse history spanning from the group's early time in New York in the 1960s when they primarily embraced an Islamic identity under the titles of the Ansaru Allah (Helpers of Allah) and Ansaru Pure Sufi. From the late 1960s, they incorporated elements of Judaism and Christianity under the names Nubian Islamic Hebrews, Ancient Holy Tabernacle of the Most High, the Children of Abraham, and the Mystic Order of Melchizedek. Prior to relocating to Eatonton, Georgia in 1993, the UNNM had interwoven Egyptian history and extraterrestrial concepts into their teachings. The Holy Tablets as revealed to Malachi Z. York emerged from and spoke to these varied and changing communal religious identities.

Like many new religious movements before him, York framed his vision as a "restoring" corrective to tradition and providing clarity about the original meaning of ancient texts rather than asserting a new teaching. He understood himself to be in a long line of Nuwaubian Moorish leaders including Noble Drew Ali, Clarence 13X, Marcus Garvey, and Elijah Muhammad. York proclaimed the Holy Tablets to be the message that would finally uplift the race and as the "scripture that is divinely inspired that will bring about a long overdue change." The Holy Tablets, originally inscribed in Cuneiform and forming the basis for the Torah, the New Testament, and the Koran, York asserted, was ultimately "by far the greatest of all, for it contains all they were trying to express but couldn't, because they didn't have the whole truth and all the facts." These other sacred texts, while important, now contained "outdated information" according to York. He proclaimed that the times called for "your history" to be "renewed by a renewer." York claimed an authority based on prior prophecies coming true. For York, the "condition of the Planet Earth" and divisions and fighting within Islam suggested that Muhammad was not the last prophet and therefore the Koran was not the last scripture. In fact, he asserted, not only has evil not been eradicated, but misinterpretations of the Koran has caused it to increase accompanied by more wars. "The Koran and the Bible has failed more than any of the other books ever written, in so far as they are misunderstood by those who claim to follow them to the letter," York maintained. Not all can hear the call for change, York taught, but only those with an "inner ear" that was capable of hearing the voice of the "Heavenly Father." (The Holy Tablets n.d. 126, 139, 144).

At the same time, York also heralded the distinctiveness of his current teachings, writing:

> But they all knew a savior was coming. Some thought it was Marcus Garvey who wanted to go back to Africa. Others thought Noble Drew Ali, others thought it was Elijah Muhammad or his teacher, W.F.D. Muhammad. Others thought it was Clarence 13X, even others thought it was Martin Luther King, some said it was Rap Brown or Stokely Carmichael from the 60s. Or Eldridge Cleaver or Bobby Seale, some thought it was Rob Karenna or Leroi Jones. Some think it's Wraith D. Fard, son of Elijah Muhammad; Others think it is Minister Louis Farrakhan or Yahweh ben Yahweh or Ben Ammi Carter. And even others think it is themselves and the list of saviors goes on...From the early 1900s all the way up to 1970 A.D. when something new started happening [sic]. A teaching unlike any other started spreading. While alluding to his place in this lineage of special leaders, York employed the familiar rhetorical strategy of avoiding self-identification as a "savior" and allowing the reader to come to that conclusion themselves.
>
> The Holy Tablets n.d. 1640–1641

Although there is no date on the Holy Tablets, York describes the 1960s with its political unrest, violence, the Civil Rights Movement, the Black Power Movement, and the formation of the Black Panthers as a key moment in the formulation of his ideas and spiritual history. Regarding this era he notes, "this made way for the first part of our liberation...what I have to give would liberate the mind of the Nubian Nation and the physical will follow." Yet, his worldview was never stagnant often transforming with the iterations of the communities of which he was a part. In the 1960s, leading Ansaru Allah, he understood himself as the al Hajj al Imam Isa Abdallah Muhammad al Mahdi and with the Nubian Islamic Hebrews in 1969, his title was Rabbonì Yeshua Bar el Haady. In the early 1980s, York self-identified as Christian referring to himself as the Lamb, then the Qutb ("Axis of the Universe") and just before migrating to Eatonton, Georgia, he was called by his Egyptian name, Neter A'aferti Atom Re (The Holy Tablets n.d. 1641). As Charles Long and Richard Brent Turner have observed, Islam and other religions have allowed African Americans to signify, name themselves, and define their own cultural identities in the face of Western colonization and stereotyping (Long 2004; Turner 1994).

Read in isolation, York's changing self-identification and absence of specific details about his spiritual history might be met with skepticism by outsiders and potential members of the community. However, placed within the lineage of other black esoteric narratives rather than raising concern, York's vague and mostly unknown past serves to legitimate and substantiate his status as a prophet. The mysterious background of the leader implicitly confirms the divine power and authority of one sent to speak on the behalf of an ancient tradition. The narrative of the Nation of Islam begins in the summer of 1930, when a mysterious peddler appeared in an impoverished area of Detroit called "Paradise Valley." While he sold clothing, silks, and other products, he also dispensed advice about physical and spiritual health. He described the "true religion of Black Men" and their real heritage dating back to Asia and Africa. Employing both the Quran and the Bible, he taught first in the homes of followers and later rented a building which he named the Temple of Islam. He called himself alternately, Wali Farrad, Farrad Mohammed, and W.D. Fard. Fard understood the power differential between whites and blacks in the early twentieth century as a temporary historical occurrence that would be rectified as African Americans gained "knowledge of self" and dethroned what he called the "blue-eyed devils." He wrote guidelines for the movement, *The Secret Ritual of the Nation of Islam*, which is passed down orally, and *Teaching for the Lost-Found Nation of Islam in a Mathematical Way* that is written in a special code that can only be interpreted by the most devoted members.

An early follower of Fard and one of his chief assistants was Elijah Poole who took the Muslim name Elijah Muhammad. The son of a Baptist minister and sharecropper in the rural town of Sandersville, Georgia, Poole moved with his family to Detroit in 1923. He and his brothers joined the Nation of Islam in 1931, and, though he only had a third-grade education, rose rapidly in the ranks of the organization. In 1934, Fard unexpectedly disappeared, which instituted a heated battle over the leadership of the community. Muhammad took the helm of one faction and relocated to Chicago in 1936, establishing Temple of Islam No. 2. In the 1940s, as the movement transitioned into an institution, Fard's status ascended from a profound teacher to "Allah," God incarnate, and Elijah Muhammad was viewed as his "messenger." Muhammad promoted economic independence and a rallying cry of "Do For Self," which scholars have characterized as "Black Puritanism" because of his emphasis on hard work, productivity, and a simple lifestyle. Under Muhammad's leadership, the Nation of Islam established over 100 temples across the United States, several grocery stores, restaurants, and other businesses. In addition, strict dietary codes forbid alcohol, drugs, pork, and unhealthy foods. All these codes were outlined in Muhammad's *How to Eat to Live* (1972). Muhammad's message resonated strongly with blacks in poor neighborhoods and prisons. In his *Message to the Black Man* (1965), Muhammad suggested that the African American psyche and self-confidence had been damaged by white racism resulting in a confused identity and self-hatred. Complete separation from whites through the formation of an independent black nation was the only remedy to restore the dignity of the black race and inaugurate the final Armageddon in which the "evil whites" would finally be banished and African Americans would assume their rightful place and rule with Allah (Jackson 2005; Clegg 1997).

In the early twentieth century, the Moorish Science Temple also emerged from a founder with an equally veiled narrative of his origins. Born in 1886 in North Carolina, Timothy Drew's parents were ex-slaves in lived in Cherokee territory. Like many leaders of black new religious movements, little is known of Drew's early life, but narratives have suggested that he ran away from home and while living among gypsies was told by God "If you go, I will follow." Although accounts vary, at the age of sixteen Drew became a sailor and eventually made his way to Egypt. By passing a mysterious "test" in the Pyramid of Cheops, Drew was given the name Noble Drew Ali and through divine inspiration he created the *Circle Seven Koran* and ascended to the status of prophet. In response to his divine call around 1913 to establish a religion "for the uplifting of fallen mankind" with a focus on the "lost-found nation of American blacks," Ali founded the Moorish Science Temple, initially referred to as the Canaanite Temple, in Newark, New Jersey.

One of the more controversial teachings of the Nation of Islam is "Yakub's History," which offers a distinctive account of the origins of the white race. According to the narrative, after the moon separated from the earth, God placed black people, "the Original Man" in Mecca. In the holy city, there were twenty-four brilliant scientists, but one of them one, "Mr. Yakub," created an "especially strong black tribe of Shaba" who are the ancestors of present-day African Americans. Between 4500 and 5000 BCE, Yacub, born with an abnormally large head as well as a superior intellect, fulfilled his destiny to wreak havoc on society. An effective orator, Yacub gathered so many converts that the established religious authorities banished him along with his 59, 000 followers to the island of Patmos, the location where John received the message that would become the Book of Revelation in the New Testament. Upset about being exiled, Yacub sought revenge against Allah by creating a "devil race—a bleached-out white race of people." Possessing scientific knowledge of recessive and dominate genes, Yacub set about breeding a progressively lighter complexioned and physically and mentally weak people. To facilitate the process, Yacub allowed only lighter skinned blacks to marry and reproduce, while those children that were deemed to be too dark were killed. According to the narrative, it took over six hundred years to proceed from black, brown, red, yellow, to finally arrive at a pure white race.

These "blond, pale-skinned, cold blue-eyed devils," according to Elijah Muhammad, were hairy "savages" that, like animals, walked on all fours, and lacked the ability to cover themselves with clothes. After six hundred years, this white race made their way from the island to the mainland and within six months of their arrival began to deceive black people and stir up intraracial tensions that turned an Edenic existence into conflict-roiled hell. Recognizing that the whites were the source of their problems, blacks captured them, placed them in chains, "generously" covered their nakedness, and led them across the Arabian Desert to the "caves of Europe." After two thousand years, God raised up Moses to lead this people. The first to respond to his message was the Jews. According to the narrative, it was God's will that white people would rise up and rule the world for six thousand years. Slavery was necessary then, to bring Africans to the New World to learn the "white devil's true nature" firsthand. It was prophesied that this white reign would continue until the chosen one, Fard, would come to the black race and instruct them about their true history and destiny. Because Fard was of African and European American descent, he was able to be both a member of the black race and move undetected among white people.

One might blanch that no reasonable person could possibly believe this farfetched narrative, yet it provides a striking reversal of the use of religious scripture to advance notions of black inferiority. Within many nineteenth-century white Christian circles, the Bible was widely interpreted to justify African enslavement. Genesis 9:20–27 chronicles an episode in which Noah, drunk from wine, lies nude within his tent. Ham, the father of Canaan, sees Noah naked and tells Shem and Japheth, who walk backward into the tent, placing a blanket on their father while averting their eyes. When Noah awoke and found out what happened he said, "Cursed be Canaan! The lowest of slaves will he be to his brothers...May God extend the territory of Japheth; may Japheth live in the tents of Shem, and may Canaan be his slave." Most contemporary biblical scholars contextualize the story within the tenth-century BCE Israelite enslavement of the "Canaanites." However, in the second century CE, the church fathers began to employ the passage to connect blackness with evil. Origen (185–254) wrote that by "quickly sink[ing] to slavery of the vices," Ham's "discolored posterity imitate the ignobility of the race" he fathered. Augustine (354–430) saw the origins of slavery in Ham's transgression, and Ambrose of Milan (339–397) wrote that Noah's chastisement only applied to the darker descendants of Ham. However, it was not until the fifteenth century and the Spanish and Portuguese enslavement of people of color that the narrative became cemented as a justification for racial slavery. Early abolitionist literature cited the "curse of Ham" as a central rationale for the Atlantic slave trade (Curtis 2002; Haynes 2007).

Ali shifted the ancestral lineage of blacks to an "Asiatic" and Moorish lineage. Black ancestry stemmed from Noah's son Ham and the Canaanites as well as the Moabites. Black Americans were not descended from slaves, Ali asserted, but from great Moorish empires that had reigned over Europe and Asia. Given this history, the "natural religion" for African Americans was Islam and not Christianity. Others had misunderstood the role of Jesus and granted him divine status; when in fact, Ali corrected, he was a prophet of Canaanite ancestry. "Only by means of a deliberate distortion of the racial background of Jesus was it possible for European (whites) to claim him as one of their own and establish him as the head of their church" (Berg 2005), Ali maintained.

Ali's narrative reconfigures and reinterprets American history beginning with the "Black Laws of Virginia" in 1682 which prohibited Muslims from being enslaved. However, George Washington and the other founders of America ignored these laws and enslaved Moors with the other "Negroes" in 1774. According to Ali, Washington removed the Moorish red banner that flew to hide this history which was eventually morphed over time into the story of his cutting down the cherry tree. As a result of this and choosing the white man's religion of Christianity, the true Moorish history and identity of African Americans had been hidden from them and they had accepted being slaves.

From this rich lineage of history making, challenging social contexts, and transformative identities emerged York's own writings and understandings about race. *What Race was Jesus?* And *The Paleman* reverses the curse of Ham to explain white, not black inferiority. "Noah predicted the physical manifestation of the pale race of Jinn after his son Ham looked at him with the thought of Sodomy. This curse was manifested through Ham's fourth son Canaan and mentally manifested through Jacob…Thus the Canaanites (meaning cave-dweller) were born and lived in caves for 600 years 'until Moses and Aaron were sent to civilize the lepers'" (The Paleman 256; Palmer 2010, 16). York traces the ancestry of whites to the Amorites, which is "mountain dwellers" in Hebrew. York describes the Canaanites fleeing to the mountains to alleviate the pain from their leprosy. As the sun grows hotter, York predicted, whites would seek refuge in underground caves inaugurating the rule of Nuwaubians on earth. York also reversed the curse of Cain. "Adam and Eve were sent to the Aegean Islands between Asia and Europe, where they started having children, and each couple's first born child was an Albino and those Albinos are called Cain in the Bible, 'Cain' being short for 'Caucasian.'" In *Spell of Leviathan 666: The Spell of King*, York describes Caucasians as the descendents of "riptides," fat people from Doers, "Mongoloids" who are the ancestors of the 48-chromo-somed Taros. The Nuwaubians, however, are the "children of beautiful angelic beings from the planet Rizq." Nubians originally had green skin as extraterres-trials that turned brown once the "Ether 9 beings" came to Earth. From this perspective, interracial marriage was disloyalty to one's race and alien ancestry (The Paleman, 256; Palmer 2010, 16).

As with other creation narratives emerging from black new religious move-ments such as the "Yacub" story of the Nation of Islam, York framed whiteness as equating to spiritual and physical weakness. The Holy Tablet states that, the:

> Meaning that the original beast, the beast like creatures, the ape like crea-tures eventually mixed with other people and brought forth an Albino race. Albinism, a curse which was given to Canaan and his descendants, is a sign of recessive or weak genes. The extreme of the physical manifes-tation in their characteristics are: blue eyes, yellow and white hair and pale complexion. We know that this curse is the Caucasian race...because the Nuwaubian man has olive tone skin, woolly hair, and dark eyes, which are genetically dominant traits...The Nuwaubian characteristics will dominate and the offspring will be recognizably Nuwaubian.
> The Holy Tablets n.d. 546–547

While white historical literature often cast blacks as envious of white culture and obsessed with white women, York framed those of European ancestry as most benefiting from interracial relationships. "The Albino is a carrier of many reces-sive traits..." "To you, many of these traits affect the person negatively. So there is nothing good to be inherited from a lack of melanin. If anyone could benefit from miscegenation, it is the Albino himself; In order to keep his dying seed alive, he had to mix with others." "And he needs some more Melanin for pigmentation to protect his weak skin from the sun" (The Holy Tablets n.d. 546–547).

Yet, unlike other emergent twentieth-century black alternative communi-ties, blackness was not the ultimate sign of the superior race, but rather York heralded the green reminisces of an ancient alien past. Drawing on the work of Clarence Jowars Smith also known as Clarence 13X, York quotes, "Remember, your olive tone parents of long ago...Remember our dark-reddish brown skin, copper tone perfected in green, as the greenest of olives because of the mela-nin that is within our genetics which we have coated in our genes." "The mela-nin that is throughout your body is the same thing that colors this planet Qi, now called Earth" (The Holy Tablets n.d. 149, 204).

Based on its predating western and eastern religious traditions, York asserted an authority for the Nuwaubian creation narrative. The creation story of the

Nuwaubians began "trillions of Earth years ago" with "supreme beings of pure green light, ethereal and sub-supreme beings of the impure, amber light, fire." Because of their ancient and extraterrestrial sacredness, full understanding of the Holy Tablets was not possible for humans. "You cannot fully comprehend their beginnings, because their time zone is much greater than your ability to comprehend at this point." The Holy Tablets bridges this gap to "open your eyes to their time zones, that are in and beyond space" (The Holy Tablets n.d., 1–6). There were three phases to the creation of life. Original or primary creation consisted of subatomic energy "registering as nothingness, yet existing, being lighter than the first form of existence hydrogen." Secondary or "evolutionary creation" entailed the "evolving of existence from density to matter to atoms to cells, to organisms, to bodies." Tertiary or "ghostational creation" consisted of the "breath of life, the living soul, the existing conscious being." The first people were the "Melanin-ites" or Nuwaubians the "original woolly-haired, dark skinned Muurs 'Moors'." Out of these original people came three species of "Mongoloids" and two species of "Caucasoid." "Nine ether," the combination of all existing gases in nature and therefore the most dominant energy and the "most potent power in all the boundless universes" was the original creator that formed the universes and "personified themselves as flesh and blood beings, they became human beings from Atoms to Adam." This ancestral lineage is recorded in the sacred texts of the Nuwaubians such as Nuwaubu which embodies "universal right knowledge," "right wisdom," and "right understanding" (The Holy Tablets n.d. 1–6).

The UNNM narrative also has a millennialist component. York prophesied that spiritual "supreme beings" called "Annunagi" or "Neteru" as known to the ancient Egyptians would descend to earth and guide humans "back towards their home, in and beyond the stars." In so doing, they would help them to "become once again, the supreme beings of the pure green light, ethereal energy that they once were." York was sent to "prepare a way" for that process to occur. This was necessary because once humans "became rulers over the planet Earth," "engrossed" in their "own desires," and "in pursuit of physical gratification and material gain," they "gradually forgot that your purpose in life was to gain your way back towards the Sustainer." York prophesized that in 2003 the alignment of the planets would indicate the return of the mother ship, Nibiru, "whose diameter is 63,408 miles" which could increase or decrease in size and would be "waiting on the other side of the asteroid belt" in the solar system. At the appointed time, "The Shams" or "passenger crafts" would come to earth for the "rebirth of the elite few, the 144,000." Being the older tradition, York suggested that Christians had co-opted this sacred number. "The Christians late took the concept of the 144,000 and the rapture, used it in their

Bible." As with William Miller of the Adventist tradition and Charles Taze Russell of the Jehovah's Witnesses, one declaration of a final prophetic date was followed by another. In the case of the UNNM, a contingency plan was also foretold (Miller 1995). "If we are blocked, we shall continue to try to abduct you...in June when the Earth positions itself, in the location of revolution of Earth year 2030 A.D." Yet, this plan of action also came with risks. "This would involve a telepathic message from Nibiru which could be dangerous to those children, who haven't raised themselves, to a certain level and would cause a shock to their nervous systems. Many would be cut off causing us to severe our etheric tie, although it may be a necessary step." The last opportunity for departure would be August 2043 when "this vortex will re-open and we must depart with or without you, so be prepared" (The Holy Tablets n.d. 1–3, 8, 151–152).

The Holy Tablets describe extraterrestrial beings that intervene in human history. These extraterrestrials interacted with human civilizations such as the Cushites which, according to York, included the Dogons of Mali in West Africa during the "evolutionary process." The Dogons "speak and teach what they have been taught by these two tribes of Extraterrestrials to this very day," York maintains. The narrative describes a complex and interwoven network of people groups that were often at odds with one another. One such group, the Anu, first came to earth 500,000 years ago and the Dragon People or Draconian and the Snake People "were already here living in the vast tunnels under Earth's/ Terra's crust, or some lived in the deep seas, to protect themselves from the frequent radiation storms, and magnetic shifts." To avert a war between the Draconians and the Rizqiyians, territorial boundaries were established and intermarrying between the groups was enforced. These ancient extraterrestrial ancestors such as the Anunnagi who used "crafts to bore tunnels to the inner world" have left markers of their existence and contribution to earth through their digging of the Tigris river and Euphrates to mine gold to save their planet. "The pyramids originally called 'mir' in ancient Tama-Ra, Egypt, in which the elders built, were the temples of initiation into the deeper sciences of mystics. The pyramids were built with lasers, a so called modern invention which existed thousands of years ago" (The Holy Tablets n.d. 91, 153, 159, 178, 1071–1076).

York connected varied historical figures to alien lineages. For example, he linked Adolph Hitler to an ancient extraterrestrial race known as the Pleidians. "These Aryan beings call themselves Pleidians, deceptive as they are. They, to this date, are influencing the minds of Humans. Their link on Earth, in latter time, was to the Third Reich, under a demon referred to as Adolph Hitler." "Hitler held the super race with great reverence and respect. These beings have light blonde hair and blue eyes. They were originally bred by gene transplants, a process called embryo implantation. The beings from Aldebaran gave Hitler a lot of technology and flying saucers, which Hitler took out to Antarctica, a continent lying chiefly within the Antarctic Circle and asymmetrically centered on the South Pole. They were responsible for the technology and plans for a superior race. Hitler was actually breeding a superior race for the Extraterrestrials" (The Holy Tablets n.d. 371–372). As with "Yakub's History," which explained the European American enslavement of African Americans for members of the Nation of Islam, so too did York provide an answer for the success of Hitler's Third Reich.

The Holy Tablets not only explained past historical events but also provided a warning about other potential future dangers particularly those presented by those with white skin and asserting a Jewish heritage.

> They, the blond haired, blue eyed, Nordic race claim that they are the descendants of the Pleiadeans, humanoids with reptilians living within them, who come claiming peace, yet they plan to rule…. "Be not deceived my children," York admonished, "for there is a massive deception going on, with the Zionist, who is trying to tie the extraterrestrial involvement with them, claiming to be the children of the light, our ancestors. Don't let these demons fool you into thinking that they are here to help you and guide you back to the right path. Remember, these are the same ones that betrayed our ancestors the woolly haired, dark skinned Rizqiyians. The Rizquiyians trusted the Pleiadeans only to be betrayed."
> The Holy Tablets n.d. 382, 384

Yet, York also had a special role to play in the enlightenment of the world. "Lo! Nuwaubians, one of the schools, which I, your Master Teacher, known as the Reformer, Al Mujaddid, Al Mukluks, Yaanuwn, Ramona, Al Imaam, and Melchizedek. I have many names for the many cloaks I wear." York saw the teachings of the Holy Tablets as essential to changing the self-identity and thinking of his followers. "I, your Master Teacher, who, you know as Nayya Malachi Zodoq York-El, have been sent to you to break the spell. I am about to Impart upon your mind, the mechanics of what you call the master organ, or simply 'the brain', which works with the mind." "And the hearts of the children to their fathers, or else, I, Nayya Malachi Zodoq York-El, will come and hit the planet Earth with an utter destruction. Elijah Muhammad was sent, and he did not do it. So I, Nayya Malachi Zodoq York-El, am here; and the whole planet Earth has been hit now" (The Holy Tablets n.d. 729, 731, 876).

Much of the Holy Tablets are York's teaching about how to correct one's thinking and actions to be in line with Nuwaubian. York writes, "I must take you through...the school of the ego. Know ye that, this is one of the hardest attribute to destroy." York provided warnings of punishment that would accompany wrongdoing. "You are exceptionally apt to get AIDS, if you let your emotions, be controlled by lust, or the luster, or the luster of it make you go out and buy, or being a sexual instrument to give you pleasure. Then you will be an AIDS victim..." "Acquired Immune Deficiency Syndrome, a new scientific term for a biological creation of A.I.D.S. It is the first of the 7 plagues. We will put all evil people and false teachers under our heels." York directed that to avoid these travails one must eradicate "the craving for sensory stimulation." Through the "Fasting of the Mind" thoughts would be "stilled and concentrated, it no longer presses one to seek further pleasures." Action was essential for transformation to occur, York advocated. "Lo! A change in character occurs only through formation of new habits. Control can be gained by non-attachment or by eliminating emotional reactions to situations and individuals." "But do not become intoxicated, for this is unhealthy for both the body, and the mind. Take in no intoxicating poisons, nor should you inhale intoxicating poisons, nor should you inhale intoxicating fumes, nor chew or inject any intoxicating substance into the shell, that houses the presence of Allah, that you manifest in flesh" (The Holy Tablets n.d. 731, 739–741, 761, 877, 1081).

Resonating with the teachings of the Moorish Science Temple and the Nation of Islam, York asserted that slavery had estranged African Americans from their true history and led to a poor racial self-image. "The Negro, mentally dead does not know what it means to accept an alien religion. For example, if a person accepts Hinduism or Muhammadism as his religion, He should know that he has accepted the east Indians or Indo-Arabs as his visible deities, in so far as, the images of authority, respect, and admiration is from a specific race. That's why they dress like them and want to look and be like them, which is other than your own self. Neither can he become equal with or have power over the East Indian, or Arabs. So he becomes their slave again..." He continues, "And you, as a race, are greatly in need of it. In order to think and do for yourselves..." "Some may wonder why I am still using the word 'Negro', when referring to mentally dead Nuwaubian people. It is because as long as you people have negative and slave minds, You are still Negroes no matter what other names you choose to call yourselves, And by calling themselves something other than Negro, Deceives you into believing that you are not Negroes any more. Therefore, I continue to call the mentally dead by the name Negro, For this emphasizes the fact that a person does not become something else just by changing his name, But instead by changing his mind." "The slave master taught the Nubian slaves that God put a curse of black skin and kinky hair upon you. Nuwaubu teaches you that it is purely false; Because Nubians had black or brown, skin and wholly-hair from the original creation; before this planet Earth; And black skin provides the best protection against exposure and disease, And wholly hair means that the sun genes, the genes of life, are much stronger in wholly-haired people, Than they are in straight-haired people. Hence, woolly hair is a sign of life and originality." "Lo! The slave mentality, and European influenced religions, be it Christianity, Judaism Or Islam, or whatever denomination or sect, should all be eliminated, and this elimination will lead to right thinking." "If a Negro, male and female, can read and study the tablet and still have the same old negative mind and same old negative spirit, that makes a person a black devil and keeps a person a Negro. That individual is incapable of being resurrected from the mental dead and is definitely detrimental to the cause of New Being progress and well-being, because that person is indeed on the side of the enemy of liberty, equality, justice, and nationalism" (The Holy Tablets n.d. 891–892, 894, 897–898, 900–901).

York pointed toward the impending threat of a mysterious race called "Leviathan" that represented the greatest obstacle to Nubian achievement.

> There is a special project under way by Leviathan to further leopardize And ghostlike your race, the world of woolly-haired people, By changing original hair, original color, And original features to those of other races. In other words, destroy beautiful woolly hair, And pretty dark brown skin by one-sided racial miscegenation, which is one-sided racial sexual mixing. They are creating a "new race" or neutral race where you can't tell their nationality. Leviathan is suing straight-haired men and women in its attempt to destroy you through the sexual use of woolly-haired women and men. Male, New Being, must also refuse to have sexual relationships with alien women and refuse to mongrelize their seed by refusing to father offspring by women of Tomah races. The hybrids born from interracial sexual mixing are not accepted in the Canaanite race, And they are not accepted by the Nubian race. "Lo! The English bible is the manifestation of Leviathan, 6 ether and ghost." "The Tomah race is using all tricks available to keep you from regaining liberty, equality, justice, and rightness".
>
> The Holy Tablets n.d. 888, 899–900

While some outsiders have equated notions of racial superiority with racism, York understood the UNNM as a religion of love. "Lo! My child, true religion consists of more than ritualistic observances, baths, and pilgrimages, but in loving. Kosmic love is all embracing and all-inclusive. In the presence of pure love all distinctions and differences, as well as hatred, racism jealousy, egoism are dispelled just as dirtiness is dispelled by the cleanliness. There is no knowledge higher than love..." The theology of the UNNM challenges stereotypical notions of the straightforward black nationalist religion that espouses hatred and black superiority. "A child of the ALUHIM recognizes that both love and hate are the two most powerful driving forces in life: And that both emotions are healthy and essential to life, And to possess only one love or hate, And to be deprived of the other is to be crippled as a bird with only one wing" (The Holy Tablets n.d. 756).

A close reading of the writings of the UNNM reveals a series of seemingly conflicted ideas: black superiority and love, racial pride but in an original green skin, and ideological resonance with the Moorish Science Temple and the Nation of Islam but ultimately identifying with an ancient alien culture. In addition to racial stereotypes, black new religious movements espousing and protecting esoteric knowledge face the legacy of "cult" movements that ended in mass suicide. In 1978, news coverage of the People's Temple where over nine hundred people took their lives in Guyana left the indelible image of bodies lying in the central pavilion of Jonestown and forever changed the landscape of religion in America. "Cult" and "brainwashing" gained new prominence in the American vernacular. Fear that maniacal leaders could manipulate the naïve and weak willed entered the public discourse. Years later, in 1993, the Branch Dravidians at Waco, Texas, were defined as a dangerous "cult" and after a fifty-one day standoff, the federal authorities forcefully entered the Dravidian complex. Although accounts of subsequent events vary, the siege resulted in the deaths of over eighty Branch Dravidians. In March 1997, in Rancho Santa Fe, California, thirty-nine members of Heaven's Gate committed suicide.

Emergent African American new religious movements are often framed within this "cult" paradigm and face the additional challenges of racial categorization and in some cases outright racism that criminalizes people groups before much is actually known about them. With twenty-four-hour news cycles reporting on and constructing stories and a skeptical audience all too willing to believe the worst, the evidence mustered to establish cult behavior mounts quickly and gathers steam. The notion that "I know a cult when I see it" masks the complexity of religion in general and the constantly shifting grounds on which identity is questioned, constructed, and reimagined. Black Norms have walked the line between maintaining their distinctiveness and embracing assimilation. If new religious traditions maintain beliefs and practices that diverge from the mainstream, they open themselves up to the range of charges of wrongdoing associated with "cult behavior." If they abandon the vision that initially brought the group together to be accepted more broadly or allow their sacred knowledge to become public, they may lose the sense of specialness that binds them together. This dilemma between maintaining authenticity while also surviving as a minority religion in America is a challenge that will likely continue well into the twenty-first century.

Upon initial consideration, the Nuwaubian invocation of extraterrestrials seems an unlikely choice for a group seeking credibility as a minority in a small town, particularly the notion that York was an extraterrestrial being from the galaxy Illyuwn. However, extending their history beyond Egypt and the earliest civilizations to a time before the formation of the earth allows the community to be at once new and ancient, uniquely American and transcending human-kind, and racially distinctive and supernatural. Taking seriously the narratives and sacred texts of emergent black religious communities may open up whole new areas of inquiry into the nature and diversity of esoteric knowledge in African American religious history.

PART 3

Late 20th Century to Present-day

∵

CHAPTER 14

Astro-Black Mythology
The Poetry of Sun Ra

Marques Redd

Introduction

I begin with a poem from the legendary jazz musician Sun Ra (1914–1993) entitled *Astro Black*:

Astro-Black Mythology
Astro-Timeless Immortality
Astro-Thought in Mystic Sound
Astro-Black of Outer Space
Astro Natural of Darkest Stars
Astro Reach Beyond the Stars
Out to Endless Endlessness
Astro-Black American
The Universe is in My Voice
The Universe Speaks through the Dawn
To Those of Earth and Other Worlds
Listen While You Have the Chance
Find Your Place among the Stars
Listen to the Outer World
Rhythm Multiplicity
Harmony, Equational
Melody Horizon
Astro Black and Cosmo Dark
Astro Black and Cosmo Dark
Astro Black and Cosmo Dark
Astro Black Mythology
Astro-Timeless Immortality
Astro Thought in Mystic Sound
Astro Black Mythology

SUN RA 2005, 74

Sun Ra's poem, bursting with real power, is a profound meditation on and enacting of the possibilities of Astro-Black mythology, a mode of thought that forces us to upturn all conventional thinking about the history, development, and ideal construction of knowledge. Most paradigms of religious studies seek to contextualize and rationalize various elements of the religious imagination, but Sun Ra's Astro-Black mythology cannot be contained by them because he returns us to the very root of the word religion, which comes from the Latin *re* (again) and *ligare* (to tie, bind, fasten). Primarily, Sun Ra seeks to fasten religion itself with the other branches of knowledge from which it has been severed—astronomy, musicology, political science, physics, mathematics, dance, etc. Furthermore, Sun Ra provides practices aimed at tying people back to something with which they had originally been one, the entire sweep of the cosmos. The goal of this paper is to use this poem to stage an exploration of the contours of this Astro-Black Mythology as it is developed throughout his written work at large.

In 2005, this poem was published in a four hundred page groundbreaking edition entitled *The Immeasurable Equation: The Collected Poetry and Prose of Sun Ra*, and the release of this volume marked an important cultural moment for those interested in American and Afro-diasporic music, literature, philosophy, and religion, to name only a few of the standard disciplines to which Sun Ra's work directly speaks.[1] For a figure of his stature, the lack of attention to his *oeuvre* evidences many of the shortcomings of the contemporary hyper-specialized, despiritualized academy, yet in truth, he seems to be repressed by orthodox academic canons of knowledge precisely because his work threatens them so deeply. To be fully absorbed by the academy, he would inevitably and irrevocably change the academy.

The Immeasurable Equation is especially useful for its insightful appendices. In the first one, John Szwed (anthropologist and musicologist) and James Jacson (drummer in the famed Sun Ra Myth-Science Arkestra) provide a list of all of the texts that Sun Ra had in his personal collection, which paints a vivid image of his personality and intellectual precursors. In Ra's library, histories of jazz sat comfortably next to books on crystals, Chinese herbal cures,

---

1   Although this paper will focus on texts from this collection, it should also be mentioned that within the last ten years there has been something of a renaissance of interest in Sun Ra's writings. Some other essential source texts are *The Wisdom of Sun Ra: Sun Ra's Polemical Broadsheets and Streetcorner Leaflets*, edited by Anthony Elms and John Corbett (Chicago: WhiteWalls, 2006); *Sun Ra: Interviews & Essays*, edited by John Sinclair (London: Headpress, 2009); *This Planet is Doomed: The Science Fiction Poetry of Sun Ra*, edited by Bhob Stewart (New York: Kicks Books, 2011).

atomic energy theory, and primers on the Japanese, Hebrew, French, and Italian languages. Most fascinating for our purposes here is proof that Sun Ra wonderfully was absorbed in and quite knowledgeable about a wide range of esoteric and occult(ed) traditions. One can find works of theosophy (Madame Blavatsky's *The Secret Doctrine*), Afrocentrism (Frances Welsing's *The Isis Papers*, George James' *Stolen Legacy*), Renaissance hermeticism (John Dee's *The Hieroglyphic Monad*), sufism (Shaykh ad-Darqawi's *Letters of a Sufi Master*), the Nation of Islam (Elijah Muhammad's *Message to the Black Man in America*), occultism (*The Qabalah of Aleister Crowley*), revisionist Egyptology (Gerald Massey's *A Book of the Beginnings*, Rene Schwaller de Lubicz's *The Egyptian Miracle*), and much more.

Szwed, the scholar who has probably written the most and the most perceptively on Sun Ra, expounds these influences with gusto in his masterful biography *Space is the Place: The Lives and Times of Sun Ra*. He says,

> As personal as his vision was, it was nonetheless drawn from many currents of Afro- and Euro-American thought, most of them unknown to the public. He spoke from a long tradition of revisionist history by way of street-corner Egyptology, black Freemasonry, theosophy, and oral and written biblical exegesis, all bound together by a love of secret knowledge and the importance it bestows upon those excluded from the usual circuits of scholarship and power.
>
> SZWED 1998, xviii

Perhaps against Szwed's conscious intention, the "those excluded from the usual circuits of scholarship and power" should not simply be read as "those racially discriminated against." This exclusion also references the status of esotericism, the subjugated knowledge *par excellence*. I will show how Sun Ra deploys this knowledge as the foundation for a *transdisciplinary*,[2] all-embracing orientation which has the possibility to revise these usual circuits of scholarship. Not wanting to repeat the details of Szwed's fascinating juxtapositions and his unraveling of these connections, I will focus on one particular figure by whom Sun Ra was influenced, Rene Schwaller de Lubicz (1887–1961), in order to comment on the larger intervention that Sun Ra makes into rethinking post-Enlightenment ideas about the construction of knowledge.

---

2 I use this phrase in the precise way elaborated by Basarab Nicolescu in his *Manifesto of Transdiciplinarity*.

Schwaller de Lubicz and Sacred Science: A New Paradigm for
Esoteric and Literary Studies

Schwaller de Lubicz, twentieth-century Alsatian mathematician and philosopher, spent a significant part of his life in Egypt studying its monuments and
culture, and in books like *Sacred Science: The King of Pharaonic Theocracy, The
Temple of Man: Apet of the South at Luxor, The Temple in Man: Sacred
Architecture and the Perfect Man*, and *Symbol and the Symbolic: Ancient Egypt,
Science, and the Evolution of Consciousness*, he argues that knowledge-activity
in the ancient Egyptian context was much more complex than that for which
it is normally given credit. Fully conversant with contemporary discoveries in
cosmology, physics, and anthropology, de Lubicz argues that Egypt's endeav-
ors—whether the erection of temples, governmental structures, literature, or
mathematical systems—derived from a mode of knowledge not concerned
with the study of external objects, but with using potent combinations of rituals and symbols to catalyze the deep transformation and expansion of consciousness, with the final goal being the divinization of the human. This "sacred
science" was a rich fusion of science, religion, and art that was directed toward
the embodiment of spiritual knowledge, and toward the internalization and
corporeal expression of intellectual and spiritual powers, rather than the
mechanistic utilization of power-knowledge for the exploitation and manipulation of the earthly environment. In his book *The Temple in Man*, de Lubicz
says, "However, there is a type of education that can awaken 'consciousness' of
states that precede and transcend material forms...Ancient Egypt is in fact one
of the major sources of these sciences: however, a true vocabulary of the
Pharaonic language—or even a provisional one—will never be possible unless
attention is given to those questions which we define as psycho-spiritual"
(Lubicz 1981, 17). This focus on consciousness from a psychospiritual perspective allows this knowledge system to resist the reduction of the world into
empty, alienated time and space; celebrate the central, transformative power
of the human imagination; and theorize human participation in an animated
universe in which the cosmos itself is seen as a manifestation of the divine.

This sacred science—forsaking conventional analytical modes of thinking in order to analogically elaborate links between human and cosmic
functions[3]—did not disappear completely with the demise of high ancient

---

3 Pharaonic science is "foremost an expression of the universal principles of organization and
   causation, which define not only the natural and cosmic creation but also the patterns and
   processes of the human mind and spirit." Schwaller de Lubicz, *Temple of Man* (Rochester:
   Inner Traditions, 1998), 20.

Egyptian civilization. Fragments of it were disseminated through various channels and formed the basis of what is now called the esoteric or hermetic tradition, composed of strains as various as Sufism, Gnosticism, Kabbalah, Freemasonry, Alchemy, and Neoplatonism. These holistic, psychospiritual knowledge systems also served to transmit a precise suprarational knowledge and intuitive vision that were used, in the words of de Lubicz, "in the expression of a vital philosophy, not a rationalist philosophy" (Lubicz 1981, 27). Simson Najovits confirms this idea when he says, "Yet, on a strictly historical basis, all the modern esoteric systems, with the notable exception of the Hindu, seem to have been influenced by the Egyptians in both real and imaginary ways" (Najovits 2004, 301).

Perhaps not surprisingly, sacred science, due to its use of symbolic methods as an instrument by which knowledge projects itself successively into generations and cycles of time, has also taken refuge in the arts as rationalism, empiricism, and scientific materialism have consolidated their position as the vanguard of Western civilization. As a scholar of British Romantic, 19th-century American, and Afro-diasporic literatures, I have come to realize that these complex symbolic networks emerging from Egyptian spiritual science have been extremely influential for the mythopoetic literary creations of literature written in English from at least the Renaissance to the present moment, in a movement stretching from Edmund Spenser's Egypto-hermetic *The Faerie Queene* (1596)—a text in which the Temple of Isis is one of the most important iconographic centers—to John Crowley's magisterial four-volume novel *Ægypt* (2007). At the moment, however, there is no analytical framework (not Marxism, feminism, deconstruction, phenomenology, structuralism, psychoanalysis, reader-response theory, etc.) that is equipped to explicate the claims of this tradition of sacred science or its long-lasting impact. This hinders us from fully understanding the non-instrumental and non-propositional *gnosis* that literature provides—its emancipatory force, and its performative effects in the world.

In this paper, therefore, I want to take de Lubicz's work as the basis for a new scholarly "methodology" in pursuing an interpretation of Sun Ra. I do not want to analyze his poem as a static formal object or mobile collection of rhetorical tropes, deconstruct it, historicize it, perform an ideology critique upon it, or situate it within any sociopolitical context or set of discourses. Alternatively, I want to view this work as a gesture toward the reconstruction of a deeply penetrating sacred science, a project which entails elaborating how the text reintegrates fragmented areas of knowledge into a new, all-encompassing unity and examining the subsequent knowledge claims it makes. As a first gesture of my own in creating a properly hermetic literary theory, my goal is not to subordinate literature to a reigning rationalist methodology, one in which poetry, plays, and novels are dissected as if they were devitalized corpses or analyzed as if they were mechanical contraptions, but to use the text to challenge all rationalist methodologies. Fundamentally, this requires viewing the literary work not as an "object," but as a text of initiation, one that augments our awareness and propels us toward regaining various elements of a larger cosmic consciousness. Sun Ra's work is a treasure of spiritual, intellectual, and artistic possibilities.

Astro-Black Mythology

The fundamental grounding point of Sun Ra's poetry is its meditation on blackness, which becomes the basis for his metaphysics and system of knowledge. In the poem, "Black on Black," Sun Ra says: "Black is the all of/ everything because of its endless acceptance/ like a black bottomless pit…Black is/ the storage house of all colors" (Sun Ra 2005, 80). All colors and vibratory energies are a part of this large, expansive blackness. As a "bottomless pit," black is the primal origin from which being itself emerges. The "all of everything," blackness is progressively the primeval ocean, chaos, outer space (birthplace of the planets, stars, and galaxies of the universe), night sky, womb, hidden doorway to the unconscious, and fundamental archetype of humanity. Black is the color of carbon, fundamental molecule of life; black holes are found at the center of our own galaxy and countless others; and a black body (as explored by thermodynamics) is a perfect absorber and radiator of all forms of light and energy.

Developing these thoughts about this primal blackness, Sun Ra adds in "The Outer Darkness (version 2)": "I speak of a different kind of Blackness, the kind/ That the world does not know, the kind that the world/ Will never understand/ It is rhythm against rhythm in kind dispersion/ It is harmony against harmony in endless coordination/ It is melody against melody in vital enlightenment/ And something else and more/ A living spirit gives a quickening thought" (Sun Ra 2005, 295). Blackness, as something the world does not know, is not simply a sociological category and cannot be comfortably assimilated into standard sociopolitical ideas about race or racial hierarchy. It is a divine, cosmic principle of the universe, a living spirit that transmits its vitalism. Embodying rhythm, harmony, and melody, it is fundamental to the energetic operation of the universe, providing the proper coordination of the multiplicity of elements that compose it and the proper foundation for the enlightenment of those elements. For Sun Ra, blackness is a multi-dimensional symbol simultaneously encoding information about the formation of the cosmos, human life, and the human psyche and linking these domains through analogy.

Sun Ra encourages us to study this Blackness, but this is not a process of study in which the subject is distinguished from the object, but fully embraces it. Turning to Sun Ra's "The Outer Darkness (version 2)," one finds an explanation: "Natural Black music projects the myth of Blackness/ And he who is not Black in spirit will never know/ That these words are true and valid forever" (Sun Ra 2005, 295). By becoming Black in spirit, one enters the "bottomless pit" of consciousness, a doorway that leads to advanced laws and rhythms that span the universe. For Sun Ra, therefore, all of life has a foundation in Blackness, although this "Blackness in spirit" is often rejected and repressed. Becoming Black in spirit is what accounts for inner vision, intuition, creative genius, and spiritual illumination.

In an interview with Ira Steingroot, Sun Ra proclaimed, "In alchemy, black is the color associated with Saturn" (Steingroot 1988, 51). It is no surprise, then, that Sun Ra constantly claimed throughout his life to have come from the planet Saturn (Szwed 1998, 183–184). And the concern with alchemy, from the Arabic *al-kīmiya'*, is one of the many threads that ties Sun Ra to ancient Egypt.[4] Sun Ra, of course, knows that Egypt's original name was *Kemet* (km.t), which translates to "The Black Land." This Blackness has the same multivalent meaning in the Egyptian context as well, where rituals are used to bring the blackness of the land in synch with the blackness of outer space, thereby insuring the success of celestial causes on terrestrial effects. As the legendary Hermes Trismegistus says in the *Hermetica*, the famous collection of third-century Alexandrian tracts, "Do you not know, Asclepius, that Egypt is an image of heaven or, to be more precise, that everything governed and moved in heaven came down to Egypt and was transferred there? If truth were told, our land is the temple of the whole world" (Copenhayer 1992, 81). For Sun Ra, Egypt, the temple of the cosmos, is a place where Blackness in spirit was the norm and where it was theorized as such for the first time.

In his pivotal musicology text *Blutopia*, Graham Lock argues that astro-black mythology "emphasizes Sun Ra's conscious creation of a mythology, and it conveniently encapsulates the two dominant facets of that mythology, the Astro of the outer space future, and the Black of the ancient Egyptian past" (Lock 1999,

---

4   For more on the question of alchemy and Egypt, see Jack Lindsay, *The Origins of Alchemy in Graeco-Roman Egypt* (New York: Barnes & Noble, 1970).

14). However, this fusion of Egypt with the space age of NASA and the moon landings is a bit more complicated. Sun Ra says in the poem "Black Myth": "But other myths of black mythology/ Radiate from beyond the measured borders of time" (Sun Ra 2005, 79). Ra is not simply bringing together ancient Egypt with the future. More provocatively, he is showing with this term how much ancient Egyptian cosmology itself is already an "astro-black mythology," an intellectual project he is choosing to pick up and extend "after the end of the world."[5] Egyptian sacred science was in large part founded on a sacred astronomy, which posits that all astronomical phenomena—the movement and cycles of the planets, stars, sun, and moon—represented the visible dimension of divine forces. With complicated calendars keeping track of the interactions of multiple kinds of cycles (solar, lunar, and stellar) and serving as the foundation for different temple traditions and modes of initiation, ancient Egyptians viewed cosmic life as a realm of conscious, vital forces existing harmoniously with mortal life, thus sparking the formation of systems of astrology, prophecy, and geomancy.

Sun Ra's term *myth-science* is a perfect term to describe this system of thought, which in turn permeates his own. In the poem "The Realm of Myth," he says, "As a science Myth has many dimensions/ And many degrees" (Sun Ra 2005, 324). With these compact lines, he flags for the reader how sacred science explores a vast array of dimensions—heavenly and earthly, physical and nonphysical, pre- and post-mortal—and is organized through degrees, with this term meaning both the degrees of the position of celestial forms and degrees of initiation through which one comes to embody this spiritual knowledge. He elaborates this position in the poem "Living Parallel": "Wisdom on its abstract planes/ Uses myth as medium to understanding/ Thus a living parable to the outward or inward truth/ Is every myth:/ ***[6]/ Knock upon the door of darkness/ And voices speak from without" (Sun Ra 2005, 228). Sun Ra's myth-science, in other words, maintains perpetual interaction between heaven and earth, linking together inward and outward truth.

In "Wisdom-Ignorance," Sun Ra explains what this knowledge leads to: "the hope/ Of continuation-living-being is myth/ Myth from equational wisdom-ignorance/ is is./ ***/The myth touches every field/ of endeavour so that the myth is the/ bridge to the/ Greater Myth" (Sun Ra 2005, 426). The Greater Myth

---

5 This phrase comes from his cult classic movie *Space is the Place*. John Coney, director (New York: Rhapsody Films, 1998).

6 This symbol will mean that lines are deleted here.

to which this sacred science leads is, as we shall see in the next section, the promise of immortality.

Astro-Timeless Immortality

Anything can give up its life,
Why don't you give up your death?
Why don't you do something different
Something that was never done before?
So that the universe will know you're here
So you can stand and speak to the universe
And say "Here I am!
I am just like you:
Endless, Immeasurable, Eternal, Impossible"
The universe has shown you the way
Go out look at the stars
They're always around
Go out and look at the sky
It's always there
Go out and look at the sun
In the morning
It's always here.
Why do you have to go?
Why should you leave the stars
And the sun and the moon
And the universe all alone?

SUN RA 2005, 71

With its revision of Matthew 10:39 ("He that findeth his life shall lose it: and he that loseth his life for my sake shall find it"), Sun Ra is directly confronting the question of immortality in this poem "Anything can give up its life." We cannot turn to disciplines such as psychology, biochemistry, and mathematics to illuminate this question. In the words of Schwaller de Lubicz, they do not give "an education with regard to a life greater than that of physical existence" (Schwaller 1998, 18). Although illogical and paradoxical from the point-of-view of these disciplines, sacred science focuses explicitly on the dynamics of reincarnation, resurrection, and the journey of the soul through alternative experiential realms of the inner/after life.

The identification with the universe that Sun Ra speaks of here—"I am just like you"—is preceded and directly influenced by the *Pyramid Texts*, the earliest cosmological writings of Egypt.[7] These texts outline a powerful physics of transformation that guides one through a transubstantiation of form toward an exalted partaking in divine existence, and here we see the ancient king's spiritual synthesis with cosmic life. He is transformed into a stellar body after ascent from the Earth:

> You shall become completed as every god:
> your head as Horus of the Duat – an Imperishable Star;
> your face as Eyes-Forward – an Imperishable Star;
> your ears Atum's twins – an Imperishable Star;
> your eyes Atum's twins – an Imperishable Star;
> your nose as the Jackal – an Imperishable Star ***
> You will not perish.
>
> ALLEN 2005, 32

Instead of leaving the universe "all alone," these texts provide a path through which one joins its permanently, and the key term "Imperishable" is elaborated and morphed by Sun Ra's word equations into "Endless, Immeasurable, Eternal, Impossible."

Further down, in Utterance #156, the protagonist Unis speaks: "This Unis has come to you, Nut; this Unis has come to you, Nut, having left his father on earth, having left Horus behind him, having grown wings as a falcon, feathered as a hawk, his ba having fetched him, his magic having provided him. (Unis), you shall part your place in the sky among the stars of the sky, for you are the lone star at Nut's shoulder" (Allen 2005, 40). This chant is the perfect context for understanding what Sun Ra is encouraging us to do in *Astro Black*, the poem with which we began: "Find Your Place among the Stars." Sun Ra is breathing new life into this ancient knowledge, discovering and perpetuating it anew in the 20th century. As he says in "The Curtain Call": "Take your curtain call and bow/ Then leave/ The scenery must be cleared/ For another day/ Another kind of Cosmo-play/ A play on words/ Of hieroglyphic chant/ A play on words of Immortalic reach/ It is a play of peoples and a different horizon's world-sun/ Therefore prepare, for you are the star" (Sun Ra 2005, 123). Throughout his work, Ra builds on the "hieroglyphic chant" of the *Pyramid*

---

7   As far as dating is concerned, these texts can only be said to be older than 2300 BC. In this paper, I will use James Allen, trans., *The Ancient Egyptian Pyramid Texts* (Atlanta: Society of Biblical Literature, 2005).

Texts with the aim of using his poetry as a technology of preparation for immortality.

One central scene in the Egyptian funerary literature is the judgment of the deceased, a stage that must be passed successfully in order that he or she may become "justified" and receive an elevated spiritual nature. The initiate enters a hall of judgment where the heart, a sacred and important organ of a highly complex psychospiritual anatomy, is placed on one side of a scale, with the other side containing a single feather representing truth, order, and justice. If the heart balanced with this lone feather, the prospect of joining the Neteru (a term usually translated as "gods," but closer in meaning to "divine principles") in the sacred land is offered; if not, the soul ceases to exist completely, dying a "second death" (which is often interpreted by some commentators as a metaphor of reincarnation, or return to physical life).

The complex Egyptian architecture of post-mortal planes and dimensions is reconfigured in Sun Ra's exploration of heightened, initiatic consciousness. He uses the words "weigh" and "way" to convey his ideas about the connection between one's style of living and the quality of one's soul. In his poem *Circle of Comprehension*, he states, "The verdict is the judgment:/.........The Weigh........./ The verdict........." (Sun Ra 2005,100). The weighing of the heart ceremony is the obvious referent here, and here Sun Ra propels the reader back to ancient ceremonies and the mode of knowledge they embodied. In *Self Radiation*, Sun Ra gives a very personal elaboration of this ceremony, particularly by thinking about his relationship to humanity at large:

> One day you will walk where I have walked;/ Yet where I have walked,/ I have walked seemingly in vain/And seemingly too all alone............/***/A lonely weigh...a lonely path...a lonely way/ Uncharted dimension-strange duality to that which is....../***/For myself is a many-multi-self/And along the way/I have left an alter-self-radiation/That will make it's presence known [*sic*]/As you walk the way/To the place of the celestial weigh............
>
> SUN RA 2005, 337

In his process of reconstructing a modern version of sacred science, one that is focused on a thematics of divine transformation and which strives to explore realms of experience (the "uncharted dimensions") forbidden and repressed by empirical sciences, Sun Ra commits to the "lonely path" of a groundbreaker. His clotted syntax and vocabulary vividly exemplify the difficulty of conveying experiences and concepts that cannot quite be expressed in alphabetical language. His path is a "lonely way," mainly because a social context capable of being fully organized by a sacred knowledge no longer seems to exist, and therefore his is a "lonely weigh," as he reaches a height of spiritual achievement emblematized by the weighing of the heart that unfortunately will not be shared with all. Yet, Sun Ra does not give up all hope. Sacred science, rather than simply accumulating alienated facts about the external world, effects an augmentation of the self of the practitioner, creating Sun Ra's "many-multi-self." He leaves an element of his personality, even now in the present after his physical death, to guide us as his readers "to the place of the celestial weigh." Reading, therefore, becomes akin to an initiation, and the poetry functions as a technology to catalyze our own psychospiritual development. Furthermore, the "celestial" added as a descriptor to the "weigh" here is intriguing, reminding us that the afterlife is not just a simultaneously post-mortal and internal space, but an extraterrestrial one as well.

Sun Ra, whose very name references the Egyptian deity who represents the life force as symbolized by solar energy, testifies to the possibility of the transcendence of human form and transfiguration of identity. Through the vibrations of mystic sound, which I will now explore, his poetry provides a means through which we as readers can also achieve that same epiphany; he points us "With fiery aim to find/ The even greater day of the even greater tomorrow.../ The Cosmo-timeless realm/ Of the Omni-Everlution-Immortalic Day" (Sun Ra 2005, 107).

Astro-Thought in Mystic Sound

Many formalist critics will be unhappy with *Astro Black*, finding it difficult to discern within it a detailed attention to poetic structure or familiar genre. To them, it might also seem to lack a rich rhetoricity that precludes its worthiness of attention. By the same token, many sociopolitical critics will find it all too easy to reject this poem, as it cannot be easily mapped into prefabricated programs of resistance or liberation. However, this poem synthesizes an art of nuance that transcends the concerns and capacities of most modes of contemporary literary criticism.

Most importantly, it is operating in a context in which the "literary" is a much more expansive category than normally considered. Sun Ra says in the essay "The Aim of My Compositions" that he wants readers to "understand that poems are music, and that music is only another form of poetry. I consider every creative musical composition as being a tone poem" (Sun Ra 2005, 448). This poem, therefore, is a complex vibratory system constructed to have a powerful effect on consciousness and the wider world at large, and in this particular instance, it is part of an entire ritual complex.

In the 1980 documentary *A Joyful Noise*, we see "Astro Black" come alive in a performance atop the roof of the Philadelphia International Center, with vocalist June Tyson singing the words of the poem while the Arkestra provides musical accompaniment (Mugge 1998). This performance works in the same vein as ancient Egyptian practice, where ritual gesture (including dance), sound (music and chant), and the observation of celestial phenomena were choreographed with the use of sacred literature to enliven the human domain with divine presence. This intense coordination emulated the process of cosmogenesis itself. Rather than alienated analysis of this abstract moment, a more participatory mode was engaged that invited the forces of creation to enter the temple.

Ancient ceremonies often opened with a hymn; inscribed in every temple and tomb, they provided an initial greeting meant to evoke the divine feeling and image of the Neter. After singing *Astro Black*, June Tyson moves into another verse brimming with double meaning: "When the world was in darkness/ And darkness was ignorance/ Along came Ra." Cheekily, Sun Ra walks out as this is intoned, his emergence paralleling the emergence of the sun, with purple wig and makeup, gold *lamé* shawl, and wire sculpture headpiece. This is completely appropriate attire. As he says in an interview with musicologist John Corbett, "Costumes are music. Colors throw out musical sounds, too. Every color throws out vibrations of life" (Corbett 1994, 313). At center stage, Sun Ra engages in brief discourse on his name: "I have many names. Names of mystery. Names of splendor. Names of shame. I have many names. Some call me Mr. Ra. Some call me Mr. Re. You can call me Mr. Mystery." In ancient Egypt, sacred names incorporated the essence of a being, and possession of such names provided both knowledge of and access to divine forces. Sun Ra extends this science of sound alchemy throughout his works.

"Mystic sound," therefore, is important for understanding the complexity of Sun Ra's text and larger artistic project, although at the moment we do not have the sophisticated methodological tools and vocabulary necessary for fully apprehending the vibratory power of language, its intricate interactions with voice, or its subtle effects on consciousness and the environment. This sound, however, is not simply relevant to the sphere of music. Sun Ra also theorizes a larger harmonics, one responsible for the physical phenomena that scientists call "reality."

Here I turn to the essay "The Air Spiritual Man," although in truth this text is really a prose poem, flouting as it does conventional presentations of syntax and obsessed with the details of language. Sun Ra says, "Music is of many forms within itself and outside itself as derivative projection creation; under that fact consideration, it is the foundation and basis of all art...Everything vibrational

is of different degrees of music. There is music everywhere infinite infinity"
(Sun Ra 2005, 452). Central to Egyptian science, religion, art, and magic (all
working in concert) was the notion that creation was a harmonically ordered
unity-in-multiplicity, and this knowledge—implicitly embodied in concrete
works of architecture and art—displayed a sophisticated grasp of rhythm,
number, and proportion that predated and heavily influenced explicit
Pythagorean articulations of the "music of the spheres." In *The Temple of Man*,
Schwaller de Lubicz notes, "A harmonic relation must exist between Cosmic
Man—who also contains the stellar world—and this incarnate man called
Microcosm. The study of this harmony is the key to esotericism. There is thus
an *esoteric science* because there is a projection of the Universe within the
human body, a *body of experience* and, so to speak, an atlas of cosmic, spatial
locations" (Schwaller 1998, 64). In this reading, the harmonic relationship that
exists between the cosmos itself and man, mapped through analogical modes
of thought, is the foundation of esotericism, and this position guides Sun Ra's
exploration of "infinite infinity." In another prose poem "I always called myself
Sun Ra," he frames the relationship between Cosmic Man and incarnate man
in his own specialized vocabulary, "The intergalactic music is in hieroglyphic-
sound: an abstract analysis and synthesis of man's relationship to the universe,
visible and invisible, first man and second man" (Sun Ra 2005, 458).

Although I have been exploring *Astro Black*'s lines sequentially, and it is
difficult to break the structures of alphabetical linear process, do not forget
that this poem, along with sacred science as such, has to be apprehended holistically, with no part divorced from the rest. This "mystic sound" is directly connected to Ra's "astro-black" trope. He explains these links in the poem "Black
Prince Charming": "The strange truth of Eternal myth/ Is the Sound; It is
the/ Sound truth...Music Sound/ And there always is music/ The music always
is/ ***/ There is black sound" (Sun Ra 2005, 82). As I return to this exploration
of blackness, I will skip a little further down in *Astro Black* and move a little
more quickly in elaborating a new dimension of his use of this term.

Astro-Black American

In the poem "The Black Rays Race," Sun Ra says, "See how the black rays of the
black race/ Have touched the immeasurable wisdom" (Sun Ra 2005, 83).
Writing at the height of various black nationalist and civil rights movements,
and clashing quite comically with groups like the Black Panthers, who expelled
him and the Arkestra from their shared living space, Sun Ra uniquely reorients
racial language and racial struggle toward the cosmos. His esoteric political

project moves in three phases: (1) recognition of mundane black American alienation, (2) assumption of "Astro-Black American" identity, and (3) revitalization of the entire human family.

This tripartite unfolding is nicely laid out in the 1971 poem "Message to Black Youth." The poem begins with a note of concern: "Never say you are unloved/ I love you/ In all the simplicity of the word/ Never say you have no friend/ How dare you feel that way!" (Sun Ra 2005, 240). This message is simultaneously addressed to an individual black youth and the entire collective of black youth, which might feel "unloved," to put it mildly, because of an entire historical legacy of economic exploitation, state violence, and unredressed ancestral enslavement. Yet with an ambivalent message of hope, Sun Ra proselytizes for a new future: "I am your unknown friend/ How long before you know/ If I deny you/ It is only love/ Seeking a way to make you hear/ The thought essence of being/ It is too late not to be your better self/ Your beauty to me is your discipline" (Sun Ra 2005, 240). Through the sacred science he reconstructs, Sun Ra opens a path toward the assumption of a "better self," effecting a shift from being the "black youth" of the poem's title to the status of "Astro-Black American." By making them *hear* the "thought essence of being," Sun Ra is expanding the mind beyond the normal strictures of time and space, placing them in direct contact with the idealized "dark black blue golden brown of you" (Sun Ra 2005, 241). Reestablishing a link with primal blackness, reborn black people can bring about the larger salvation of humanity, unable to find the hidden doorway of blackness to a spiritual unity with nature: "Other youth take heed/ prepare/ discipline-precision/ ***/ Other youths if real in the myth shall partake" (Sun Ra 2005, 241). One implication is that black Americans, stripped of a nation and national belonging and formed by an amalgam of cultural fusions, can point the way to an integral future by serving as the model of a post-national, planetary sensibility and pointing the way beyond that to a post-planetary one.

Although black liberation projects have often been founded on disciplines such as the law, economics, political science, and sociology, Sun Ra gives this project a new paradigm. In many respects, he is the hidden, unacknowledged precursor of Barbara Holmes' fascinating study *Race and the Cosmos: An Invitation to View the World Differently*. She says very persuasively:

> we cannot be reconciled to one another by using the language of oppression, victimization, and overcoming. We need new connections to universal and cosmic realities to divest oppressors of historical narrative advantages and to offer victims alternatives to entrenched and internalized narratives of violation. For besieged minority and marginalized

communities locked into discussions of power and victimization, scientific languages offer flashes of insight about race, identity, and the moral life within the broader context of the cosmos.

HOLMES 2002, xvi

In other words, the study of cosmology provides a new framework from which to rewrite sociopolitical categories and histories, reframing them from a wider, more expansive perspective. Sun Ra pursued that project for the majority of the latter half of the twentieth century, and it is curious that there is no direct engagement with him in that text. Whereas Holmes is fascinated by the latest accomplishments of quantum mechanics, string theory, and astronomy, Sun Ra emphasizes that the achievement of a sacred science requires wholly transfiguring those frameworks so that our relationship to knowledge and its expression is considerably altered.

In "This world is not my home," Sun Ra strikingly "invites us to view the world differently":

> You got to reach out and touch beyond the stars./You got to reach out and touch beyond the stars above that./ You got to walk/through the universe./You got to touch the edge of the universe./***/Continue to be a slave./Are you going to continue to be a slave?/Are you going to continue to be a slave?/Are you a slave to planet Earth?/You said you're free, Prove it to me.
>
> SUN RA 2005, 383–384

Sun Ra is pushing African Americans to take on a new identity in a revolutionary way. This revolution, however, is not about political struggle, but about relocating out of the earth and its squabbles altogether. The history of slavery is directly referenced here, but that historical situation is broadened out into an ontological dilemma—will you be a slave to the Earth?—which is a more fundamental slavery as it keeps us from recognizing the full potential of development that sacred science affords. The properly Astro-Black American identity is fully assumed when one is emancipated—not legally, but in a new way, breaking earthly chains and projecting outward to the edge of the universe itself.

As this progression moves forward, from Black American to Astro-Black American, Sun Ra projects even future stages of evolution to come after that: "I know I'm a member of the Angel race,/ My home is somewhere else in outer space." (Sun Ra 2005, 381). In the essay "I am not of this planet," Sun Ra explores this hyper-transformation in more depth. He begins by saying, "I am not of this planet. I am another order of being" (Sun Ra 2005, 460). It is this different order to which Sun Ra wants everyone to aspire.

The Universe is in My Voice

In the *Temple of Man*, Schwaller de Lubicz says, "Every living function of the human being is but a symbol of an organically realized cosmic function. Swallowing, rejecting, assimilating, sleeping, sitting, talking, desiring, imploring, praying, and so forth, are nothing but incarnated cosmic functions" (Schwaller 1998, 76–77). The fundamental insight of sacred science is its understanding of the human body as a living synthesis of the essential vital functions of the universe. With the proclamation that "the universe is in my voice," Sun Ra embodies this Anthropocosmic understanding. Throughout his poetry, as I have shown in this essay, Ra turns to ancient Egyptian sacred science, a fundamental origin of esoteric thinking, as a source for elaborating his thinking about cosmic blackness, immortality, harmony, and the role these concepts play in leading to social revitalization.

Sun Ra's work is that of a permanent imagination, and it is difficult to comment on it without being contaminated by its styles and procedures, which is necessarily a tribute. Brent Edwards, in his powerful commentary on Sun Ra, "The Race for Space: Sun Ra's Poetry," discusses what he calls Sun Ra's "poetics of recombination or an exegetical poetics" (Edwards 2005, 46). Explaining these terms, he says that "Ra is most interested in phonetic (rather than graphic) recombinations and substitutions as a route to the allegorical" (Edwards 2005, 47). One can see this at work in the first line of a poem like "The Flesh"—"Israel......Is Ra El?......Ra is El...." (Sun Ra 2005, 172)—where Sun Ra pulls an Egyptian kernel ("Ra") out of Israel, a metonym for a monotheism that seeks to reject and repress it and simultaneously proclaims the ancient god, along with himself, to be El, the supreme god. In indulging in some of this linguistic play, I want to close this essay by shifting from thinking about the "universe in Sun Ra's voice" to the "*university* in Sun Ra's voice."

I graduated with a PhD from the University of California at Berkeley in 2011, and it thrills me that Sun Ra taught a course there precisely forty years prior entitled "The Black Man in the Cosmos," with a reading list spanning African American folklore, Rosicrucianism, Blavatsky, the poetry and prose of Henry Dumas, and *The Egyptian Book of the Dead*. Not surprisingly, the results were mixed. Sun Ra ruefully reflected on his experience in an interview with John Farris, connecting the universe and university in his own manner:

Well, I haven't had a chance to present my music to this planet because they don't have a place for someone like me. They got a place for soldiers and politicians and senators, presidents, kings and queens, not for my kind of person. I'm from another dimension. So you don't have a single government in the world that gives any other type of being any rights. They have humanitarian societies, but they don't have any kind of stipulations where a being from another dimension can be accepted and treated properly. So that's the reason they are down here in this great big universe, isolated with their freedoms. They are quite free from everybody else, isolated and alone with all these problems that are easily solvable if they get help from outside. Not even in the universities do they have places for somebody from another dimension. See, I tried the university. I asked them if they had a place for me. They didn't. Like I told them, it wasn't a university because a university presents everything to its students. But Berkeley didn't have a place. I was teaching there, supposed to be teaching there, they got so upset at what I was saying till they wouldn't pay me for three months. They said I wasn't even there, I was in Egypt. But they didn't have no place for what I was saying because it was another kind of truth. This planet is used to dealing with hope and faith. I'm not dealing with that. I deal with equations and every student I had, I told them what books to find it in.[8]

Coming from another dimension (whether transcendent or extraterrestrial), Sun Ra is bringing his Astro-Black Mythology to heal an earthly isolation from the rest of the universe and solder us firmly to the neglected movements of the larger cosmos. This knowledge has implications for refounding the larger organization of society around spiritual truths, but due to the entrenched power of the military-industrial complex ("soldiers"), "representative" democracy ("senators and presidents"), and defunct monarchy, this knowledge is marginalized; it does not have a place in the social world. Yet even in the academic world (and of course, part of the problem is that these domains can be so easily delimited from each other), the university rejects it, in this case because supposedly Sun Ra was shirking his teaching duties by being in Egypt. If he was not there in person, he most certainly was in spirit, as he was extending the project of sacred science into the 20th century. This "other kind of truth" does not fit within predetermined disciplinary niches within the academy, and Berkeley's knee-jerk rejection of Sun Ra is likely an aftereffect of Sun Ra's implicit prior

8   Alton Abraham, Collection of Sun Ra, [Box 2, Folder 4], Special Collections Research Center, University of Chicago Library.

rejection of it, even as he agreed to work in and through its system. For someone so extradimensional, what would categories like musicology, African American Studies, or even African American Esoteric Studies mean? He reformulates the project of the academy as such anew through his idealized equations. He uses harmonic scales, not just as the basis of his music and poetry, but to demonstrate the workings of the cosmos, and then invoke in us an instinctive awareness of (even a longing for) the unity from which harmony derives.

From Ra's perspective, humanity had crossed over into the space age, marked in particular by the landing on the moon. Ra realized that the advanced accomplishment of a certain mode of scientific endeavor and the experience of space travel would activate primal memories. Standing on the threshold of the blackness of outer space, people would be forced again into an awareness of the blackness of inner space. Ra took upon himself the goal of helping the world properly assimilate and deal with this Blackness, without being overwhelmed by its power, and with his Astro-Black Mythology he moves us toward the hidden doorway that will reconnect us to nature, the universe, and the depths of the collective past. As he says in "The Visitation," "My image of paradise is chromatic-black./ And chromatic-black again" (Sun Ra 2005, 414).

CHAPTER 15

Conjurational Contraptions
Techno-Hermeneutics, Mechanical Wizardry, and the Material Culture of African American Folk Magic

Stephen C. Wehmeyer

Introduction

The diverse corpus of vernacular magical, divinatory, and healing practices associated with the Afro-American Gulf South, variously called "Hoodoo," "Rootwork," "Conjure," etc. provides a fascinating glimpse into a world of "everyday esoterica." Here, profound mysteries drawn from spirit filled African and Afro-Caribbean religions, from the sacramental traditions of the Catholic Church, and from the *grimoires* and mystical texts of European occultism are blended together in a rich, multi-flavored *gumbo* and applied to the most prosaic and quotidian of struggles. How does one secure a job? Stop a lover from straying? Win at cards or dice? Keep the law away from a bootlegging business? Practitioners of Hoodoo envision a world of constantly competing human desires, which move and are moved by an uncountable array of malign and benign spiritual forces. These forces can be marshaled, directed or brought to bay through the skillful application of powerful substances whose symbolic or aesthetic qualities afford them meaning in the communicative register of Conjure.

One of the most substantial published compilations of Hoodoo lore and practice emerges from the field research of avocational Folklorist Harry Middleton Hyatt, who, in the late 1930's, initiated a long-term project documenting African-American folk traditions with emphasis on ritual practice and supernatural belief. His work resulted in the creation of a monumental folklore collection: a massive five-volume compendium published between 1970 and 1978 entitled *Hoodoo—Conjuration—Witchcraft—Rootwork*. Folkloristic methodologies and approaches—in particular the analysis of beliefs and practices collected in face to face interaction with everyday folks—are crucial to the study of African American religious experience. As Mark Leone and Gladys Marie-Fry maintain, in interdisciplinary dialogue with other branches of the humanities or social sciences, Folklore studies can serve to introduce "context, meaning...emotion, and enormous breadth"—establishing traditional frameworks for phenomena that at first glance appear unique or idiosyncratic (Leone/Marie-Fry 1999: 375). Folkloristic perspectives allow ordinary—often

© KONINKLIJKE BRILL NV, LEIDEN, 2015 | DOI 10.1163/9789004283428_017

marginalized—voices to be heard on their own terms, and can vastly enrich the database of what we know about lived religious and esoteric experience. Of comparable value is the continued re-examination and re-analysis of extant collections of African American folk belief (as I am attempting here). While such collections are invariably influenced by the biases and preconceptions of their collectors—and Hyatt is no exception in this regard—his propensity for voluminous, largely unvarnished documentation yields an archive that is remarkably detailed, rich, and expressive, affording opportunities for those who come after to mine this work in the service of increasingly nuanced, complex, and accurate perspectives on African American esoteric belief and praxis.

Like comparable, albeit less comprehensive collections of conjure lore (Puckett's *Folk Beliefs of the Southern Negro*, or Hurston's "Hoodoo in America," for example) the Hyatt collection includes detailed descriptions of vernacular rituals intended to harm or to heal with a diverse pharmacopeia of herbs, roots, oils, candles and other *materia sacra*. These substances Yvonne Chireau maintains, are selected for both "sympathetic associations and for aesthetic purposes. Red pepper to produce heat or irritation, lodestone to draw desirable forces...bone fragments to symbolize the passage of powers from the otherworld...The inventory of conjuring materials has remained remarkably consistent for hundreds of years" (Chireau 2003). In his seminal work *Conjuring Culture,* Theophus Smith convincingly argues that Conjure articulates the world as *pharmacosm*—a universe composed of healing and harming—*tonic and toxic*—substances, acts, and entities. These concrete symbols are the stuff out of which a network of complex relations is defined, negotiated, and transformed, establishing what Smith identifies as the hallmarks of "conjuring culture(s)" (Smith 2004).

Thus far, scholars who write about Conjure have tended to emphasize, indeed to privilege, the explicitly *natural* elements of the Hoodoo pharmacopeia—essentially keeping the roots front and center in discussions of rootwork. As Zora Neale Hurston would have it: "'Roots' is the Southern Negro's term for folk-doctoring by herbs and prescriptions, and by extension, and because all hoodoo doctors cure by roots, it may be used as a synonym for 'hoodoo'" (Hurston 1931, 117). This tendency supports perceptions of Conjure as a practice largely associated with slave resistance and marronage, and with the idea that African slaves counter an oppressive *toxic* cultural institution with herbal wisdom drawn from a healing—*tonic*—natural wilderness. In the fundamental dialectic of African and Afro-Caribbean religions—that of Village and Bush—the botanical, animal, and mineral powers of the Bush, the Bayou, *El Monte*, etc. are the tools with which one addresses the social problems of the Village or the City (Apter 1992; Brown 1999; Wehmeyer 2005). Hurston, for example, comparing what she plainly views as "adulterated" conjure in New Orleans with its "purer" form in South Florida, maintains that the former "makes use of the altar, the candles, the incense, the holy water, and blessed oil of the Catholic church. But in Florida, no use is made of such paraphernalia. Herbs, reptiles, insects, and fragments of the human body are their stock in trade." David Brown glosses Frederick Douglass' famous narrative about the root given him by Conjureman Sandy Jenkins. "For Douglass, **the root** was a token of unmatched power, and, one might infer, a sign of African-derived cultural identity in service of the cause of effective resistance to the slave system" (Brown 1990, 5). In light of comments like these, one might be tempted to gloss this *system of esoteric thought and practice* as a simple dialectic which conflates magic, resistance, the natural world, and African heritage, and pits this powerful concoction against an oppressive, hegemonic, White, industrialized society. Black vernacular esotericism is thus pigeonholed as an essentially rural, organic, and ethno-botanical phenomenon.

In reality, however, Conjure defies a simplistic, essentialist analysis. A number of scholars notably Polk (1999), Chireau (2003), Morrow-Long (2001), and Davies (2010) have attested to the centrality in Conjure work of *grimoires* and other writings drawn from Western occultism, inviting further conversations that expand and complicate our understanding of the historical *Roots* (pun intended) of Conjure. Toward a similar end, a close examination of Hyatt's ethnographic record reveals a substantial number of instances in which Rootworkers or their clients describe complex *machines, gadgets, and technological paraphernalia* employed for various esoteric operations—including treasure hunting, exorcism, love magic, hexing, and forcing thieves to return stolen goods. In light of what I think is a substantial lacuna in the scholarly treatment of Black vernacular esotericism, I'd like to examine some of the descriptions of magical machinery found in the Hyatt collection, exploring an aspect of Hoodoo's material culture that has been underemphasized, if not plainly ignored by prior researchers. Even a selective exploration of technological tropes in Conjure belief and ritual helps to challenge what might easily become a crippling trend towards a kind of hyper-natural essentialism.

In his examination of the ways in which practitioners of Haitian Vodou evolve new theologies of the *lwa*—Vodou's spirit pantheon—based upon exegeses of paper chromolithographs of Catholic saints, Donald J. Cosentino imaginatively coins the term "chromo-hermeneutics" to describe the process by which these mass produced images are subjected to intense scrutiny and narrative elaboration. Ultimately, he suggests, the chromos become powerful sources "of revelation, open to counteranalyses like rival Christian or Muslim hermeneutics of the same sacred texts" (Cosentino 1997, 303).

In this vein, I think that the verbal descriptions of esoteric technology found in Hyatt—sometimes richly detailed, often enticingly cryptic—reveal a comparable imaginative and interpretive process operating within the practice of Hoodoo/Conjure. This process might be termed "Techno-Hermeneutics"— a tradition of belief and practice in which *machines* of various sorts become metaphors for articulating, interpreting, and working with an omnipresent world of spirit. We need, I believe, to expand the pharmacosm of Hoodoo to include technological elements as well as natural, botanical ones. If the Hyatt material is any indication, both simple and complex machines provide important "tools to think with" in the articulation, mediation, and manipulation of tonic and toxic relations. Exploring the ways in which these practitioners *conjure* with *technology* of various sorts moves us to consider the ways in which they *conjure technology* itself—the ways their beliefs consume and circumscribe machinery and technology, investing these objects and images with spiritual potency and situating them firmly within what Smith might call a *conjurational* worldview.

Mechanical Monetary Mojo: Professor Frank's Treasure Finding Machine

In the early 1940s, one Reverend Young from Mobile Alabama, describes an encounter with a professional Conjure doctor in New Orleans who has been enlisted to help in the recovery of some buried treasure. "Professor Frank" appears before Young clad in a resplendent ritual robe and cap, before an altar decked with horseshoes and other mystic images, and proceeds to read from *The Sixth and Seventh Books of Moses*—thus far, a relatively standard performance for connoisseurs of conjure. But then the Professor does something Young finds both unexpected and powerful:

> He took [us] in his back yard…had a rod that resembles a lightning rod. It was round and was made so it would go up and down at a certain length, a certain depth…*it was like a drill in one end and it was curved like a curved lightning [rod] wire. And he had some wires attached to it [the drill] -he apparently had these wires [also attached] on de wall of his house, possibly the electric wires, and place this machine out in de middle of de yard.* Worked it a certain way that it worked [drilled] itself down in de yard, and stood off from it, *waved his hand like magic and said some peculiar words three different times, and then flames of fire like lightning flamed up three different times at de top of this rod. Well, the man as well as mahself, we stood there amazed because it was - well, now you understand it. But*

after that he said that regardless of where dis money was buried, if it was an old well, if it was in water anywhere, or it was on dry land, dis machine would be sure to find it [emphasis mine].

HYATT 1970, entry 427

Reverend Young's "amazement" is understandable, given this elaborate performance of conjure ritual culminating in the incorporation of a wondrous machine into an overtly magical rite. Like the robe, the altar, the esoteric incantations, Professor Frank's flaming, sparking contraption is yet another sign of his power. It is an indication that he is master of mysterious forces simultaneously mystical and mechanical in nature. The substantial drama of this conjure performance might make us wonder whether Professor Frank is a mountebank, using his machine as an element of stagecraft to bedazzle a credulous client. That may certainly be true, but for our purposes, what matters most is that a machine like this one is presented as an entirely appropriate, even desirable, tool in the conjure doctor's arsenal. That this machine, while remarkable, is not is not a jarringly anomalous element, but rather an integral part of the process of occult treasure hunting, points to the propensity for techno-hermeneutic thought in Conjure. Reverend Young's account is certainly not unique within the Hyatt corpus. Treasure hunting seems one particular area in which conjure lore is rife with descriptions of complex machinery. Another of Hyatt's informants, from Old Point Comfort, Virginia, offers a description of a mechanically augmented dowsing apparatus:

They are supposed to have a machine. It's a round thing like a clock and has three points sticking out. One was set for gold, one for silver and the other for brass. It has two handles of hickory. You hold them two handles and walk along like you witch for water. When you walk over hidden money one of them points goes down.

HYATT 1970, entry 402

The following example, from St. Petersburg Florida, involves a pendulum-like machine that facilitates spirit contact in the service of locating buried treasure, harmonizing the mechanistic and animistic elements in Hoodoo cosmology:

Ah've seen one - it's a little article that hangs on a cord that - *the cord is made of 'lectric* [*wire*] - *it's got 'lectrified* [*needs electric power*] -but chew hand dat cord an' dat ball dat hangs - it a seven-pound ball an' it hangs on it. See, if dat money's anywhere roun' there...Wal now, yo' jest put thar an' give it a turn, jest turn it jest de least bit dat-a-way ant yo' talks to it... *Well, dey says, "Spirit" - jest lak whosomever dey name that buried dat money, dey call de first letter of yore name. You say, "Point me to dis money." An'* dat thing will jest wave an' wave till it git dere.

HYATT 1970, entry 407

This unusual object is presented as both an electrified dowsing instrument, and a pendulum for animistic interaction with the spirit world. As with Professor Frank's machine (the use of which is preceded by invocations from a spirit-commanding text) technological gadgetry and spirit contact are not seen as antithetical, but as complimentary aspects of the same ritual.

An interviewee from Waycross Georgia, addresses the traditional Euro-American belief that buried treasure is often guarded by vengeful ghosts or other malevolent supernatural figures, and that the would-be treasure hunter must read a sacred text and inscribe magic circles on the earth to keep the ghosts at bay (see Hand 1980). Hyatt's informant likewise insists that the treasure finding ritual requires a magic circle—but in this case, one made of *electrified wires*:

Ah ain't nevah done none, but ah hears dey have a needle - a search needle. Read de Bible - King Solomon - an' at de time dat chew is diggin', he have to read dat Bible. *Den yo' have - have to have yo' a dynamo concern, an' yo' have to have wires connected round from dat dynamo - round dat place - an' den dat'll keep dat devilment from coming in dere.* So dey tell me.

HYATT 1970, entry 406

Note that in this latter instance, the technological elements do not entirely supplant earlier traditions of occult treasure finding but are adapted and incorporated into them—perhaps even improving their efficacy. Incantations from the Bible remain, but the invisible supernatural power of a traditional magic circle composed of cabalistic names or substances of power is here re-imagined as electricity coursing through a circle of copper wire—all the better to keep any "devilment" away.

Hex-Tech: Cursing and Curing with Machines

In the Hyatt corpus we find a number of instances of occult machines employed to harm an intended victim. One example, narrated by another informant from Waycross, Georgia, illustrates how concepts of occult technology might be seamlessly integrated with the practice of traditional herbal "root work." Hyatt's informant describes the weakening of an enemy accomplished by securing his handwriting and signature on a piece of paper "dressed" with "Trumpet Root" (probably *Campsis Radicans*, an herb native to the American Southeast) and Cinquefoil or "Five Finger Grass"—a notable Hoodoo specific used for controlling and compelling:

> If yo' be from heah to New York, or yo' be from heah to Tallahassee, or yo' kin be heah to South Ca'lina, a man would take yore handwriting an' he kin work wit yo' in yore handwriting. Well...he dress dis piece of paper... between lines - yo' write between lines. He dresses it all between lines an' wheresomevah he put 'em, right on down to de closin'. Now after he dress it, why yore name is done signed dere. Well, all right, as long as he wise enough to send to New York to git *a magic drawing glass an' kinda work on dat crystal, balance on it like de movin' picture show* [*the fadeout?*] *an' stick dat clean up in dat magic drawing glass - wasn't but one thing done, an' say could draw yo' right on down, draw yore handwriting right on down to nuthin.* After while den yore fingers git right kinda cramped crossed yore muscle parts...*Dere people wise in de world to send off to New York an' git dese magic drawing glasses an' take it an' work it by 'lectricity - like yo' working* [*the recorder*] *right heah now* - set it ovah behin' like dis is heah, an' dey say, "Draw yore han' down...Yes sir, it will keep yo' down, too - where yo' can't use yore finger, can't shet yore hand, can't pick up yore hat."
>
> HYATT 1970, entry 1165

This tantalizing description makes us wonder what sort of contraption this magic drawing glass actually was. Some of the details call to mind a magic lantern, the focusing apparatus of which could indeed be used to "draw handwriting down to nothing."[1] My own suspicion is that the Magic Drawing Glass was a Balopticon, an electric projector marketed by Bausch and Lomb in the early 20th century, which was not only capable of projecting and manipulating glass slides, but opaque images as well.

Alternately, machines akin to the treasure hunting devices described previously could be used to ferret out hidden magical charms that have been "put

---

1   The use of magic lanterns in western esoteric practice, particularly late 19th and 20th century Masonic lodge instruction and initiation, is well-attested, and the idea of a projection machine that can weaken or kill its target also suggests the fearsome *Tepaphone* described by Czech Hermeticist Franz Bardon in his occult novel, *Frabato the Magician*.

down" to harm another. Consider this example collected from an informant from Wilmington, North Carolina in the early 1930's, in which the healer uses a machine to find hidden evidence of aggressive rootwork:

> I had a aunt, she got hurt, and it started up in her head and it jes' keep on worryin' her head. ...It [was] somepin wrapped up in a little bondle [bundle] and they had it over the door. It was some kinda powder and some sharp instruments in there, look kinda like pins...*It was a rootman find it. He took a little somepin like a watch and laid a fifty cents on that, and anywhere they got anything down, it was a little hand turned [either a compass or buried-treasure finder], and that little hand turned toward that door and he went and got it.* He took that [cunjuring object] - I don't know what he did wit it. He gave her some sweet milk and sheep bur and sulphur mixed together. And then she got well.
>
> HYATT 1970, entry 245

Clockwork Conjure

In addition to unusual instruments like those described above, more commonplace elements of technology are also absorbed into the *materia magica* of Conjure. We find alarm clocks, watches, and other time-pieces employed to bring separated lovers together, cause insanity, or exorcise malevolent spirits. The prevailing theme seems to be that the continual, relentless movement of the clockwork combined with steady rhythmic ticking serves to *drive* or *animate* a sacred assemblage towards a specific purpose. We can see this particular idea underlying two examples from Louisiana, the first intended to draw an individual to the operator, the second, to render an enemy "teetotally crazy":

> *Yo' take de pitchure of a person...an' yo' take a little small clock an' yo' stan' dat clock 'side of de person's pitchure. Yo' take a fruit of every kind...a orange an' a apple an' a pear an' a banana or bunch of grapes, an' yo' surround dat pitchure...*den yo' take [a blue candle], an' yo' put it befo' dat pitchure an' yo' light dat light - *an' ev'ry beat of dat clock, as dat clock beats, it's drawin' dat party.* But yo' turn dat pitchure wit de head down - upset 'em yo' see... an' when yo' light dat light yo' call de individual's name dat's on de pitchure. An' de individual dat chew want tuh come back, yo' call dere name. *Now, ev'ry beat of dat clock is goin' tuh bring dat person nearer to de othah - Algiers, Louisiana.*
>
> HYATT 1970, entry 14368

You write their name nine time on a piece of writing paper you never have used, with an indelible pencil...When you write that name, you got their mind...*If you got a old time clock in your home - Well, you just put that up in there straightways - where that [pendulum] swings. In nine days time you begin to commence to lose control of your mind. And it just run on like that, until you just go teetotally crazy and they have to take you and put you in the crazy house - New Orleans, Louisiana.*

HYATT 1970, entry 15426

Note, in both of these cases, that it is the persistent audible beat of the clock or the constant movement of the clockwork that is understood to effect the workings of the charm.

Another of Hyatt's informants blends technological sorcery and numismatic magic in a rite of exorcism (for a "place of business") involving a pendulum clock along with two coins frequently incorporated into conjure charms—an Indian head penny and a silver dime:

Ah'm goin' tuh drive out witchcraft wit dat clock. Now ah'm goin' git me an old Indian head penny, an' ah'm goin' git me a silver dime...An' ah'm goin' tuh nail dat penny right down on de bottom where dat pendulum will swing ovah it - an' don't 'low [allow] nobody tuh bother it. An' den dat dime, dat silver dime, ah'm goin' place it up right near where some of dose little wheels will sort of pass by it. An' ah'm goin' time dat clock...to clear off dis whole place of business heah jes' by yore sound – tick tock tick – of every kind of a spirit dat's come in heah tuh do harm, of all de witches an' witchcrafts an' all dat. Ah want chure sound to be a troublin' spirit tuh 'em, an' ah want 'em tuh go from heah runnin'. Well, dat silver dime, it jes' ketch all dat sound; dat penny down dere, dat jes' keep 'em on de move - an' dat pendulum run out every witch dere is in dis State—Waycross, Georgia.

HYATT 1970,entry 14902

In one of Hyatt's more fascinating interviews, a Conjure man from New Orleans describes a pantheon of hoodoo spirits, including one called "Unkus" who appears as a "little man with a *clock* in his belly":

He don't look more than that high [8 or 9 inches] with a *little clock on his belly*. A clock to keep time - right in his belly. He's the spirit of the atmosphere. And he got a nose just like a white man...and *he just stand there with a clock in his belly*. And you can tell what time it is - when he come and when he go, any time he appear. And everything you tell him, he

going to do it. You must be very unsuccessful, unlucky, when you kin get
the spirit of Unkus. And he going to assist you.

    HYATT 1970, entry 17613

I have elsewhere explored the ways in which the name of this spirit, and its
attendant rituals suggest connections to the Bakongo *minkisi* tradition, long
considered one of the most important streams of African esoteric thought influencing African American Folk Magic (Wehmeyer 2000).[2] Labeled as fetishes—
feticos or *"made things"*—by Portuguese colonists, these sacred images house
spirits embodied in powerful herbal and animal substances packed into their
protruding stomachs and capped with shining mirrors or glass indicating the
vital activity of the concealed medicines. The other elements of the ritual man-
dated by Hyatt's informant, including the sacrifice of infant pigeons and the
inscription of sacred signs marked on the earth also suggest strong African, and
specifically Bakongo, heritage for this example.[3] But Unkus Man's vivid description of a clockwork homunculus is a powerfully modern techno-hermeneutic
reinterpretation of this traditional spiritual aesthetic.[4] In light of the previously
discussed traditions of clockwork conjure, what more apt and powerful way to
represent the secret yet relentless workings of spirit than the hidden gears and
flywheels ticking and spinning away behind the clock-face?

Vehicular Witchery: Conjuring with Wheels

Clock-faces, whirligigs, pinwheels—any rotating wheel-like objects—may be
said to occupy a position of some prominence in African-American vernacular
aesthetics, particularly in yard art or other traditions of semiotic display
(Thompson 1983; Gundaker 1996, 2005). Grey Gundaker argues that all of these
may be classed as "signs of circular motion," and serve to evoke:

> ...the rising and setting of the sun – the cyclical dimensions of time in
> nature – and the continuities underlying change. As signs of progress and

---

2   See also Thompson (1983), MacGaffey (1988), and Brown (1990).
3   Perhaps most convincing, however, is the fact that the singular form for the Kikongo word for
    these spirit containers, known both in African and New World recensions of Kongo religion-
    Nkisi—shares a marked phonetic resemblance to the name of the spirit in Hyatt: "Unkus."
    (Wehmeyer, 2000).
4   This description might be augmented by acquaintance with figural clocks which were quite
    popular in the South in the 1930s and '40's.

accomplishment, wheels are also a reminder of the defeat of complacency through progressive action.

GUNDAKER 2005, 31

Thompson likewise attests to the persistent presence of symbolically loaded
wheels in African American sacred and secular assemblage, citing numerous
examples of tires, wagon wheels, hubcaps and other spinning symbols as visual
cognates to the ring shout—a fundamental trope in Black vernacular ritual
(Thompson 1998, 42–43).

It should come as no surprise then, that although perhaps among the sim-
plest of technological objects, the wheel enjoys a robust position in Conjure
lore as an ideal tool for manipulating and effecting powerful *returns* or *dis-
patches*—forcing a thief to return stolen goods, ensuring the return of a way-
ward lover, or sending an enemy far away. Selections from the Hyatt corpus
involving wheels are essentially variations on a common ritual practice.
Various objects or substances, like splinters from a doorsill, dust from a foot-
print, or shoe-leather are placed in the hub of the wheel. The wheel is then
either turned towards the operator with an incantation which will assuredly
force the desired party to return, or else it is permitted to roll away from the
operator, with the intention that its constant motion will make the unwanted
party "roll off."

The following examples, from Brunswick and New Orleans, for example, are
regional and cultural variants of a ritual described in one chapter of the *Sixth
and Seventh Books of Moses*, an occult text already established as having considerable influence on the rites of conjure:[5]

> If a thief had been to yo' home an' dey stolen anything, yo' go an' cut chew
> three splinters off de do'[door]. *Yo' take de wagon wheel an' take de nut off
> it an' put dose three splinters in dere an' put de wheel back on, an' den yo'
> turn de wheel slower. Yo' say to de thief, "Thief, thief, bring back de stolen
> goods,"* Yo' call his name three times. *"An' as shuah as de Virgin Mary shall*

---

5 The version of the Sixth and Seventh Books of Moses published by deLaurence, Scott, and Co.
   (Chicago, IL) in 1910, includes the following ritual prescription against a thief: "Therefore, in
   the name of the Father, Son, and Holy Spirit, *take three small pieces of wood from the door-sill
   over which the thief passed in leaving the place where he committed the theft, place them within
   a wagon-wheel, and then through the hub of the wheel say the following words: 'I pray thee, thou
   Holy Trinity, that thou mayest cause A, who stole from me B, a, C, to have no rest or peace until
   he again restores me that which he has stolen.'* Turn the wheel round three times and replace
   it again on the wagon" (p. 133).

not bring forth another son named Jesus, yo' shall bring back de stolen goods"—*Brunswick, Georgia.*
HYATT 1970, entry 13405

Yo' can take a wheel off a wagon an' dere's a word yo' use, but ah can't speak, but ah know it's in Hebrew. *An' yo' spins dis wheel.* An' at a certain time dey'll [thief will] bring it back—*New Orleans, Louisiana.*
HYATT 1970, entry 8947

Thieves are not the only objects of Conjure's traditions of cyclical sorcery. Desired romantic partners or unwanted suitors can be constrained to come and go at the will of the operator by rotating the wheel:

Wanta turn a woman roun'If she gone away from dere, turn dat wheel - turn it right now, if yo' wanta turn her back. If yo' wanta run her off, turn it right an' let her go' an' if yo' wanta bring her back, jes' turn it back to de center - jes' turn dat wheel back—*Florence, South Carolina.*
HYATT 1970, entry 13795

A subsequent example calls to mind the ritual involving the "magic drawing glasses" discussed earlier, as it too incorporates herbal *and* technological elements by "dressing" the wheel with dust from the victim's foot print and with the poisonous irritant *arum triphyllum* or "Indian Turnip" (Hyatt 1970, entry 13407). Another from New Orleans makes use of shoe leather—a common ingredient in Hoodoo rituals intended to *move* a friend, foe, or paramour (Hyatt 1970, entry 13408).

This widespread employment of wheels in conjure work sheds light on a lurid mystery involving a famous (perhaps notorious) rootworker from New Jersey known as Dr. Hyghcock.[6] Mentioned in a litany of working clairvoyants by one of Hyatt's informants, Hyghcock was a healer and spiritual leader, offering consultations, church services, love magic, and—as the police would claim, abortions—to a largely female constituency in the Trenton/Camden area during the early 1920's. Under trumped-up charges of murder, Police arrested

---

6 "Doctor" is one of the more common titles taken by rootworkers in the Southeast, perhaps most famously by the legendary South Carolina healer, "Dr. Buzzard." The title is more than self-aggrandizing affectation, however—it is a term used almost ubiquitously by those who believe in conjure to denote knowledge and expertise in the craft. Whether they take it upon themselves or not, specialists are often referred to by others as "Root Doctors" or "Conjure Doctors" (see Jackson 1976; and Brown 1990).

Hyghcock and raided a complex of rooms and tunnels he'd excavated under his Trenton home. According to reports and interrogation transcripts published in newspapers nationwide, Hyghcock's secret rooms were filled with "Wires, bells, complicated signaling devices" and "networks of ropes and pulleys." An article in the Camden Courier maintains that one room "held a large cartwheel daubed with streaks of white paint on each spoke, mounted on a short upright axis set into the ground, permitting its rotation. Above the wheel was suspended a stuffed bird. The legs could be made to twitch and the wings to flap by the manipulation of a set of strings attached to them" (*"'Voodoo' is held for murder"* 1925). Another room tellingly contained "a baptismal font, a large Bible, and a carriage wheel with various colored spokes. *The wheel spins from an iron peg driven into the wall*" (*Voodoo Man confesses Bigamy* 1925.) [Emphasis mine]. Sensational press accounts call these objects "the wheel of vengeance" and "the wheel of fate" correspondingly (*Secrets of Vicious Voodoo Doctors* 1926). Yet we might readily assume these wheels were employed in rites like those described by Hyatt's informants, especially since the Camden Courier-Post subsequently reports the following incantation found in one of Hyghcock's confiscated notebooks:

> In the name of the father, son, and holy spirit, you devil, you, I want you to go just as far as God all Mighty's wind and water and fire can possibly carry, who carry you away no more no more to return throughing [sic] over your shoulder holding your right hand, *Wheel turn quick*. Don't look back March away) [Emphasis mine].
>
> Mystic's 'Library' full of weird jargon 1926

Peering *behind* the prurient and sensationalistic media accounts of Hyghcock's elaborate underground constructions, we find resonances with the sophisticated traditions of African-American yard-art documented by Thompson and Gundaker—art which often encodes esoteric knowledge and revelation. Vernacular visionaries like Henry Dorsey, whose electrokinetic yard sculptures incorporate fan-blades, hubcaps, tires and other whirling images are *conjuring* with technology—establishing these wheels as what Thompson calls "personal idioms of transcendence" (Thompson 1983). And yet that idiom is far from purely personal, as we see conjure doctors like Rev. Hyghcock, and Hyatt's informants interpreting and re-interpreting the self-same objects in comparable ways.[7]

---

7   We must also consider the techno-hermeneutic aspects of Minister Louis Farrakhan's ecstatic vision of the UFO-like "Mother Wheel," which Stephen C. Finley articulates as an "internalized image of perfection" which can be read as "that unchanging, transcendental technology that ultimately defines black bodies everywhere" (Finley 2012: 450, 448).

Steamfunk Spirits—Mechanical Mojo in Afro-Atlantic Speculative Fiction

The investiture of technological and mechanical objects with esoteric and spiritual significance, the employment of the image of technology as a code for spiritual presence and power, the creative integration of mechanical and botanical elements in one metaphysical system—these are the hallmarks of techno-hermeneutics in African-American vernacular esotericism. While these traditions continue to exert strong influences on the narratives and material arts associated with African American spiritualities, they can be discerned as well in the works of African-American dramatists, and writers of science fiction and magical realism. In the staging instructions for *A Black Mass* (1965), LeRoi Jones/Amiri Baraka indicates that the scene should include "the outline of some fantastic chemical laboratory...with weird mixtures bubbling, colored solutions (or solutions that glow in the dark)...signs in Arabic and Swahili on the walls. Strange drawings, diagrams of weird machines" (Jones 1969). The play is Jones' masterful retelling of the Nation of Islam's cosmogonic myth of the ancient Islamic Wizard-Scientist Jacoub, whose unholy experiments create White people, and bring evil into the world. In this play, which Alondra Nelson has convincingly glossed as a "Black Frankenstein" (2006), Jones blends the imagery of science and technology with ideas of magic, sorcery and spiritual craft. Nation of Islam sacred history holds that Yakub/Jacoub was inspired while playing with magnets as a child, and Jones imaginatively expands this technological imagery to include a "fantastic chemical laboratory" and "diagrams of weird machines." The *sounds* of sorcery in this play are likewise mechanical—klaxons and sirens. It is clear that Jones is critiquing and, to some degree, condemning these occult technologies as disruptive and evil, but they are no less spiritually powerful for being spiritually dangerous. What matters most is that they are inextricable from his vision of magic and sorcery (even of the most sinister sort).

In more recent decades, "Afrofuturist" writers and authors of Afro-centric speculative fiction have also explored intersections between traditional Afro-Atlantic esotericism and images and icons of technology. Nalo Hopkinson's work, in particular, demonstrates a developing techno-hermeneutic trajectory. In her first novel, *Brown Girl in the Ring* (1998), Hopkinson envisions a dystopian future Toronto in which a disenfranchised multi-ethnic underclass *opposes* a technologically advanced, largely White, hegemony with an earthy blend of pan-Caribbean supernatural belief, folk-healing, and trance-possession ritual. In subsequent writings, this dichotomy begins to break down, as Hopkinson begins to *conjure with* technology herself, imagining esoteric aspects of African-derived mystery religions as technological realities in an Afrofuturist vision. In her novel *Midnight Robber,* for example, Anansi—Ashanti/Caribbean spider-trickster—and Nana Buruku, Yoruba earth goddess and ground-of-all-being, become fused as "Granny Nanny"[8] a nano-technological neural network facilitating communication between the human colonists on Planet Toussaint (Hopkinson 2000). Contemporary Afro-centrist fantasy author and blogger Balogun Ojetade has issued a passionate call for Black voices in the wildly popular steampunk genre of speculative fiction, as a corrective to what he sees as a romantic whitewashing (literal and figurative) of the 19th century in a genre which tends to skirt "issues of racism, sexism, classism, colonialism and imperialism" (Ojetade—*What is Steamfunk?,* 2012). Ojetade's own contribution to the emergent *Steamfunk* subgenre, *Moses: The Chronicles of Harriet Tubman,* is replete with steam-powered dirigibles, a swashbuckling Harriet Tubman, and *Knolls*—menacing supernatural creatures like animated hillocks made of roots and earth, each bearing "a bronze clock the size of a dinner plate" in its chest (Ojetade—*Moses,* 2012). Ojetade's conjuring with technology in the realm of popular fiction brings us squarely back to the mysterious clockwork homunculus described by Hyatt's *Unkus Man,* and suggests how powerfully these tropes resonate with African American visions of the otherworldly, supernatural, and esoteric.

I've provided only a handful of examples here, and limited analysis, but I think at this juncture a number of key points are evident. These are not isolated, anomalous elements in the Conjure corpus. Their geographic distribution, multiple variation and persistence through time suggest that we are dealing with stable traditions in Black Vernacular esotericism—no less stable or influential than the botanical traditions more popularly associated with Rootwork. These traditions, moreover, resonate with comparable currents in African American visual, literary, and dramatic arts. This complex, yet entirely sensible interweaving of technological and spiritual themes, this use of technological symbols to express subtle spiritual knowledge—this propensity for "techno-hermenutics"—challenges essentialist visions of Hoodoo as an exclusively or even primarily "natural" esoteric practice, and further challenges stereotypical perceptions of its practitioners as simple folk steeped in rural natural wisdom. The Conjure Woman or Rootsman needs to be seen instead as a sophisticated *bricoleur,* to whom even the most modern conveniences and gadgets provide tools for exploring and working the world of spirit. Like its musical cousin, the Blues, Conjure is an accretive, adaptive art, and defies attempts to rigidly restrict its boundaries or instrumentation. Ultimately, the

---

8   Or sometimes "Granny 'Nansi"—shorthand for the "Grande Nanotech Sentient Interface."

recognition of techno-hermeneutic traditions as an essential current in African American folk magic helps to free us from a crippling insistence that Black esoteric thought and practice is fundamentally anachronistic, exclusively naturalistic, and disengaged from modernity. The "conjurational contraptions" found in the folk record invite us to consider a sophisticated vernacular esotericism whose narratives and material culture are marked, not just by roots, but by gears, wheels, and wires as well.

CHAPTER 16

Portraying Portraits

The Intersectionality of Self, Art, and the Lacanian Gaze in the Nahziryah Monastic Community

Margarita Simon Guillory and Aundrea Matthews

Introduction

Who on Earth...Who in the world...are the Purple People? These two questions
serve as the title of the main book outlining the belief system of the Nahziryah
Monastic Community (NMC). These interrogatives also act as the driving force
behind the materialization of this essay. Both authors are intrigued by this
group's fluid ritualistic activities and convoluted belief system, particularly
their use of material culture to articulate ideas about beingness and selfhood.
After exhaustive rounds of investigation, these same authors, much like the
group that they studied, began to ask specific questions. Why have groups like
the Nahziryah Monastic Community received little scholarly treatment in
African American religious studies? More importantly, how can an exploration
of the NMC's use of material culture to articulate a complex conception of selfhood premised on the dissolution of social categories like race further diversify
African American religion?

This essay considers such questions in that it explores this group's usage of
art to convey an esoteric understanding of selfhood. Specifically, self-portraits
act as objects of reflexivity affording members and non-members the ability
to experience an expansion of consciousness i.e. self-progression. The four
sections of this chapter seek to unpack this aesthetic reflexivity in the manifestation of self as conceived among the "Purple People." The first section
offers a historical narrative of the Nahziryah Monastic Community. The second section unpacks this group's convoluted conception of self—a notion of
self premised on intersectionality between consciousness, physical/psychical
differentiation and mergence. The third section employs Lacanian notions of
gazing and *mirroring* to provide a brief examination of the occurrence of
intricate encounters occurring between NMC conceptions of self, self portraits, and individuals via the creation of a "reciprocated gaze." This gaze is
defined as an interpretative view created through the interaction of the object
(e.g., self portrait) and individual to apprehend a non-differentiated notion of
selfhood. The last section discusses the major implications of this chapter on

© KONINKLIJKE BRILL NV, LEIDEN, 2015 | DOI 10.1163/9789004283428_018

Western Esotericism in particular and African American religious studies in general.

History and Belief System of the Nahziryah Monastic Community

The historical trajectory of the Nahziryah Monastic Community (NMC) begins with a single figure, Reverend Baba Nazirmoreh K.B. Kedem (All Blessings and Respect Due). Reverend Nazirmoreh (ABRD), according to the order's newsletter *The Purple Veil*, is the direct descendent of a patrilineal line of mystics: both his father and grandfather were masters of esoteric knowledge. Reverend Nazirmoreh's (ABRD) patrilinear inheritance remains latent until early adulthood, when at that time he happens upon a small book while rummaging through the basement of an old house. The book, more specifically the book's title, acts as a projection screen displaying the purposes of both his past lives and present life. This basement experience confirms for Reverend Nazirmoreh (ABRD) the presence of a hereditarily transmitted spiritual gift. The revelation, furthermore, catapults him onto an esoteric path. He immediately enters intense training in the teachings of the "Ancient Ones," which results in his initiation. (*The Purple Veil* 1994) Interestingly enough, the biographical account offered by the NMC does not list either the location of this training or the name of the "high adept" who initiates Reverend Nazirmoreh (ABRD), but despite this, his establishment of the NMC as a monastic order in 1970 as a result of his initiation has been documented. (*The Drama* 2005, 10–11) Reverend Nazirmoreh (ABRD), in addition to organizing the NMC, simultaneously forms the Nazir Order of the Purple Veil—the initiated order of the NMC whose members are distinguished by the wearing of purple garments (to be discussed later in this section). Thus, from the very beginning, he puts into place a porous organizational structure that would allow for varying degrees of membership and initiation in the NMC. The maturation of this structure occurs when the NMC relocates to Louisiana.

In 1985, Reverend Nazirmoreh (ABRD) moves the NMC from an undisclosed "wilderness" location to the urban terrain of New Orleans. While in the Crescent City, he expands the structural organization of the NMC by introducing three additional degrees of membership: (1) student-visitor, (2) helper-supporter, and (3) direct-student. These non-residential levels afford individuals the ability to take advantage of NMC's resources without a commitment to the monastic way of life as practiced by residential members. Direct-student membership, unlike the first two, is the candidacy level, which precedes full time residential membership into the NMC. Equally important to these structural changes, Reverend Nazirmoreh (ABRD) opens two centers known as the Veil of Truth Center for Metaphysical and Esoteric Learning in New Orleans. These NMC centers, open to both members and non-members, provide resources (e.g., meditative exercises and esoteric literature) meant to foster positive self-imaging and to garner multiple understandings of metaphysical and esoteric knowledge. Despite the NMC's accomplishments in New Orleans, Reverend Nazirmoreh (ABRD) moves the NMC to St. Joe, Arkansas, a small town located in the Ozark Mountains. This move represents a return of the NMC back to their wilderness roots of the early 1970s. The Veil of Truth centers continue providing services in New Orleans until 1999, at that time, Reverend Nazirmoreh (ABRD) relocates the Center for Metaphysical and Esoteric Learning to St. Joe. Presently, the full operation of the NMC, including the Nazir Order of the Purple Veil, Veil of Truth Center, Nazir Art Crafts, and Retreat for Meditation and Holistic Living, is located in the Ozarks.

Relocation of the NMC to the Ozarks is deliberate in that such isolation allows members of the monastic order to practice a specific mode of living. Daily meditation, adherence to a vegan-vegetarian diet via organic gardening, and respectful interaction with nature through practices such as recycling are key markers of the NMC way of life. The core of this life, however, is Truth-centeredness. Each of the NMC's publications includes the following words of Reverend Nazirmoreh (ABRD): "Our beliefs, our way of life are founded in Truth. Truth which is beyond any one religion. Truth which is found in all religions" (*Letters from an Open Book* 2005, 11). Truth, as conceived of in this way, is incapable of being fully contained in one religion, but rather finds a place in multiple belief systems. For Reverend Nazirmoreh (ABRD) practicing a specific way of life like that offered by the NMC serves as a way to apprehend Truth.

The teachings of Reverend Nazirmoreh (ABRD) highlight four primary principles characterizing Truth. Belief in a single Creator is the first Truth principle. The Creator is not just the originating source of all existence but rather transcends present temporality in that the Creator is the author of "all that is, was, and ever shall be" (*Who on Earth...*2006, 74). This interconnection between creativity and beingness leads to the second principle known as the "Truth of Being." Each member of the NMC understands themselves as "beings of the Divine Essence of all that is, was and ever shall be" (*Letters from an Open Book* 2005, 11). Their existence is not determined by social categories like race, gender, and class but by their inextricable connection to the Divine Creator, whose very essence shapes members of the NMC identity. Members in this way are representative of the emanating essence of the Creator. They are the Divine Essence. Additionally, beingness is thought of as complex and multidimensional.

Although members believe in the multidimensionality of being, they are taught to bring into harmony the "physical, mental, and spiritual aspects of [their] being" (*Letters from an Open Book* 2005, 11). This harmonization of beingness leads to a state of *at-one-ment*, the third Truth principle of the NMC. Attainment of at-one-ment requires NMC members and non-members seeking guidance from Reverend Nazirmoreh (ABRD) to transcend all limitations. In an email correspondence with a non-member who self-identifies as a "gay black male," Reverend Nazirmoreh's (ABRD) attempts to explain this fourth Truth principle of transcendence:

> Keep purple within your view...it is a color of the highest spiritual vibratory rate. It will assist to *transcend* this simple dimension—and enable you or assist you to view the cosmos; within the cosmos with a clearer vision; seeing the glimpses of your true spiritual essence. Beyond the body. Beyond the mind. Beyond the penis. Beyond the black. Beyond the male. Beyond the female.
>
> *Who on Earth...*2006, 39, emphasis added

From the onset Reverend Nazirmoreh (ABRD) instructs this young man to keep his eyes focused on the color purple, for it embodies the "highest vibratory rate." Continual focus on these elevated vibrations, therefore, is the key in transcending limitations. This NMC belief of transcendence through vibratory color symbolism aligns with electromagnetic spectrum theory, which considers interconnections between vibration, wavelength, and light dispersion. In theory, purple, because of its high vibration and short wavelength, possesses the ability to disperse light at a very fast pace. A direct correlation between dispersion and transcendence is set up in such a way that purple's vibratory rate, as Reverend Nazirmoreh (ABRD) suggests, results in greater insight. This endowment of "clearer vision" allows the sensitized individual, or in the case above, the young man to see "glimpses" of his "true spiritual essence." Insight into his true nature, then, acts as a driving force, empowering him to push beyond socially constructed categories of gender, sexuality, and race. This push against such categories is representative of the essentiality of identity (de)construction in NMC doctrine. As Reverend Nazirmoreh (ABRD) states in the previous quote, the individual must deconstruct one's commitment to identity formation based on social norms by "transcend[ing] the simple dimension." Such deconstruction allows individuals to construct a form of identity premised on their "true spiritual essence,"—an essence whose origin is not found in society but in a single Creator. This focus on identity serves as a connective strand conjoining each the NMC's four principles of Truth. To this end, divinely oriented identity (i.e. selfhood) construction is a core element in the doctrinal and ritual activities of the NMC.

From "Self" to "Self": Notions of *Selves* in the Nahziryah Monastic Community

Embedded within the doctrine of the NMC is a bipolar structural model of selfhood. This model contains two contrasting conceptions of selfhood posited as self and Self. The small "s" self is representative of the ego and occupies the lowest level in the NMC's model, while the large "s" Self symbolizes complete dissolution of the ego, which leads to the highest level of ascension (highest level of selfhood). Consciousness connects these two poles. Consciousness is not stagnant, but rather it is a varying state of awareness, which drives and directs the movement of an individual from small "s" self to large "s" Self. A full understanding of the NMC's conception of selfhood requires exploring inter-connections between multi-varied selfhood and consciousness, for this reason, the following section exams in greater detail the two self-poles and associated processes utilized in the progression of NMC members from self to Self.

The lowest level of selfhood is equated with the ego, or sense of self. The small "s" self is a "me" form of identity based on individuation—a process of becoming an individual by promoting one's qualities of uniqueness in rela-tionship to that of others. Thus, separateness is the necessary catalyst utilized in the formation of this mode of self. Defining this form of self is important in NMC literature. Perhaps more significant, however, is how the ego functions. In the words of Reverend Nazirmoreh (ABRD), the ego is the "mundane physical material programmed conditioned consciousness distractions" (*Who on Earth*...2006, 43). Here, before Reverend Nazirmoreh (ABRD) discusses the pri-mary function of the ego, he considers the materiality of the ego. The ego is not reduced to a psychical component of the personality; instead it is equated to the body, which leads to an understanding of self as a "mundane physical material vehicle" (*Who on Earth*...2006, 31). For Reverend Nazirmoreh (ABRD), this materialized ego is a source of contention for it constantly interjects dis-tractions into the consciousness. These interjections, according to him, result from the construction of identities that are premised on physical markers. Race, gender, and sexuality in this sense are not considered social categories solely, instead they are distractions formed by an individual commitment to an embodied ego. These distractive self-representations, in the words of Reverend Nazirmoreh (ABRD), "hold masses spellbound in the Veil of Illusion and limit[s] the mind" (*Who on Earth...*2006, 66). Thus, ego-based distractions lead to both an illusory self-image and restricted consciousness. According to NMC doctrine, the latter is the result of a process known as crystallization. An individual possessing a crystallized state of consciousness resists the apprehension of knowledge and lacks the basic understanding of self-identification beyond distractions offered by the embodied ego. This state, then, represents the lowest level of consciousness, a state characterized by a limited degree of awareness. NMC members are instructed to move beyond an illusory, limiting form of small "s" self towards a higher level of selfhood, large "s" Self, which counteracts the restrictive process of crystallization.

Movement towards a form of self premised on ego dissolution is dependent on the apprehension of the NMC's four Truth principles. In an email exchange with a non-member, Reverend Nazirmoreh (ABRD) discusses the interrelationship between these principles and the formation of an ego independent form of Self:

> I am not this body, I am not this mind, I am not the commonly accepted programmed conditioned crystallization in one area, at one degree of projection/information/direction/being. I am One with all Existence, all Being, all Beings, all Religions, Directions, Life Living—toward the consciousness expansion and further spiritual development of all Existence of all Beings transcending the limitation/crystallization/isolation of commonly accepted normality of programmed conditioned limitations/isolations/ego confrontation.
>
> *Who on Earth...*2006, 5

Reverend Nazirmoreh (ABRD) in this quote forefronts the bipolar structural model of selfhood present in NMC doctrine by addressing processes involved in the formation of each form of self: small "s" self and large "s" Self. Again, he recognizes crystallization as a limiting agent for it restricts the growth of the individual consciousness, yielding an ego-controlled mode of self. This process not only isolates the individual, but it also leads the person to commit to a self-definition that is determined by commonly (i.e., socially) "programmed conditioned limitations." For Reverend Nazirmoreh (ABRD) such a commitment must be confronted in order to apprehend the large "s" Self that moves beyond the body, mind, and ego dominance. Confrontation of this type, according to Reverend Nazirmoreh (ABRD), requires a commitment to fluid processes and belief systems like those respectively expressed as "consciousness expansion" and the principles of Truth.

"We expand our consciousness and our understanding when we," according Reverend Nazirmoreh (ABRD), "align with higher Truths of being" (*Who on Earth*...2006, 3). Thus, expansion of one's consciousness is not a spontaneous process but is dependent on individuals aligning themselves with the NMC's four principles of Truth: (1) Existence of a single Creator who is the origin of Divine Essence; (2) Humans are representatives of this essence; (3) Beingness is multidimensional and undergoes harmonization yielding a state of at-one-ment; and (4) Oppositional limitations to at-one-ment are confronted by transcendence. For Reverend Nazirmoreh (ABRD), those seeking large "s" Self must first recognize the interrelationship between the Creator as Divine Essence and humans. The former is the universal radiating source of essence, while the former, in the words of Reverend Nazirmoreh (ABRD), "are the Divine Essence: the breath of life dwelling within physical, material vehicles while traveling in and on this particular plane of existence" (*Who on Earth*...2006, 11). This form of humanness acknowledges a divinely oriented nature without denying materiality. Individuals who orient themselves toward this form of beingness express an alignment with the first two NMC principles of Truth. More importantly, however, their alignment initiates a process of spiritual development known within the NMC community as *consciousness expansion*—defined here as work exerted to overcome the mind/body split.

This desire to overcome a Cartesian split results in the expansion of one's consciousness. Furthermore, it serves as another step in the movement towards large "s" Self in that the individual now seeks to enter into a state of at-one-ment, the third Truth principle. A considerable amount of NMC doctrine is committed to explaining what this term means, how it can be apprehended, and the results that follow the apprehension of this state. The primary NMC literary tract *Who on Earth Are the Purple People* defines at-on-ment as the harmonization of the "physical, mental, and spiritual aspect" of an individual's being (*Who on Earth*...2006, 3). The resulting state is the product of what Reverend Nazirmoreh (ABRD) calls *merging*. His discussion of this process in a short essay entitled, "Merging," is worth quoting at length:

> You reach a degree in which you say, 'I'm not involved, I'm not involuted and not individuated. I've reached a level of consciousness by knowing that I'm a part of All That Is, Was and Ever Shall Be. I am a part of the universal wholeness and oneness of all existence, and all things...' You reach a degree of awareness whereas you feel the need of knowing to unite with your brothers and sisters, beyond the body, beyond the mind, beyond the physical, race, nationality, sex, and so

on and so forth...You reach a degree beyond division and attune to the
Oneness of All.
*Who on Earth...*2006, 9

Reverend Nazirmoreh (ABRD) begins this excerpt by listing two countertuitive
processes: involution and individuation. These processes lead to the formation
of identities premised on turning inwardly and differentiating oneself from
others, respectively. Identity formation of this kind is ego driven and prevents
persons from reaching at-one-ment. According to Reverend Nazirmoreh
(ABRD) if these same individuals, however, openly accept and constantly
reflect on the third Truth principle of at-one-ment, then they would move
towards a higher "level of consciousness." For him, this movement correlates to
consciousness expansion. It is this expanded consciousness garners individuals with the power to move beyond or transcend (4th NMC Truth principle)
societal categories such as "race, nationality, and sex." Rejection of social division coupled with the acceptance of "universal wholeness and oneness of all
existence" symbolizes the process of merging and the resulting state of at-one-
ment. Persons operating at this degree not only have apprehended the third
and fourth principle, but they also have aligned themselves with the first two
NMC Truth principles. They realize their connection to the Divine Essence.
These individuals, then, understand that they are, in the words of Reverend
Nazirmoreh (ABRD), "a part of All That Is, Was and Ever Shall Be." It must be
noted, however, that Reverend Nazirmoreh (ABRD) warns those seeking alignment with the four Truth principles of the continuous struggle they will face
with the ego. He states:

> So even the realization and the knowing of that and reaching that degree
> of awareness, you're still bombarded by thought energies and your still
> struggling, you see. You feel beautiful and very much attuned, at One.
> And then the energies get you bombarded—because you're still center-
> ing in 'me' to a certain extent. And that's a part of the ego too.
> *Who on Earth...*2006, 9

For Reverend Nazirmoreh (ABRD) the recognition of one's interconnection
to the Divine Essence and the ability to transcend societal, physical, and
mental limitations in order to achieve at-one-ment does not free NMC members and seeking non-members from the counteractive force of the ego.
These individuals will continuously "struggle" with a barraging ego attempting to form a small "s" self. Due to this constant threat, the NMC has put
in place various methods, which can be utilized to oppose this psychical

bombardment of the ego. Meditation, esoteric/exoteric healing, and material culture manipulation represent examples of such methods made available to both members and non-members who seek to form a higher form of Self (i.e., large "s" Self).

Portraying Portraits: Self-Portraits, the Lacanian Gaze, and the Articulation of Self

While meditative and eso/exo-teric practices represent paths taken to reach a large "s" Self, material culture usage is the most commonly employed way to apprehend this self-definition. Material culture here is primarily concerned with the employment of "instrumental objects" (Morgan 2010, 72). These objects afford individuals the ability to exercise agency. They also are, in the words of David Morgan, "objects of intrinsic value enabling humans to imagine their relationship to people, institutions, histories, or gods they experience as sacred" (Morgan 2010, 72). Thus, material culture involves the mediumistic usage of objects to enact agency and relationality. For members and seeking non-members of the NMC, specific objects are mediating agents that allow them to reach a higher form of Self. For instance, harmonizers are examples of instrumental objects utilized by these individuals to move towards a state of at-one-ment. These multi-colored objects composed of resin, metal, and crystal combat "unharmonious emanations such as negative thought atmosphere pressures—chaotic frequencies [that] compromises one's abilities to be in tune and in touch with one's inner being" (Nahziryah Monastic Community 2013). Users may wear these objects as pendants or place larger versions in their home. Either way, harmonizers act as an ionic compound producing positive and negative charges that are representative of harmonic vibrations. These vibrations counter lower frequencies of chaos and disorder normally associated with ego activity. More importantly, harmonizers balances one's mental, physical, emotional, and spiritual aspects. Belief in the re-aligning power of harmonizers illustrates an alignment with the third Truth principle of at-one-ment. Accordingly, as discussed in the previous section, individuals aligning themselves with NMC Truth principles are endowed with power to transcend individuation in such a way as to construct an identity premised on universal wholeness—unification with the Divine Essence and representatives of this essence (i.e., humans). To this end, they use harmonizers to apprehend a sense an agency that affords them the ability to move towards a more expanded conception of Self.

While harmonizers represent the latest objects offered by Reverend Nazirmoreh (ABRD) to apprehend a large "s" Self, Nazir art crafts have been employed since the late-1970s by practitioners to gain this form of self. Thus, art crafts serve as the oldest medium of material culture used in the NMC to acquire spiritual attunement in order to move towards an expansive Self. Nazir art crafts include but are not limited to colorful garments, crocheted head-pieces/pouches, and handcrafted jewelry. The 2012 Nazir Art Catalog states the following in regard to the production of these items: "Rev. Nazirmoreh (A.B.R.D.) often will say...'Nazirmoreh would like to see this made' and pro-ceed to describe the vision to brothers and/or sisters of the community. It is then up to us to produce it" (Nazir Art Crafts Catalog, 2012). NMC art crafts, then, are divinely-inspired visions made concrete realities respectively through Reverend Nazirmoreh (ABRD) and select NMC members. Both parties act as creative mediums in that they are the intervening substance responsible for the manifestation of the crafts. Like them, these crafts also serve as mediating vehicles, for they propel interested individuals towards a higher form of Self.

For over three decades, clothing and jewelry were the most commonly used articles of material culture used in obtaining Self through spiritual attunement. Most recently, however, paintings and portraits have become instrumental means in obtaining this same form of Self. For example, cosmic paintings are readily displayed in the monastery's art gallery and readily available on-line for purchase. Painted by Reverend Nazirmoreh (ABRD), these acrylic works of art are "spontaneous and absolutely one-of-a-kind; they are ONE with the All in All, in truth, light and love" (Nazir Art Crafts Catalog 2012, 28). According to Reverend Nazirmoreh (ABRD), these paintings are projections of the emanat-ing essence of the Divine Creator. Reverend Nazirmoreh (ABRD) only considers himself a projector; accordingly, he views the canvass as an essence-projecting screen. These paintings because they are concrete manifestations of the Divine Essence can be employed as meditative pieces. Specifically, individuals are advised to meditate on the cosmic meaning captured in the paintings. Such meditation places the individual in a position to move towards the transmit-ting oneness of the painting. Such a posture initiates consciousness expansion. This process empowers the person to move from an ego-dominated form of self towards a more ego-independent mode of Self.

In addition to these acrylic paintings, NMC portraits are also available for those seeking to articulate a large "s" Self. A female NMC member creates these portraits in the NMC's painting studio. The NMC catalog describes her as "a direct student/disciple of the Reverend Baba Nazirmoreh (A.B.R.D.) [who] has lifetimes of experience and training for expressing through the means of visual art." Thus, her apprenticeship with the spiritual head of the NMC conjoined with her experience as an artist serves to validate her. The description contin-ues by interrelating the artist to the creative product:

The objective is not to focus on the artist's renowned fame and notoriety—but to focus on the artwork which is produced *through* the artist not *by* the artist. Herein lies the key; to be an instrument for invoking the more spiritual and noble elements of our being.

NAZIR Art Crafts Catalog 2012, 35

Purpose over notoriety is the overall focus of this excerpt. Interested individuals are made aware of the artist's temporal capabilities but not at the expense of emphasizing her spiritual gifts and abilities. The artist's ability to tap into her inner beingness places her in a position where she can adequately allow artwork to be divinely "produced through her." Like Reverend Nazirmoreh (A.B.R.D.)'s cosmic paintings, the origin of these hand painted portraits is attributed to the Divine Creator, but the process of manifestation works through the human vessel. Not only does this artistic NMC nun possess the ability to tap into her own spiritual essence, she, according to the quote, acts as "an instrument for invoking the more spiritual and noble elements" of both NMC members and seeking non-members beingness. To this end, while the artist creates a product of materiality, it is ultimately meditation on this creative product, i.e., painted portrait, which moves individuals towards a higher form of self-actualization.

Although painted portraits in the image of animals and nature scenery are readily available, self portraits are the most requested images used in self-expansion. An interested individual is asked to send a headshot of himself or herself to the artist. The artist then paints a picture of the individual unto either a canvass using acrylic paint or on a NMC natural fiber scroll using a specialized mixture of acrylics, watercolors, and ink. These creations are called self-portraits, even though the painting is not of the artist herself. The reasoning behind this augmentation of the traditional conception of the term is captured in the overall objective of these painted portraits. A detailed description found in the NMC catalog of art crafts clearly articulates this purpose:

To emphasize and point out the noble and positive attributes of ones' higher self. The sometimes serious; the sometimes joyous side of ones' being, however, touching upon that which is beyond personality; that which transcends the me, mine, selfish aspects of the self.

NAZIR Art Crafts Catalog 2012, 33

The artist, while she captures the likeness of the subject's emotional posture, moves beyond just direct transference. Specifically, she utilizes the actual picture to depict an image of the person's highest form of Self. This higher Self is exalted, honorable, and without negativity. It evades the individuated trappings of the ego in that it "transcends the me, mine, selfish aspects of the self." In this way, individuals interested in obtaining a large "s" Self through the use of a self portrait enters a process that moves beyond mere interaction between the material object and the individual but now involves the indirect participatory action of the NMC artist. Lacanian psychoanalysis, specifically his theory of the gaze and mirroring, helps to unpack this convoluted progression from an ego dominated to a more expanded conscious form of self.

Progression through self portrait usage begins with the activation of the gaze. According to Lacan, the gaze is "constituted by way of vision, and ordered in the figures of representation, something slips, passes, is transmitted, from stage to stage, and is always to some degree eluded in it" (Miller 1978, 73). The gaze's interconnection between figural representations and its transmissibility are two properties of interest in discussing how individuals use NMC derived self portraits to possess a higher Self. Transmission of the gaze begins with a subject. In the case of NMC self-portrait usage, the resident artist drives the gaze. Specifically, it is her *desire* to capture a certain image of the person requesting a self-portrait from the NMC. Lacan grapples with this desire of the artist in his work *The Four Fundamental Concepts of Psycho-Analysis*. He asks, "What is the desire which is caught, fixed in the picture, but which also urges the artist to put something into operation?" (Miller 1978, 93). "Certainly, in the picture," Lacan answers, "something of the gaze is always manifested" (Miller 1978, 101). Likewise, for the NMC resident artist the resulting portrait of the individual's higher Self is a concretized form of the gaze of the artist. The painted portrait, then, is "a trap for the gaze" (Miller 1978, 89).

In painting the portrait, the NMC artist focuses on the face of the individual, particular the eyes. For this reason, the artist requests that interested individuals "send a close-up photograph (minimum size 5" x 3") which preferably shows clearly the windows to the soul (your eyes)" (Nazir Art Crafts Catalog 2012, 32). This interaction between the artist and photo vividly captures a modified notion of Lacanian notion of the gaze. For Lacan the gaze originates with the object i.e., photo. Thus, when the artist looks at the photo, it is "already gazing back at [her], but from a point in which the subject cannot see it" (Evans 1996, 72). The gaze in this way is on the side of the object. However, in the interaction between the requested photo and the NMC artist occurring in the monastery's studio the latter initiates the gaze with the former. It is the artist's desire to capture the noble and positive aspects of the higher Self; hence, intense focus on the facial features of the person serves as the driving catalyst in the creation of the gaze. Unlike Lacan's theory, the gaze in this way is both on the side of the object, but more importantly, it is on the side of the subject or the NMC artist. The resulting self-portrait, then, captures a form of the gaze posited here as the *reciprocated gaze*—a form of gaze occurring between the artist and photo during the painting process resulting in the creation of a self portrait, which captures an image of a large "s" form of Self.

The relinquishment of this self-portrait to the requesting individual further problematizes the Lacanian theory of the gaze. The interjection of this individual into the equation of the gaze is captured in the stated benefits cited in the NMC's catalogue:

> The energies and surroundings of Nahziryah Monastic Community are conducive to attuning to the subjects' inner being—so that the portrait will portray that which is subtle but powerful means—invoking higher qualities and states of awareness. May you utilize *your* portrait as an aid in expansion and further spiritual development.
>
> NAZIR Art Crafts Catalog 2012, 33

This description describes the benefits of a NMC portrait. Specifically, the self-portrait subtly captures the "subjects' inner being." The portrayal of these subjective qualities are the direct result of the "energies and surroundings" of the physical space of the NMC and indirect result of the artist ability to, as stated earlier to "invoke the more spiritual and noble elements of [one's] being" (Nazir Art Crafts Catalog 2012, 35). While both the NMC and artist acts as conduits for the creation of the self portrait, the requesting individual is directed to use the portrait as "an aid in expansion and further spiritual development." Specifically, NMC doctrine instructs the individual to meditate on the higher image of Self portrayed in the portrait. It is through this act of reflection that the individual joins the initial photo and the NMC artist in an augmented form of the Lacanian gaze. Unlike Lacan's understanding of the gaze as an indication of subject detachment, reflection on a NMC produced self-portrait draws the subject into a modified, triangular notion of Lacanian gaze. The individual reflects on an image that is the concrete manifestation of the NMC artist's desire to capture a higher form of the person's Self. Thus, the object of reflection captures both the reciprocated gaze occurring between the artist and initial photo and the reflecting subject and the self portrait. Unlike Lacan's negation of the subject, the gaze in this sense *is* "on the side of the subject" i.e. the reflecting individual (Evans 1996, 72). The individual's interaction with her/his self portrait not only captures a reciprocated act of gazing, but also this specific usage of material culture illustrates how this act affords the same person the ability to move towards a higher mode of Self, one free of ego dominance.

Interconnectivity between acts of gazing and remembering initiates the movement of the individual towards this large "s" notion of Self. Remembrance requires the individual to first meditate on his/her self-portrait. Gazing upon this image as it gazes back drives the process of remembrance. During this reciprocated gazing, the individual concentrates on the *likeness* of the image. This likeness, according to NMC doctrine, symbolizes oneness in that the "portrait draws upon that which is one with the Divine Essence and Universal Love" (Nazir Art Crafts Catalog 2012, 33). Meditative interaction with the self portrait allows individuals to reflect or remember who they are in reference to the Divine Creator. The NMC self-portrait in this way acts as a modified version of a mirror in that it shows the individual an image of his/her selfhood in its highest state. In a piece entitled *The Mirror*, Reverend Nazirmoreh (ABRD) states that the mirror "reveals who you truly are" (Nazirmoreh 1991, 4). It "assists one to remember one's Self...to remember who one truly is—a spark of the Divine Essence of all that is, was and ever shall be" (Nazir Art Crafts Catalog 2012, 33). The subject "gazes into the catalyst of the mirror" (O'Connor 1985, 169) and catches sight of a higher form of Self premised on oneness with the Divine Essence. As with Lacan's notion of the gaze, the NMC's usage of self-portraits as mirrors further problematizes his conception of the mirror stage. For Lacan this stage involves the individual appropriating the specular image as oneself. This appropriation leads to the formation of the ego. Therefore, Lacan establishes a direct relationship between the process of mirroring, ego construction and the image (pre-cursor of subjectivity). While Lacan recognizes the relationship between the latter two as confrontational, assumption of the image is still considered the necessary step required for ego construction—a fragmented form of the body that eventually leads to the formation of the subject. The NMC's utilization of the reflexive properties of the mirror, however, unlike Lacan, seeks to bring about subjectiveness through ego dissolution. It is the deconstruction of the ego that leads to the construction of an ego-independent, more expansive form of selfhood. Meaning that the actualization of the highest form of self i.e. large "s" Self in the NMC cosmological system occurs at the expense of the ego and supporting processes like crystallization.

Interactional gazing between the self-portrait and the individual places the latter in a position to move towards a large "s" Self. More importantly, this encounter aligns the individual with the four NMC Truth principles introduced earlier in the essay. Alignment serves as a catalyst that propels the meditating person beyond an ego-dominated view of self towards a more expansive form of self. Reflecting on the image, the individual acknowledges the existence of the Divine Essence and his/her connectivity to this same source. They are one. Recognition of oneness arms the individual with the power to begin the process of transcending beyond an ego dependent, individuated self-definition that results from the crystallization of one's consciousness. This recognition comes by way of constant interactional gazing with the "other" captured on the reflective surface of the self-portrait. The person in this interaction is forced to come to terms with their current state because the self-portrait provides a precursor of who they will become by transcending the limitations of the ego. The individual remembers who (s)he is in relationship to the originating source of essence presented in NMC doctrine as the Divine Essence, and as a result moves "beyond the body, beyond the mind, beyond the mundane physical material programmed conditioned consciousness distractions, the ego" (*Who on Earth*...2006, 43). The person gradual moves beyond a Cartesian split towards the harmonization of mind, body, and spirit. This state of at-one-ment, because the NMC recognizes it as the ultimate sign of consciousness expansion and spiritual development, is the primary goal of meditative gazing with one's self-portrait. Constant appropriation of the image both fuels the desire to apprehend a harmonizing state and enacts the faculty of remembrance in that it *mirrors* a depiction of one's highest Self.

Like the NMC's utilization of the self-revelatory property of painted portraits, this essay similarly acts as a mirror revealing two images of African American religious studies. The first is an *outer* methodological image. This representation captures a commitment to historical interpretations found operating in the study of African American religions. While historical understandings of these religious traditions are significant, the traditional privileging of this interpretative view misses more subtle characterizing elements present in these same religions. The utilization of Lacanian theory in this essay acts as a "deeper unconscious mirroring" that apprehends such predicates which in the past has evaded historical reflection (O'Connor 1985, 169). Apprehension of this form leads to a second *internal* image. The "underlying configuration" of this essay uncovers those hidden impulses, which are often under-appreciated in African American religious studies. Specifically, this essay examines how an African American monastic order employs material culture to articulate a convoluted conception of selfhood, an ego independent view of self that transcends societal constructs of race, gender, and sexuality. To this end, "Portraying Portraits," much like other essays included in the current anthology, uses uncommonly applied interpretative lenses like psychoanalysis to consider intersecting quadrants, such as art and identity construction, of esoteric traditions that have received little scholarly treatment in African American religious studies in particular and Western Esotericism in general.

CHAPTER 17

Those Mysteries, Our Mysteries

Ishmael Reed and the Construction of a Black Esoteric Tradition

Marques Redd

Introduction

The goal of this volume, according to its editors, is to carve out an intellectual space for the study of what they term *Africana esotericism*. This field will ana-lyze esoteric traditions and practices found among people of African descent, challenge the historiography and epistemology of the field of Western esoteri-cism, and provide methodological innovations for the study of religious phe-nomena. A major trailblazer for this scholarly quest is the novelist Ishmael Reed. His fiery novel *Mumbo Jumbo*, published in 1972, is one of the first attempts to chart the space of global Africana esotericism, particularly through the links he draws connecting ancient Egyptian metaphysics; West African reli-gious systems, particularly the Yoruba and Fon; Haitian vodun or voodoo, syn-thesized in the 17th and 18th centuries as a result of syncretic mingling of West African tribes in the Caribbean; hoodoo, formed in the USA during the 19th and 20th centuries through the movement of the African American diaspora through the country; and Neo-HooDoo, Reed's contemporary synthesis of hoo-doo-voodoo forms with popular culture.[1] Quite powerfully, he does not theorize Africana esotericism as a sub-field within the supposedly larger territory of Western esotericism, but he subsumes Western esotericism as a sub-field within the study of the more primal field of Africana esotericism. This paper will hone in on this major intervention and meditate on its implications for esoteric stud-ies, Africana studies, and the possible convergence between the two.

Before exploring the novel in more detail, I will provide a brief plot sum-mary for those unfamiliar with the text. *Mumbo Jumbo* tells the story of the anti-plague Jes Grew,[2] which sweeps the USA in the 1920s. This phenomenon represents the spirit of a pan-African ebullient culture and is an infectious

---

1 Throughout this paper, I will be using the following edition—Reed, *Mumbo Jumbo* (New York: Atheneum, 1988). This five-part sequence is usefully explored in Reginald Martin, *Ishmael Reed and the New Black Aesthetic Critics* (Houndmills: The MacMillan Press, 1988), 107.

2 Reed explains why he uses the term "anti-plague": "Some plagues caused the body to waste away; Jes Grew enlivened the host...Terrible plagues were due to the wrath of God; but Jes Grew is the delight of the gods" (6).

personification of jazz, freedom, energetic dance, and enlivening spiritual possession. Opposed to the burgeoning force of Jes Grew is a shadowy organization called the Atonist Path, which employs the Wallflower Order, a militarized fraternal organization, and other assorted groups like the Knights Templar, freemasons, and Teutonic Knights as its aids in attempting to stamp it out. The biggest supporters of the Jes Grew phenomenon are Papa LaBas, "noonday HooDoo, fugitive-hermit, obeah-man, botanist, animal impersonator, 2-headed man, You-Name-It" (Reed 1988, 45), and his assorted followers and allies. The central plot's mystery involves their search for the location of Jes Grew's sacred text, which will serve as the permanent home and foundation of Jes Grew. Unfortunately, at the end of the novel, this quest is not successful, and Jes Grew disperses.

Mumbo Jumbo and the Disciplines

In an interview with Jon Ewing, Ishmael Reed says, "*Mumbo Jumbo* has come to be regarded as a manifesto. I wrote it as a novel, but it's taken seriously" (Dick and Singh 1995, 120). In this essay, I will be taking Reed's novel quite seriously as well. With its dense intertextual web, encyclopedic breadth, and complexly entangled allegorical plots, *Mumbo Jumbo* directly engages in the type of methodological experimentation and disciplinary boundary transgression appropriate for an exploration of Africana esotericism, a mode of knowledge that cannot be contained within pre-fabricated disciplinary constructions as it synthesizes the entire spectrum of experience from our ancient origins in primal blackness to our future destinies in the black reaches of outer space.[3] The novel is the perfect methodological model of what an advanced scholarship looks like that synthesizes the right brain's function of thinking holistically through myth and symbol and the left brain's Cartesian, separative, and analytical logic which is heavily over-emphasized in western academic production (and, alas, in this essay).

---

3   See my contribution on Sun Ra for a further elaboration of this idea. Toward the end of
    Mumbo Jumbo, Reed says of Jes Grew, the embodiment of Africana esoteric power: "Jes Grew
    has no end and no beginning. It even precedes that little ball that exploded 1000,000,000s of
    years ago and led to what we are now. Jes Grew may even have caused the ball to explode...
    You see, life will never end; there is really no end to life, if anything goes it will be death. Jes
    Grew is life" (204). Jes Grew, in other words, is written in the stars, carried in the individual
    and transpersonal consciousness, and links together ancient, contemporary, and future
    worlds.

Mumbo Jumbo is a cultural polyphony. Its main text is broken up with illustrations that often do not refer seamlessly to the text next to which they are juxtaposed, newspaper articles, photographs, tarot cards, telegrams, citations from academic sources, charts, handwritten notes, as well as other visual and linguistic insertions. These registers of discourse allow Africana esoteric traditions to display their power in multiple dimensions simultaneously, illustrate their struggle with various forms of repression, and demonstrate how African systems of spiritual cultivation train its initiates to find glimpses of the divine everywhere. For example, there is an image of a vodun ceremony with a group of participants dressed in all white, a Brazilian carnivalesque scene with figures dressed in all kinds of costumes parading down the street, a quote from Louis Armstrong ("The spirit hits them and they follow"), special reports that speak to the global dimensions of Africana esotericism ("IN HAITI IT WAS PAPA LOA, IN NEW ORLEANS IT WAS PAPA LABAS, IN CHICAGO IT WAS PAPA JOE. THE LOCATION MAY SHIFT BUT THE FUNCTION REMAINS THE SAME"), and more (Reed 1988; 7, 77).

Deconstructing the boundaries between fiction and reality, *Mumbo Jumbo* is also a compendium of Africana esotericism with its many references to historical events—such as the resistance of "voodoo generals" against the American Marine invasion of Haiti beginning in 1915; institutions—namely Prince Hall Freemasonry, which opened a major esoteric conduit for African-American men; locales—like the Place Congo in New Orleans, an 18th-century meeting place that allowed for the reconstruction of old and creation of new Africana esoteric traditions; and people—like the famed voodoo practitioner Marie Laveau and the occult magician Black Herman. Herman is actually a major character in *Mumbo Jumbo*, who helps LaBas perform an exorcism on a character possessed by a hot spirit and is LaBas' main assistant in the quest for the text of Jes Grew. In his book *The African Unconscious: Roots of Ancient Mysticism and Modern Psychology*, Edward Bynum argues from anthropological evidence that the "template of humankind—the psychic and genetic roots of all present-day humanity—was nestled in East Africa for at least 2.5 million years before leaving the continent" (Bynum 1999, 3). Because of this, the deep-structure archetypes of the species and the origin of all human philosophical, scientific, and artistic traditions can be found in an "African unconscious" that is deeply embedded in us all on the psychological and genetic level. With this mapping of the contours of Africana esotericism, Reed's work has the potential to reorient the study of black religion away from its predominant focus on various appropriations of Christianity toward movements that are the closer to the original psychospiritual paradigms that gave birth to the unfolding of human civilization itself and will be explored in more detail later in the essay.

As a historico-aesthetic textbook, Reed's novel moves beyond casual allusions to major Africana esoteric signposts to make serious knowledge claims from an Africana esoteric position, which are supported through the use of an impressive scholarly apparatus. There are footnotes throughout the text and a five-page "Partial Bibliography" appended after the epilogue, which brings together topics across disciplinary lines ranging from witchcraft and American history to the history of jazz, dance, epidemiology, and Egyptology. Although *Mumbo Jumbo* makes concessions to the conventions of modern North Atlantic scientific knowledge production (yet here I would emphasize the ironies of the "partial" bibliography), Reed mocks them as well by parodying the voice of the academic gatekeeper: "Well can you prove this? I mean don't you think we need evidence for this? Who's your source?" (Reed 1988, 141). In place of these standards, which emerge from a focus on a narrow left-brained, mono-dimensional logic and sadly seem to view knowledge only as a reproduction of the status quo, he posits Africana esoteric experiences as a new center of transdisciplinary knowledge creation:

> Evidence? Woman, I dream about it, I feel it, I use my 2 heads. My Knockings. Don't you children have your Knockings, or have you New Negroes lost your other senses, the senses we came over here with? Why your Knockings are so accurate they can chart the course of a hammerhead shark in an ocean 1000s of miles away...Why, when the seasons change on Mars, I sympathize with them.
>
> REED 1988, 25–26

By questioning "evidence," Reed places hegemonic western rationality in suspension, situates it, and defines its boundary conditions. In its place, he asserts the power of an embodied, intuitive, visionary knowledge, one directly in touch with African traditions, which have been circumscribed by the Middle Passage and invalidated by the work of external and internalized racism. This kind of clairvoyance gives immediate access to a variety of interlinked phenomena, from the biological and oceanographic to the extraterrestrial, and thereby reinscribes existing knowledge orders. Africana esoteric "knowledges" depend on dreams, "sympathetic" magic, and "2 heads," or a perfectly achieved balance of left and right brain thinking.

The dynamism of *Mumbo Jumbo* derives from the seriousness with which Reed pursues the project of turning this pre-disciplinary mode of knowledge into a post-disciplinary one. Reed does not just provide representations of Africana esoteric knowledge systems and phenomena, but he plays with textual effects that are meant to bleed over into the "real" world outside of the text in order to influence us as readers. The novel is not just an aesthetic object, but a material fetish brimming with esoteric power. He says:

> I think that's one of the elements in African religion, the seer, the prophet, the necromancer. One almost feels as though one is receiving a vision or revelation in this work. I think the books can be seen as amulets. An amulet, you know, is something you carry around and people say they carry my books around. With *Mumbo Jumbo* I advise if you don't read it, put it over your door! That comes out of the idea of the holy book, the sacred book. There are powers that really influence people in strange ways in those books...people do respond to those books in strange ways and there may be powers that we unleash in the books, in the words and language rhythms, which affect people in ways we don't know about.
>
> DICK and SINGH 1995, 185

Implicit here is a challenge to develop new methodologies, ones that can operate with subtlety in order to understand how literature (and the arts in general) not only works to provide political commentary or a sense of aesthetic satisfaction, but plays upon human faculties to provoke a heightened experience of reality, influencing consciousness through complex harmonic principles. Reed is also presenting a model for a new kind of academic inquiry, one that is fully immersed in the topic it is studying without pandering to hegemonic standards of alienated, "objective" distance. He forgoes strict attention to empirical detail for a more imaginative and mythologically engaged recreation of the past and participation in it. As the characters diligently search for Jes Grew's text—"For what good is a liturgy without a text?" (Reed 1988, 6)—it becomes clear that *Mumbo Jumbo* itself is being written as a text that can replace the one that has been lost, becoming on a metanarrative level its own sacred text. In other words, Reed is writing himself directly into the Africana esoteric tradition of which he is providing an overview.

Esotericism *Africanized*

Well, and keep in mind where those Masonic Mysteries came from in the first place. (Check out Ishmael Reed. He knows more about it than you will ever find here.)

THOMAS PYNCHON, *Gravity's Rainbow*

One of the major secrets *Mumbo Jumbo* bequeaths to the reader is its serious challenge to the historiography of esotericism. Antoine Faivre's *Access to Western Esotericism* is the first systematic treatment of esotericism to appear in English, and it tells a magisterial story about the development of various esoteric strains from antiquity to the twentieth century (The French edition *Accès de l'ésotérisme occidental* was published in 1986, over a decade after *Mumbo Jumbo*). Outside of one extremely brief mention of Paschal Randolph on page 94, however, there are no figures or movements of the African diaspora examined in the text at all, which effectively shuts out an entire range of experience from the consolidation of this new field. An offhanded comment of Reed's captures quite nicely this state of affairs: "I once leafed through a photo book about the West. I was struck by how the Whites figured in the center of the photos and drawings while Blacks were centrifugally distant" (Reed 1988, 209–210). *Mumbo Jumbo* can be read as a corrective project before and against the grain, one that does not petition for greater inclusion, but forcefully reframes and rebalances the entire narrative. The text is an energy vortex that absorbs many strains of esoteric history, brings them into a narrative cosmos firmly grounded in ancient Egypt, and filters and translates them through Reed's revisionary gusto.

In Faivre's text, there is a deep ambivalence about Egypt. On one hand, his narrative begins and crucially locates itself in Hellenistic Alexandria, in particular with the fascinating collection of religious tracts called the *Corpus Hermeticum* (drafted in the 2nd and 3rd centuries AD). These texts feature disquisitions on the nature of the divine, mind, nature, and the cosmos from the teacher Hermes Trismegistus, a syncretic Greek avatar of the Egyptian god of writing Thoth. On the other hand, he makes sure to draw a line of distinction between Alexandrian and pharaonic Egypt and diminish the importance of earlier Egyptian culture for the study of esotericism. He says:

> Today and for the last three centuries there are enthusiasts who see in the religion of ancient Egypt an esotericism, present in the form of mysteries, symbols, initiations, and information hidden from the profane. Now, even presuming that the enthusiasts are correct, what they describe would never be but a form of religiosity shared by many other religious systems, and it is hard to see why that should be termed 'esotericism.' It appears more pertinent and legitimate to study forms of egyptomania and egyptophilia proper to Western esotericists themselves, because if there is an Egyptian esotericism, it exists first of all in our modern imaginary. Whether or not the latter since the seventeenth century, reflects

what ancient Egypt really was concerns the historian of Western esoteric currents only very indirectly.

FAIVRE 1994, 17

To put it bluntly, this is a very reactionary position to take, and even mainstream Egyptologists assert that the tractates of the *Corpus Hermeticum* "stand in an age-old Egyptian tradition that began with the Admonitions of Ipuwer, the Prophecy of Neferti, and similar texts from the Middle Kingdom. There are also direct allusions to ancient Egyptian religion" (Hornung 2001, 51–52). Faivre's position here, which intends to set a foundational academic agenda, reeks of a smarmy condescension (note the dismissal of his "objects" of study as mere "enthusiasts"), conceptual incarceration, and intellectual imperialism that plagues the western academy at large and promises to stunt the growth of the study of esotericism.

Edward Bynum's *The African Unconscious* provides a better way of framing the conversation. Working toward the construction of a true global humanities curriculum, Bynum builds his thinking about the development of human culture on the movement and development of the human species as a whole, and he asserts that "only in Africa can we find the complete record and genetic blueprints of our species. This template...is the source stock of all other unfolding branches of the human family" (Bynum 1999, 5). Bynum argues that this template also forged a primordial African consciousness that has given rise to the various iterations of human culture, and he outlines its basic tenets: the active perception of transformations in all of the life processes and creation; the intuition of a vitalism in all things; the apprehension of rhythm and pattern repetition as intrinsic in nature; the perception of so-called magical-religious permutations in nature; the cultivation of an internally latent spiritual-evolutionary force; emphasis on group, tribal, or community consciousness as opposed to egoic or individualized consciousness; the literal movement of the life process by way of rhythm and vitality through the body; and the transmission of this living system through linear and non-linear means (Bynum 1999, 86–100). These characteristics actually provide a stunningly thorough definition of esotericism, and we can use them to judge how sophisticated an esoteric system is in its attempt to influence and elevate human consciousness. Furthermore, Bynum's framework convincingly shows how to create cultural genealogies that tie various esoteric traditions back to ancient Egypt and Egypt to its indigenous African roots (In some respect, we can think of Bynum's work as a cultural version of the Genographic Project, which is an attempt to map the complete history of human migration given the markers of descent we all bear connecting us to the earliest humans in Africa).

This is exactly Ishmael Reed's project, suturing the severed links between Africa, Egypt, and esoteric traditions. Moreover, *Mumbo Jumbo* provides a dazzling esoteric reading of the history of esotericism, one that fuses myth and history in an attempt to understand the development of complex spiritual patterns. To bring all of the novel's loose ends together and explain the longstanding conflict between the Atonist Path and the supporters of Jes Grew, Papa LaBas begins an outrageously long monologue, "Well if you must know, it all began 1000s of years ago in Egypt" (Reed 1988, 160). He then proceeds to a retelling of the Osiris myth cycle in order to explain events that have happened in the 1920s of the novel's present. At its most simple, Osiris is the harbinger of civilization who is murdered by his brother Set and reconstituted through the magic of his wife Isis. Reed's version vivifies the myth with the spirit and language of 20th-century African American culture. Osiris is the celebrant of an ecstatic Egyptian religion brimming with dancing, singing, fertility rituals, and agricultural celebrations. He is the master of its various rhythms, known as the "Black Mud Sound" (which links it to the blues of the Mississippi Delta) (Reed 1988, 161). Furthermore, he—along with Thoth, the god of writing—is the codifier of dances that inspire and are inspired by natural cycles: "Osiris did his basic dances for many days until Thoth had them all down. A Book of Litanies to which people in places like Abydos in Upper Egypt could add their own variations. Guides were initiated into the Book of Thoth, the 1st anthology written by the 1st choreographer" (Reed 1988, 164).

Osiris' brother Set, by contrast, thrives on destruction and alienation. In Reed's words, "He went down as the 1st man to shut nature out of himself. He called it discipline" (Reed 1988, 162). He fetishizes "progress," "invading foreign countries and killing," and "famine pestilence and earthquakes" (Reed 1988; 164, 174). Like the contemporary "Stop-And-Frisk" police, he enjoys telling people, "Move that chariot to the side of the road, O.K. where's your license" (Reed 1988, 165). Moreover, he cannot dance: "Even Hully Gullying children on the street would point out Set as the man who can't shake it 'til he breaks it" (Reed 1988, 163).

Osiris leaves Egypt to spread his system of celebrations around the world, and he visits Teotihuacan, the Olmeca, Navaho Indians in North America, Aztec festivals, and various West African peoples. During his absence, Set takes over the throne, revels in violence, and plots the death of Osiris. On Osiris' return, Set dismembers his body into fourteen pieces and spreads them across the land. However, he is not able to completely stamp out his "living Spirit," which continues to spread throughout the world (Reed 1988, 167).

Through his adroit use of mythical discourse, Reed is able to condense many multi-dimensional levels of meaning. He provides complex insight into a wide range of phenomena, such as the psychological development of the individual, the spiritual evolution of society, the conflict between left and right brain functions, the battle between forces of entropy and self-organization on the level of thermodynamics, and the history of the African diaspora. For our purposes, we can think of Osiris as the founder of the *prisca theologia*, which must be African if it is the most ancient form of spiritual truth. He discovers and systematizes the first system of spiritual cultivation, which is constructed to be a complete science of living. Through rituals that plug into celestial and terrestrial cycles, he raises his consciousness to the highest division of his spirit and increases his spiritual power to its highest potential, and therefore is a metaphor for the fully realized spiritual initiate. Moreover, Osiris also prefigures the founders of all subsequent hermetic utopias, as he is able to bring civilization—here defined as a spiritually controlled way of life—to the people through the effects his spiritual system has on government and economics and thereby increase social harmony, peace, and prosperity.

The reach of this system extends across the world as Osiris travels broadly to meet different tribes. This journeying mirrors the routes of migration out of Africa undertaken by the human species as it branched out, diversified, and cross-fertilized in various waves. The presence of Osiris, to use the terminology of Bynum, explains "how the genetic, psychic, spiritual, and cultural origins of our species...are traceable to a collective and common African origin in spite of apparent differences between peoples based on 'race', language, cultural style, spirituality, geographic location, and even era in history." Furthermore, his presence demonstrates "how the many pathways to our literally felt and experienced psychospiritual awakening and unification with the energy of the universe are inextricably connected to the genetic, psychic, spiritual, and cultural processes that are rooted in the African origin of our species" (Bynum 1999, xxv). For Reed, western esotericism is also woven on the loom of this primordial collective African unconscious. He purposefully emphasizes that Osiris is the force behind the "Book of Thoth," which will become the source of the vast corpus of hermetic writings when Thoth becomes Hermes of the Greek tradition. Reed makes the point explicit when he adds that after Set's attack on Osiris, Thoth goes "into exile in the hills where he wrote magical books under a pseudonym which survived until the 'civilized' Romans burned the library at Alexandria" (Reed 1988, 167). We are now completely out of the Eurocentric frame imposed by figures like Faivre, can place esoteric traditions in a larger context by understanding its links with Africa, and can even start to compare them with complex indigenous spiritual systems found throughout the world.

Set, who becomes jealous of the praise given to Osiris, is a symbol of the dedication of our cerebral faculties to the service of the base, unenlightened self. Driven by his lust for power and the rebelliousness of the lower consciousness against the spiritual order imposed by Osiris, Set kills him, hacking his body into pieces and scattering them throughout the land. This suggests that all of the esoteric systems that are now carefully distinguished (e.g. alchemy, astrology, theurgy, etc.) at one point functioned as a complete, integral system of initiation before being broken up. In addition, the fragmentation of this system corresponds to the dispossession of African people from their land by conquerors and their dispersion throughout the world. We can see the Osiris-Set conflict not only in the invasions of the Hyksos and Arabs at various points of Egyptian history, but also much later in historical time in the transatlantic slave trade. Like Osiris, Africans were tricked into a wooden prison, cast out to sea, and spread in fragmented units into a new world.

We can also see in Set's fragmentation of Osiris' body the separation of religion from the state and education, God from nature and humanity, humanity from itself, spirit from physical matter, and the divine from the mundane. Reed says, for example, that "in Egypt at the time of Osiris every man was an artist and every artist a priest." Only with the rise of Set do we get "The First Poets," as "Art" becomes a category alienated from the community and the divine (Reed 1988, 164). This insidious system of dividing and segregating all things and people from each other and the whole leads to the formalization of the major enemies of esoteric traditions—monotheism and rationalism—and eventually brings us to the contemporary academy.

After this murder, Set usurps the Egyptian throne and proceeds to terrorize the world. He creates the first empire and replaces the system of maintaining social order through moral cultivation with a policing system. Building on an earlier point, this corresponds to the violent incursions of Eurasian people into the Mediterranean, Western Asia, India (as narrated in the Vedas as the Aryan invasion), Africa (as narrated in the Bible as the conflict between the Hebrews and the Egyptian children of Ham), and eventually to the rest of the southern and western hemispheres. The conquerors appropriated the psychospiritual teachings and cultural elements of the ancient civilizations in light of their own biases and misunderstanding, and they deployed them for vastly different ends. To explore this point in greater detail, Reed turns at this point in the narrative to retell the story of Moses, who for him is emblematic of a severe repression of the African unconscious that sets the pattern for certain forms of European monotheism and esotericism.

Reed's representation of Moses is influenced by texts like Sigmund Freud's *Moses and Monotheism*, which argues that Moses' religious innovations built upon the monotheistic efforts of Akhenaton, who reigned in Egypt from approximately 1353–1336 BC and also makes a brief appearance in Reed's novel.

In the words of Egyptologist Jan Assmann, "The monotheistic revolution of Akhenaten was not only the first but also the most radical and violent eruption of a counter-religion in the history of mankind" (Assmann 1997, 25). These figures traumatically destroyed beloved icons, suppressed traditional "knowledges," drew a strict line between revealed monotheistic "truth" and "pagan idolatry," and forced humanity to seek salvation not within but from an entity outside of and alienated from itself.

Reed's Moses is one in a long line of puritanical, morbidly anti-human, and power mad figures who has been exposed to the vital power of Egyptian religion, but severs his connection with it and establishes a repressive system to tamp it down. Although he does start out with the intention to learn about the Osirian mysteries, his autocratic character traits get the better of him. He makes a Faustian deal with Set (boldly imagined by Reed as the force behind the burning bush, linking him to Yahweh) to gain tyrannical control over Egypt. Empowered by him, Moses confronts Isis to forcefully take the knowledge of the Book of Thoth, and he obtains the Text under the wrong phase of the moon, which illustrates his refusal to exist in harmony with the astral patterns charted out by Africana esoteric "knowledges." With the deformed version of the mysteries he obtains, he organizes a concert and performs for the Egyptian people, but the music he plays promotes chaos and violence instead of pleasure and dancing. When the Osirians rise up against him in protest against his lack of respect for their traditions and deities, Moses uses the Book to unleash a nuclear attack on Egypt. Using terms drawn from Haitian vodun, Reed explicates this moment as a turning point in the Book's history, where *petro*, the way of the Left Hand practiced by Moses and associated with deities of violent, aggressive action, becomes the equal in strength of *rada*, the rituals of the Right Hand aligned with protective, benevolent guardian powers. Moses at this moment is a *bokor*, or charlatan, rather than a *houngan*, a true practitioner of what LaBas terms The Work. Fearful of this display of power, Moses decides to hide the book in a tabernacle, and it becomes known as one of the "lost books of Moses" (Reed 1988, 187). The Left vs. Right Hand dynamic is another iteration of the charted conflict between the left and right brain. Reed is narrating here the trauma that is the eventual outcome when the African unconscious is repressed, or in other words when the left brain functions of separation, segregation, and polarization start to dominate thinking, behavioral patterns, and cultural expressions.

Through the figure of Moses, Reed shows that monotheism engages in a constant dynamic of attraction toward and repulsion from Africana esotericism. Reed interprets the famous biblical scene of the Golden Calf as a relapse into a "pagan" practice supposedly left behind; it is an episode of "dancing before the despised Bull God Apis, the animal which carries the living spirit of Osiris" (Reed 1988, 187). In other words, regardless of the attempt to fully suppress the Egyptian rites, they still reemerge in some form. Surprisingly, however, Reed argues that this push-and-pull engagement with and rejection of Egypt (seen in Faivre) is also replicated in some of the major forms of European esotericism. Moses, of course, is a figure just as important for esoteric thinkers as he is for orthodox Abrahamic monotheists, and he has been appropriated by alchemists, freemasons, kabbalists, sufis, and more. If one looks at masonic scholarship, for example, one will find an argument claiming Moses to be their first scholar:

> Moses, from his peculiar education, was well acquainted with the rites, the ceremonies, the hieroglyphs, and the symbols used by the Egyptian priesthood. Many of these he introduced into Masonry, and thus began that system which, coming originally from the Egyptians and subsequently augmented by derivations from the Druids, the Essenes, the Pythagoreans, and other mystical associations, at last was developed into that science of symbolism which now constitutes so important and essential a characteristic of modern Freemasonry.
>
> MACKEY 1996, 132

Reed uses narratives like these to construct a bifurcated esoteric tradition. One life-enhancing conduit goes from ancient Egypt to systems like vodun (which explicitly keep a balance between the Left and Right Hands), and another life-denying current travels from ancient Egypt through Moses into certain European sects, which often use esoteric power to oppress more than uplift.

This linkage of western esotericism and monotheism contradicts another important line of the historiography of western esotericism, which sees these discourses as the antithesis of the other. Lee Irwin, in his "Western Esotericism, Eastern Spirituality, and the Global Future," voices a widely accepted position when he claims that "esoteric traditions have tended to develop often in contrast to more orthodox and 'external' paternal religions whose orthodox members have tended to regard esotericism with some suspicion and, at times, have attacked such societies with strategies of repression" (Irwin 2001, 1). From Reed's perspective, European esoteric groups have often been aggressors with strategies of repression of their own, particularly toward the African unconscious and black people. And instead of monotheism being the normative exoteric framework within which esoteric thinking develops, Reed sees both the Abrahamic tradition and European esotericisms as a heretical falling away from the plenitude of ancient Egypt's sacred science, albeit with differences in degree as the esoteric traditions are usually the result of the inability of mono-theistic frames to completely repress the African unconscious from which they emerge.

Around the year 1118, as Reed's narrative continues, the Book of Thoth is found by Hinckle Von Vampton, the librarian of the Knights Templar, a medi-eval, esoteric Christian order usually revered as the preserver of ancient knowl-edge and relics such as the Ark of the Covenant and the Holy Grail (According to legend, Moses' tabernacle was the foundation of the Temple of Solomon, over which the Knights built their headquarters). Having learned to cheat death with an Arab formula and bent on Crusades and world conquest, Von Vampton is the major enemy faced by Papa LaBas in the book's present. The Knights Templar translate the Book's hieroglyphics, but it refuses to reveal its true meaning to them. Reed says, "They began to translate the hieroglyphics but the Book was not going to be their whore any more and gave them the worst of itself. It was saving all of its love and Rada for when it united with its dance and music. What they derived from the Book were strange ceremonies... They practiced these Petro rites in secret and this is when their fortunes reversed" (Reed 1988,188). As a result of this misreading and general lack of proper training, the Knights Templar and their Atonist descendants, the free-masons, practice a misguided version of the mysteries with the Left Hand, emblematized by Von Vampton's worship of the god Baphomet in the form of a hideous, bejeweled little black doll. However, this practice is powerful enough to move members of these societies, such as Warren Harding and Woodrow Wilson according to the novel, into positions of power in politics, the media, and other institutions that the Jes Grew supporters struggle against in the 1920s present of the novel.

This summary, albeit lengthy, only scratches the surface of the fantasia on western esoteric history Reed elaborates here, which also touches in whirlwind fashion on figures like John Milton and Julian the Apostate. After LaBas' long summary of this chain of events, one of his supporters—the Prince Hall Freemason Buddy Jackson—proclaims about Von Vampton:

> We learned what we always suspected, that the Masonic mysteries were of a Blacker origin than we thought and that this man had in his possession a Black sacred Book and how they were worried that we would find out and wouldn't learn that the reason they wanted us out of the mysteries was because they were our mysteries! Get to that. They were accusing us of trespassing upon our own property...1 of the brothers told us 1 night that even the Catholic Mass was based upon a Black Egyptian celebration.
>
> REED 1988, 194

Here one can see quite clearly how the novel usurps conventional historiography of the western esoteric tradition. This passage is a grand pyramidion for the narrative that LaBas provides—the Masonic mysteries are Africana esoteric mysteries. Reed not only inscribes esotericism with a new history, firmly located in a primordial blackness, but marks several strains of European esotericism as watered-down appropriations of the original source. He renders western esotericism belated and secondary in order to clear space for the primacy of Africana esotericism. In this reading, Faivre himself, by severing the links between ancient Egypt and esotericism, would be akin to the Von Vampton figure here anxious to stop black people from trespassing on their own territory.

This racial psychosis, extremely evident in several American esoteric traditions, comes in for a direct critique from Reed. At a party in Harlem, Papa LaBas and Black Herman meet Abdul Hamid, a noted magazine editor. In conversation, Hamid turns his sights to Mormonism:

> The most fundamental book of the Mormon Church, the Book of Mormon, is a fraud. If we Blacks came up with something as corny as the Angel of Moroni, something as trite and phony as their story that the book is the record of ancient Americans who came here in 600 B.C. and perished by A.D. 400, they would deride us with pejorative adjectival phrases like 'so-called' and 'would-be.' They would refuse to exempt our priests from the draft, a privilege extended to every White hayseed's fruit stand which calls itself a Church. But regardless of the put-on, the hype, the Mormons got Utah, didn't they?
>
> REED 1988, 38

This comment speaks to the racialized situation of esotericism. Black esoteric traditions often are often marginalized and dismissed by the academy, government, and other social institutions, while white ones (even those without the same spiritual force) are lauded. Mormonism is an interesting case for this critique, as it embodies the same dialectic of fascination with and repulsion from ancient Egypt seen with Reed's Moses. The connections between Mormonism and Egypt are intense. The *Book of Mormon* itself is purported to have been originally written on golden tablets in "reformed Egyptian" characters. These were translated by Joseph Smith, who also kept mummies and papyri, supposedly containing the writings of the patriarchs Joseph and Abraham in his possession.[4] Yet, even with this deep influence by ancient

---

4   For more on Egypt and Mormonism, see Robert Ritner, "'The Breathing Permit of Hor' among the Joseph Smith Papyri," *Journal of Near Eastern Studies* 62 no. 3 (2003): 161–180.

Egypt, the church was quite racist, and black people were excluded from participation in temple ceremonies and Priesthood ordination until 1978. Ironically, Mormonism as a religion is deemed an "American original" (Bloom 1992, 77), whereas African American thinkers and religious speculators who draw on the legacy of ancient Egypt are often derided for confusedly living in "mythical pasts and imagined homes" (Howe 1999). Reed's novel and the entire project yielding the current volume are constructed to help us move beyond this impasse.

A new "global humanities" (including the studies of religion and esotericism) must be founded on a paradigm of unity. It must study the deep structures of our psychospiritual traditions (scientific, religious, and artistic) and explicate how their efflorescent diversity emerges from a common root. In many ways—natural evolution, cross-fertilization, repression, syncretistic reemergence—Africana esotericism is the trunk of our human cultural tree. In the words of Bynum, "The peaceful resolution of our worldwide ethnic madness will be the deep recognition of our African rootedness. In it is our template, our common connection to the Earth, the nonlocal intelligences, and the stars" (Bynum 1999, 318). The self-knowledge of our species is still in its infancy, and a return to fully understanding our ancient origins can possibly lead to sublime new vistas of future destinies.

Conclusion

> Crazy dada nigger that's what you are. You are given to fantasy and are off in matters of detail. Far out esoteric bullshit is where you're at.
>
> ISHMAEL REED, *Yellow Back Radio Broke-Down*

In his groundbreaking work of literary criticism *The Signifying Monkey*, Henry Louis Gates says, "Reed's Signifyin(g) on tradition begins with his book's title. *Mumbo jumbo* is the received and ethnocentric Western designation for the rituals of black religions as well as for black languages themselves...*Mumbo Jumbo*, then, Signifies upon Western etymology [and] abusive Western practices of deflation through misnaming" (Gates 1988, 220–221). This term, however, has not only been applied to the black vernacular in a derogatory manner; it has also been used to describe the secret rituals and texts of esoteric traditions. Only a select few get past the "mumbo jumbo" of the societies in order to reach the sublime heights to which they lead. Through this canny use of a title, Reed is attempting to effect a powerful fusion between Africana and Esoteric Studies. In the novel, he powerfully weaves the history of

Africana esotericism with that of its western counterpart, reformulating that history in the process. The study of Africana esotericism, therefore, would not be a simple sub-field within the larger study of esotericism as it is currently constituted, but the ground from which to understand the entire tradition differently.

Although this paper has focused on how Ishmael Reed has brought an *Africana* perspective to esotericism, a future exploration can turn to look at how he also brings an *esoteric* perspective to Africana studies. Reed finished the novel in Berkeley, California, in 1971, which places him right in the middle of heated battles about the institutionalization of Africana Studies within the university. From Reed's perspective, however, the struggle to radically rethink the foundations of knowledge was not fully sustained. This could be attributed to the turning away from autochthonous African traditions (Egyptian metaphysics, Yoruba cosmology, Haitian voodoo, etc.) in order to attain a sense of academic legitimacy by importing intellectual systems from Europe. Ironically, at the moment of the institutionalization of Africana Studies, this opened space of possibility was disciplined into a discipline, and the importance of Africana spiritual "knowledges" was lost.

Mumbo Jumbo can be interpreted as a concerted effort to define, determine, and defend the territory of Africana Studies from an esoteric perspective. As such, Reed subjects "lecturing on Freud and Marx and all the old names" (Reed 1988, 216) to intense scrutiny, particularly because the influence of these two "hermeneuts of suspicion" permeated so broadly at the time. His critique unfolds in four stages:

(1)   He parodies Freudianism and Marxism ruthlessly in order to expunge their influence from the domain of Africana Studies. For example, he claims that Freud's "real talent lies in the coinage of new terms for processes as old as the Ark"—"exorcism becomes Psychoanalysis, Hex becomes Death Wish, Possession becomes Hysteria" (Reed 1988; 208, 213).

(2)   He then illuminates how both of these systems have an ambivalent relationship to esoteric traditions. In Marx's case: "And as for secret societies? The Communist party originated among some German workers in Paris. They called themselves the Workers Outlaw League. Marx came along and removed what was called the ritualistic paraphernalia so that the masses could participate instead of the few" (Reed 1988, 26)

(3)   Furthermore, Reed challenges these systems on their own territory by outlining how Africana esoteric systems explain the phenomena they claim to understand in a richer, more complex manner:

The loa [or vodun deity] is not a daimon in the Freudian sense, a hysteric; no, the loa is known by its signs and is fed, celebrated...The attendants are experienced and know the names, knowledge the West lost when the Atonists wiped out the Greek mysteries. The last thing these attendants would think of doing to a loa's host is electrifying it lobotomizing it or removing its clitoris, which was a pre-Freudian technique for 'curing' hysteria.

REED 1988, 50

(4)   Finally, Reed supplants Freudianism and Marxism by outlining a specifi-cally esoteric theory of liberation that moves beyond class struggle and sublimation. A major element of his program is the call for an esoteric attack on oppressive institutions:

You remember in that Art History class at City College. The pact that we made that day...that we would return the plundered art to Africa, South America and China, the ritual accessories which had been stolen so that we could see the gods return and the spirits aroused. How we wanted to conjure a spiritual hurricane which would lift the debris of 2,000 years from its roots and fling it about. Well, we are succeeding with these raids into the museum, for what good is someone's amulet or pendant if it's in a Western museum.

REED 1988, 87–88

As Reed clearly knows, modern, post-Renaissance academic knowledge has been consolidated through the dismissal and denunciation of both Africana Studies and Esoteric Studies (See Wouter Hanegraaff's *Esotericism and the Academy: Rejected Knowledge in Western Culture* for more about how esotericism has been marginalized by a tradition of Enlightenment polemics, and see the complete work of Sylvia Wynter for how Africana knowledges have been margin-alized in the same manner). I became interested in working on intellectual proj-ects such as this one because I, like Ishmael Reed, wanted to see what possibilities a convergence of these branches of study had for rewriting the structure of the academy as such. After a few years as a tenure track professor, however, I have serious doubts that this synthesis can organically emerge from within the cur-rent university system, as it is too deeply entrenched in outworn paradigms that are crumbling even on their own terms. The essays published in this volume, therefore, will be my first and most likely my last scholarly contributions.

The more esotericism is properly studied, the more one becomes an esoteri-cist. And the more one becomes an esotericist, the differences between the

21st-century American corporate university and the ancient *Per Ankh* (Egyptian for "House of Life") become too stark to bear. In Reed's myth, the Book of Thoth is written to be a foundation for life-enriching ritual. In the modern academy, the academic book has displaced and rationalized meaningful ritual. From this hyper-specialized and hypo-spiritualized system, the only training provided to students is intellectual, leaving other parts of the human spirit unengaged. The disciplines of the university are all fragmented from each other, with no articulated relationship to link them together. Furthermore, there is little unity joining classes even offered within the same discipline. And when students are finished, they are usually initiated into nothing higher than a lifetime of debt.

The critiques of the corporate academy are well known, so I do not need to go through them here. My personal solution has been to leave and start afresh. Now in the desert of Arizona, I am on my own quest to reconstitute the limbs of Osiris, to see if it is possible to synthesize and, more importantly, live by all of the spiritual sciences of which the ancient Egyptians were master, including (but not limited to) shamanic astronomy, divination, sacred geometry and architecture, astral projection, dream interpretation, ancestor communication, glyphic meditation, talismanic magic, numerology, cosmic music, aromatherapy, rootwork, gemology, chanting, breath/energy/body work, sacred sexuality, cosmology, afterlife training, magical art, ceremonial healing, alchemy, and theurgy. If those mysteries are our mysteries, we need to create new institutions (or new versions of old institutions) that can protect them and help them to flourish. If we do not, who will?

CHAPTER 18

Rockin' for a Risen Savior

Bakongo and Christian Iconicity in the Louisiana Easter Rock Ritual

Joyce Marie Jackson

Introduction

I grew up in the sanctuary of a black Baptist church where women were always in the majority in terms of attendance, "feeling the spirit" (shouting) and ritual performativity. By supporting and nurturing one of the most crucial spaces of creativity, resistance and rejuvenation of African American people—the black church—black women are, in large part, responsible for the continuance of cultural and spiritual rituals in the church. Historically, black male leaders have insisted on adopting the patriarchal ministry of their white Christian forbears, even during the times when they strove to purify the white instruction of racist theology and to transform it into liberation theology. It is a peculiar irony of the black church that, while not all but many, men and women of various denominations, are still solidly installing black men in the upper realms of privilege and power, women are still consigned to subordinate positions. Nonetheless, women of the church constantly present challenges to this authority, pulling from a well of Africanist cultural performance practices— dancing, singing, shouting, and exalting—to forge a personal relationship with God. The black "folk church" is already a delineated performance venue in which pastor and congregation engage in a spirited performance which undulates with oratory, poetry, rhythm, music, dance and shouting, in essence a sacred but dramatic theatrical ritual. Pearl Williams- Jones characterizes the folk church as:

> at once a mystical, inevitable body of believers unified by a common Christian theology as well as a visible body and community of Black people united by common cultural ties. We may consider the black folk church as being an institution controlled by blacks which exists principally within the Black community and which reflects its attitudes, values and lifestyle. It is a church of everyday people and one of any denomination....
>
> WILLIAMS-JONES, 1977, 21

© KONINKLIJKE BRILL NV, LEIDEN, 2015 | DOI 10.1163/9789004283428_020

Many of the ritual practices, which we commonly associate with the black folk church, such as freely structured services, dance, improvisational music, the emotional and musical delivery of style of sermons and prayers, and spontaneous verbal and non-verbal responses by preachers and congregations, have essentially merged from African values and aesthetics. Denominational affiliation is secondary to ritual in the black folk church. In essence, the type of ritual determines if a church is a "folk" church or not.

Since the church is the most conservative institution in the African American community, it is logical to assume that ritual services, including the mode of worship and style and function of music, would be preserved there in their truest form. Many cultural ties of the African ancestral lineage have been maintained within the enclave of the black folk church.

In this chapter, it is my intention to respond to a misunderstanding of the black church that was articulated by some early scholars such as Gunnar Myrdal in "The Negro Church: Its Weakness, Trends, and Outlook." His work in 1944 basically stated that the black church had become an outdated, impractical, dysfunctional institution whose conservative politics supported black poverty. His work set the stage for negative views and was followed by others who concluded that assimilation into mainstream American culture would solidify the demise of the old-time black folk church. Even at the end of 1960s some scholars were still predicting the end of the black church as a development favorable to the black community's survival (Cone 1971, 349; Washington 1971, 301–309).

Although the impact of the black church within African American communities is richly documented since the early 1960s, this study is a living testament to the unique ritual in a rural community in Louisiana that maintains its identity and strength through the women of the community.

The Easter Rock ritual has two distinct frames and as I will emphasize later, African influences are found in a syncretized form, blended with diverse non-African icons in a unique configuration. In the *Old Ship of Zion: The Afro-Baptist Ritual in the African Diaspora,* Walter F. Pitts, Jr. first delineates this binary structure that persists either in their original or modified form in the Black Atlantic World. Through the earlier labor of Pitts and others, it is affirmed that the African roots of African American religion and culture were never fully nor effectively severed and by their existence challenged the inevitability of dad-to-day subordination.

To understand these rituals, and their significance in their respective church communities, I draw heavily on Walter Pitts' dual ritual frames concept, which combine to create the total ritual structure. In his *Old Ship of Zion,* he refutes the impression, both scholarly and popular, that ritual behavior in the

American black church is an ecstatic jumble. He carefully develops his argument and explains, after rigorous comparisons of various rituals in the diaspora, the specific elements that are needed to construct the frames. With some alterations, these binary frame structures are also essential for the Easter Rock ritual.

I am also exploring how black women, through the maintenance of these binary ritual structures, operate radical Africanist performance modalities in the folk church which challenge church patriarchy, but also helps with church sustainability. Although this ritual is not the exclusive domain of women, men can participate, but it is one that achieves its fullest expression and vibrancy by the women of the churches in the region. By extension, I will show how black women have reconfigured the ritual icons from what I believe to be Bakongo icons to Christian icons to make the ritual palatable to Christian beliefs due to the fact that it is a pre-emancipation ritual as well as esoteric to the Baptist and for that matter to the Christian faith.

I also draw on historical records and recent ethnographic field data I collected from the Easter Rock tradition bearers and many years of personal observations and participation in the Easter Rock ceremony in a Baptist church in Winnsboro, Louisiana. In addition, I draw from a pool of other field experiences of circular rituals I have examined in other areas of the Black Atlantic World (Senegal, Ghana, Bahamas, Trinidad and Georgia) and performance centered theory from an interdisciplinary context of ethnomusicology, folklore and cultural anthropology.

The ritual is centered on Easter and involves spiritual-based music and the performance of circular movements or "ring shout."[1] Historically, it is clear that they have African antecedents, but my primary focus is on Bakongo and Christian icons that are tangible and not so tangible in the ritual. I am also examining iconic symbolism and, performance practices.

There is a number of studies on African diasporic sacred ritual traditions. On diasporic sacred rituals in the Caribbean, we have a large number to pull from on Haitian Voodoo (Metraux 1972, Hurston 1938) Cuban Santeria (Murphy 1988; Clark 2007), Trinidadian Spiritual Baptist (Glazier 1983; Henry 2003), the

---

1 The ring shout is a black religious dance usually done in a counterclockwise movement and has strong African performance practices. Historically, the dance consisted of movement in a circle by a group or band of singers, where their feet never crossed and usually were not lifted from the ground. These dances were performed in praise houses, slave quarters and consequently in the black folk church. There are numerous accounts of the ring shout in literature of the ante-bellum period. For a more detailed discussion, see Epstein (1977), Levine (1977), Stuckey (1987) and Blassingame (1979).

big drum ritual of Carriacou, Granada (McDaniel 1998) and in South America we have Brazilian Comdomblé (Omari-Tunkara 2005; Daniel 2005). On United States soil we have studies such as *Together Let Us Sweetly Live: The Singing and Praying Bands* (2007) by Jonathan C. David. This work also examines a folk and ring shout tradition, which began in the early nineteenth century in Delaware and Maryland. This tidewater community tradition is a fusion of Methodist prayer meeting worship and African singing, dancing and worship performance practices. David first presents the reader with an extended introduction where he supplies the ethnographic context and history of the tradition. The remainder of the nine chapters tells the story of the singing and praying bands through the oral narratives of various group members. His methodology is problematical because of his editing techniques. Usually we look at a first-person narrative to be a primary source of information without additions by the scholar. The scholar usually attempts to analyze and interpret, but hardly ever changes the words if the narrative is supposed to be an oral history, oral narrative or ethnographic interview. David actually changes some of the narrative and provides his explanation:

> ...readers should see these narratives as portraits that I, the folklorist, painted, using the informant's own words and stories. These portraits do indeed resemble the speakers; individuals to whom I read their chapters recognize themselves, their stories. Yet the portraits also bear as much of the unmistakable technique of the writer as a painting bears the brush-stroke of the painter.

Nevertheless, it is a descriptive approach to examining another sacred folk ritual that is still vibrant today and the study also illustrates the patterns of black folk life in the Chesapeake Bay region.

The McIntosh County Shouters near the sea island coast of Georgia are another group maintaining the shout ritual. These shouters in the Bolden community first came to the broader public's attention in *Shout Because You're Free: The African American Ring Shout Tradition in Coastal Georgia* (1998) by Art Rosenbaum. The book has an insightful introduction and three chapters that interweave the history of the shout and its African origins, with slavery and Emancipation, along with oral histories and comments from tradition bearers, folklorists and other outside observers as well as descriptions of present-day shouts. In addition, the ethnomusicologist, John S. Buis includes notes, musical transcriptions and lyrics of twenty-five shout songs performed by the McIntosh County Shouters. These studies are important for relating the history of the tradition and for documenting their importance in the community, but with an exception of a few, the above studies and others in the diaspora seldom offer a gendered reading of power relations inherent in the performance of such rituals.

The totalizing nature of meta-narratives ignores the heterogeneity of human experience and they are also created and reinforced by power structures. My aim here is to present a more modest or localized narrative which can replace the meta-narrative by bringing into focus a singular annual event. This particular ritual event is grounded in locally legitimated history and current human experience. Because of the prominence of women in Easter Rock ceremonies, I look at women's roles as dynamic agents of growth, change and continuity in the church. My offering here responds to dominant meta-narratives about African American religion and patriarchy by examining how women shape and redefine their status with respect to the development of new and reconfiguration of old iconic symbolic representations and organizational possibilities resulting in various concepts of authority and power.

The location of discrete moments within ritual musical performance where women find agency in an otherwise male dominated cultural system provides an alternative lens through which to theorize authority and power within the "black folk church." Here black church women are not passive minions of black male church leadership, but rather active agents in the cultivation of female authority through developing what James C. Scott calls, "hidden transcripts" (Scott 1990, xii). That this source of empowerment emerges within performance highlights the generative power of ritual often associated with diasporic traditions.

Before my 2006 publication of an article on the Easter Rock, previous studies consist of three articles and a brief mention of the ritual in a fourth. The earliest study, "Easter Rock: A Louisiana Negro Ceremony" (Seale 1942, 212), describes the ritual as it was performed in the 1940s. The authors, Lea and Marianna Seale observed the ritual three times in two plantation churches and interviewed two of the oldest blacks living in Concordia Parish. From their opening statement, "An Easter Rock is one of those pagan rites clothed in Christian symbolism which are not altogether uncommon among the Negroes of the South" (Seale 1942, 212), we immediately see the biases of that day and era by the authors' use of the phrase "pagan rites" which is normally used in a pejorative manner. However, the article's value lies in the fact that it is the earliest primary account of the ritual, including song lyrics. Chronologically, the second article, "Easter Rock Revisited: A Study in Acculturation" (Oster 1958), was English professor Harry Oster's, report of his 1956 observations of the Easter Rock ritual. His observations were in the same church near Clayton, Louisiana in Concordia Parish that had previously been observed by the Seales.

He states, "Since the authors of the original article did not describe the African origins of certain features of the service, I shall trace the background out of which these primitive elements came" (Oster 1958, 22). He does provide some background information relating the Easter Rock vocalizations to the "shout," along with interpretation of aspects of the ritual, speculations about African survivals, the text of a sermon and lyrics to songs and degrees of acculturation which differ from those in the Seales' article.

The article by cultural geographer Hiram Gregory, "Africa in the Delta" (Gregory 1962) only discusses the Easter Rock for a page and a half: he describes the Easter Rock ritual as a "prime example of acculturation" in the Louisiana Delta. Through his description, we have another eye witness account of the ritual at a later date and also in another area of the Delta: Gregory made observations at the Primitive African Baptist Church near Waterproof, Louisiana and at the Pittsfield Plantation Church near Ferriday, Louisiana. Therefore, his work indicates that the Easter Rock was not exclusive to one location in the Louisiana Delta. Although in 1962 he recognized that the Easter Rock was "a stylized form of religious observance" he commented that the "dance is now vanishing rapidly from the Delta scene" (Gregory 1962, 17). However, I cannot agree with his assertion, that "Today the loss of meaning of the ritual is ample evidence of the changing status of culture" (Gregory 1962, 19). While the original African significance and meaning may have long been forgotten, the ceremony carries biblical meaning that is enduringly real and important to those who still participate in the ritual and gendered meaning. Although Gregory was unable to elicit from the participants at the ritual any adequate explications, this too does not mean there are none. In my experience of researching this tradition since 1994, I have learned that many of the elderly community members who used to participate no longer attend the Rocks. It is from these elders that I acquired greater insight into the meanings and interpretations of various elements of the Rock. In all, I interviewed over twenty people over the course of several years. In all three of the historical articles discussed above, it is clear that field techniques and the researcher's goals for continuing, influenced their observances and descriptions of the Rock. Gregory also claimed that, "adequate explanations are not given" (Gregory 1962, 18), which led him to the premature conclusion that, "The results of the process of acculturation are now apparent. The African elements have fused with the Anglo-American elements.... The Easter Rock, now only a revered tradition, once was the mystic dance of the practitioners of voodoo" (Gregory 1962, 22). He made this statement with absolutely no explanation or evidence to corroborate it. In over a decade of researching this tradition, none of the practitioners I have worked with has ever mentioned Vodun in relation to the Easter Rock, not even people who spoke against the tradition. When I have asked people who practice this tradition, they clearly indicate that it has nothing to do with Vodun. They are Baptist and even though Vodun is a traditional African-derived religion, they do not identify with its practices. Gregory's attempt to link the Easter Rock to Africa through Vodun is misguided, although African traditional and spiritual elements are present in the Louisiana Easter Rock.

More recently, Janet Sturman, an ethnomusicologist, published the third article that focuses entirely on the Easter Rock, based upon two years of participant observation of the annual Rock ritual in Clayton, Louisiana in Concordia Parish. Sturman also conducted many interviews with participants. Along with providing a detailed description, history, and analysis of the Easter Rock tradition, her main focus is on the role of assertion in the contemporary efforts to revive the Easter Rock at that particular church. She contends that "the Easter Rock transforms the forbidden into the permissible and asserts an identity that paradoxically derives power from both dimensions" (Sturman 1994, 24). My article and the most recent published on the Easter Rock, "Rockin' and Rushin' for Christ: Hidden Transcripts in Diasporic Ritual Performance" (2006), analyzes the Rockin' ritual in northern Louisiana during Easter and the Rushin' ritual in Andros Island, Bahamas during Christmas and New Year. These women-led religious rituals rooted in musical performance and theological similarities are syncretic in nature and are retained in two seemingly unrelated regions of the African diaspora. The work illustrates how they constitute esoteric practices, sustained by the women in the communities and informed by centuries of cultural resistance to plantation society and dominant religious institutions. The article also shows how they are concealed within the larger context of wider known religions including Baptist and Pentecostal and that "ritual adoptions, maintenance and deletions are solely the prerogatives of the women leaders, whose decisions concerning ritual change are most frequently calculated in the hidden transcripts of preserving the sacred ritual, teaching ritual values, and recruiting young adults" (Jackson 2006, 118).

Before discussing the Easter Rock, I need to define the parameters of the term ritual and how it is used in this study. First, ritual is a repetitive social practice composed of a sequence of symbolic activities, in the form of dance, song, speech, bodily actions, and the manipulation of certain objects. Second, it is set off from the social routines of everyday life. Third, rituals in any culture adhere to a characteristic, culturally-defined ritual schema, which means that members of a culture can tell that a certain sequence of activities is a ritual. Finally, ritual action is closely connected to a specific set of ideas that are often encoded in myth (Schultz and Lavenda 1998, 35). For example, these ideas might concern the nature of evil or the relationship of human beings to the spirit world. The reason for which a ritual is performed will guide the way these ideas are designated and symbolically enacted in any given ritual. Ritual events involve ways of embodying in action certain ideas that are important in society. Through that action, the ideas are reflected or transformed and some of these ideas are sanctified.

E.R. Leach informs us, "ritual action and belief are understood as forms of symbolic statements about the social order" (Skorupski, 1976, 19). To take an example from the African American context, during the Civil Rights Movement when a state of disequilibrium occurred, it was customary for blacks to gather at a black church to meet, pray, and sing before going out to face whatever adversity—a march, sit-in, boycott, or freedom ride on an interstate bus. This was a non-violent act, and to some people, it also appears passive; on closer inspection, we can see that the prayer and singing ritual are actions toward release of anxiety and tension, leaving the participants and leaders with better mental control to plan strategies to deal with the adverse situation they were facing. In addition, the praying and singing meeting serves also to unite the community against the anticipated brutality. In this way, any subsequent pain and grief becomes communal and therefore less heavy on the individuals directly afflicted. What initially appears to be a passive reflex is in fact a courage-promoting ritual.

While there is no single or simple definition to ritual, it is clearly an essential part of all human societies. As we come to examine the religious rituals of Easter Rock, we need to bear in mind E.R. Leach's remark that "no interpretation of ritual sequences in man is possible unless the interpreter possesses detailed knowledge of the cultural matrix which provides the context for the rite in question" (Quinn 1973, 104).

Focus upon the importance of ritual allows us to see that woman in the black folk church base their leadership and power on direct control of ceremonial and ritual events rather than exercise overt resistance against gender domination. James Scott examines the dynamics of power, resistance, and subordination and according to his findings, the use of anonymity and ambiguity—gossip, folktales, songs, theater, and jokes—allows the powerless an ideological resistance to domination. He draws most of his evidence from slavery, serfdom and caste subordination while also examining patriarchal domination, colonialism and racism.

Under the premise that structurally similar forms of domination will bear a family resemblance to one another, slavery and gender domination can thus be considered together. Although slavery is more dramatically violent and gender domination more subtly imposed, both are forms of domination.

Scott declares: "The ideologies justifying domination of this kind include formal assumptions about inferiority and superiority which, in turn, find expression in certain ritual or etiquette regulating public contact between strata" (Scott 1990, x, xi). Since I have acquired evidence from participants that the Easter Rock predates the Civil War era when the institution of slavery was still flourishing, I concur with Scott that "there is something useful to be said across cultures and historical epochs when our focus is narrowed by structural similarities" (Scott 1990, x). This sacred and circular ritual was practiced during the slavery era, when the slave master dominated everybody, and everybody participated in the ritual whether it was open or clandestine. Then, when emancipation ensued along with Jim Crow and the early 20th century, the rituals were relegated to the next subordinate group, the women in the church, who continue to be subordinated by the men in the church.

Ethnographic Gaze on Rockin'

Today, the town of Winnsboro is located on LA Highway 15, thirty-seven miles from Monroe, Louisiana and fifty-five miles from Natchez, Mississippi. The distance from Baton Rouge is about one hundred and fifty miles normally takes a little over three hours due to two lane roads for part of the route. This particular year I came to Winnsboro three days before the Easter Rock ceremony at The Original True Light Baptist Church, which is located on Highway 4 in back of the town. At the time, the Original True Light Baptist Church had a very small congregation and was in need of extreme repairs. However, the owners allowed the church to stay open as long as the congregation attended services and made minor repairs to keep it habitable, so the community continued to come to church services and the yearly Holy Saturday Easter Rock ceremony each year.

In my observations over several years the ritual is never incorporated into a regular church worship service, they are always performed at night and they are community events and not just for one congregation. They are organized, directed, and maintained by women and they do everything including baking the cakes, mending and/or making the white dresses, purchasing oil for the lamps, boiling and coloring the Easter eggs or purchasing candy eggs, spring-cleaning and decorating the church, preparing the children, mending or constructing the banner, making programs, and contacting and inviting potential participants to the program. During my visits, there was one woman, Ms. Haddie Addison, who orchestrated the entire event. If someone did not implement her delegated task, in Ms. Addison's words, she had to "take up the slack." Ms. Addison has been the guiding force for many years after she "inherited" the

Rock from her mother when she decided she was getting too old for the complex responsibility of organizing all and doing most of the tasks. Since her daughter had worked with her through the years and she had trained her well, she knew she was leaving the Rock in capable hands.

I visited the homes of several participants and observed them as they prepared for the annual celebration. These women require several days of preparation before the Easter eve ritual. The preparations included, dressmaking and altering dresses, cake baking, and refurbishing the banner. I also visited the church the day before the ritual because the coordinator of the Easter Rock, Haddie Addison and a few of the other women rockers had to rearrange the pews against the walls, give the church its Easter cleaning as in sweeping and dusting and decorate with pastel colored crepe paper streamers.

On the day of the ritual, people begin to gather outside of the church, visiting with each other, while a few women make last minute preparations inside the church. I enter the church and take a seat in one of the pews that have been pushed against the sides of the sanctuary, leaving a wide area in the middle of the floor for the rocking circle. Two long tables, positioned in the middle of the floor are draped in white cloth with pastel crape-paper streamers, as are the windows, entrances, and pulpit of the church. The cue for the ceremony to begin is when the mistress of ceremony takes her place at the dais on the floor beside the elevated pulpit. This is the first structured frame of the ritual. While it is a woman who directs the ritual, she does not do so from the pulpit. Even during this female-driven occasion, the minister is still the only one in the pulpit. The mistress of ceremony leads the congregation in a typical devotion and worship service. An elderly male deacon initiates the call to worship from the dais, performs an opening prayer and leads the congregation in a lined-out hymn.[2] Rev. Mc Dowell gives the greetings from the pulpit and a female visitor

---

2 A lined-out, long-meter, or Dr. Watts hymn is an older tradition of congregational singing. A deacon or one of the members of the congregation "lined-out" or in the case of black Baptist churches, "raised" the text and melody of the hymn, by intoning or chanting a phrase at a time. The congregation follows by singing the words and melody they had just been given. This tradition was very effective in congregations where literacy was rare, however the lining-out style of hymn singing continued to be a preference among certain congregations. The singing is slow and has a surging choral sound, thus the designation of long-meter. In addition, in the African American oral tradition, the naming of an entire genre of songs and singing style after a major composer or musician is a way of acknowledging that a composer or musician set the standard by which all others working in that genre will be measured. Dr. Isaac Watts' lyrics resonated within the collective memory of the congregation so that even today the lining-out style is referred to by many as the "Dr. Watts style."

from another church gives the acceptance from the dais. Someone sings a solo and another person then gives the occasion. Several congregation members and visitors from other churches perform solos, and some elderly women shout when they are "filled with the Holy Spirit." When emotions finally die down, there is a break in the service.

After the break, a deacon or another elderly person starts another lined-out hymn. This performance starts the second frame of the structured ritual that I consider as part A. Some of these practices are common in the devotional segment of a regular church service, however in the devotional setting, they are preparing the congregants for the minister's sermon; in this setting, they are preparing the congregants for the Easter Rock, the annual celebration for the risen Christ. After the deacon and the congregation have sung two verses, a third verse begins and the lights are turned off. These are the specific cues for the Rock to begin.

A procession of twelve women starts from the back of the sanctuary, moving toward the center to encircle the table. In the earlier days these women were the elderly "mothers of the church" and were purported to be members of the benevolent society (Pollard 1997; Gregory 1962).[3] As they process in a counterclockwise direction around the table, the rockers begin to sing the spiritual "Oh When the Saints Go Marching In" in a dirge-like style, and the surrounding congregation augments the singing. The entire ceremony is done *a capella,* with only handclapping and foot stamping to accompany the songs. The leader of the procession carries the circular banner with streamers flowing from it, and twelve women follow each other carrying burning kerosene lamps.

After circling several times, the women place the lamps on the table in a straight line. They then repeat these actions to place the twelve cakes on the table. Traditionally, all the cakes had white icing, but now it is a mixture. While

---

3   In a Baptist church, the phrase "mothers of the church" usually refers to the elderly women who sit in the front pews of the church. They are also referred to as the stewardesses or deaconesses, essentially the female counterpart to the male deacons of the church. These women are charged with the preparation for communion, working with baptismal candidates, praying for the sick and "shut in," and other advisory tasks. They are normally attired in white dresses and hats, if not every Sunday, definitely on communion Sunday. In some churches, these same women belong to "the society," that is, the benevolent society. These societies are organizations established in black communities during Reconstruction and grew out of the need to provide for the sick, properly bury the dead and care for the families of deceased members. The societies may be female, male, or mixed and many of them still exist today.

singing the same song and without missing a step, they continue to proceed around the table while someone passes the cakes to them through the door in the back of the church. They slowly place the twelve cakes on the table, and continue their marching around the table. After the cakes have all been placed on the table, the rockers make a few more rounds. Then the tempo accelerates, the song changes, and the steps of the rockers quicken and change.

At this key moment, the rockers are transitioning into the second and heightened phase of the Rock still within the second frame that I designate as part B. Now they begin to sing, "Oh David," an old up-tempo spiritual that is no longer performed except for this ritual. Since this spiritual is faster, the rockers began to move more quickly, performing the distinctive rocking step. This step constitutes a step-slide and skip from one side to the other and some participants do the steps without taking their feet off the floor. At this point the person behind the banner carrier retrieves the two ropes connected to each side of the banner. Symbolically, that person is helping to carry the banner or cross. This phase of the Rock can continue indefinitely with practitioners alternating between sitting and rocking. In an earlier time, the ritual continued until the "sun shouted," or sunrise. Even now, this second phase is highly charged with emotion, where some of the rockers and congregants "catch the spirit," either shouting or going into trance. The repetitive rhythm that the congregants' feet make while dancing or rocking around the table is the equivalent of the driving percussive texture of the African drum. In the Rock, as is in many African-derived sacred rituals, repetitive beaten rhythms whether from the drum or the sound of the feet on a hard floor, have a tendency to cause some participants to shout, go into trance, or invoke the spirit. After the Rock has gone on for quite some time, the song may be changed to, "Elijah Rock." It depends on who is leading the song and sometimes who is carrying the banner at the time. However, this does not mean that the banner carrier always leads and determines the song.

After the rockers have circled for an undetermined length of time depending on the movement of the spirit or degree of fatigue, they cease rocking for a while and subsequently resume the program. At this transition, the mistress of ceremony announces that it is time for the congregation to "honor God by giving," that is, it is time for the collection. The mistress of ceremony volunteers two members to collect the offering while all other participants march around the church to give their offering, while singing a congregational hymn. Afterwards, a deacon prays over the funds in the collection plate, and the program continues. During this transitional period, announcements are made and guest singers from different churches perform a few more solos; some singers are even requested to sing certain songs. These vocalists are well known by members of the congregation and for having one or two "signature songs."[4] After the soloists perform, the deacon once again begins a long-meter hymn with the congregation; after singing a while, they turn off the lights, which signals that the Rock is beginning again.

The rockers again fall in line, and begin to rock around the table for this second phase of the ritual. The line begins like the first one, with the banner carrier in front. This time, the participants rock for an interval, while singing the same songs. Then the mistress of ceremony invites other members of the congregation and guests to join in the Rock. In earlier years, this ritual lasted all night, but currently, and for at least the last decade, the ritual usually ends between nine thirty and ten o'clock. After the program and ritual has ended, the coordinator "gives words of thanks" and everybody is invited for the repast, which consists of the twelve ritual cakes and red fruit punch. During the earlier years when the Rock lasted all night, the women brought more substantial food, like fried chicken and potato salad to actually feed people during the night. The ceremony would last until it was time to go to Easter Sunrise service.

The north Louisiana Rocking ceremony at the present time takes place only on Easter eve. However, in earlier days, Rocks in Concordia Parish were not exclusively for Easter. There are some accounts by the elders where Rocks were held on New Year's Eve such as the Ship of Zion ceremony and some were held in November as the Harvest Rock ceremony (Sturman 1994, 28). There have also been accounts of another Delta congregation that sponsored Rocks on a weekly basis to attract youth to the church and to participants claim that the Rock is relegated solely to Easter in their area.

Rockin' Frames and Icons

The main thesis of Walter F. Pitts' book is that, in the Afro-Baptist church worship there are two ritual frames (Devotion and Service) that have a correlation to some African initiation rites and that these two contrasting frames, as retained in the Afro-Baptist service, function as in some African contexts, to transport worshipers psychically from a hostile and precarious world to a smaller and more secure one that will equip them to face the hostile

---

4   A vocalist's "signature song" is a song that is frequently performed by one person with a specific stylized version. In the black folk church, when a particular vocalist rises to sing a song, the congregation anticipates a certain culturally sanctioned performance. The song is designated as their song and other members of the church usually avoid singing it.

environment again. Pitts argues persuasively with the assistance of Victor Turner and by virtue of his own participant observations and subsequent initiation into the mysteries of the Afro-Baptist world. The variations in ways of speaking at different points in the ritual and the genre of music that was performed at certain times were the determinants of frames. For instance, the first frame uses standard twentieth-century English and Jacobean English in the prayers, while the second frame—the sermon—draws on Black Vernacular English. The music styles are parallel to the speech styles in the same frame. The transformance of participants emotions and psyches during the ritual frames and the experience of *communitas*, a transitory moment of social reversal and leveling. The evidence of resistance is also very significant.

In the Easter Rock, the binary frames are divided as part A when the devotional service or program takes place. The congregants are greeted; a welcome, acceptance and purpose are given. In addition, various songs are performed (hymns, gospels, long-meters) and maybe poetry is recited and this part is more Eurocentric. The performed songs are usually hymns and Dr. Watts or long-meter with an occasional black gospel song. Also there is a structured written program. Part B starts when the long-meter song is performed, the lights go off, and the oil lamps come on. The actual Rock or shout movements and the spiritual song "Oh David" follow this and the second frame is more Afrocentric. The round banner with the streamers and the song of resistance, "Oh David" are evidence of the Afrocentric nature.

From the accounts of participants in Winnsboro, the Rock ceremony has an abundance of symbolic meanings and pageantry pertaining to the passion of Christ and other biblical scriptures. Various elders who once participated in the Rock gave me their interpretations based on many years of participation as well as on information their ancestors gave to them. This information has been transmitted through several generations, so some of the symbolic representations have taken on multiple meanings, depending on who is giving an account of the ritual. For example, for some the twelve women processing represent and are referred to as the twelve saints, while others refer to them as the twelve disciples of Christ. The cakes represent the twelve tribes of Israel and the unleavened bread at the Last Supper. Easter eggs are placed on the table, according to the elders, to symbolize new birth and the stone that was rolled away from the tomb of Christ on Easter Sunday morning.

There is a predominance of the color white; all the women who first process are wearing white dresses, the tables are draped in white cloths, and the base of the banner is white—signifying purity. The red fruit punch that is served to congregants after the Rock represents the blood of Jesus Christ. Several participants recalled that homemade wine was used in earlier days (Bowie 1995).

The round banner on the staff and the person carrying it symbolize Christ carrying the cross. The banner puller who processes behind the banner carrier and pulls rhythmically on the two streamers or light ropes connected to the banner, symbolizes Simon the Cyrenian who helped Jesus bear the cross on his way to Golgotha.[5]

The banner itself warrants more analysis, as it is apparently a circular representation of the perpendicular shape of the cross. The perplexing question, which this sacred icon posed, is: Why have participants used a circle mounted on top of a staff to represent the cross when they could have easily made a wooden cross which represents the Christian symbol? After I posed this question to each elderly person in the community that I interviewed, I still did not receive an answer. Basically, I was told about the ways the banner has changed over the years from basic white slipcovers to a white banner with colored streamers flowing.

Since this is a pre-Civil War ritual and it is obvious that this ritual has antecedents in West Africa, I suggest that the Easter Rock circular cross icon as well as the counterclockwise circular dance were maintained by enslaved Africans on plantations in Franklin, Concordia, Catahoula, and Tensas Parishes.

At this point, it is generally known that at the time of Emancipation, slaves were still overwhelmingly African in culture. Although the official end of the Transatlantic slave trade occurred in 1808, it would take some time for Africans to assimilate into African Americans. In order to proclaim this self-definition, it would be a time-consuming process involving and informed by a number of factors including non-maintenance of the slave environment and society, cultural and social interaction, material conditions of servitude, reinterpretation of religious ritual and folklore.

Sterling Stuckey, a leading historian, has explored the folklore of American slaves by examining it through a cross-cultural Pan-African lens. In his seminal work, *Slave Culture,* he establishes what he refers to as the "black ethos in slavery." Essentially, he substantiates the centrality of an African ancestral ritual—the Circle Dance—to the black religious and artistic experience. He writes:

> The majority of Africans brought to North America to be enslaved were from the central and western areas of Africa—from Congo-Angola, Nigeria, Dahomey, Togo, the Gold Coast, and Sierra Leone. In these areas,

---

5   Golgotha is the site of the crucifixion, which is referred to as "the place of the skull," in the Bible (Mathew 27:33; Mark 15:22; and John 19:17). The site of the crucifixion is also referred to as Calvary (Luke 23:33). The cross was laid on the back of Simon, a Cyrenian, so he could bear it for Jesus (Mathew 27:32; Mark 15:21; and Luke 23:26).

an integral part of religion and culture was movement in a ring during
ceremonies honoring the ancestors. There is, in fact, substantial evidence
for the importance of the ancestral function of the circle in West Africa,
but the circle ritual imported by Africans from the Congo region was so
powerful in this elaboration of a religious vision that it contributed dis-
proportionately to the centrality of the circle in slavery. The use of the
circle for religious purposes in slavery was so consistent and profound
that one could argue that it was what gave form and meaning to black
religion and art.

STUCKEY 1987, 10–11

Circular dances are also linked to the burial ceremony, which is the most
important of all African rituals. According to art historian Robert F. Thompson,
in Bakongo burial ceremonies, mourners moved around the body of the
deceased in a counterclockwise direction with their feet imprinting a circle on
the earth (Thompson 1988. 28, 58). In 2004, I observed three funerals in the
coastal region of Ghana in Woe between Keta and Anloga, all of which included
some form of circular dancing or processing in relationship to the deceased
body. The funeral of a 108-year-old man was dense with circular movements of
individuals, groups, and individuals with animal sacrifices, all moving around
the deceased in a counterclockwise direction.

The Easter Rock circular dance could also be symbolically linked to burial as
interpreted through Christian doctrine of the ritual burial of Jesus Christ after
his crucifixion. The Easter Rock ritual is a condensed celebration of the last
three days of Christ on earth: the crucifixion, burial and resurrection. Because
of the regional climate and temperature of the water, this is also the time in
many southern rural Baptist churches when baptisms were held in the river,
lake or creek. The candidate is symbolically buried under water in Christ, where
sins are washed away, and he/she is raised up to walk in the newness of life.

Furthermore, the circular cross and staff symbolizes a movement from one
state of being in the Kongo religious system to a higher one. In addition, the
circular cross is the sign of the four moments of the sun, which is the Kongo
emblem of spiritual continuity and renaissance (Thompson 1988, 28, 58).

Searching for Kongo in North LA

In looking for evidence of ethnic slave groups in Spanish Louisiana, Gwendolyn
Midlo Hall states in *Africans in Colonial Louisiana*, that "The Africans brought
to Louisiana under Spanish rule came from four main areas: Senegambia, the

Bight of Benin, the Bight of Biafra, and Central Africa" (Hall 1992, 284, 286). In searching specifically for the Kongo in Louisiana, I looked at Hall's work focusing on the Point Coupee post between 1771 and 1802 (also coinciding with Spanish rule). She noticed that, "Throughout most of this period, the slave population increased sharply while the white population declined" (Hall 1992, 281). In 1795, another slave ship, the *La Paloma* was recorded in point Coupee bringing slaves probably to replace those exiled or executed after 1795 revolt. All of the slaves on board were Congo, and they were sold by a merchant of New Orleans name Jean Raymond et Cie (Hall 1992, 280). Hall also concludes that, "Documents generated by African slave trade to Spanish Louisiana do not help. While French slave trade to Louisiana was highly centralized and well documented, the Spanish slave trade was neither. There was little direct involvement by the Spanish government" (Hall 1992, 379). It also appears that we have little documentation of groups in north Louisiana.

Continuing the search for the Kongo, David Geggus in his article, "The Haitian Revolution," calculated that the Congo were the largest African group in St. Domingue during the late eighteenth century. This group constituted one-third of the slave population in the plains and well over half in the mountains (Geggus 1989, 23). His documentation along with Alfred Hunt's work focusing on the *Influence of the Haitian Revolution on the Antebellum South,* also asserts a large introduction of the Kongo in Louisiana by way of the emigration during the revolution (Geggus 1989, 19).

According to the WPA history and the Louisiana Chronicler many of the Anglos that moved into Franklin Parish and subsequently to Winnsboro in 1844 moved from somewhere else bringing their slaves with them. Unfortunately, only Natchez was named as one of those places. This was basically a cotton plantation area and during the late 1800s it was not as lucrative as the Mississippi River Road plantations further south, so they did not have a large number of slaves. The number increased after the railroads were established to facilitate the transportation of the cotton. At his point, it is only my speculation that slaves were brought in from southern Louisiana, Natchez, Mississippi and or the Carolinas. Of course, it all depended on where the settlers came from during this period to populate the land.

Conclusion: Binary Transcripts

In conclusion the majority of the icons are Eurocentric, however the most strikingly powerful ones, the music and the banner or representation of the cross, are Afrocentric. The calendrical time of year, the Lenten season, is always observed the last forty days leading up to Easter and many church leaders call the twelve disciples "the forefathers," which indicates that this practice had a solid link to the actual beginnings of Christianity. Therefore, the numerological representations of twelve saints (women), twelve disciples (cakes) and ten virgins (lamps) were symbolic of people and aspects of the Christian Bible. Also, the symbolic icons of Easter eggs (new birth or tombstone) and wine or red fruit punch (blood of Jesus Christ) were also straight from biblical references. In addition, the color white (purity, clean) for the women's ritual attire, the tablecloth and historically the cakes, are also biblical but this color is also prevalent in other African-based religions rituals including Vodou, Santeria, Candomblé as well as other Christian rituals.

People adopt, absorb and maintain what they consider relevant. The influence of the domestic slave trade, black-white cultural borrowing and diffusion were all factors in the creation of black sacred music. At least two types of sacred music evolved: those songs and hymns that were learned from whites and those representing the slaves' own creativity and originality—their prayer and shout songs. In addition, from past spiritual traditions, African Americans inherited mysticism, a sense of drama, and an oral communication in song already rich in symbolic imagery. This background merged with biblical apocalypse, narrations, and miraculous interpretations along with the sense of human frailty also brought forth the poetry from within.

The binary frames in the Easter Rock are not exactly the same as in Pitts' work, but the variation of speech and song styles that define the two frames are crucial in maintaining the oral ritual for over a hundred years without a written liturgy. A fleeting moment of antistructure provides for a catharsis and a release of tension from structural constraints. It also offers *commmunitas* to the participants. The women are there in large numbers, they sing more, the dance around the church and they are the ones to go into trance more, therefore they gain the most benefit if you look at the ritual from a psychological rather than a social perspective.

While my primary aim was not the excavation of African survivals but rather the explication of the actual character and diversity of the icons in this ritual as manifest among African American women. Ultimately, I believe that much of the originality and special richness of the Easter Rock ritual rests in the fact that it was forged by women of African ancestry in the crucible of oppression, first during slavery and later under patterns of segregation, discrimination and economic disparities. Only powerful African cultural elements were retained and effectively mobilized as part of African American women's response to spirituality and life.

I argue, however, that much of the current importance of these African elements derives not from their possible source but in the part that they have played in the past and continue to play in the crafting of a special mechanism for social survival, emotional comfort and transcendent expressions of agency and power under patriarchal circumstances. The Africanism in the construction of the banner or cross, the most significant icon, gives a special and unique temperament to the Baptist Easter Rock, contributing a feature that helps account for experiential differences between this Baptist ritual and others.

The creativity of these women chanters and rockers carried their community's heritage over many decades and historical transitions. Their musical performance and iconic aesthetics continue to articulate the reality of their existence, and as preservers of ritual music and icons, these women preserve their authority and power within the church and the community. In so doing they remain within their cultural parameters while simultaneously dealing with hidden transcripts in their ritual performances.

CHAPTER 19

Pole Dancing For Jesus
Negotiating Movement and Gender in Men's Musical Praise

Alisha Lola Jones

Introduction

Since 2011, "pole dancing for Jesus" has gained in popularity as a provocative expression of praise across racial and gender boundaries. Amidst media coverage of this trend, Jungle Cat's performances to gospel music evoked especially passionate responses from viewers. His performance was controversial because he combined the symbolic meanings of the pole, with dance, and the pursuit of a deeper spiritual connection to God. However, viewers' language about Jungle Cat's performance was markedly different from the characterization of the Texas housewives who also praise pole danced. The public's reception of his combination of these symbols and signifiers was related to their perceptions of his racialized and gendered body.

This essay examines the extent to which black men's musical praise informs discourses about sexual ambiguities within gospel music performance. Drawing on an ethnomusicological analysis of a praise pole dancing performance by Jungle Cat and a series of correspondence with him, I contend that his performances reveals tensions that characterize Christian worship by men striving to join body and spirit. I do virtual ethnography of his worship practice via the Internet, through which I move beyond the local or denominational theology that shape black men's worship experiences. The reception of Jungle Cat's performance via the Internet illustrates what Barry Taylor calls an "entertainment theology," which "highlights the evolution of theology from a didactic or studied approach to the question of God to a more global *communal conversation* about the sacred in general" (Taylor 2008, 19). Virtual exchanges are connected to notions of transcendence and spirituality because they enhance the personal nature of modern worship, providing ideal spaces of expression and moments of participation that are not determined by geography and real time. Undeniably, globalization accelerates the distribution through technology of gospel performances, products, and practices. It is a place where people are not physically present but are connected nonetheless. The virtual domain's role in modern worship is a space in which black religious scholars must increasingly explore.

In posting his worship, Jungle Cat positions himself for assessment of the meaning of his performance. Many spectators struggle to decipher Jungle Cat's YouTube videos, which feature a mix of gendered signifiers and body language that comes across as sexually ambiguous. In addition to virtual ethnography Jungle Cat's performance, I will examine a constellation of interpretations: the implications of his liturgical dance, constructions of masculinity, mysticism in Christian practice and the media's reception of his worship.

Virtual Ethnography

As I viewed the opening credits of the YouTube video,[1] it curiously read: "Jungle Cat, I Need You To Survive, Hezekiah Walker." This is a popular gospel song by Bishop Hezekiah Walker, a leading choir director. The choir softly sings in unison, with whispery vocals, and in a slow tempo. After they sing the chorus once, Bishop Walker leads a call and response using the chorus. Then they modulate, as they repeat the "special" or vamp of the song until the end, when they return to the last couplet of the chorus. I noted the dancer's stage name and braced for the possible irony of the performance. While the familiar slow melody of the song began playing in the background, the man with dreadlocks and a hat, wearing a grayish "wife beater," jeans, and Timberlands®, meanders to the pole that was erected in the center of what looked to be his dimly-lit living room. Jungle Cat's dreadlocks sway from side to side, as he limberly mounted and swirled around it. His gestures are both upward on and outward from the pole. Throughout the performance, he progressively demonstrates his pole tricks facility to the playing music, as the following lyrics unfolded:

> I need you, you need me.
> We're all a part of God's body.
> Stand with me, agree with me.
> We're all a part of God's body.
>
> It is his will that every need be supplied.
> You are important to me, I need you to survive. (2x)
>
> I pray for you, you pray for me.
> I love you, I need you to survive.
> I won't harm you with words from my mouth.
> I love you, I need you to survive…
>
> WALKER 2002

---

1   "Guy Does Pole Dancing To Hezekiah Walker's "I Need You To Survive," http://www.youtube .com/watch?v=v_H5kG9dOoE, last accessed July 23, 2013.

It was at this point that I giggled, sighed, and echoed the phrase: "It is his will that every need be supplied..." I found humor in the connection made firm with the use of his body language (one's range of movements and comportment) to convey community, yearning, reciprocity, solidarity, and closeness. The lyrics of the song refer to closeness among humans. He also nurtures a divine-human shared memory of suffering, as he uses his body with the pole to assemble a signified cross. Yet, his gestures often extend upward, a direction within liturgical dance that signifies reaching to God. Pole dancing to this song, with the incorporation of the aforementioned elements, provokes online spectators to respond to his devotion using the pole, which is a symbol conventionally understood to be a profane object of female seduction and objectification.

How might dance styles conventionally deemed "profane" be reclaimed through performance as a means for intimacy with God? I would like to address here what is at stake in the exploration of using profane dance styles and symbols in worship. In Mircea Eliade's seminal work, *The Sacred and the Profane: The Nature of Religion* traces the early development of the sacred and the profane concepts. Eliade defines the sacred as something that manifests and shows itself within religious experiences as wholly different from the profane. The profane is a modern concept to black religiosity that White oppression imposed upon African-American worship styles that held white worship styles as superior. Jon Michael Spencer (1992) connects the introduction of the profane concept to African worship contexts to the era of Puritanism through the Second Great Awakening. According to Samuel A. Floyd, "In traditional African culture there was no formal distinction between the sacred and the profane realms of life or between the material and the spiritual..." (Floyd 1995,15). If profane and sacred realms were not always distinct in the foundations of African worship, what are the ways in which dance has traditionally been received? Scholarly perspectives on liturgical dance and constructions of masculinity in black worship from music history, ethnomusicology, and black religious studies can shed light on what is at stake for those seeking intimacy with God through musical movement.

Scholarly and Historical Perspectives

Dance in Black Worship

Musicologists have done well, however, to research sacred music making of the antebellum period, during which time European Americans who adhered to Victorian codes considered Christian slaves' sounds and movements of "black church" worship to be "heathenish." In her seminal work, *The Music of Black Americans* (1997), Eileen Southern recounts the early conceptualization of music and movement that allowed for the ring shout in extracurricular black worship. Regulations for "shouting" were very rigid and did not allow for the variety of improvisatory expression that we might observe today, due to the socio-cultural codes of the time.[2] As a result of these beliefs, much of the preservation of older sacred and secular dance music repertoire was lost due to dance's association with damnation. "Most of the song collecting took place on plantations where slaves, having been converted to Christianity, came to regard dancing as sinful and no longer indulged in it" (Southern 1997, 130–131). Since this era, black gospel participants have revised their readings of the Hebrew/ Old Testament biblical text. Indeed they have adapted to imagery that celebrates David as an iconic figure in masculine praise to God.

Ethnomusicologist Melvin L. Butler has noted that in church and concert settings, gospel performers often utilize a Davidic model of worship. For example, artists such as Fred Hammond have produced songs recounting how David danced, as a representation of his close relationship with God. As Butler states, "(O)ne of his most successful albums of the 1990s is entitled *The Spirit of David*, in reference to David's character, his commitment to praise and worship, and repentant heart" (Butler 2011). David's display of "dancing before the Lord with all his might" (2 Samuel 6:14) is held to be the exuberance to which masculine worshippers ought to aspire. The Davidic model concentrates on the participant's sense of closeness to God, regardless of human's approval.

David as a model for masculine movement has been critiqued however as a romantic aspiration by theologian Cheryl Kirk-Duggan, in her chapter "Salome's Veiled Dance and David's Full Monty: A Womanist Reading on the Black Erotic in Blues, Rap, R & B and Gospel Blues." Kirk-Duggan uses a womanist biblical interpretation of David dancing, to name it as "David's Full Monty." She argues "David's Full Monty" is "a metaphor for the erotic, communicates divine observance and human acknowledgment to the aesthetics of the sensual, sexual body in worship of God in tribute of life, connecting politics, pomp, and power" (Kirk-Duggan 2006, 222). Kirk-Duggan's interpretation of movement offers a useful tool for considering erotic connotations of dancing before a God constructed as male. Her line of interpretation will

---

2 "For the participants, the shout was not under any circumstances to be construed as a dance, and strictly observed rules insured that the line between 'shouting' and dancing was firmly drawn. Only songs of religious nature were sung, and the feet must never be crossed (as would happen in the dance). Among strict devotees, the feet must not even be lifted from the ground. Presumably, any song could function as a shout song or 'running spiritual'. In practice, however, the slaves preferred some songs to the exclusion of others, and a special body of these songs was developed among them" (Southern 1997, 130–131).

inform my assessment of Jungle Cat's homoerotic mysticism, as I will discuss later.

There is specifically a yawning gap of critical inquiry within "the black church" into the ways in which black men currently practice musical movement. In order to analyze Jungle Cat's musical movement specifically, one must engage black religious plurality in constructions of masculinity, as applied it is to gesture. Christianity is presumed to be the sole religious practice of black in America. Yet, black religion has always encompassed a participation in other world religions, apart from and along with Christianity. Scholars such as Charles Long (1986), James Evans (1992), Anthony Pinn (1998), and Gayraud S. Wilmore (1957) have done well to explain the extent to which black religiosity encompasses what Gayraud S. Wilmore calls African Traditional Religions (ATRs) and other expressions of religious plurality (Wilmore 1957, 4). Black religion scholarship offers a conceptualization of overlapping faith networks and plurality that informs my analysis of black worshippers in virtual forums.

Constructions of Masculinity in Black Worship

With regard to constructions of masculinity in worship, in *Adam! Where Are You?: Why Most Black Men Don't Go To Church,* Jawanza Kunjufu interviews men in Chicago to research the reasons they choose not to attend church. Kunjufu interrogates the growth of black male absenteeism in the church. One of 21 interviewees' responses to reasons for black male absenteeism in church reveals men's homophobic beliefs about music ministers' sexuality and manhood. Men involved in music ministry are perceived to be less manly because of the demonstrative nature of their musical movement. Kunjufu notes,

> Several of the brothers said that the church is made up of women, elders, and sissies. 'You notice most of the brothers that play the organ or piano or sing in the choir, how they got their butt going up in the air. They love waving their open hand. No wonder they believe in turning the other cheek, they probably want to be kissed on it. They can't defend themselves…One brother said, "That's why I let my girls go to church but not my boys. I want my boys to be like me. I want my boys to be strong. I want my boys to be macho. I don't want my boys crying…I want my boys to be straight. I don't want my sons being taught by a homosexual teacher or being propositioned by one."
>
> KUNJUFU 1997, 67

This testimony depicts men's anxiety about other's perception. They express a dislike for males to exhibit open gestures and emotional vulnerability. Some men see churches as a threat, in large part because their "sissified" musical spaces are perceived to be a magnet and harbor for men of either gay or ambiguous sexual orientation.[3] Men are not to be "soft" or emotionally expressive, especially not while other men are spectators (Burt 2007, 14). Such perceptions are based on a Victorian reading of the worshipers' body language as emblematic of a gay or ambiguous sexual orientation. The men interviewed believed that interactions with these demonstrative, musical men place impressionable boys and young men at risk, diminish their masculinity, and spiritually contaminate them.[4] Men's aspiration toward the aforementioned Davidic model of experiencing undignified worship that nurtures a relationship with God is dissonant with this anti-open worship that focuses on negotiating humanity's homophobic perceptions of what male praise should look. The manner with which Jungle Cat worships evokes the questions: for whom (or to whom) is worship offered? In Jungle Cat's worship as a black man, there is a unification of a gender and race, and body and spirit, in a realm that socio-culturally sets aside closeness as symbolically more congruent for women in a heteronormative construct.

Within mysticism discourse, one can write about mysticism or mystics. Scholars such as B. McGinn have observed that among the myriad of different Christian denominations and other world faiths, mysticism is a common ground experience (McGinn 1992, xvi). Mysticism is "every religious tendency that discovers the way to God direct through inner experience without the mediation of reasoning. The constitutive element in mysticism is the immediacy of contact with the deity" (Deissmann 1957, 149). I would like to deploy B. McGinn's definition of mysticism as the "direct consciousness of the presence of God" (McGinn 1992, xvi). The scope of this paper centers on Jungle Cat as a mystic because ethnomusicological research focuses on the people who perform and their musical context(s).[5] In my conversations with

---

3   E. Patrick Johnson explores the stories of gay men in gospel performance in the chapter "Church Sissies" in his book *Sweet Tea: Black Gay Men of the South* (Johnson 2011).

4   As a result of Victorian codes, Gay Morris examines how male dancers were viewed as suspicious because of their choice to dance. In other words the very desire to move as only ladies were to do was held as effeminate (Morris 2001, 246).

5   With regard to research that focuses on mystics, Steven Fanning argues that focusing on mystics as opposed to abstract mysticism is more profitable. He writes "The effect of a focus on mystics is to make one aware that the direct experience of the divine has come in many different ways and paths and has been expressed in a variety of forms. Thus rather than there being a favored paradigm of mysticism alongside the many areas of commonality shared by the mystics" (Fanning 2001, 3).

Jungle Cat, he privileges his black Pentecostal spiritual formation. Yet, he has researched mysticism in Christianity, other religions such as Hinduism, and the use of the pole for worship in eastern faiths. Within Jungle Cat's story, we find the ways in which black religious practice does not form in isolation. In what ways can we understand men's intimacy with a God conventionally constructed as male, through insights from Jungle Cat's Christian mystic practice?

Jungle Cat's Story: Mysticism in Christian Practice

Jungle Cat (born Tavon Hargett) is a self-identified, sheltered country boy from North Carolina who moved to Washington, DC for a change of scenery. A librarian by day and a pole fitness instructor by night, his story is that of cultivating a community of love and positivity. Hargett considers himself Apostolic Pentecostal—part of a network of churches, which permit improvisatory bodily responses to worship. He qualifies his religious identity as spiritual, non denominational and open to the wisdom of various faith traditions. Since 2003, Hargett practiced tantric celibacy as a self-identified heterosexual man. According to Tantra expert Elsbeth Meuth "tantric celibacy" has meanings such as conscious celibacy, tantric sublimation, tantric self-love, or solo practice (autoeroticism). She interprets tantric celibacy as "sexual energy channeling and transmuting for other purposes than the bedroom."[6] She also referred me to Stuart Sovatsky's writing on tantric celibacy as "a sex-positive, body-affirming attitude, for it is a path of sublimation, not repression" (Sovatsky 1999, 5). In Sovatsky's estimation, Tantric sublimation is the negotiation of a paradox—Eros literally becomes sublime.

On St. Patrick's Day in 2009, he started teaching himself pole fitness and is presently an instructor affiliated with the American Pole Fitness Association. According to Jungle Cat, he had never seen stripping nor had he been to a strip club before he started teaching himself pole fitness. In addition, he mentioned familiarity with the Indian sport of *Mallakhamb*, in which both men and women master using the pole in gymnastic feats. Performing his first praise on Easter Sunday 2009 in his home helped Jungle Cat to deal with his "church home" sickness. The following is an excerpt from my phone interview with Jungle Cat conducted in May 2011:

---

6   Personal communication with Elsbeth Meuth via email on July 18, 2013.

Alisha: Why did you start doing praise pole dance?

Jungle Cat: I will never forget my first praise dance. It was on Easter and it was like, I didn't feel like going to...I don't think I actually had like a church at that time. So it was Easter Sunday and I wanted to do something...but I didn't know what to do....

I didn't want to just walk in, you know, in some random church. I wanted to have something to myself. So I put on some gospel music, like I always do. Um and, It just felt, It just felt natural. It was no question. I never questioned it. I didn't have any reason to question it because I know how I worship. It was just like I was on the pole doing it...I didn't have any second thoughts. It was all genuine. I felt the presence of the Lord! Like it was just powerful for me. After I was done, I was in tears. I felt so good... And I posted it...So I just put it there so that I could look at it later and get encouraged by it. Because more people were encouraged I felt better about myself.

Being a Christian is hard. It is hard for everybody...Just because someone says that it is wrong, don't mean it is. That is where *they* are coming from.

Liturgical Dance as Nurture

I maintain that Jungle Cat's Baptist and Pentecostal practice structures his options for modes expressing his spirituality through movement. His embodied spirituality moves beyond the "lethal blows" of society and culture with which black men cope, as an extension of black worship through movement and emotional vulnerability. Corporate black worship often creates what pastoral theologians Seward Hiltner and William A. Clebsch conceive as a tripartite "pathway to nurture" that inform the negotiation of masculinity. A pathway to nurture is comprised of healing, sustaining, guiding and later Charles R. Jaekle added to the formula *reconciling*.[7] In "Black Christian Worship as Nurture" from *Black Church Studies*, we find that black worship incorporates resources for a culturally relevant nurture of a divine-human relationship consistent with a Davidic model.

---

7 "*Healing* pertains to binding up of wounds or restoring bodily wholeness and mental functions caused by disease, impairment or loss. *Sustaining* consists of the provision of comfort and strength needed by needed by people to endure difficult circumstances. *Guiding* refers to helping people through the provision of principles of educing within people choices, courses of actions and resources in times of trouble. *Reconciling* seeks to reestablish broken relationships or to bring people in positive relationship with others and God" (Hiltner and Clebsch 2007, 183).

The method by which music nurtures people in Black worship includes emotion-laden, expressive, and art-full involvement. Bodily responses of clapping, swaying, dancing and miming, and uses of drama are powerful ways of arousing kinesthetic meanings of faith in God. This approach to music in worship engages and forms people's emotional and kinesthetic intelligence that opens the way for them to grasp hope and perseverance in the face of an uncertain future with passion and conviction as Christians.

FLOYD-THOMAS et al 2007, 191

The worship as nurture paradigm can be extended to those who fellowship virtually through multi-media. The kinesthetic knowledge helps believers access the unspoken matters in their lives, building what is called "improvisational movement vocabulary." In worship, the performer's improvisational movement vocabulary is a semiotic and sensuous method of conveying knowledge to other participants. On the sensuousness of worship Ashon Crawley writes about the complexity of the conveyance, "The 'space' of the Black Pentecostal tradition is multivocal: it is a space where the sensuousness of the black body finds meaning through the conferral of power and authority while, simultaneously and contradictorily, the space disciplines and polices particularly dangerous modes of power and authority of the agential self, through confusing and abusive discourse about sexuality" (Crawley 2008, 309). The participant's confusion can be attributed to disorientation about by whom the meaning should be evaluated. Transferring corporate practice of kinesthetic knowledge to private devotion provides resources for men to confess their faults, live out loud, and seek God. There is however knowledge lost in translation as one's improvisational movement vocabulary is transferred to unchartered virtual realms that lack the shared knowledge cultivated in corporate worship.

As Jungle Cat shares what is in his heart toward God, he acknowledges that those unfamiliar with his improvisational movement vocabulary have misunderstood him. I argue that the reasons for the misunderstanding are two-fold: the unconventional use of his racialized and gendered body, and lack of exposure to a Davidic approach to dance. Black men's dance performance is peculiar in that they embody race and gender that is often invisible within United States' power structures. Their negotiation and control of visibility in gospel music performance is illuminated by male dance scholarship, which utilizes theories of the gendered gaze in film pioneered by Laura Mulvey. As the result of remnant Victorian respectability codes, men's dance has been interpreted within society as effeminate because male dancers occupy the feminized space of the stage (Morris 2001). "To summarize this extremely briefly, in response to the spectator's gaze (and the presumption is that it enforces a dominant heterosexual male point of view) men in film look actively and thus avert objectification, while passivity allows women to be turned into eroticized spectacle" (Burt 2001, 221). Such values are rooted in the practice men are to gaze and women are to appear. There is a disruption in power when black men step into the male gaze (Burt 2007) because viewing a man's movement is an erotic act. Consequently, viewing him move causes a cognitive dissonance for those who apprehend the change in social order.

Cognitive dissonance is heightened when Jungle Cat's image and gesture defies the images to which the spectator is socialized. To behold black men's spiritual intimacy with God counteracts pervasive black male images that focus on his physical abilities. Citing G. Dent, Ronald L. Jackson writes, "Because mass media and popular culture are predominantly littered with these negative images, it appears that they are unwilling to see Black bodies positively, and this affects everyday looking relations" (Jackson 2006, 2). These negative images are coupled with the notion that "the physical expression of masculinity in dance in the twentieth century has become associated with homosexuality. If the male dancing body is always already queer, this transgression against normative definitions of gendered and sexual behavior carries with it the penalty of punishment" (Burt 2001, 233). Thus, to view the black male dancer as heterosexual may trigger a cognitive dissonance for the post-colonial beholder. As a result of the *fantastic hegemonic imagination* (Townes 2006) and folklore about black men's bodies, mass media has reduced them to their physical attributes such as their penis, physical strength, and sexual prowess. Succinctly, black men's visibility evokes a simultaneous navigation of white male ideals, envy, surveillance, and law. While the beholder organizes their perception of the male body and potential arousal from that body, men in particular negotiate the fine line between their internal suspicion of homosexuality and homosocial bonding anxiety.

While many online commentators have chided him for his "praise pole dance," the comments that defend his praise have come to make this endeavor worthwhile for him. Jungle Cat's performance disrupts however the order of the gaze by submitting his inscripted male body to be interpreted. Literature on the construction of race in the American imagination has posited that the black male body is a locus for race and representation that is constantly interpreted (Baker-Fletcher 1996; Bordo 1994; Dyson 1994; Hall 1997; hooks 1995). Ronald L. Jackson argued "the interpretations of mass-mediated inscriptions of the body reveal the hidden contours of psychic and institutional investitures that drive, indeed motivate, the producers of the inscriptions"

(Jackson 2006). Jackson defines inscription as the ways in which the body is socially understood and treated as a discursive text that is read by interactants. He explores the extent to which the black male body is read in the American racial imagination of corporeal politics. Although theologically oriented scholars such as Dwight Hopkins (2006) and Michael Eric Dyson (1996) have considered the implications of these inscriptions in black Christian religiosity, there has not been consideration about the ways in which these inscriptions have been interpreted in traditional gospel performance. Further, there have not been any linkages made from black gospel embodiment to broader African diaspora understandings of black male corporeal politics in worship.

I also believe the spectator's misunderstandings stem of his body language, in part, from the fact that Jungle Cat sees his movements as a form of Davidic worship that nurtures a divine-human relationship, in which the triune divine encompasses a theology of incarnation. To dance before God is to deal with one's imagination of God's corporeality. Central to black Christian tradition, the belief that Jesus Christ as "God with us" is an illustration that God has shared in the fullness of humanity's materiality and made the body a sacred site for God's gesture of love toward humanity.

> For example, Jesus Christ, in Black Christianity, is body revelation of sacred life force. 'Jesus Christ clearly signifies that God loves us in or bodies as uniquely embodied creatures.' Simultaneously, the blues moan and groan out another revelation of sacred life force. In the blues, physicality and spirituality exist as a dynamic quilting of the life force among Black folk. The folk perceive a powerful, 'spiritual function of the human body.' The sacred and the secular the divine and human coalesce. 'For black people the body is sacred, and they know how to use it in the expression of love.'
>
> HOPKINS 2006,189

Consequently, the struggle, on the part of many black congregations, to discuss issues of gender and sexuality is ironic to many scholars in black religious studies. Particularly since Christianity is, as Dyson notes, "grounded in the Incarnation, the belief that God took on flesh to redeem human beings. That belief is constantly trumped by Christianity's quarrels with the body. Its needs. Its desires. Its sheer materiality. But especially its sexual identity" (Dyson 1996, 306). Realizing the phenomenon of the Incarnation becomes even more complex as men explore their sense of God's materiality as a male body within worship.

Existential phenomenologist Lewis Gordon asserts that the metaphoric maleness of God arguably gets in the way of men's worship in many charismatic black churches. Especially for congregations that adhere to hegemonic structures that socio-culturally render black men's bodies invisible (Gordon 2009, 19). In "Homoeroticism and the African-American Heterosexual Male," Stephen Finley (2007) considers Gordon's assertion and engages Kunjufu, Howard Eilberg-Schwartz, and Jeffrey J. Kripal to expand on the implications of the metaphoric maleness of God, in the psychoanalysis of particularly African-American men. Finley argues that in the monotheistic Christian religious tradition, the symbolically gendered attribution of God causes the language of many men to break, entangling their references in social constructs of gender, sexuality, and desire. Thus, the space to relate to God is confined. In his book, *God's Phallus: And Other Problems For Men and Monotheism*, Howard Eilberg-Schwartz argues that over time the traditions upon which Christian imagery is based have necessitated a disembodied God, one that needed to be dismembered: "What if this uneasiness flows from the contradiction inherent in men's relationship with a God who is explicitly male?" (Eilberg-Schwartz 1991, 1). Eilberg-Schwartz's inquiry is key to unraveling the ways in which religious symbols, such as God's phallus and maleness, get in the way of what men are feeling as they demonstrate their relationship to the metaphorically male God of ancient Judaism.

Christian mystical heterodoxy and orthodoxy is followed along gendered and sexed lines. "The bottom line seems to be a theological and structural one: where God is imaged as a male with whom the male mystic erotically unites, the symbolism will by definition, be homoerotic for males" (Kripal 2001, 19). Because of the Christian tradition a major dilemma is the homoeroticism evoked by the love of a male human for a male God. I pause to make a distinction between "homoeroticism" and "homosexuality." Citing Stephen Finley, I define homoerotic as "symbolic same-sex relationships in which the desire is for union with the other of the same gender and in which a sexual acting out is not a requirement" (Finley 2007, 311). Howard Eilberg-Schwartz defines it as "the love of a male human for a male God" (Eilberg-Schwartz 1994, 2). Moreover, in mysticism discourse, Jeffrey Kripal also distinguishes between homoeroticism and homosexuality:

By this I do not mean to imply that most male mystics who employed erotic language to speak about their religious experience also engaged in homosexual acts, or even that most of these same mystics would have desired such acts within some culturally and historically specific register: an individual's use or appropriation of homoerotic symbolic structure does not necessarily reflect a subjectively felt set of same-sex desires or, more problematically still a "homosexuality"...By "homoerotic," then I mean to imply the textual existence of a male-to-male symbolic structure in which mystical encounters are framed along same-sex lines, often with the human male coded as female in a heteroerotically structured encounter.

KRIPAL 2001, 18

The metaphoric language that permeates the characterization of the divine-human relationship in biblical tradition is a corporeal, erotic, and sexual, where in heteronormative terms God is a man and humanity is imagined as a woman.[8] Eilberg-Schwartz proposes that the metaphoric entanglements that manifested in ancient Judaism presented a cognitive dissonance that would attempt to erase the homoeroticism suggested in the male relationship with God. The erasure of God's body over time has manifested in the prohibition against depicting God (veiling the body of God) and the perceived feminization of men. "By imagining men as wives of God, Israelite religion was partially able to preserve the heterosexual complementary that helped define the culture" (Eilberg-Schwartz 2001, 37). Likening God to man reifies patriarchy, controlling women's bodies and spaces. As a result, when men enter into "women's spaces," their corporeality becomes inverted, swallowed up in the feminine role of the divine-human relationship, which then presents problems for men's conception of the self.

In order to address the problems of the self-concept in the divine-human relationship, Finley considers what Eilberg-Schwartz calls the *symbolic domains*, "a set of representations or conceptions and statements about God" (Eilberg-Schwartz 2001, 7). The challenge of unpacking, organizing and re-imagining God seems to be overwhelming, in order for a man to feel comfortable and close, especially in a public demonstration of their relationship to God. It is this complexity compels me to ask again the question posed by Lewis Gordon, "Can men worship God?" Can men find ways to publicly open up to God? One would have to consider the social-cultural signification of embodied masculinity as impenetrable, within a faith tradition of a God who indwells.

---

8 Eilberg-Schwartz explains, "Marriage and sexuality are frequent biblical metaphors for describing God's relationship with Israel. God is imagined as the husband to Israel the wife; espousal and even sexual intercourse are metaphors for the covenant. Thus when Israel follows other gods, 'she' is seen to be whoring. Israel's relationship with God is thus conceptualized as a monogamous sexual relation and idolatry as adultery. But the heterosexual metaphors in the ancient texts belie the nature of the relationship in question: it is human males, not females, who are imagined to have the primary intimate relations with the deity" (Eilberg-Schwartz 1994, 3).

According to Gordon Lewis, within a heteronormative society men's bodies are constructed and disciplined to assume a "closed identity," blocking entry into the body. Male bodies are perceived to protrude and to be without holes. They are not permitted to physically lose themselves, be overcome by or entered by any entity. Contrary to a full-bodied masculinity, this social construct also limits the body language of men, as their affect of admiration is stirred in worship. To be entered suggests that a man's masculinity is lessened in the required surrender of a divine-human relationship. To assume a masculine posture is in essence to lose one's capacity for worship, the space for God to indwell a man, and an opportunity for the Holy Spirit to "enter in" him. Stephen Finley concludes that "The impervious, fully armored, Black male body is an impediment to finding meaning in the Black Church in that worship of God is a homoerotic entry into the body" (Finley 2007, 18). Thus, in a Western context, worshipping God becomes a moment in which psychoanalytically a man's masculinity gets in the way of divine-human intimacy, prohibiting him from a deeper consciousness of and unity with God. Yet, Jungle Cat has transcended the threat of losing his capacity for the Spirit to enter in him. As a result of nurturing his connection to the divine, he become vulnerable emotionally and cries. Such a posture defies mass media's looking relations that distributes negative images more than transcendent black male dancers. In order to gauge the transgressive nature of his movement, let's consider to what does media reception of Jungle Cat's mystic use of the pole differ from other worshippers?

Racialized and Gendered Reception of Devotional Pole Use

I find it curious to compare media coverage of Jungle Cat's performance to white women's similar devotional uses of the pole. Jungle Cat makes a subversive move to reclaim his agency, despite the wrath and doubting of a predominately male media gaze upon his spirituality through critical coverage of his dancing in the Washington Post, Huffington Post and New York Times. I note the disparity in the media reception in describing Jungle Cat's corporeal worship as a possibly blasphemous black male dancer.[9] For example, a writer from

---

9   The absence of Jungle Cat's sexual suggestiveness was covered in "Pole Dancing For Jesus," http://www.huffingtonpost.com/2011/09/14/pole-dancing-for-jesus_n_962804.html, last accessed October 22, 2011. Awesome Luuvie's blog post alludes to the homoerotic overtones in his praise pole dance, "As he glorifies HIS name by sliding down a phallic metal structure. Y'ALL BETTER GIVE GLORY TO YOUR CHRIST THROUGH...*pause* POLE

GmagazineNow, the entity that snatched and reposted the YouTube video of Jungle Cat, offered an intriguing description of the video, attesting, "I could not stop laughing at the irony of a man pole dancing to a gospel song. Is this guy committing blasphemy? Let me know your thoughts."[10] When this video was posted on various media sites such as huffingtonpost.com and kysdc.com, he received his share of detractors, and personal threats from other videos. Yet, he offers a gestural response through Walker's gospel song. The lyrics, "I need you, you need me. We're all a part of God's body. Stand with me, agree with me…" urge a reconciliation and connectivity despite distance, difference and bottom-mired social station. God is not just above. God is a part of us all.

While coverage of his praise spread, there were articles about free pole dance classes that are exclusively for (mainly white Christian) housewives who bring their church bulletins to the class in order to gain admittance to a fitness studio in Houston, Texas. Their expression about the intimate connections explored in such classes are given a romantic space in the coverage that allows the instructor to share about how her former life as a stripper informs her ability to get in touch with the divine in an all female class.[11] The women are enacting a homosocial bonding amongst themselves in erotic worship to a male God.

In international coverage, Anna Nobili headlined as "a lap dancer turned nun angers Pope." She self-identified as "a ballerina for God" in Rome, Italy. Nobili twirled around a wooden crucifix before male cardinals and bishops but was eventually reprimanded by the Pope. Within a tradition where leadership is organized in homosocial groups, she facilitated a co-ed ritual, in order for God to "enter in" them corporately. Subsequent to her performance, her monastery was shut down for "suspicious activity," not befitting their holy designation. These contrasting media receptions of women dancing at the foot of the

---

DANCE! -_- Apparently, praise dancing in flowing white clothes while a fan blows at the annual bazaar just doesn't cut it anymore." http://www.awesomelyluvvie.com/2011/09/gospel-pole-dancing.html, last accessed October 22, 2011. In "Meet the Pole-dancing Man" male pole dancing is characterized as weird, http://jezebel.com/5525636/meet-the-pole+dancing-men, last accessed October 22, 2011. "Men strip pole dancing of another taboo," http://www.washingtonpost.com/wp-dyn/content/article/2010/04/26/AR2010042603094.html?wprss=rss_health, last accessed October 22, 2011.

10   "Guy Does Pole Dancing To Hezekiah Walker's 'I Need You To Survive'"…http://www.youtube.com/watch?v=v_H5kG9dOoE, last accessed October 22, 2011.

11   "Woman offers Christian Pole Dancing Class in Houston," http://theurbandaily.com/special-features/wtf-special-features/theurbandailystaff2/christian-pole-dancing-class-houston-video/, last accessed October 20, 2011.

figurative and proverbial cross reveal distinct social sensibilities about homosocial bonds forged in religiosity and eroticism that are demarcated along gender and color lines.

A Queered Gaze of Worship

Jungle Cat's male body creates, in lieu of the presumed female body on the pole, what E. Patrick Johnson argues to be the queer gaze in heated worship. "Jungle Cat" moves in the view of worshipping men who would expect an enactment of this kind by Texan housewives or a ballerina for God. Yet, Jungle Cat is, "The black body being eroticized when overcome by the Holy Ghost" (Johnson 1998, 403). Johnson makes the connection between the ecstatic and orgasmic moments that are performed in worship. He acknowledges that within sensuality there are referential resources of spiritual satisfaction. This satisfaction is informs possibilities within the pursuit of deeper connections with the divine.

One of his biggest fans is his mother. Hargett acknowledges that there were moments when he wanted to stop and give up but he recounts praying about his pole dance participation and still feels led to do it for God's glory. His objective is to get more men into the sport so that women participants can have partners for styles such as pole tango. Hargett feels most comfortable pole dancing to slow gospel music, and in July 2011, he pole danced to gospel music accompaniment in a National Competition for the first time, using Byron Cage's rendition of "This Is The Air I Breathe" (Cage 2005).

Conclusion

In this essay, I have attempted to explore the ways in which men in gospel music spheres are using music and movement as a means of worshiping, in a language that they can recognize. They deploy and reconstruct symbols that speak to them and their audiences in multivalent ways. Tapping into wider body vocabulary broadens their ability to join flesh and spirit in the act of worship in both public and private spaces. Whether or not the church's public square is willing to provide room, men of various sexual orientations are finding ways to cultivate their openness. Often it is fashioned within the privacy of their homes, in which they are free to allow the issues and emotions of their heart to flow. It is certain that the intentions of the movements will get lost in translation. Speech in many ways has insufficient capacity to respond to worship in a manner that confesses all the deepest sentiments. Moreover, rigid notions of masculinity constructed as an enclosure may be proving too confining for men "whom the Son has set free" (John 8:36). Perhaps devotional such as practices praise pole dancing for Jesus ultimately releases men to claim what they can wield for God's glory.

CHAPTER 20

Wonder Working Power
Reclaiming Mystical and Cosmological Aspects of Africana Spiritual Practices

Barbara A. Holmes

Introduction

There is Power in the Blood
There is pow'r, pow'r, wonder working pow'r
In the blood of the Lamb;
There is pow'r, pow'r, wonder-working pow'r
In the precious blood of the Lamb.

Would you be free from your passion and pride?
There's pow'r in the blood, pow'r in the blood;
Come for a cleansing to Calvary's tide;
There's wonderful pow'r in the blood.

LEWIS E. JONES, 1899

This essay considers the cultural and cosmological aspects of mystical African Diasporan practices in black religious life. Specifically, I am exploring the idea of "wonder working" power as an important and retrievable legacy in the African American community. As I began this essay it became evident that despite my desire to adhere to academic dispassionate discourse, the mystery would not allow it. Woven throughout this essay are the dangling ends of esoteric fragments, enticing and unfinished. The mysteries of faith are historical, cultural, cosmological and experiential. Therein lies my methodology with a grateful nod to phenomenology. As a constructive ethicist focused on moral flourishing, I am influenced by contemporary culture, rhetoric, cosmology and the contemplative and esoteric practices of the black church. Even when we deny the existence of worlds beyond our reach, we wonder, and therein lays our hope. During the 20th century, the African American community mastered the art of protest and resistance to oppression, achieved measures of success on individual and communal levels, but ultimately could not connect the dots. Freedom is not only social and political, it also requires wonder. If we are to be free and whole, spirited and generative, we need the ability to imagine options beyond the limits of natural progression. We need wonder working

© KONINKLIJKE BRILL NV, LEIDEN, 2015 | DOI 10.1163/9789004283428_022

power. I define wonder working power as the ability to transcend the malaise of the age you were born into; the willingness to grasp and appropriate incongruity and myth as precursors to insight; and the audacity to traverse cosmic divides using only unlikely resources, creative imagination and a transcendent life perspective.

African diasporan people are not strangers to wonder. Stories of divination and uncanny connections to the natural world in West Africa continue to ignite the imagination. On North American shores, enslaved Africans told stories of women and men who flew back to Africa, lifting off from sweltering cotton fields like birds of the spirit.

> The theme of human aerial flight permeates the mythology of Black America. Examples of the metaphor are found in major musical genres, myths and poetry in Black cultures that span the Caribbean and southern North America, embracing generations to testify to the depth of the cosmological and conscious projection of systems of flight, escape and homeland return.
>
> MCDANIEL 1990, 28

It doesn't matter whether or not the accounts of flying humans are myth, magic or verified testimonies. The stories seem to be indicative of belief systems rooted in mystery. While slavery heightened the need for physical escape and narrative relief, today, we have the same need for wonder working power. African Americans are ostensibly free but inwardly bound by desires rooted in consumer lust. The search for wholeness has morphed into the relentless acquisition of material goods. Yet our best efforts to curb our consumerism and love our neighbors tend to wither under the weight of unenlightened self interest.

The antidote to selfishness and cynicism may be wonder. It is my belief that some of the roots of wonder may be tucked into the historical memory and rituals of the African American religious experience.

Mystics in the Family

I come to my interest in this work because my Aunt Lee, a Catholic/Gullah mystic, and other women in the family before her, were shamans, mediators of reality and visionaries. They saw beyond the veils that shroud the worlds. It seems that gifts of healing, foreknowledge and inter-dimensional communication (to name a few) are inherited by some of the women in our family.

While my Aunt regularly saw and talked to relatives who had passed into the life beyond life; in my generation, those of us who inherited her aptitudes have chosen to sublimate them into traditional religious beliefs. We join churches and try to fit the gifts of foresight and dream knowledge into the ordinary expectations of congregational life. Only with others of our "kind" do we whisper about the visitations and messages from the other side. Sublimation may delude us into thinking that we have distanced ourselves from the strangeness of it all; but it cannot extinguish or hide the syncretistic layering of ancient African practices and Christian belief. I know that the world is not as it seems because I grew up with extended boundaries of reality that included the blessings and warnings of relatives long gone. Because mysticism was part of my everyday life, I have a sense of wholeness that comes from knowing that there is more to the life journey than my feeble strivings. I was taught that in the midst of the ordinary, we are also invited to dance with mystery, to be conduits for divine intentions and for the energy and power of the cosmos.

I am suggesting in this essay that mysticism is an essential part of the well-being of humankind, particularly for historically oppressed communities. On the road to freedom, besieged people place their confidence in political and judicial systems and in leaders of one type or another. Why not trust the power invested in us by the creatrix/conjurer/spirit? Why not embrace the gifts of discernment and second sight, affinity to nature and the secrets of the night skies that came to the Americas with captured Africans? I use the terms "discernment" and "second sight" to refer to the ability to receive knowledge beyond the limits of ordinary human perception. I described these gifts in *Race & the Cosmos: An Invitation to View the World differently.*

> When midwives in the slave quarters delivered a child, they always looked to see if the child was born with a veil of membrane over its face. Being born with the gossamer veil was a sure sign that the child's vision would reach to the heavens. Barefaced tots had flat world eyes that screeched to a halt at apparent edges, but not the veiled ones. Behind those lids would scroll the cosmic visions of worlds unseen, and quantum dreams of wriggling, resonating infinitesimal things.

The child with second sight journeys from the "life before life" into the everyday world with tangible tethers to the unseen. They often arrive with gifts of healing or the ability to hear the whispers of the human heart. They respond to others as if they were turned inside out, as if all that is within was exposed.

The Necessity of Mysticism

African Diasporan people came to the Americas with mystery tucked into their innards. They bore the lash and murderous enslavement while harboring the power of transcendence in their souls. You may snatch children from their mothers and separate kidnapped siblings across vast seas, but mystery travels well and cannot be extinguished in the holds of tight packed ships. Often, those ships were named after the powerful Christian God, who seemingly sanctioned this rupture in their lives.

Given the circumstances, Africans in captivity presumed that this new God had wonder working power. It takes a powerful force to override centuries of culture and civilization in favor of forced journey. As they traversed the "bitter waters," they would experience the power of communal contemplation and the wonder of survival. Essentially, captive Africans were born again in the holds of slave ships. Their moans became birthing sounds, "the first movement toward a creative response to oppression, the entry into the heart of contemplation through the crucible of crisis" (Holmes 2004, 75; Noel 1994, 73).

Although enslaved Africans hoped that freedom would come, it would not be enough for one enlightened person to bring news of a deliverer. Wonder working power had to manifest in tangible ways. Moreover, the community of believers had the responsibility to witness, verify, and participate in the process: together they would enter the space of potential divine encounter, and engage spiritual emissaries collectively. As strange as it may seem, belief systems that affirmed multiple realities reminded Africans in the diaspora, that despite their circumstances, they were deeply connected to a powerful and life sustaining system. Cosmologist Brian Swimme says this about the potential of power:

> You do not know what you can do, or who you are in your fullest significance, or what powers are hiding within you. All exists in the emptiness of your potentiality, a realm that cannot be seen or tasted or touched. How will you bring these powers forth?
>
> SWIMME 2001, 51

To fully inhabit the potential of wonder working power requires the realization that westerners have truncated their options and diminished the potential for engaging invisible spaces. In this regard, Africans on the continent had a much "thicker" view of reality than postmodern African Americans. They acknowledged power beyond their own embodiment as a fact of human existence, and embraced a continuum of life that included both the mystical and the mundane. Reliance on medicinal herbs, mediating gods, and ancestral guides completed a rich panoply of potential power.

This expanded view of reality became a life saving resource during the years of captivity. Knowledge of cosmology and star systems aided escapees, while belief in the spirit world and in the power of divine presence emboldened slave resistance to oppression. Finally, encounters with Christianity affirmed their reliance on wonder working power.

Mysticism for the 99%

Like other faiths, Christianity draws its power from mysticism. What is extraordinary about this power is its accessibility to ordinary people. To confirm this focus, the proclaimed Messiah arises from ordinary circumstances, yet displays abilities that often overturn the "laws of nature." In the midst of everyday life, the dead are resurrected; the sick are healed, the blind see, and upon command storms cease. Moreover, the strange prophecy to local people in the community, who observe such happenings, is "greater things shall you do." Christianity is not a religion that requires long apprenticeships to shamanic leaders, vision quests or the generational acquisition of secret knowledge; its "wonder working" power is available to everyone.

The clues to attaining this spiritual power are in the sacred text for all to see: love one another, believe, have faith, be transformed by the renewing of your mind, and present your body a living sacrifice for the cause of Christ. In other words, according to the Bible, anyone committed to the basic tenets of Christian faith can exercise wonder working power. Yet we don't. To observe African American Christian practice in its postmodern form is to witness an intense effort to quell the potential for transcendence in favor of predictable and familiar rituals. This occurs even in charismatic religious gatherings where displays of emotion, prophecy, and the exercising of gifts are welcome.

In Holiness worship services, encounters with the Holy Spirit are encouraged, but the "yes" songs are always ready to encourage safe returns and contain unbridled spirit possession. Leaders of charismatic congregations know the difference between joyful celebratory praise, and those occasions when the air crackles and the Spirit is in control. Then, music tempos slow, humming begins and those under the thrall of altered spiritual states of consciousness are musically prodded back to reality.

In denominational black churches, congregants invoke the presence of the Holy Spirit, through song and litany, but are more than a bit nervous about what it would mean if the powers inherent in this manifestation of the

Godhead were unleashed. We are Christians because we believe mystical narratives that form the foundation of the faith, but we are rooted in our own science-inflected and technologically awed world. These moorings strain our ability to exercise wonder working power for the benefit of the community and the world. An understanding that science has its own mysteries and mythologies, might allow room for the re-emergence of deeply sedimented wisdom and the operation of "gifts." The importance of the full exercise of spiritual abilities cannot be over emphasized.

Members of historically oppressed groups need all of the help that they can get to assuage nihilism. Why not tap the power of the universe and the discernment of the departed. The reluctance to explore mystical aspects of black religious life seems directly related to the legacy of slavery. One consequence of oppression is that for many generations to come, people want to "fit in." They don't want to draw attention to themselves, except to tout their accomplishments and ability to be enfolded into the society that once oppressed them. As a consequence, religious expressions tend to be reflective of and attuned to the preferences of the colonizing culture. In a visit to Kenya, I was surprised to see people drinking hot tea in the blistering heat of the Turkana desert, wearing formal and heavy black protestant robes, and singing songs of praise from a western hymnal instead of using the rhythms of their ancestors.

I should not have been surprised. It is not unusual that the effects of colonization last longer than the actual occupation. It is also predictable that assimilated communities will "riff" on the main ideas and religious norms of their colonizers. But creative appropriations of ancient rituals are seldom seen. Every election season, African Americans arrive at political conventions in choir robes clapping and exuding charismatic cheer. This form of religious expression does not threaten the powers of the dominant culture. By contrast, trance dances prevalent in storefront gatherings never make prime time. Such displays make a mockery out of the prevailing presumptions about control. Moreover, one can only assume that if Americans did not understand the "prophetic preaching" of the Rev. Dr. Jeremiah Wright, a familiar trope in a traditional setting, they are not ready for more.

In western society, part of the social contract is the unspoken agreement that we will not focus on or accent realities that contradict basic presumption about the world and how it works. Accordingly, we tend not to see or understand expressions of mysticism when they occur right before our eyes. An example comes to mind. At a recent church conference, a small, conservative, and primarily Anglo protestant denomination in the Midwest proudly displayed its cultural night. They were delighted to have Afro-Cuban members sharing their worship service. Congregation members smiled and took photographs as the drummers and dancers began a worship ritual that induced a trance-like state.

With their eyes rolled back in their heads and their movements becoming effortlessly synchronized, the dancers invoked spiritual power from sources in Christianity, but also from African diasporan culture that would have surprised the sponsoring congregation. I was a guest, a woman of Gullah origins familiar with the varied permutations of Christianity that emerged from the cultural cauldrons of faith and mystery. I knew what I was seeing.

This was no ordinary praise dance. The rhythms and incantations in "mother tongue" pointed toward the embodiment of ancient rituals known by the body and spirit if not by the mind. The power of the performance and the complete lack of understanding that surrounded it brought tears to my eyes and reminded me that before African diasporan people were Christian and before our African ancestors arrived in the Americas; they knew how to negotiate life's mysteries in ways that we have forgotten. However, it is important to note that while mystery is an integral part of an Africana worldview, Africans have no special or exclusive relationship to it. Engagement with mystery is observable in most indigenous populations. As Charles Finch notes, "Everywhere in Africa, there exist men and women who claim to be able to see into the future... and communicate with other beings—human and nonhuman—through psychic means" (Finch 2001, 254). But can wonder working power and psychic abilities be conflated?

The word "psychic" as a description of esoteric practices is rejected by most African American churchgoers. But the fact that African American worship tends to avoid alternative spiritual expressions in mainline churches does not mean that deeply sedimented practices do not emerge. Even in storefront holiness and Pentecostal gatherings, the "wonder working" power of ancient rituals may be evident when least expected. Scholar and poet Jim Perkinson recounts such an instance:

> A videotape of a black North American Pentecostal preacher is shown to a number of Candombles in Bahia, Brazil. The Bahians watch the video with mute interest until the preacher moves from "warm-up" to "takeoff" in his delivery, shifting from simple communication to searing incantation from quietude to incandescence. Suddenly, [the Bahian listeners] lurch into agitated outburst, "Xango! Xango! Xango!" They do not speak English, nor do they know anything of Pentecostal worship. They simply know the arrival gestures of this *orixa* in the flesh of human "being," and the body language is all the eloquence they need.
>
> PERKINSON 2001, 566–94

The Bahian observers were not familiar with the "hoop" or the bombastic sermonic conclusion prevalent in some styles of black preaching, but they recognized the physicality of the *orixa*. Every move that the preacher made announced the arrival of Xango! I do not know how these things occur, but I do know that when gifts of ancestral memory emerge in our lives the best response is receptiveness and gratitude. We are all spiritual beings having an embodied experience. Accordingly, we share access to the collective unconscious and have the ability to host, invite or suppress these occurrences. However, suppression of spiritualities inscribed on the soul are a sure bet for soul weariness and confusion.

To be clear, I do not mean that evocative worship and trance dancing is a necessity for wellbeing in African American communities. My suggestion is that African diasporan legacies have been preserved in the fringe gatherings of marginal religious communities, storefront congregations, cultural signs and symbols, and even in the rituals of the mainline churches. In these places, it is clear that assimilation into western society diminished but did not extinguish Africana tendencies to include both the seen and unseen worlds in religious life. We need to retrieve this legacy because the ills of addiction, materialism, and violence have a spiritual as well as social component. The truth of the matter is that we have applied our best social remedies; perhaps the time has come to welcome and host the mysteries of life.

For African Americans, Christianity is anchored not only by its message of liberation but also by its depiction of wonder working power. My ancestors were wonder working people in their ordinary lives. They kept their heads above the waters of racism and discrimination and could make two salmon cakes feed fifteen working women and men. When they encountered the wonder working, water walking, crowd feeding Jesus, conversion was a redundancy; instead there was a natural recognition of kinship. Wonder working power does not presume or exclude divinity. You don't have to be a robed prophet or sect leader to connect to a resource endemic in the cosmos. Only a limited western perspective presumes that human beings, their needs and desires are the beginning and end of reality.

Scientists tell us something completely different. According to current research, there are at least 11 dimensions in the life space, but human beings can only access four (length, width, depth and time), the rest are beyond our grasp (Greene,2000, 16). In the western scientific mindset, "access" is synonymous with the ability to inhabit, test, analyze and verify. Indigenous people (even today) seem to have better ways to reach the unreachable. They inhabit other worlds when they ride the cadences of drums, and journey during ceremonies and rituals beyond the boundaries of human expectation. Musicologist and Ewe tribe member W. Komla Amoaku describes the power of African music to alter human body and spirit. He says,

> For me it is the involuntary alteration that occurs in my psyche, the spiritual upliftment, my transcendental imaginations of a spirit world, my oneness with the gods and spirits of departed relatives and that temporary transformation of my physical body into spirit.
>
> AMOAKU 1985, 37

Indigenous people know that wonder working power is accessible to everyone, and is rooted in the belief that life is an intersecting and multidimensional spiritual and material realm.

Wonder Working Power: I Know it was the Blood

> I know it was the blood,
> I know it was the blood,
> I know it was the blood for me;
> One day when I was lost
> He died on the cross,
> I know it was the blood for me.
>
> TRADITIONAL?

The "blood songs" are a familiar part of the black church hymnody. In fact, they are such powerful signifiers in the black church tradition that it is easy to forget that Jesus did not bleed to death. The songs assert the actual and symbolic power of the sacrifice of a Jewish carpenter, on behalf of those who believe. There is power in his blood not because of its magical substance, or because the elements of communion are ingested ritually, but by virtue of the divine/human relationship. Beyond theological debates about the symbolism of communion or the transubstantiation of the elements, blood songs speak to the mysteries of Christian life that lurk just below the surface of familiar rituals.

> It is as if we enter a different door of our reality, when someone gives her or his life for us. Why this should be is a mystery, but it is the mystery, I think, behind all the great myths in which there is human sacrifice— not on an altar, but on the road, in the street—for the common good.
>
> WALKER 2010, 39

Alice Walker alludes to the power of sacrifice for the good of the community. This is a mystery that challenges our intense focus on scientific objectivity. Try as we might, we cannot eliminate mystical aspects of the world. To the contrary, suppressed mysteries tend to emerge again in our storytelling, dream fantasies, songs and films. Most recently we are reminded that the idea of blood sacrifice retains its power for those familiar with Christian rituals and for those who prefer vampire stories. In the world of film, vampires have taken over the blockbuster legacy of Harry Potter.

In fact, Bible study teachers are wondering if they should include vampire sagas to enhance the interest of young people. Bible teacher and author Jane Wells notes that vampires make us aware that the supernatural surrounds us whether we are aware of it or not; and that Christ's love for us or Edward and Bella's love for one another results in and even requires sacrifice (Crumm 2011, 2).

> Vampires are hot stuff right now...The idea of achieving immortality through blood is central to both traditions—the Christian through the life-giving blood of Christ, and the vampire, through drinking the blood of victims. Vampire legends are rich with Christian symbols, most notably the crucifix (believed to protect mortals) and the consecrated bread and wine of Communion.
>
> EVANS 2010, 2

Most African American black church congregations make clear distinctions between the blood sacrifices of Christ and the bloodlust of Edward the vampire based on historical interpretations of good and evil. The power and meaning of "the blood" is directly related to the divinity of Jesus. There is both a cultural and cosmic aspect to the death of God's son. On the cosmic level, the blood sacrifice of the one related to the Creator changes an enigmatic earth experience into a purposeful journey. On the cultural level, James Cone in *The Cross and the Lynching Tree* speaks of the identification of oppressed people with the brutality of the cross.

> When blacks sang about "blood," they were wrestling not only with the blood of the crucified carpenter from Nazareth but also with the blood of raped and castrated black bodies in America—innocent, often nameless, burning and hanging bodies, images of hurt so deep that only God's "amazing grace" could offer consolation.
>
> CONE 2011, 75

For Cone, the invocation of the blood is syncretic. The remembrance of divine sacrifice and triumph is also a re-membering of broken black bodies through the resurrection power of the despised and rejected Jesus. For African America congregations the message is clear: it takes wonder working power to transcend brutality and transform shed blood into consecrated love.

Experiencing Wonder Working Power

Growing up in the mid-twentieth century focused most of my energy on achievement and success. The Civil Rights movement was winding down and the race toward all that had been denied began. During the decades of siege, all we had was church. In this safe space, we practiced modalities of integration by straightening our hair and affirming our commitment to upward mobility. Because we wanted to fit into mainstream society, most of the mystical aspects of African American religious life were submerged or relegated to the storefront churches. In retrospect, the politics of respectability played an important role in this suppression. It was in marginal religious communities that I first encountered acceptance of, remembering and inducement of the esoteric.

Religious life in the black community has always been layered. It was never one thing instead of another. It was a mix of everything plus more. Even during the most ordinary and boring denominational order of business, mystery lurked. Sometimes during ordinary church services, the veil between the expected and the *numinous* would part for a moment and we would experience presence, awe and the incredible sensation of being known and loved. But those moments were few and far between. When I refer to the numinous I am evoking the theories of Rudolf Otto, who described the mystery that undergirds most religious experiences as *numinous*. Otto describes the *numinous* as *mysterium tremendum et fascinans*—a phrase that encapsulates awe, terror, and fascination. It is an encounter with the "wholly other" that confounds and attracts (Otto, 2000, 13, 19, 23, 25, 31).

But, I am also evoking the *numinous* as the reality of ancestors who cannot be cited, but whose legacies were passed down through my family and others as proof positive that presumed limits of body and spirit can be transcended. This transcendence as worship practice during preaching and singing may be the reason that African American religion attracts great attention in public life. However, this interest in black worship can be problematic. As an example, the black choir is a ubiquitous symbol of commodified joy at political conventions and on television commercials, but in private worship services can also be the vehicle for evoking "presence" and entry in to the awe/terror/fascination continuum. This essay responds to over simplified dominant meta-narratives about African American religion by reminding future generations that the "performance" of worship has at its core a catalytic source of ancestral, community and individual experiences that include access to wonder working power.

In my memoir (pending) *Called: A Spiritual Journey*, I tell the story of my encounter with a marginal religious community in Dallas, Texas, that conjured, hosted and manifested alternative spiritual powers. This multi-racial group believed in the power of blood sacrifice without the benefit of currently popular *Twilight* vampire and werewolf sagas. The songs and testimonies attested to the power of Christ's blood to redeem, resurrect, empower and transcend the boundaries of human suffering. Because it was believed that nothing is beyond the limits of the wonder working power of the blood, extraordinary things happened.

While I was with this group, levitations, healings, and exorcisms, were all as ordinary as Bible study. For a woman steeped in the bourgeois routines of mainstream black churches, the experience was life-changing. I have never seen the world in the same way since. When I first encountered this group, I was new to Texas, having recently relocated from Macon, Georgia to join the J.C. Penney Company's legal department. Although I was excited about the possibilities; this was a new city, and I was lonely and adrift. A Sunday excursion to find a church close to my corporate apartment, led me to a tiny stone building in one of the wealthiest sections of Dallas.

My curiosity was piqued because the building and its grounds did not fit the neighborhood surroundings. The mud parking lot and pickup trucks were out of place in the upscale neighborhood. Instinctively, I sensed that something odd was afoot. It didn't take long for my suspicions to be confirmed. A gentleman appeared on the curb and beckoned me out of heavy traffic toward the side driveway. When I looked back he was gone. As I entered the building, the pastor, a big redbone man galloped toward me saying "She's here!" A dozen people, more or less, were looking at me with interest. The church had worn velvet pews and only a handful of members. I didn't really have time to assess my situation because I was in the middle of the aisle, penned in by the pastor and his wife. Both prophesied to me, telling me aspects of my life that they had no way of knowing, and foretelling my career shift from law to ministry. Amazingly, all of their prophetic predictions came true!

As strange as it may seem, they were waiting for me. Months ago, the pastor had prophesied that the class would consist of twelve members, with one coming from Georgia. I was the last to stumble into a tutelage that would last for one year before my ministry was launched. I said nothing and kept my eyes closed as the pastor and his wife spoke to my need and uttered words that seemed to point the way toward my future. I wanted be respectful, but from my point of view, they were making ridiculous statements. I was a bored and unhappy corporate lawyer, but a lawyer nonetheless. I had no intention of going into ministry; I was simply trying to attend a church service.

I wondered if this ministerial couple was crazy! And even if they were, what source of collective wisdom were they mining to access the deepest secrets of a stranger's heart? This was not prophesy as an educated guess, the pronouncements were certain and accurate. While they talked to me, the congregation (such as it was) sang, walked, and verbally affirmed his words. As I saw it, I had two choices: I could flee or listen. But if I listened, where would I put this mystical approach to matters of faith. It was impossible to incorporate the manifestations of spiritual power into the fabric of my rather ordinary spiritual life, with its taken-for-granted presumptions and expectations.

To further complicate matters, I was not reacting in ordinary ways to the events that were unfolding. The fact that I grew up in a staid congregational church in the shadow of Yale University, should have catapulted me toward the door for a quick escape. But strangely enough, escape was the last thing on my mind. It was too late for that! I was enveloped by a sense of destiny and well-being, and hooked by the intoxicating display of spiritual gifts.

The truth of the matter is that I am inclined toward the esoteric and mysterious in all religions. I need a God who exceeds the limits of human theological musings. I am in love with the God who acts counter-intuitively and who challenges and disrupts in stillness and in burning bushes. I am confounded by faith communities who avoid even hints of mystery in their worship and rituals. In my experience, the mysteries of spiritual power manifest wherever faithful people are willing to host the in-breaking of alternative realities.

The impetus to invite and/or host such occurrences does not depend on belief or objective verification. The mysteries of faith are a matter of personal and communal experience so profound that they pervade your spirit for the rest of your days. Years afterward, one can attribute such events to carnival manipulations, misunderstandings, or faulty sight, but the heart knows. The world is not as we suppose. Despite scientific findings that unveil a quantum world of possibility, we are still more comfortable with certainty and static descriptions of self and society. The dynamism that reveals human capability far beyond limits of skin and space is often sacrificed in favor of a prevailing story of order. Africana spiritual practices on the continent and in the Diaspora invoke deep mystery, reveal untapped sources of human power, and give clues to the secrets of the universe.

While I sojourned with this group, so many unexplainable events occurred that the mystical became ordinary. We could not wait to go to church (daily) to see what would happen. On Sundays, ordinary services were held so that visitors would not be freaked out. But on weekdays, services varied from lament rituals, to exorcisms, trance, prophecy and levitation. The expectation was that all options were open. Moreover, a powerful God waited for our entreaties and could move in ways that on occasion would suspend the laws of nature, ever so briefly.

The one who was crucified had wonder working power. The lamb slain from the foundations of the earth would not politely wait for us to read our bulletins and find the pages of the hymns. The blood songs in this place first beckoned then baptized us with mists of memory and promise, and then reminded us of where we have been and where we can go.

Summary: To Chart a New Path Toward Spiritual Power

In recent decades, African Americans focused on the struggle for political power, freedom and acceptance. In some respects the mission has been accomplished. But in our striving we may have harvested more than we expected. Along with success came debt, consumerism, alienation of youth, neighborhood violence and a historical black church that is losing relevancy as the fight for freedom wanes. Every path toward belovedness of self and neighbors has been tried, from academic and professional achievement to creative expressions of talent and finally ascendancy to the presidency of the United States.

Still there is a sense of bewilderment and loss. Cornel West calls it nihilism... a lovelessness that leaves the afflicted bereft (West 1994, 22). In the face of such soul pain, perhaps it is time to seek unexpected solutions to resolute problems. Quantum physics exposes a world that seems to observe us as we observe it. The Princeton Global Consciousness Project alludes to shared wisdom or foreknowledge that can be accessed, as evidenced by synchronized computer readings hours before the 9/11 tragedy (Nelson, accessed 8/5/13).

How did my Aunt Lee communicate with dead relatives? How did the priest at a local Catholic Church (recently returned to the States from decades of service in West Africa) levitate during communion before the eyes of a stunned congregation? I don't know. But the fact that I don't have absolute answers doesn't mean that the boundaries of my knowledge or the accepted wisdom of the community limit the potential of mystical power and opportunity.

We accent the reality that we can access, but there are worlds beyond our reach. Today we need to reclaim the mystical legacy of Africana and indigenous people all over the world, whose intuitive ways of knowing inspire a broader spectrum of spiritual power. In recent years, it has seemed that western societies have reached the limits of political, religious and sociological maneuverings. If this is the case, perhaps the recovery of African American esoteric spiritual resources will revive the difficult work of becoming more spirited humans in pursuit of the beloved community.

The Continuing Quest to Map Secrecy, Concealment, and Revelatory Experiences in *Africana* Esoteric Discourse

"There Is a Mystery..."

Stephen C. Finley, Margarita S. Guillory and Hugh R. Page, Jr.

> The earth beneath my feet is the great womb out of which the life upon which my body depends comes in utter abundance. There is a work in the soil a *mystery* by which the death of one seed is reborn a thousand-fold in newness of life.
>
> HOWARD THURMAN (1953, 210)

> Subsequently, *secrecy* itself is embedded in African religious culture across the Diaspora. Among the Yoruba, for example, there is no exact word for "religion"; its closest concept is found in their word *awo*, [which means] secret...In Haiti, the konesanz resides in the *mystery*...
>
> YVONNE DANIEL (2005, 253)

The Mystery Unfolds

The epigraphs above consider the inexplicable nature of *mystery*, a theme that each of the preceding essays engages in some way. Theologian Howard Thurman contemplates the centrality of mystery in the cycle of life and death, while anthropologist Yvonne Daniel recognizes mystery and secrecy as important tropes in African Diasporic religions. In beginning this project several years ago, we were acutely aware of the importance of this trope. We were also mindful of several additional realities that would impact our work. We understood that secrecy, particularly the extent to which it has shaped, in whole or in part, the religious sensibilities of African Africans, was only beginning to be understood fully. We realized that the same could be said for mystical experience, the impact of which is far reaching among African Americans, but the critical examination of which—in historical and contemporary perspective—remained in its infancy.[1] We also knew that neither methodological parameters

---

1 Work like that of Barbara Holmes (Holmes 2004) on the Black contemplative tradition has broken new ground in this area.

laying the groundwork for the integral and trans-disciplinary study of the aforementioned phenomena as part of the African American *ethos*, nor a rationale for a distinct sub-field dedicated to such work, had yet to be articulated. Addressing these *lacunae*, and situating African American notions of secrecy, concealment, mysticism, and enlightenment in relationship to the so-called Western Esoteric Tradition became, therefore, the overarching goals of this pioneering collection of essays.

Secrecy and the Embrace of Mystery in African American Esotericism

As many of the essays in this volume make clear, secrecy serves as a primary agent in the crystallization of African American religions. It gives definite form to the religious experiences of African Americans. Secrecy, here, represents "anything that is kept intentionally hidden…it also denotes the methods used to conceal, such as codes or disguises or camouflage, and the practices of concealment" (Bok 1982, 5–6). Varying degrees of hiddenness, therefore, characterize secrecy. More importantly, secrecy is not representative of a static form, but it is processual in that it involves utilizing multi-varied processes to conceal information, practices, and sources, which have been set apart and deemed candidates for hiddenness. With regard to African American religions, concealment affords not only the protection of secretive dimensions, but also allows for the transmission of foundational tenets that assures the overall preservation of religious tradition.

Instances of concealment, transmission, and preservation can be found operating within the complex terrain of African American religions. Material objects and symbols have been used to preserve elements of secrecy in these religions. For example, slaves used an iron pot to conceal religious activities occurring in hush harbor meetings. According to various interviews of former slaves, "the pot was usually placed in the middle of the cabin floor or at the doorstep, then propped up to hold the sound of praying and singing from escaping" (Raboteau 2004, 215). The ordinary 'cooking' pot as a concealing agent offered slaves a sense of safety from the prying eyes of the plantation overseer and preserved the sanctity of the meeting place where they freely practiced their unique expressions of Christianity. Like material objects, symbols were also employed to maintain secrecy in African Diasporic religions. For example, Muslim slaves (mainly taken from Senegambia) in Jamaica, South Carolina, and Georgia adapted Christianity to Islam. God was equated to Allah while Jesus Christ represented the prophet Muhammad. These slaves concealed their Islamic belief system through the creative usage of Trinitarian symbols. Additionally, Christian cosmological images were appropriated, and are still being appropriated, to enshroud the identities of African-derived deities. In Haitian Vodou and New Orleans Voodoo, Saint Anthony of Padua represents, *Papa Legba* and *Papa Laba*, while Saint Michael emblematizes *Ogou Badagri* and *Joe Ferraille*, respectively. People of African descent manipulated material objects like the pot and Christian cosmological imagery in order to hide certain religious orientations. This hiddenness allowed for the transmission and preservation of worldviews and rituals both complex and diverse. Secrecy in this way is a connective fiber that runs through African Diasporic religions, a category that includes African American religious traditions of an esoteric nature.

While the studies assembled here seek to demonstrate how secrecy acts as a means to connect a variety of African Diasporic religions, the volume as a whole also offers a view of the interconnection between secrecy and mystery through its overall engagement of esoteric currents and traditions. Specifically, an examination of esotericism in African American religious experiences (i.e. African American Esotericism) places in the foreground secrecy's dual ability: to hide and to reveal. This duality endows secrecy with the capacity to indicate the presence of a second dimension, or in the words of Georg Simmel, "a second world along side the obvious world" (Simmel 1906, 462). The potential of this second dimension becomes actualized in the tensional interplay of secrecy's dual strategy of concealment and manifestation:

> Secrets may end when they are exposed, but when complex, arcane lore is revealed, such as knowledge about the nature of the cosmos, that information continues to perplex. [In this way] they imply something nearer to mystery, to the dense, opaque, polysemous complexities of the universe....
>
> BEIDELMAN 1993, 43 and 47

Revelation of that which is secret leaves a residue of ambiguity that perplexes and points to the presence of another obscure, and at times inexplicable, dimension. Ambiguity serves as a sign of mystery. In other words, secrecy, by way of ambiguity, reveals *mystery*. Thus, the former points to the overarching presence of the latter.

It is the presence of this mysteriousness and its relationship to secrecy that serves as the focal point of this volume. The academic study of African American Esotericism not only identifies secrecy as a connective fiber in African American religions, but this approach also examines how secrecy points to another more obscure ligament: *mystery*. Specifically, secrecy functions in esoteric currents and traditions practiced by African Americans as a strategic way of denoting the existence of an "impulse of mysteriousness." Scholars like Anthony Pinn and W.E.B. Du Bois have considered the role "impulses" play in the religious experiences of African Americans. In *Terror and Triumph*, Pinn, for example, ascribes meaning to the very nature of African American religion by way of an impulse. "There is a deeper, elemental impulse, an inner stirring," Pinn maintains, "that informs and shapes religion as a practice and historical structure" (2003, 174). Thus, for Pinn this impulse, is an *internal* feeling, which finds externalization in African American religions. Du Bois posits the impulse as a "stirring" and a "deep religious feeling" (1903, 206).

Like Pinn's notion, Du Bois' conception of the impulse and exploration of African American esotericism, recognize the connective function of this urge in the religious experiences of African Americans. Unlike these scholars, however, esoteric studies as an academic field moves the impulse beyond "feeling" and focuses on how it propagates mysteriousness—an ambiguous state, form, essence, or "spiritual realization [that moves] beyond the rational" (2005, 51). The inclination toward mysteriousness manifests itself palpably in African American esoteric traditions. More importantly, these traditions display how this powerful drive encapsulates secrecy's tensional interplay of concealment and revelation. In this way, a disciplined and rigorous approach to esotericism affords a robust view of the transmission of the complex idea of mysteriousness, including the complexities and processes associated with this otherwise hidden dimension, in African American esoteric traditions. Given that such an endeavor must limit itself to neither a single historical moment nor a monolithic set of methodologies, the essays in this volume—and the emerging new field they are helping to shape—push against parameters that have been established in the field of Western Esotericism.

Reinscribing the Boundaries of Western Esotericism

Both Antoine Faivre and Wouter Hanegraaff have made significant contributions in defining the term "esotericism." Esotericism, according to Faivre, is a "form of thought" characterized by six predicates: (1) *Correspondences*; (2) *Living Nature*; (3) *Imagination and mediation*; (4) *Transmutation*; (5) *Concordance*; and (6) *Transmission* (Faivre 1992, xv–xx). Correspondence represents the interconnectivity between dimensions of visibility and invisibility, while nature is the very embodiment of that which is hidden. Accordingly, the faculty of imagination affords a view of the intersectional activity of correspondences. Imagination is a catalyst of transmutation that leads to the apprehension of gnosis (secret knowledge). The last two predicates of concordance and transmission, unlike the previous four, are extrinsic in that their presence or lack thereof does not determine esoteric discourse. For Faivre, then, four of the six characteristics act as essential building blocks in defining esotericism, and more importantly, they delimit what texts, traditions, and currents are considered esoteric. Thus, it is the transmission of particular constituent ideas that constitutes acceptability. Such parameters are helpful in delimiting parameters for the study of some, though not all, manifestations of the esoteric. Unfortunately, when such criteria are applied without nuance to African American traditions, one may be left with the sense that they do not "possess an *air de famille*" (Faivre and Voss 1995, 49).

Hanegraaff acknowledges the analytical value of Faivre's conceptual framework, but problematizes his idea of correspondence as an intrinsic constituent of esotericism. "Faivre's first—and arguably central—intrinsic characteristic, the worldview of correspondences," Hanegraaff maintains, "was severely compromised, to say the least, under the impact of a mechanical and positivist worldview based on instrumental causality" (Hanegraaff 2004, 508). Here, the idea of correspondence illustrates a privileging of Hermetic-derived "enchanted" conceptions of the world at the expense of considering the impact of societal processes like secularization on religion in general and esotericism in particular. According to Hanegraaff, this privileging restricts the definitional parameters of esotericism as well as diminishes the importance of how 19th and 20th century esoteric currents creatively underwent re-configurations in response to secularization. Consideration of a correlation between esotericism and secularization, in addition to a centeredness on gnosis and symbolic language usage, represent the primary markers characterizing Hanegraaff's conception of Western esotericism. Hanegraaff, while widening the definitional dimension of esotericism, continues, much like Faivre, to characterize esotericism as a "specific mode of thinking" (Hanegraaff 1995, 106). Again, the transmission of certain ideas serves as the identifying mark used to determine the inclusion or exclusion of traditions, works, and experiences understood to be esoteric. The excavation of such *realia* becomes the driving force in selecting a methodology to be applied in their study.

Both Faivre and Hanegraaff maintain that these esoteric ideas originate within a specific era, namely the European Renaissance and affirm the importance of historical methodology. Faivre's description of what such an approach entails is minimalist (Fairve and Voss 1995, 49). Hanegraaff's, by contrast, is more detailed. For him, the historical development of esoteric ideas over time, or as he calls it, the "diachronic approach," serves as the primary focus in the study of esotericism (Hanegraaff 1995, 109–111). This privileging of esoteric ideas and their temporal development provides the impetus for Hanegraaff's empirico-historical approach to esotericism. Such an approach, according to him, allows for the examination of the history of esoteric ideas, which includes: the origination of these ideas during the Renaissance; traditions and currents that serve as conduits for such thought; and the adaptability of esoteric ideas due to the influences of social processes like secularization and scientific materialism. Such an interpretative stance for Hanegraaff avoids a commitment to bipolar analytical approaches of religionism and reductionism (Hanegraaff 1995, 99). Such an approach moves the study of esotericism beyond the "Yates Paradigm" of perennialism and avoids the embrace of an approach to religion that is reductionist. It also offers scholars a way of appreciating the more granular dimensions of esoteric thought. Such puts Hanegraaff in a position to offer a more robust notion of esotericism:

> An esoteric *tradition*, on this foundation, may be defined as a historical continuity in which individuals and/or groups are demonstrably influenced in their life and thinking by the esoteric ideas formulated earlier, which they use and develop according to the specific demands and cultural context of their own period. A diachronic study of such an esoteric tradition, recognizing the irreversibility of historical time, must be *genetic*. It traces the filtration of ideas over time *not* with prior intention to demonstrate their trans- or meta- historical similarity or unity, even less with the intention to demonstrate historical "anticipations" of cherished ideas, but with the intention of clarifying the complex ways in which people process—absorb, (re) interpret, (re) construct, etc.—the ideas of the past accessible to them.
>
> HANEGRAAFF 1995, 109

Thus, the diachronic analysis of genetically transmutable concepts—i.e. "esoteric ideas"—leads to the inscription of boundaries that foster disciplinary coherence. However, an exclusively historical approach of this kind brings with it an understanding that only certain traditions are part of the esoteric "gene pool" as well as an implicitly positivist orientation that reifies boundaries known to be quite permeable. It is this permeability to which the essays in this volume call attention: esoteric tributaries—historical, current, and emerging—extant among peoples of African descent. Its essays also collectively locate them in close proximity to—but do not construe them as subsumed or totalized by—those traditions that are part of the Western Esoteric Canon. Our goal has been to bring together for the first time exemplary research on

African American esotericism that invites critical examination of basic terminology, definitions, primary sources, and methodology. Its entries amount to a *mosaic* representing the diversity and unity of work conducted on African American Esotericism thus far, and a map indicative of the esoteric landscape in which future forays might take place.

Although recognizing the role that religion has played as the central organizing paradigm thus far in research on Western and *Africana esoterica, Esotericism in African American Religious Experience* leaves open to debate the taxonomies used to classify the constellation of phenomena being examined, while calling attention to several things. The first is the role of methodology and authorial location in the study of African American *esoterica*. The second is the relationship between esoteric texts, aesthetics, and popular culture. The third is the importance of being attentive to embodiment and ritualized performances of the esoteric. The fourth is the role of symbol, number, and language in the transmission of esoteric teachings. The fifth is the experiential dimensions of African American esoteric traditions.

A Reassessment and New Engagement

Overall, this collection of essays is a prolegomenon for a new history of African American religion that treats *Africana* Esotericism as integral to it. They wrestle with the issue of how people of African descent understand the revelatory continuum for which full disclosure and concealment are the poles. They lay bare a phenomenon that is neither linear nor monolithic, but complex and fluid. They also reveal the ways in which hegemonic impulses have privileged and classified as mainstream a select number of religious traditions and practices while rendering others—particularly those having taken shape within the larger African American *milieu*—marginal. These forces operate in both the academy and the larger community and serve to structure both interpretive discourses and practices in ways that reflect, undergird, and perpetuate the ideologies and interests of those who consider themselves to be stewards of the sacred and of the disciplines focused on its critical study. These essays also seek to articulate a particular theory of religion that challenges popular materialist and constructivist perspectives dominant in Religious Studies. These theories posit religion as an artifact at once cultural *and* academic—i.e., as a phenomenon whose origins are found in the lived experiences of indigenous peoples *and* the humanistic and social scientific models employed in studying them.

Unfortunately, to date, many of these models pay little attention to the *embodied* nature of the spirituality and religious life and are based on essentialist paradigms and binary thinking that jettison consciousness as a topic that does not lend itself to empirical study. Conversely, *Africana* esotericisms in the United States are characterized by an "aesthetic" that is complex and fluid: one that is implicitly concerned with black *beauty*; *(re)calibrating* and *(re)creating* black bodies; and *connecting* meaning to *transcendent sources* (i.e., that unnamed *something* for which there is an enormous esoteric lexicon). Therefore, the articles in this volume point to the need for ways of thinking and talking about esotericism and other African American cultural phenomena that treat the body, consciousness, and culture as living *matrices* in which ideas take shape and from which many African Americans derive solace, meaning, and power.

Moreover, these essays suggest that esoteric traditions enliven the African American imagination by suggesting the existence of a *mystery*, a *something incapable of precise description*, a *je ne sais quoi* mediated by and structured through *Africana* bodies, minds, experiences, senses, hopes, dreams, aspirations, and life ways. However, this *mystery* is *not* coequal with the aforementioned verities individually or collectively. This *ultimate reality* is variously construed as at once profoundly immanent and indescribably transcendent; and—what's more—as capable of providing enlightenment. By and large, mainstream epistemologies fail to offer plausible explanations of this *hyperreality* and typically fall short in accounting for the vitality of phenomena reflecting it: e.g., UFO lore, folk healing practices such as conjure and root-work, numerology, and belief in astral projection. Instead, many extant scholarly paradigms tend to treat such things exclusively as social, material, or psychological constructs. By contrast, the essays in this volume seek to: identify and define a distinctly *esoteric milieu* within that part of the *Africana* world situated in North America; focus on particular manifestations of esoteric thought and practice in the African American cultural landscape; lay the groundwork for future research on these and related *realia*; and advance dialogue about what might be termed *manifestations of the esoteric* in the Black Atlantic and beyond.

Finally, related to embodiment, aesthetics, and the sense of connectedness to this *something* that is radically other—yet unnamed—*Africana* esotericisms are further distinguished from many Western esoteric strains in that they engage social, existential, and experiential conceptions of *race*. *Africana* esotericisms do something revolutionary and the notions of race and blackness in that they subvert received social meanings and the structural realities based upon Western racial ontologies, and they re-imagine and transmute race and blackness—rather than a biological and social hierarchy that is socially *real*—race and blackness become metaphysical categories that re-signify Africana peoples as the embodiment of something universal in the world. Indeed, as Paul Gilroy (2000) indicated about the concept of race:

It cannot be readily re-signified or de-signified, and to imagine that its dangerous meanings can be easily re-articulated into benign, democratic forms would be to exaggerate the power of critical and oppositional interests. In contrast, the creative acts involved in destroying raciology and transcending "race" are more than warranted by the goal of authentic democracy to which they point. The political will to liberate humankind from race-thinking must be complemented by precise historical reasons why these attempts are worth making (12).

Yet, the transmutation of "race" and "blackness" into something subversive, and, at the same time, into something beautifully new that is located in a metaphysical space in which all races converge, a blackness, a chiasm that transgresses established boundaries and norms, that not only represents the universe, it points to the *universal*.

And, like Gilroy articulates, these metaphysical notions of race and blackness as *transcendence, transmutation*, and *transgression* are absolutely in the interest of "authentic democracy," for Africana esotericisms, as revealed in these pages and essays, point to contact with—and consciousness of—something immanent and transcendent, a *numinous* that is symbolized by blackness and signified by black bodies but is *excess* or *surplus* (Finley 2012, 457). It is present and available for everyone. Hence, the experience, to which many of these essays witness, is radically democratic and egalitarian. One will note such conceptions, explicit and implied, in religious thought and experience of Africana esotericism that are explored and expressed in this volume.

Positionality, both the contributors to the volume and the *oeuvre* to which their contributions collectively belong, is a pivotal concern for this project on *Africana esotericisms* for several reasons. First, the designation of certain lore, ideas, or ritual practices, as strictly *esoteric* can only be undertaken from a vantage point that considers other comparable cultural artifacts as *exoteric* (i.e., *non-esoteric*). In many African settings as well as within the cultural epistemologies fashioned by peoples of African descent living in the Americas and elsewhere, strict bifurcation of knowledge into categories of this kind—religious or otherwise—is not normative.

Second, the extent to which any set of social customs may be considered either *Africana* or *African-American* in nature is fraught with difficulty, each being a contested descriptive category. Cultural insiders and outsiders classify *realia* appropriately belonging to one or another of these experiences in various ways. Many notions of *esoterica* today appear to be articulated in a manner that gives pride of place to Judaism and Christianity as the normative *exoteric* traditions from which most significant Western *esotericisms* develop. *Africana* tributaries feeding this large and diverse *stream* tend to receive short shrift in scholarly literature on the subject (cf., the limited treatment of such topics in Hanegraaff 2005). As a result, the dominant paradigm for understanding the nature and scope of the *esoteric* from either Western or global perspectives is extremely narrow from both religious and geographical vantage points.

Third, the role of *Africana* figures in shaping both the Western Esoteric Tradition and what might be termed the *Africana* Esoteric Tradition, has yet to be excavated fully, described, and analyzed. Moreover, the disciplinary architecture for the latter has yet to be articulated fully. Such realities cannot help but shape the framework within which any conversation about the place of the *esoteric* in either *Africana* or African-American life takes place.

Finally, we do not understand this anthology as a final and definitive statement on Africana Esoteric Tradition. Instead, we consider our role—as editors—and that of our contributors being to sketch some broad and inclusive parameters for what we hope will be a vibrant conversation about esotericism(s) throughout Africa and the African Diaspora for many years to come. The intentional *ellipsis* in this volume's subtitle refers to the work yet to be done in response to the "mystery" of which the late Howard Thurman spoke. Perhaps, more poignantly, it is a signifier of a dynamic *Africana* ethos in which the flow from extant esoteric headwaters continues unabated, and the newer tributaries constantly forming that feed a torrential *Africana* imaginary at once rich, diverse, and global.

Afterword

Anthony B. Pinn

Much of what scholars and students of African American religion have high-lighted over the past century of formal discourse has revolved around easily identifiable communities, doctrines, and creeds. Of primary importance have been the functional dimensions of experience that are explainable in terms of how embodied bodies engage the world. For evidence of this one need only think in terms of major works in religious history, theology, or ethics that center on the activities of physical institutions and that understand the expression of the religious in line with the belief-based programs and practices of those institutions. In this regard, African American religion has been under-stood as oriented toward socio-political and economic transformation based on the geography of how bodies encounter and occupy time/space—first assumed lodged in the content and intent of "hush arbor" meetings. From these and other clandestine gatherings scholars move forward to visible orga-nizations and practices, privileging in this discourse those that take a decid-edly Christian orientation. This is not to say some scholarship hasn't mentioned "non-Christian" structures of meaning, but such acknowledgement tends to do little to challenge the normative claims shaping so much of what has constituted African American Religious Studies as a Christian—if not church based—enterprise.

Gayraud Wilmore's *Black Religion and Black Radicalism* (1979) certainly suggests such an arrangement, as does Albert Raboteau's *Slave Religion* (1978). More recent and more focused treatments such as Wallace Best's text *Passionately Human, No Less Divine* (2007) or Frederick Harris's *Something Within* (1999) appear to abide by the same logic. Furthermore, black and womanist theologies—constituting a self-proclaimed rethink-ing of African American religious discourse—also tend to make a similar move whereby the functional dimensions of African American religion become its defining elements. Think in terms of James Cone's early work— *Black Theology of Liberation* (1969)—but this seems just as true with respect to the writings of second and third generation scholars such as Dwight Hopkins (2005) and Victor Anderson (1995 and 2009). Womanist scholars such as Katie Cannon in *Womanist Ethics* (1989) and Emilie Townes in *Womanist Ethics and the Cultural Production of Evil* (2006) also privilege the same dimensions of what it has meant to be African American and religious. If nothing else, such studies imply the central importance of empirically generated materials and realities. One might expect this approach to the extent so much of the contemporary study of African American religion generates from and is informed by the epistemological and pedagogical assumptions of the civil rights movement. In a word, the socio-political and economic dimensions of cultural formation (including the religious) as expressed through particular structures become privileged terrain for investigation. And what about African American religion scholars cannot uncover in this way is assumed of limited significance for a people struggling against death delivering forces. For instance, interest in (black) consciousness on the part of many scholars of African American religion does not entail esoteric considerations by in large, certainly not beyond that which is lodged in notions of the exotic or derogatory discourse on "cults" and "sects."

Stemming from this approach is a soft mode of theorizing premised on the generic and easily recognizable form of the religious. In its most obvious appearance this involves the privileging of a passive theory of religion whereby the assumed markings of African American religion are constituted by the historical development of African American Christianity and are lodged in the workings of the primary framing of that Christianity—the Black Church. Hence, African American Christianity is the working theory of religion. This approach is passive because there is no effort to interrogate this assumption. And there is no discernable concern to push beyond such assumptions of a reifiable 'something' called African American religion. One of the most impactful challenges to this thinking was provided by Charles Long (1986), who, in a Tillichian manner, promotes a sense of African American religion as direction for life—the framing of our existence in line with an ultimate concern and the orientation promoted by that concern. This theorizing, in *Significations*, privileged a history of religions approach—one by means of which Christianity is not rendered normative but rather more general markers of what it has meant to be African American and religious are sought and explored. There is in this take on the religious a comfort with paradox and recognition of the manner in which the very cultural arrangements and markings of a people speak to a quest for meaning.

This quest for meaning has more recently taken on a deeply central role through an understanding of religion as constituting this very quest for meaning—framed in terms of complex subjectivity (Pinn, 2002, 2010). That is to say, religion (in this case African American religion) is at its core is a quest for complex subjectivity, an effort to wrestle with the fundamental questions of human existence. In this regard, in a manner more explicit than in some cases, religion is not understood as a privileged category of experience. There is nothing *sui generis* about it. Rather, mindful of Long, religion is a way of interrogating or 'naming' human experience's particular charge or direction. Such thinking assumes the importance of those elements of human experience or meaning that are not fully captured through embodied movement in the world, through—that is—empirically arranged developments. Yet, it seeks to hold this in tension with persistent regard for the ways in which bodies occupy time and space. Such thinking opens the study of African American religion to a variety of source materials seldom engaged otherwise. For instance, there are ways in which this approach de-privileges the written word, and gives equal attention to the other "texts"—such as the visual arts and expressive culture—through which African Americans over the course of centuries have articulated their quest for life meaning. Theology—through this theory—and other modalities of study are shifted away from allegiance to any particular tradition—or even theism—and are more intentionally committed to interrogation of the complex and contradictory arrangement of orientations and postures toward the world that constitute the "religious."

While this has been a vital development as a way to better recognize the tone and texture of the religious, it is something of a call for additional work. This alternate theory of religion as the quest for complex subjectivity is meant to promote a detangling from earlier assumptions that prevent creative and imaginative engagement with new questions and new concerns. Yet, in itself, it does not go far enough in that it still betrays more interrogation of the embodied nature of religion than the other possibilities it surfaces. Although not jettisoning this approach, greater tension between embodied realities and other 'markers' of the religious would be beneficial. What of the imaginaries guiding and informing these physical works? What of the more esoteric groundings for the religious—the workings of consciousness that are not so easily named and handled through our tools of the "trade"?

Within the history of the study of African American religion attention to consciousness is not missing altogether. Although present, it is usually the case that it has been limited to pastoral care and counseling conversations. As a result, how African Americans feel about their religiosity, particularly with respect to the texture of salvation in Christian communion, has been tapped to some extent—but little more than this. So conceived, typically presented is a rather flat depiction of African American religious thought and life. Yet, what is it about the existential and ontological predicaments of life for people of African descent that would foster complacency with such limiting presentations of life concern and meaning? Recognizing this difficulty has been a slow process in part because it is only natural for the scholar of religion to tap what is most obvious and move from those spaces of life to more challenging terrains.

Mindful of this, *Esotericism in African American Religious Experience: "There is a Mystery"*...entails an important contribution to the advancement of scholarship. It marks out something of a next phase of investigation. It is a pattern of study and appreciation of the religious that is hinted at in work produced more than a decade ago (based on the scholarly productivity of certain contributors that is expanded but not constituted anew here), but that is expanded in vital and vibrant ways. New voices and established scholars participate in this volume and in that way demonstrate a blending of generational shifts (and sensitivities) in the study of African American religion. Through such an arranging of contributors, the editors speak both implicitly and explicitly to the location of this turn in the study of African American religion in ways that place it firmly in the intersections—spaces marked by plasticity and flexibility. What one gathers from this text is a deep appreciation for complexity and a limited desire to understand the study of African American religion as the unpacking of this complexity—the simplifying of cartography of African American mappings of meaning. Instead it finds in this complexity—the inability to fully capture through empirical materials—profound potential for the attentive scholar of religion. And it seeks to maintain this complexity. By so doing, this approach opens up to exploration a fuller range of source materials—sensual in a very different way. Or, as the editors remark there is something about the religious that involves "*mystery*, a *something incapable of precise description*, a *je ne sais quoi* mediated by and structured through *Africana* bodies, minds, experiences, senses, hopes, dreams, aspirations, and life ways."

Readers must be mindful that this is not simply a shift with respect to source materials and/or the methodological tools used in the study of African American religion. Rather, and of great importance, it involves a different posture toward what is explored and what is "found" through exploration. The effort is to de-privilege any particular arrangement of traditions, thoughts, or movements. Instead, it seeks to work based on an assumption that everything it means to be African American and religious cannot be captured. In important ways, this elusiveness, this existence beyond concrete detection, is part of the very nature of the religious.

What you have undoubtedly noticed in these pages is the manner in which it privileges the often-considered "marginal" arrangements of religious life in African American communities; but it doesn't do this as a matter of apologetics. No, it assumes rightly the importance of these markers of the religious and instead of pleading their relevance, the authors simply unpack and explore the manner in which they speak to vital but less frequently discussed dimensions of African American encounter with the world. Finally, in thinking about this book and its intent, I'm reminded of James Baldwin's words:

> The purpose of art is to lay bare the questions that have been hidden by the answers.
>
> "The Creative Process," 1962, 16

However phrased, the implications for scholarship are sure. All this makes for a solid and insightful text—one that requires careful consideration, and one that should spark lively conversation and debate with respect to issues of theory, method, sources, and description.

Bibliography

Abraham, Alton. Collection of Sun Ra, [Box 2, Folder 4]. Special Collections Research Center. University of Chicago Library.

Albanese, Catherine L. *A Republic of Mind and Spirit: A Cultural History of American Metaphysical Religion.* New Haven: Yale University Press, 2007.

Alexander, Michelle. *The New Jim Crow: Mass Incarceration in the Age of Colorblindness.* London and New York: The New Press, 2010.

Allen, Ernest Jr. "Identity and Destiny. The Formative Views of the Moorish Science Temple and the Nation of Islam," in: *Muslims on the Americanization Path?* edited by Yvonne Yazbeck Haddad and John L. Esposito, 163–214. New York: Oxford University Press, 1998.

Allen, James, trans. *The Ancient Egyptian Pyramid Texts.* Atlanta: Society of Biblical Literature, 2005.

Amoaku, Komla, W. "Toward a Definition of Traditional African Music: A Look at the Ewe of Ghana," in: *More Than Drumming: Essays on African and Afro-Latin American Music and Musicians*, 1985.

Anderson, Alan C., and Deborah G. Whitehouse. *New Thought: A Practical American Spirituality.* New York: Crossroad Publishing, 1995.

Anderson, Jeffrey E. *Conjure in African American Society.* Baton Rouge, LA: Louisiana State University Press, 2005.

Anderson, Victor. *Beyond Ontological Blackness.* New York: Continuum, 1995.

——. *Creative Exchange.* Minneapolis: Fortress, 2009.

Apter, A. *Black Critics and Kings: The Hermeneutics of Power in Yoruba Society.* Chicago: University of Chicago Press, 1992.

Ariès, Philippe. "The Reversal of Death: Changes in Attitudes toward Death in Western Societies," in: *Death in America*, edited by David E. Stannard, 134–158. Philadelphia: University of Pennsylvania Press, 1974.

——. *The Hour of Our Death.* New York, NY: Oxford University Press, 1981.

Asad, Talal. *Genealogies of Religion: Discipline and Reasons of Power in Christianity and Islam.* Baltimore: Johns Hopkins University Press, 1993.

——. *Formations of the Secular: Christianity, Islam, Modernity.* Palo Alto, C.A.: Stanford University Press, 2003.

Ashcroft-Nowicki Dolores. *Ritual Magic Workbook.* London: Aquarian Press, 1984.

Assmann, Jan. *Moses the Egyptian: The Memory of Egypt in Western Monotheism.* Cambridge: Harvard University Press, 1997.

Baer, Hans A. *The Black Spiritual Movement. A Religious Response to Racism*, Knoxville: University of Tennessee Press, 1984.

Baker-Fletcher, G. "Black Bodies, Whose Body?: African American Men in XODUS," in: *Men's Bodies, Men's Gods: Male Identities in Post-Christian Culture*, edited by B. Krondorfer. New York: New York University Press, 1996.

Baldwin, Davarian. *Chicago's New Negroes: Modernity, the Great Migration and Black Urban Life*. Chapel Hill: University of North Carolina Press, 2007.

Baldwin, James. "The Creative Process," in: *Creative America*, New York: Ridge Press, 1962.

Banks, A. *Race, Rhetoric, and Technology: Searching for Higher Ground*. New Jersey: Lawrence Erlbaum Associates, Inc., 2006.

Bardon Franz. *The Practice of Evocation*. Germany: Dieter Ruggeberg/Wuppertal, 1970.

Barkun, Michael, *A Culture of Conspiracy: Apocalyptic Visions in Contemporary America*, Berkeley: University of California Press, 2003.

Bastide, Roger. *The African Religions of Brazil: Toward a Sociology of the Interpenetraion of Civilizations*. Baltiomore: Johns Hopkins University Press, 1978 [1960].

Batterson, Mark. *The Circle Maker: Praying Circles Around Your Biggest Dreams and Greatest Fears*. Reprint ed. Grand Rapids, MI: Zondervan, 2012.

Beidelman, T.O. "Secrecy and Society: The Paradox of Knowing and the Knowing of Paradox," in: *Secrecy: African Art that Conceals and Reveals*, edited by M.H. Nooter. New York, NY: Museum for African Art, 1993.

Bell, Catherine. *Ritual: Perspectives and Dimensions*. New York: Oxford University Press, 1997.

Bell, Bernard W. *The Contemporary African American Novel: Its Folk Roots and Modern Literary Branches*. Amherst, MA: Massachusetts UP, 2004.

Bennett, John. *Transformation*. Charles Town W. Va.: Claymont Communications, 1978.

Berg, Herbert. "Mythmaking in the American Muslim Context: The Moorish Science Temple, the Nation of Islam, and the American Society of Muslims." *Journal of the American Academy of Religion* 73: 3 (2005), 685–703.

Best, Wallace. *Passionately Human, No Less Divine*. Princeton: Princeton University Press, 2007.

Beynon, Erdmann Doane. "The Voodoo Cult among Negro Migrants in Detroit." *The American Journal of Sociology* 43: 6 (1938), 894–907.

Bible. Galatians 1: 6–9. New Revised Standard Version.

Black, Pen. *GODS, EARTHS and 85ers*. CreateSpace Independent Publishing Platform, 2011.

Blakey, Michael L. "The New York African Burial Ground Project: An Examination of Enslaved Lives, A Construction of Ancestral Ties." *Transforming Anthropology* 7: 1 (1998), 53–58.

Blassingame, John. *The Slave Community: Plantation Life in the Antebellum South*, 2nd ed. New York: Oxford University Press, 1979.

Blavatsky, H.P. *The Secret Doctrine: the Synthesis of Science, Religion and Philosophy*, Theosophical University Press Online Edition, 1888, http://www.theosociety.org/pasadena/sd/sd-hp.htm.

——. *Isis Unveiled: A Master Key to the Mysteries of Ancient and Modern Science and Theology, Vol. I.* Pasadena, CA: Theosophical UP, 1988.

Bloom, Harold. *The American Religion: The Emergence of the Post-Christian Nation.* New York: Simon & Schuster, 1992.

Boesel, Chris, and Catherine Keller. *Apophatic Bodies: Negative Theology, Incarnation, and Relationality.* New York: Fordham, 2009.

Bogdan, Henrik. *Western Esotericism and Rituals of Initiation*, Albany: State University of New York Press, 2007.

Bok, Sissela. *Secrets: On the Ethics of Concealment and Revelation.* New York, NY: Pantheon Books, 1982.

Bordo, S. "Reading the Male Body," in: *The Male Body: Features, Destinies, Exposures*, edited by L. Goldstein. Ann Arbor: University of Michigan Press, 1994.

Bowie, R. *Personal Interview with the Author.* March 14. Winnsboro, Louisiana, 1995.

Braden, Charles. "New Thought," in: *These Also Believe: A Study of Modern American Cults & Minority Religious Movements.* New York: MacMillan Company, 1956.

Bragdon, Claude. "Annotated Correspondence," 1918, http://www.lib.rochester.edu/index.cfm?PAGE=3515.

Brathwaite, Edward and Glissant, Edoard. *The Cultural Creolization of the World.* Label France, 2000.

Braude, Ann. *Radical Spirits: Spiritualism and Women's Rights in Nineteenth-Century America.* Bloomington: Indiana University Press, 2001.

Brown, D. "Conjure/Doctors: An Explanation of a Black Discourse in America, Antebellum to 1940." *Folklore Forum* 23: 3–46, 1990.

——. "Altared Spaces: Afro-Cuban Religion and the Urban Landscape in Cuba and the United States," in: *Gods of the City: Religion and the Urban American Landscape*, edited by R. Orsi, 155–230. Bloomington: Indiana University Press, 1999.

Brown, Henry. "Letter from Brother Brown." *The Christian Recorder*, December 8. Accessible Archives: African American Newspapers, 1866.

Brown, Lois. *Pauline Elizabeth Hopkins: Black Daughter of the Revolution.* Chapel Hill, NC: North Carolina UP, 2008.

Brown, William Wells. "Letter From WM. W. Brown." *The Liberator*, August 17. American Periodicals Series Online, 1855.

——. *Clotel; Or, The President's Daughter.* New York, NY: Modern Library, 2000.

Butler E.M. *Ritual Magic.* USA: New Castle Publishing Company Inc, 2001.

Butler, Jon. *Awash in a Sea of Faith: Christianizing the American People.* Cambridge: Harvard University Press, 1990.

——. *New World Faiths: Religion in Colonial America*. New York: Oxford University Press, 2008.

Butler, Melvin L. "The Spirit of David: Negotiating Faith and Masculinity in Black Gospel Performance," http://divinity.uchicago.edu/martycenter/publications/webforum/122010/The%20Spirit%20of%20David_Butler%20Final%201.pdf, last accessed April 12, 2012.

Burt, Ramsay. "Dissolving in Pleasure: The Threat of the Queer Male Dancing Body," in: *Dancing Desires: Choreographing Sexualities On & Off the Stage*, edited by Jane C. Desmond. Madison: University of Wisconsin, 2006.

——. *The Male Dancer: Bodies, Spectacle, and Sexuality*. London and New York: Routledge, 2007.

Bynum, Edward. *The African Unconscious: Roots of Ancient Mysticism and Modern Psychology*. New York: Teachers College Press, 1999.

Cage, Byron. "This Is The Air I Breathe," from *An Invitation To Worship*, Detroit: PAJAM, 2005.

Cannon, Katie. *Womanist Ethics*. Atlanta: Scholars Press, 1989.

Chesnutt, Charles W. *Conjure Tales and Stories of the Color Line*. New York: Penguin, 1992.

Chireau, Yvonne P. *Black Magic: Religion and the African American Conjuring Tradition*. Berkeley: University of California Press, 2003.

Cicero, Chic. *Secrets of a Golden Dawn Temple*. Woodbury: Llewellyn Publications, 1995.

Clark, Mary Ann. *Where Men Are Wives and Mothers Rule: Santería Ritual Practices and Their Gender Implications*. Gainesville: University Press of Florida, 2005.

——. *Santeria: Correcting the Myths and Uncovering the Realities of a Growing Religion*. Westport, Connecticut: Praeger Publishers, 2007.

Clark Veve A., "From Field Hands to Stagehands in Haiti: The Measure of Tradition in Haitian Popular Theatre." PhD diss., University of California Berkeley, 1984.

Clegg, Claude Andrew, III. *An Original Man: The Life and Times of Elijah Muhammad*. New York: St. Martin's Press, 1997.

Clymer, R. Swinburne. *Book of Rosicruciae*. Quakertown, PA: Philosophical Publishing Company, 1947.

Coleman, James W. "Communications." *The Christian Recorder*, September 18. Accessible Archives: African American Newspapers, 1873.

——. *Faithful Vision: Treatments of the Sacred, Spiritual, and Supernatural in Twentieth-Century African American Fiction*. Baton Rouge, LA: Louisiana State University, 2005.

Cone, James. *A Black Theology of Liberation: Twentieth Anniversary Edition*. New York: Orbis Books, 1986.

——. *The Cross and the Lynching Tree*. Maryknoll, N.Y.: Orbis Books, 2011.

Coney, John, director. *Space Is the Place*. New York: Rhapsody Films, 1998.

Copenhaver, Brian, trans. *Hermetica*. Cambridge: Cambridge University Press, 1992.

Corbett, John. *Extended Play: Sounding Off from John Cage to Dr. Funkenstein.* Durham: Duke University Press, 1994.

Cornelius, Janet D. When I can Read My Title Clear: Literary, Slavery and Religion in the Antebellum South. Columbia, SC: University of South Carolina Press, 1992.

Cosentino, Donald. *Sacred Arts of Haitian Vodou.* CA: University of California Los Angeles, Fowler Publications, 1995.

——. "Repossession: Ogun in Folklore and Literature," in: *Africa's Ogun: Old World and New,* edited by S. Barnes, 290–314. Bloomington: University of Indiana Press, 1997.

Cox, Robert S. *Body and Soul: A Sympathetic History of American Spiritualism.* Charlottesville: University of Virginia Press, 2003.

Crawley, Ashon. "'Let's Get It On!' Performance Theory and Black Pentecostalism." *Black Theology* 6: 3 (2008), 308–329.

Crumm, David. Why Christians Should Love Twilight Vampires, Werewolves and the Bible." *Huffington Post,* http//www.huffingtonpost.com/david-crumm/why -christians-should-love-twilightb110, posted 11/23/11, accessed12/12/11.

Culianu Ioan. "Magic in Medieval and Renaissance Europe," in: *Sullivan Lawrence. Hidden Truths.* NY: MacMillan Publishing Company, 1989.

Curtis, Edward E., IV. *Islam in Black America: Identity, Liberation and Difference in African-American Thought.* New York: SUNY, 2002.

——. *Black Muslim Religion in the Nation of Islam, 1960–1975.* Chapel Hill: University of North Carolina Press, 2006.

Cusic, Don. *The Sound of Light: A History of Gospel Music Book.* Bowling Green, O.H.: Popular Press, 1990.

Dakake, Maria, "Hiding in Plain Sight: The Practical and Doctrinal Significance of Secrecy in Shi'ite Islam", *Journal of the American Academy of Religion* 74: 2 (2006), 324–355.

Daniel, Yvonne. *Dancing Wisdom: Embodied Knowledge in Haitian Vodou, Cuban Yoruba, and Bahian Candomblé.* Champaign, IL: University of Illinois Press, 2005.

David, Jonathan C. *Together Let Us Sweetly Live: The Singing and Praying Bands.* Champaign: University of Illinois Press, 2007.

Davies, Owen. *Grimoires: A History of Magical Books.* Oxford, UK/New York: Oxford University Press, 2009.

Davis, David Brion. "Some Themes of Countersubversion: An Analysis of Anti Masonic, Anti-Catholic, and Anti-Mormon Literature", in: *Conspiracy. The Fear of Subversion in American History,* edited by Richard O. Curry and Thomas M. Brown, 61–77. New York: Holt, Rinehart and Winston, Inc., 1972.

Deissmann, Adolf. *Paul, a Study in Social and Religious History,* translated by William E. Wilson. New York: Harper & Row, 1957.

Deiter, Hans. *Greek Magical Papyri in Translation.* Chicago: University of Chicago Press, 1996.

Delany, Martin R. *Principia of Ethnology: The Origin of Races and Color, with an archaeological compendium of Ethiopian and Egyptian civilization...* Philadelphia, PA: Harper and Brothers, 1879.

Denino Best. Wallace. *Passionately Human, No Less Divine: Religion and Culture in Black Chicago, 1915–1952*. Princeton: Princeton University Press, 2005.

Derrida, Jacques. *Circumfession*. Chicago: University of Chicago Press, 1993.

———. *Points: Interviews 1974–1994*. Stanford: Stanford University Press, 1995.

———. *A Taste for the Secret*. Malden: Blackwell, 2001.

Deutsch, Nathaniel. "'The Asiatic Black Man': An African American Orientalism?" *Journal of Asian American Studies* 4: 3 (2001), 193–208.

Deveney, John Patrick. *Paschal Beverly Randolph: A Nineteenth-Century Black American Spiritualist, Rosicrucian, and Sex Magician*. New York, NY: New York State UP, 1997.

Dianteill, Erwan. *La Samaritaine Noire: Les églises spirituelles noires américaines de la Nouvelle-Orléans*. Paris: Éditions de l'EHESS, 2006.

Dick, Bruce and Amritjit Singh, eds. *Conversations with Ishmael Reed*. Jackson: University Press of Mississippi, 1995.

Diouf, Sylviane. *Servants of Allah: African Americans Enslaved in the Americas*. New York: NYU Press, 1998.

Dorman, Jacob S. "'I Saw You Disappear with My Own Eyes': Hidden Transcripts of New York Black Israelite Bricolage." *Nova Religio* 11: 1 (2007), 61–83.

Dowson, Ross. *The Vanguard Organ of the International Left Opposition of Canada*, 1932, http://www.marxists.org/archive/dowson/vanguard32_36.html.

Drake, St. Clair, and Horace R. Cayton. *Black Metropolis: A Study of Negro Life in a Northern City*. Chicago: University of Chicago Press, 1993 [1945].

DuBois, W.E.B. *The Souls of Black Folk*. Chicago, IL: A.C. McClurg, 1903.

———. *Writings*. New York: Library of America, 1987.

Durkheim, Emile. *The Elementary Forms of Religious Life*. New York: The Free Press, 1915.

Dyson, Michael Eric. *Race Rules Navigating the Color Line*. Reading, MA: Addison-Wesley Publishing Company, Inc., 1996.

Edmonds, Ennis and Gonzalez, Michelle. *Caribbean Religious History*. NY: NYU Press, 2010.

Edwards, Brent. "The Race for Space: Sun Ra's Poetry." *Sun Ra: The Immeasurable Equation: The Collected Poetry and Prose*, edited by James Wolf and Hartmut Geerken. Wartaweil: Waitawhile, 2005.

Eilberg-Schwartz, Howard. *God's Phallus: And Other Problems for Men and Monotheism*. Boston: Beacon Press, 1994.

Elihu Pleasant-Bey. *Exhuming a Nation: Biography of Nobel Drew Ali: Appendix, The Holy Koran of the Moorish Science Temple of America*, Noble Drew Ali. Memphis: Seven Seal Publication, 2004.

Eliade, Mircea. *The Sacred and the Profane: The Nature of Religion*. Orlando, FL: Harcourt, Inc., 1987.

Emanuel, James A. "The Christ and the Killers," in: *Langston Hughes: Critical Perspectives*, edited by Henry Louis Gates, Jr. and Kwame Anthony Appiah, 172–196, 1993.

Essien-Udom, E.U. *Black Nationalism: The Search for an Identity*. Chicago: University of Chicago Press, 1995.

Esters, Israel Malik. 2011–2012. Telephone Interviews by Author. June 22 and July 3 2011 and January 15, 2012.

Evans, Dylan, ed. *An Introductory Dictionary of Lacanian Psychoanalysis*. New York: Routledge, 1996.

Evans, Elrena. "There's Power in the Blood," 2010, http://www.christianitytoday.com/ct/2010/february/26.37.html, posted 2/19/10, accessed 12/12/11, 2.

Evans, James. *We Have Been Believers: An African American Systematic Theology*. Minneapolis: Fortress Press, 1992.

Evanzz, Karl, *The Messenger: The Rise and Fall of Elijah Muhammad*, New York: Vintage Books, 1999.

Faivre, Antoine. "Introduction 1," in: *Modern Esoteric Spirituality*, edited by A. Faivre and J. Needleman. New York: Crossroad Publishing Company, 1992.

———. *Access to Western Esotericism*. Albany: SUNY Press, 1994.

———. "The Notions of Concealment and Secrecy in Modern Esoteric Currents since the Renaissance," in: *Rending the Veil: Concealment and Secrecy in the History of Religions*, edited by Elliot R. Wolfson, 155–176. New York: Seven Bridges Press, 1999.

———. *Theosophy, Imagination, Tradition: Studies in Western Esotericism*. Albany, NY: State University of New York Press, 2000.

———. *Western Esotericism: A Concise History*. Albany, NY: State University of New York Press, 2010.

Faivre, Antoine, and Karen-Claire Voss. Western Esotericism and the Science of Religions. *Numen* 42: (1995), 48–78.

Faivre, Antoine and Wouter J. Hanegraaff. "Western Esoterism and Science of Religion: Selected Papers Presented at the 17th Congress of the International Association for the History of Religions, Mexico City, 1995." *Peeters* 1998.

Fanning, Steven. *Mystics of the Christian Tradition*. New York: Routledge, 2001.

Farrakhan, Louis. *The Announcement: A Final Warning to the U.S. Government*. Chicago: FCN Publishing Co., Gardell, Mattias. 1996. *In the Name of Elijah Muhammad: Louis Farrakhan and the Nation of Islam*. Durham, NC: Duke University Press, 1989.

———. *Let Us Make Man*. Atlanta, GA: Uprising Communications, 1996.

Finch, Charles S. *Star of Deep Beginnings: The Genesis of African Science and Technology*, 264, Decatur, GA: Khenti, 2000.

———. *Nile Genesis: an introduction to the opus of Gerald Massey*, 2006, http://gerald-massey.org.uk/massey/cmc_nile_genesis.htm.

Finley, Stephen C. "Real Men Love Jesus?": Homoeroticism and the Absence of Black Heterosexual Male Participation in African American Churches." *CSSR Bulletin* 36.1, 2007a.

———. "Homoeroticism and the African-American Heterosexual Male: Quest for Meaning in the Black Church." *Black Theology: An International Journal* 5: 3 (2007b), 305–326.

———. "Re-imagining Race and Representation: The Black Body in the Nation of Islam." PhD diss., Rice University, 2009.

———. "he Meaning of *Mother* in Louis Farrakhan's 'Mother Wheel': Race, Gender, and Sexuality in the Cosmology of the Nation of Islam's UFO." *Journal of the American Academy of Religion* 80: 2 (2012), 434–465.

———. "From Mistress to Mother: The Religious Transformation of Tynnetta Muhammad in the Nation of Islam," in: *Ain't I a Womanist, Too?: Third Wave Womanist Religious Thought*, edited by Monica A. Coleman. Philadelphia: Ausburg Fortress Press, 2013.

———. "Hidden Away: Esotericism and Gnosticism in Elijah Muhammad's Nation of Islam," in: *Histories of the Hidden God: Concealment and Revelation in Western Gnostic, Esoteric, and Mystical Traditions*, edited by April DeConick and Grant Adamson, 259–280. London: Equinox Publishing, 2013.

Floyd, Samuel. Ring Shout! Literary Studies, Historical Studies, and Black Music Inquiry. *Black Music Research Journal* 1: 11 (1991), 265–287.

———. *The Power of Black Music: Interpreting Its History and from Africa to the United States*. New York: Oxford University Press, 1995.

Frater, U.D. *Practical Sigil Magic*. Woodbury: Llewellyn Publications, 1990.

Frazier, E. Franklin and C. Eric Lincoln. *The Negro Church in America/The Black Church Since Frazier*. New York: Schoken Books, 1974.

Frothingham, Octavius. *Gerrit Smith: A Biography*. New York, NY: Putnam, 1909.

Gallagher, Eugene V. "'Cults' and 'New Religious Movements.'" *History of Religions* 47, 2 (2007/2008): 205–220.

Gamache, Henri. *The Magic of Herbs Throughout the Ages*. New York, NY: Power Thoughts Publishing Company, 1942.

———. *The Master Key to Occult Secrets*. Reprint of 1942 ed. Bronx, NY: Original Publications, 1983.

———. *Mystery of the Long Lost 8th, 9th, and 10th Books of Moses*. Plainview, NY: Original Publications, 1993.

———. *The Master Book of Candle Burning*. Reprint of 1942 ed. Plainview, NY: Original Publications, 1998.

———. *Terrors of the Evil Eye Exposed*. Buena, Park, CA: Astral Books, 2010.

Gardell, Matias. *In the Name of Elijah Muhammad: Louis Farrakhan and the Nation of Islam*. Durham: Duke University Press, 1996.

Gates, Henry Louis. *The Signifying Monkey: A Theory of African-American Literary Criticism*. Oxford: Oxford University Press, 1988.

Gibbons, Tom H. *Rooms in the Darwin Hotel: Studies in English Literary Criticism and Ideas, 1880–1920*. Nedlans, WA: University of Western Australia Press, 1973.

Gilkes, C. *"If It Wasn't for the Woman..." Black Women's Experience and Womanist Culture in Church and Community*. New York: Orbis Books, 2001.

Gilroy, Paul. *Against Race: Imagining Political Culture Beyond the Color Line*. Cambridge, MA: The Belknap Press of Harvard University Press, 2000.

Glazier, Stephen D. "Spiritual Baptist Outreach from Trinidad." *Cultural Survival Quarterly* 7: 3 (1983), 38–40.

Godwin, Joscelyn, Christian Chanel, and John P. Deveney. *The Hermetic Brotherhood of Luxor: Initiatic and Historical Documents of an Order of Practical Occultism*. York Beach, ME: Weiser, 1995.

Gomez, Michael. *Black Crescent: The Experience and Legacy of African Muslims in the Americas*. New York: Cambridge University Press, 2005.

Gordon, Lewis. *Bad Faith and Antiblack Racism*. New York: Humanity Books, 1999.

——. "Can Men Worship?: An Existential Portrait in Black and White," in: *Existentia Africana: Understanding Africana Existential Thought*. NY and London: Routledge, 2000.

Gordon, R. Negro "Shouts from Georgia," in: *Mother Wit from the Laughing Barrell*, edited by A. Dundes. Englewood Cliffs, N.J.: Prentice-Hall, 1972.

Grandin, D.S. "John Randolph." *The Liberator*, November 5. American Periodicals Series Online, 1858.

Gregory, Hiram. Africa in the Delta. *Louisiana Studies* 1: 1 (1962), 17–23.

Greene, Brian. *The Elegant Universe; Superstrings, Hidden Dimension, and the Quest for the Ultimate Theory*, 16. New York, Vintage Press, 2000.

Greer, John Michael. *Inside a Magical Lodge*. Woodbury: Llewellyn Publications, 1998.

——. *Circles of Power*. Woodbury: Llewellyn Publications, 1997.

Gregory, Steven. *Santería in New York City: A Study in Cultural Resistance*. New York: Garland, 1999.

Grey, William. *Western Inner Workings*. Newbury: Red Wheel/Weisers, 1983.

Griffin, Farah Jasmine. *"Who Set You Flowin'?": The African-American Migration Narrative*. New York: Oxford University Press, 1996.

Grossman, James R. *Land of Hope: Chicago, Black Southerners, and the Great Migration*. Chicago: The University of Chicago Press, 1989.

Gundaker, Grey. *Signs of Diaspora, Diaspora of Signs*. USA: Oxford University Press, 1998.

Gundaker, G. and J. McWillie. *No Space Hidden: The Spirit of African American Yard Art*. Knoxville: University of Tennessee Press, 2005.

Guragain, Khem. "African American Literary Tradition and Toni Morrison's Aesthetic Perspectives." *The African Executive*, 2009, http://www.africanexecutive.com/ modules/magazine/articles.php?article=4324.

———. "Guy Does Pole Dancing To Hezekiah Walker's 'I Need You To Survive,'" http:// www.youtube.com/watch?v=v_H5kG9dOoE, last accessed October 21, 2011.

Haley, Alex. *The Autobiography of Malcolm X*. New York: Ballatine Books, 1973.

Hall, Gwendolyn Midlo. *Africans in Colonial Louisiana: The Development of Afro-Creole Culture in the Eighteenth Century*. Baton Rouge: Louisiana State University Press, 1992.

Hall, Manly. *The Secret Destiny of America*. Los Angeles: Philosophical Research Society, 1944.

Hall, S. *Representation: Cultural Representations and Signifying Practices* (*Culture, Media and Identities*). Thousand Oaks, CA: Sage, 1997.

Hand, W. "The Quest for Buried Treasure: A Chapter in American Folk Legendry," in: *Folklore on Two Continents: Essays in Honor of Linda Degh*, edited by N. Burlakoff and C. Lindahl, 112–119. Bloomington: Trickster Press, 1980.

Hanegraaff, Wouter J. Empirical Method in the Study of Esotericism. *Method and Theory in the Study of Religion* 7: 2 (1995), 99–129.

———. *New Age Religion and Western Culture: Esotericism in the Mirror of Secular Thought*. Albany, NY: State University of New York Press, 1998.

———. "Esotericism," in: *Dictionary of Gnosis and Western Esotericism*, edited by Wouter J. Hanegraaff, 336–340. Leiden: Brill, 2006.

———. *Esotericism and the Academy: Rejected Knowledge in Western Culture*. Cambridge: Cambridge University Press, 2012.

———. *Western Esotericism a Guide for the Perplexed*. New York, NY: Bloomsbury Academic, 2013.

Harley, Gail M. *Emma Curtis Hopkins: Forgotten Founder of New Thought*. Syracuse: Syracuse University Press, 2002.

Harms, Daniel, ed. *The Long Lost Friend: A 19th Century American Grimoire*, Completed Annotated ed. Woodbury, MN: Llewellyn Publications, 2012.

Harris, Frederick. *Something within*. New York: Oxford University Press, 1999.

Harris, Leslie M. "From Abolitionist Amalgamators to 'Rulers of the Five Points': The Discourse of Interracial Sex and Reform in Antebellum New York City," in: *Sex, Love, Race: Crossing Boundaries in North American History*, edited by Martha Hodes, 191–212. New York, NY: New York UP, 1999.

Hart, Kevin. "The Experience of Non-Experience," in: *Mystics: Presence and Aporia*, edited by Michael Kessler and Christian Sheppard. Chicago: University of Chicago, 2003.

Haynes, Stephen R. *Noah's Curse: The Biblical Justification of American Slavery*. New York: Oxford University Press, 2007.

Heidegger, Martin, and Edward Robinson. *Being and Time*. New York: HarperPerennial/ Modern Thought, 2008.

Heidegger, Martin, trans., Matthias Fritsch and Jennifer Anna Gosetti-Ferencei. *The Phenomenology of Religious Life*. Bloomington: Indiana University Press, 2004.

Heidegger, Martin, trans., Albert Hofstadter. *The Basic Problems of Phenomenology*. Bloomington: Indiana University Press, 1982.

Henderson, Suzanne Marie. "The African-American Experience of Orisha Worship." PhD diss., Temple University, 2007.

Henry, Frances. *Reclaiming African Religions in Trinidad the Socio-political Legitimation of the Orisha and Spiritual Baptist Faiths*. Barbados: University of the West Indies Press, 2003.

Hezekiah Walker and The Love Fellowship Choir. "I Need You To Survive." *Family Affair II: Live At Radio City Music Hall*. Verity Records, 2002.

Higginbotham, Evelyn Brooks. *Righteous Discontent: The Women's Movement in the Black Baptist Church, 1880–1920*. Cambridge: Harvard University Press, 1993.

Highgate, E. Goodelle. "Letter From New Orleans." *The Christian Recorder*, March 17. Accessible Archives: African American Newspapers, 1866.

Ho, Fred Wei-Han, and Bill V. Mullen, eds. *Afro Asia: Revolutionary Political and Cultural Connections between African Americans and Asian Americans*. Durham, N.C.: Duke University Press, 2006.

Hodd, Tom. "Literary Modernism and Occult Scholarship: The Rising Academic Tide," in: *Review of Literary Modernism and the Occult Tradition and Modemist Alchemy: Poetry and the Occult by Timothy Materer*. *The Antigonish Review*, edited by Leon Surette and Demetres P. Tryphonopoulos, 115, 2010, http://www.antigonishreview .com/index.php.

Hollywood, Amy. *Sensible Ecstasy: Mysticism, Sexual Difference, and the Demands of History*. Chicago: University of Chicago Press, 2002.

——. "Practice, Belief, and Feminist Philosophy of Religion," in: *Thinking through Rituals: Philosophical Perspectives*, edited by Kevin Schilbrack. New York: Routledge, 2004.

Holmes, Barbara A. *Race and the Cosmos: An Invitation to View the World Differently*. Harrisburg: Trinity Press International, 2002.

——. *Joy Unspeakable: Contemplative Practices of the Black Church*. Minneapolis: Fortress Press, 2004.

Hooks, Bell. *Killing Rage: Ending Racism*. New York: Henry Holt & Co, 1995.

Hopkins, Dwight. *Being Human*. Minneapolis: Fortress, 2005.

——. "The Construction of the Black Male Body: Eroticism and Religion," in: *Loving the Body: Black Religious Studies and the Erotic*, edited by Anthony B. Pinn and Dwight N. Hopkins. New York: Palgrave Macmillan, 2006.

Hopkinson, N. *Brown Girl in the Ring*. New York: Warner Books, 1998.

——. *Midnight Robber.* New York: Warner Books, 2000.

Hopkins, Pauline. *Of One Blood; or, the Hidden Self.* New York, NY: Washington Square, 2004.

Hornung, Erik. *The Secret Lore of Ancient Egypt: Its Impact on the West.* Ithaca: Cornell University Press, 2001.

Howe, Stephen. *Afrocentrism: Mythical Pasts and Imagined Homes.* London: Verso, 1999.

Hucks, Tracey E. "Approaching the African God: An Examination of African-American Yoruba History from 1959 to the Present." PhD diss., Harvard University, 1998.

——. "'Burning with a Flame in America': African American Women in African-Derived Traditions." *Journal of Feminist Studies in Religion* 17: 2 (2001), 89–106.

Hughes, Langston. *The Big Sea: An Autobiography.* New York: Hill and Wang, 1940.

——. *The Langston Hughes Reader.* New York: Braziller, 1958.

——. *The Collected Poems of Langston Hughes.* New York: Vantage, 1994.

——. *The Collected Works of Langston Hughes: Essays Vol. 9.* Columbia: University of Missouri Press, 2002.

Hunt, Matthew O., and Larry L. Hunt. "Regional Religions?: Extending the 'Semi-Involuntary' Thesis of African-American Religious Participation." *Sociological Forum* 15: 4 (2000), 569–594.

Hurston, Zora Neale. "Hoodoo in America." *Journal of American Folklore* 44: (1931), 317–417.

——. *Tell My Horse, by Zora Neale Hurston.* n.p.: Philadelphia, J.B. Lippincott [c1938], 1938. *Louisiana State University*, 1938.

——. *Dust Tracks on a Road.* New York: HarperPerennial Press, 1991 [1942].

——. *Seraph on the Suwanee.* New York: Charles Scribner's Sons, 1948.

Hutchinson, George. *In Search of Nella Larsen: A Biography of the Color Line.* Cambridge: Belknap Press of Harvard University Press, 2006.

Hyatt, H.M. *Hoodoo – Conjuration – Witchcraft – Rootwork: Beliefs Accepted by Many Negroes and White Persons, These Being Orally Recorded among Blacks and Whites. Vols. I–V.* Hannibal: Western Publishing, Inc, 1970.

Irwin, Lee. "Western Esotericism, Eastern Spirituality, and the Global Future." *Esoterica* 3: (2001), 1–47.

Jackson, Joyce Marie. *"Rockin' and Rushin' for Christ: Hidden Transcripts in Diasporic Ritual Performance." Caribbean and Southern: Transnational Perspectives on the U.S. South* 38: (2006), 89–123.

Jackson, Ronald L. II. *Scripting the Black Masculine Body: Identity, Discourse, and Racial Politics in Popular Media.* New York: State of New York University Press, 2006.

Jackson, Sherman A. *Islam and the Blackamerican: Looking toward the Third Resurrection.* New York: Oxford University Press, 2005.

Jacobs, Claude F. "Spirit Guides and Possession in the New Orleans Black Spiritual Churches." *Journal of American Folklore* 102: 403 (1989), 45–56+65–67.

Jacobs, Claude F., and Andrew J. Kaslow. *The Spiritual Churches of New Orleans: Origins, Beliefs, and Rituals of an African-American Religion*. Knoxville: The University of Tennessee Press, 1991.

James A. Miller, Susan D. Pennybacker, and Eve Rosenhaft. "Mother Ada Wright and the International Campaign to Free the Scottsboro Boys, 1931–1934." *The American Historical Review*, April 2001, http://www.historycooperative.org/journals/ahr/106.2/ah000387.html (30 Dec. 2011).

Jantzen, Grace. *Power, Gender and Christian Mysticism*. Cambridge: Cambridge University Press, 1996.

Johnson, E. Patrick. "Feeling the Spirit in the Dark: Expanding Notions of the Sacred in the African-American Gay Community." *Callaloo* 21: 2 (1998).

——. *Sweet Tea: Black Gay Men of the South*. Chapel Hill: The University of North Carolina Press, 2011.

Johnson, Paul C. *Secrets, Gossip, and Gods: The Transformation of Brazilian Candomblé*. Oxford: Oxford University Press, 2002.

——. "Secretism and the Apotheosis of Duvalier." *Journal of the American Academy of Religion* 74: 2 (2006), 420–445.

Jones, Arthur C. "Black Spirituals, Physical Sensuality, and Sexuality: Notes on a Neglected Field of Inquiry," in: *Loving the Body: Black Religious Studies and the Erotic*, edited by Anthony B. Pinn and Dwight N. Hopkins, 235–248. New York: Palgrave, 2004.

Jones, Jimmie Lee. Personal Interview with Author. September 14. Monroe, Louisiana, 1996.

Jones, L. *Four Black Revolutionary Plays*. Indianapolis/New York: The Bobbs-Merrill Company, 1969.

Jules-Rosette, B. "Privilege without Power: Women in African Cults and Churches," in: *Women in African and the African Diaspora*, edited by T. Terborg-Penn and A. Rushing, 99–119. Washington, D.C.: Howard University Press, 1989.

Karen, McCarthy-Brown. "The Vèvè of Haitian Vodou: A Structural Analysis of Visual Imagery." PhD diss., Temple University, 1976.

Kerman, Cynthia Earl and Richard Eldridge. *The Lives of Jean Toomer: A Hunger for Wholeness*. Baton Rouge: Louisiana State University Press, 1987.

Kerr, David. "Similarities between the Philosophies of George Ohsawa and George Gurdjieff: Notes." Web, http://www.9starki.com/davidk1.htm, last accessed 15 September 2014.

Kieckhefer, Richard. *Forbidden Rites: A Necromancer's Manual of the Fifteenth Century*. PA: Penn State Press, 1998.

King, C. Daly. *The Oragean Version*. Unpublished, 1951, http://sarmoung-mastersof wisdom.sitiwebs.com/page55.php.

King, Karen L. *What Is Gnosticism?* Cambridge: Harvard University Press, 2003.

Kirby, Vicki. *Telling Flesh: The Substance of the Corporeal*. New York: Routledge, 1997.

Kirk-Duggan, Cheryl. "Salome's Veiled Dance and David's Full Monty: A Womanist Reading on the Black Erotic in Blues, Rap, R & B and Gospel Blues," in: *Loving the Body: Black Religious Studies and the Erotic*, edited by Anthony B. Pinn and Dwight N. Hopkins. New York: Palgrave Macmillan, 2006.

Kirschke, Amy Helene. *Aaron Douglas: Art, Race, and the Harlem Renaissance*. Jackson, Miss. : University Press of Mississippi, 1995.

Knight, Michael Muhammad. *The Five Percenters: Islam, Hip Hop and the Gods of New York*. Richmond: Oneworld, 2008.

Kripal, Jeffrey J. *Roads of Excess Palaces of Wisdom: Eroticism & Reflexivity in the Study of Mysticism*. Chicago: The University of Chicago Press, 2001.

———. "Mystical Bodies: Reflections on Amy Hollywood's 'Sensible Ecstasy.'" *The Journal of Religion* 83: 4 (2003), October, 593–598.

———. *Esalen: America and the Religion of No Religion*. Chicago, IL: Chicago UP, 2008.

———. *Authors of the Impossible: The Paranormal and the Sacred*. Chicago, IL: Chicago UP, 2010.

Krippner, Stanley. "The Role Played by Mandalas in Navajo and Tibetan Rituals." *Anthropology of Consciousness* 8: (1997), 22–31.

Kubik, Gerald. "African Graphic Systems." *Muntu* 4: (1986), 71–137.

Kucich, John. *Ghostly Communion: Cross-Cultural Spiritualism in Nineteenth-Century American Literature*. Hanover, NH: Dartmouth College Press, 2004.

Kunjufu, Jawanza. *Adam Where Are You?: Why Most Black Men Do Go To Church*. Chicago, IL: African American Images, 1997.

Lacan, Jacques. *The Four Fundamental Concepts of Psycho-analysis*, edited by Jacques-Alain Miller, translated by Alan Sheridan. New York: w.w. Norton and Company, 1978.

Lackey, Michael. "Zora Neale Hurston's *Herod the Great*: A Study of the Theological Origins of Modernist Anti-Semitism." *Callaloo* 34: 1 (2011), 100–120.

LaMenfo, Mambo Vye Zo Kommande (Scheu). *Field notes from Haiti and New Orleans*. Private. "Lap dancer turned nun angers Pope," 2003–2007, http://www.telegraph.co.uk/news/worldnews/europe/italy/8536052/Lap-dancer-turned-nun-angers-Pope.html, last accessed December 14, 2011.

Lavenda, Robert, and Emily Schultz. *Anthropology: What Does it Mean to Be Human?* New York: Oxford University Press, 1998.

Leach, Edmund R. *Political System in Highland Burma: A Study of Kachin Social Structure*. Cambridge, Mass.: Harvard University Press, 1954.

———. Introduction, in: *Dialectic in Practical Religion*, edited by E. Leach. Cambridge: Cambridge University Press, 1968.

Lee, Martha F. *Conspiracy Rising: Conspiracy Thinking and American Public Life*. Santa Barbara: Praeger Publishers, 2011.

Leitch, Aaron. *Secrets of the Grimoires*. MN: Llewellyn Publications, 2005.

Lemann, Nicholas. *The Promised Land: The Great Black Migration and How it Changed America*. New York: Alfred A. Knopf, 1991.

Leone, M. and Marie-Fry, G. "Conjuring in the Big House Kitchen: An Interpretation of African American Belief Systems Based on the Uses of Archaeology and Folklore Sources." *Journal of American Folklore* 112: 445 (1999), 372–403.

Leroy-Frazier, Jill. "Othered Southern Modernism: Arna Bontemps's *Black Thunder*. *Mississippi Quarterly* 63: (2010), 1–2, http://www.thefreelibrary.com/Othered+South ern+modernism%3A+Arna+Bontemps's+Black+Thunder.-a0248904591.

Lessig, Laurence. "The Regulation of Social Meaning." *University of Chicago Law Review* 62: (1995), 943–1045.

Lévinas, Emmanuel. *Totality and Infinity: An Essay on Exteriority*. Pittsburgh: Duquesne University Press, 1969.

Levine, Daniel M., and Ann Gleig. "New Age Movement," in: *African American Religious Culture*, Vol. 1, edited by Anthony B. Pinn, 265–273. Santa Barbara, CA: ABC-CLIO, 2009.

Levine, Lawrence. *Black Culture and Black Consciousness: Afro American Folk Thought from Slavery to Freedom*. New York: Oxford University Press, 1977.

Lincoln, C. Eric, and Lawrence H. Mamiya. *The Black Church in the African American Experience*. Durham, N.C.: Duke University Press, 1990.

Lindberg, David C. *The Beginnings of Western Science*. Chicago: University of Chicago Press, 1992.

Lindsay, Jack. *The Origins of Alchemy in Graeco-Roman Egypt*. New York: Barnes & Noble, 1970.

Lock, Graham. *Blutopia: Visions of the Future and Revisions of the Past in the Work of Sun Ra, Duke Ellington, and Anthony Braxton*. Durham: Duke University Press, 1999.

Long, Carolyn Morrow. *Spiritual Merchants: Religion, Magic, and Commerce*. Knoxville: University of Tennessee Press, 2001.

Long, Charles H. *Significations: Signs, Symbols, and Images in the Interpretation of Religion*. Philadelphia: Fortress, 1986.

Long, Charles H. *Significations: Signs, Symbols, and Images in the Interpretation of Religion*. 2nd Edition. Aurora, CO: The Davies Group, 2004.

MacGaffey, W. "Complexity, Astonishment, and Power: The Visual Vocabulary of Kongo Minkisi." *Journal of Southern African Studies* 14: (1988), 188–203.

Mackey, Albert. *History of Freemasonry*. New York: Random House, 1996.

Malcolm, X. *The End of White World Supremacy: Four Speeches*. New York: Arcade Publishing, 1971.

Marion, Jean-Luc. *In Excess: Studies of Saturated Phenomena*. New York: Fordham, 2002.

Martin, Reginald. *Ishmael Reed and the New Black Aesthetic Critics*. Houndmills: The MacMillan Press, 1988.

Marsh, Clifton E. *From Black Muslims to Muslims: The Resurrection, Transformation, and Change of the Lost-Found Nation of Islam in America, 1930–1995*. Lanham, MD: The Scarecrow Press, Inc., 1996.

——. *The Lost-Found Nation of Islam in America*. Lanham, MD and London: Scarecrow Press, Inc., 2000.

Martin, Darnise. *Beyond Christianity: African Americans in a New Thought Church*. New York: New York University Press, 2005.

Masuzawa, Tomoko. *The Invention of World Religions: Or How European Universalism Was Preserved in the Language of Pluralism*. Chicago: University of Chicago Press, 2005.

Mauss, Marcel. "Techniques of the Body (1935)," in: *Techniques, Technology and Civilization*. New York: Durkheim Press, 2006.

Mbiti, John. *African Religions and Philosophy*. New York: Frederick A. Praeger, 1969.

McCutcheon, Russell T. *The Discipline of Religion: Structure, Meaning, Rhetoric*. London and New York: Routledge, 2003.

McDaniel, Lorna. "The Flying Africans: Extent and Strength of the Myth in the Americas," in: *New West Indian Guide/Nieuwe West-Indische Gids* 64: 1/2 (1990), 28–40, Leiden.

——. *The Big Drum Ritual of Carriacou praisesongs in Rememory of Flight*. Gainesville, Fla: University Press of Florida, 1998.

McGinn, B. *The Foundations of Mysticism*. London: SCM Press, 1992.

McLoughlin, William Gerald. *Revivals, Awakenings, and Reform: An Essay on Religion and Social Change in America, 1607–1977*. Chicago: University of Chicago Press, 1978.

McMurray, Anaya. "Hotep and Hip-Hop: Can Black Muslim Women Be Doum with Hip-Hop?" *Meridians* 8: 1 (January 1, 2008), 74–92.

——. "Meet the Pole Dancing Man," http://jezebel.com/5525636/meet-the-pole +dancing-men, last accessed December 14, 2011.

——. "Men Strip Pole Dancing of Another Taboo," http://www.washingtonpost.com/ wp-dyn/content/article/2010/04/26/AR2010042603094.html?wprss=rss_health, last accessed December 14, 2011.

Métraux, Alfred. *Voodoo in Haiti*. New York: Schocken Books, 1972.

Meyer, Joyce. *The Secret Power of Speaking God's Word*. New York: Warner Faith, 2004.

Meyer, Marvin and Mirecki, Paul, eds. *Ancient Magic and Ritual Power*. Leiden: E.J. Brill, 1995.

Meyer, Marvin and Smith, Richard, eds. *Ancient Christian Magic: Coptic Texts of Ritual Power*. New York: HarperCollins Publishers, 1994.

Miller, James A. *Remembering Scottsboro: The Legacy of the Infamous Trial*. Princeton: Princeton University Press, 2009.

Miller, Timothy, ed. *America's Alternative Religions*. Albany: State University of New York Press, 1995.

Miyakawa, Felicia M. *Five Percenter Rap: God Hop's Music, Message, and Black Muslim Mission*. Bloomington: Indiana University Press, 2005.

——. "Receiving, Embodying, and Sharing 'Divine Wisdom': Women in the Nation of Gods and Earths," in: *Women and New and Africana Religions*, edited by

Ashcraft-Eason, Lillian, Darnise C Martin, and Oyeronke Olademo, 29–52. Santa Barbara, Calif.: Praeger, 2010.

Morgan, David, ed. *Religion and Material Culture: The Matter of Belief.* New York: Routledge, 2010.

Morris, Gay. "What He Called Himself: Issues of Identity in Early Dances by Bill T. Jones." *Dancing Desires: Choreographing Sexualities On & Off the Stage.* Madison: The University of Wisconsin Press, 2001.

Mugge, Robert, director. *A Joyful Noise.* New York: Winstar, 1998.

Muhammad, Elijah. *The Supreme Wisdom: Solution to the So-called Negroes's Problem,* Vol. I. Phoenix, AZ: Secretarius MEMPS Publications, 2008.

——. *Message to the Blackman in America.* Atlanta, GA: Secretarius MEMPS Publications, 1965.

——. *The Fall of America,* Chicago: Muhammad's temple of Islam No. 2, 1973.

——. *Our Saviour Has Arrived,* Phoenix: Secretarius MEMPS Publications, 1974.

——. *History of the Nation of Islam,* Atlanta: Secretarius MEMPS Publications, 1993a.

——. *The Science of Time: The Day When Self Tells the Truth on Self,* Phoenix: Secretarius MEMPS Publications, 1993b.

——. *The True History of Jesus' Birth, Death, and What It Means To You and Me,* Phoenix: Secretarius MEMPS Publications, 1993c.

——. *That Which You Should Know...The Secrets of Freemasonry,* Phoenix: Secretarius MEMPS Publications, 1994.

——. *Yakub: The Father of Man-Kind,* Phoenix: Secretarius MEMPS Publications, 2002a.

——. *The God-Science of Black Power,* Secretarius MEMPS Publications, 2002b.

——. *Everything Was Going So Well Then...We Accepted Jesus: How Christianity Deceived the Black Nation.* Phoenix: Secretarius MEMPS Ministries, 2002c.

——. *Why Must Elijah First Come?* Phoenix: Secretarius MEMPS Publications, 2005.

——. *The Theology of Time.* Phoenix: Secretarius MEMPS Publications, 2006.

——. *Christianity Versus Islam: When Worlds Collide.* Phoenix: Secretarius MEMPS Publications, 2008a.

——. *The Mother Plane.* Phoenix: Secretarius MEMPS Publications, 2008b.

——. *My People Are Destroyed: Proper Instructions in the Time of Judgment.* Phoenix: Secretarius MEMPS Publications, 2008c.

——. *The True History of Master Fard Muhammad, Allah (God) in Person.* Phoenix: Secretarius MEMPS Publications, 2008d.

——. *The God-Tribe of Shabazz,* E-Book. Phoenix: Secretarius MEMPS Publications, 2012.

Muhammad, Jabril, ed. *Closing the Gap: The Inner Views of the Heart, Mind & Soul of the Honorable Minister Louis Farrakhan.* Chicago: FCN Publishing Company, 2006.

——. *Is It Possible that the Honorable Elijah Muhammad Is Still Physically Alive?* Phoenix, AZ: Nuevo Books, LLC, 2007.

Muhammad, Tynnetta. *The Comer by Night 1986*. Chicago, IL: The Honorable Elijah Muhammad Educational Foundation, Inc, 1986.

——. "In Search of the Messiah – King Solomon Examines the Queen of Sheba." *Unveiling the Number* 19: (2003) 17 July, viewed 12 November, 2009, http://www .finalcall.com/artman/publish/printer_903.shtml.

——. "Masonic Roots May Be Traced to Moses (Musa) 4.000 B.C. and Ancient Egypt," *Unveiling the Number 19*, in: *Final Call*, 21 December 2010. Viewed on 20 November 2012, http://www.finalcall.com/artman/publish/Columns_4/article_7512.shtm.

Munson, Gorham. "The Significance of Jean Toomer." *Destinations, A canvas of American Literature since 1900*. New York: J.H. Sears & Co, 1928, http://www.nsm .buffalo.edu/~sww/toomer/toomerworks.html.

Murphy, Joseph M. "Mystic's Library is full of Weird Jargon." *Camden Courier-Post* (April 10, 1925), retrieved from http://www.dvrbs.com/people/CamdenPeople -DrHyghcock.htm.

——. *Santería: An African religion in America*. Boston: Beacon Press, 1988.

Nahziryah Monastic Community. *The Purple Veil*. New Orleans: NMC, 1994.

——. *The Drama*. St. Joe: NMC, 2005a.

——. *Letters from an Open Book*. St. Joe: NMC, 2005b.

——. *Who on Earth...Who in the World...Are the Purple People*. St. Joe: NMC, 2006.

——. *Nazir Art Crafts Catalog*. St. Joe: NMC, 2012, http://www.nmcnews.org/softcopy -catalogs.html.

Najovits, Simson. *Egypt: Trunk of the Tree*. Volume II. New York: Algora Publishing, 2004.

Nance, Susan. "Mystery of the Moorish Science Temple: Southern Blacks and American Alternative Spirituality in 1920s Chicago." *Religion and American Culture* 12: 2 (2002), 123–166.

Narayanan, Vasudha. *Hinduism*. Oxford: Oxford University Press, 2004.

Nashashibi, Rami. "The Blackstone Legacy, Islam, and the Rise of Ghetto Cosmopolitanism." *Souls: A Critical Journal of Black Politics, Culture, and Society* 9: 2 (2007), 123–131.

Nazirmoreh, K.B. Kedem. *The Mirror*. New Orleans: NMC, 1991.

Nelson, A. "*A Black Mass* as Black Gothic," in: *New Thoughts on the Black Arts Movement*, edited by L.G. Collins and M.N. Crawford, 138–153. New Jersey: Rutgers University Press, 2006.

Nelson, Roger. "News From the A.M.E. Churches." *The Christian Recorder*, July 7. Accessible. Archives: African American Newspapers, 1866.

——. The Global Consciousness Project Home page, noosphere.princeton.edu/index .html, accessed 8/5/13.

Nicolescu, Basarab. *Manifesto of Transdisciplinarity*. Albany: State University of New York Press, 2002.

Noel, James A. "Call and Response: The Meaning of the Moan and Significance of the Shout in Black Worship," *Reformed Liturgy & Music* 28/2: Spring 1994, 72–76, 73.

Nuruddin, Yusuf. "The Five Percenters: A Teenage Nation of Gods and Earths," in: *Muslim Communities in North America*, edited by Yvonn Yazbeck Haddad and Jane Idleman Smith, 109–130. Albany: State University of New York Press, 1994.

O'Connor, Francis V. "The Psychodynamics of the Frontal Self-Portrait," in: *Psychoanalytic Perspectives on Art*, edited by Mary Mathews Gedo, 169–221. London: The Analytic Press, 1985.

Oliver, B. and M. Murphy. *The Works Progress Administration History of Franklin Parish*. Louisiana. Unpublished article, 1937.

Omari-Tunkara, Mikelle Smith. *Manipulating the Sacred: Yoruba Art, Ritual, and Resistance in Brazilian Candomble*. Detroit: Wayne State University Press, 2005.

Oster, Harry. Play On Your Harp David. *The Harry Collection.* AFS 12575, LWO-5059, Box I, Recorded March 11, 1957, Napoleonville, La, 1957 (sung by Rebecca Smith, born in 1885).

———. Easter Rock Revisited: A Study in Acculturation. *Louisiana Folklore Miscellany* 1: 3 (1958), 21–43.

———. With the Louisiana Folklore Society. n.d. *A Sampler of Louisiana Folksongs, Sung by Tradition Performers.* LSF-1201.

Otto, Rudolph. *The Idea of the Holy*, translated by John W. Harvey, 5. Oxford: Oxford University Press, 1923.

Ouspensky, Peter D. *In Search of the Miraculous: Fragments of an Unknown Teaching*. New York: Harcourt, Brace, 1949.

———. *Tertium Organum: The Third Canon of Thought, a Key to the Enigmas of the World*, translated from the Russian by Nicholas Bessaraboff and Claude Bragdon. Guildford: White Crow Books, 2011.

Outlaw, Lucius T. *On Race and Philosophy*. New York and London: Routledge, 1996.

Page, Hugh R. Jr. "The Bible and Africana Esotericism – Toward an Architectonic for Interdisciplinary Study," in: *Semeia Studies: Esoteric Interpretations of Genesis*, edited by Susanne Scholz and Caroline Vander Stichele, 1–3. Atlanta: Society of Biblical Literature (Forthcoming). Semeia Studies.

Palmer, Susan. *The Nuwaubian Nation: Black Spirituality and State Control*. Ashgate, 2010.

Pérez, Elizabeth. "Narrative, Seasoning, Song: Praxis, Subjectivity, and Transformation in an African-American Lucumí Community." Ph.D. diss., University of Chicago Divinity School, 2010.

Perkinson, Jim. "Personal Items." *The Christian Recorder*, August 26. Accessible Archives: African American Newspapers, 1875.

———. "Ogu's Iron or Jesus' Irony: Who's Zooming Who in Diasporic Possession Cut Activity?" *Journal of Religion* 81/4: October (2001), 566–594.

Peterson, Joseph. *The Lesser Key of Solomon*. MA: Weisers, 2001.

Pietz, William. "The Problem of the Fetish, Illa." *Res* 16: (1988), 105–123.

Pilsbury, Parker. "Utica Philanthropic Convention." *The Liberator*, September 17. American Periodicals Series Online, 1858.

Pingree, David. "Some of the Sources of the Ghāyat al-hakīn." *Journal of Warburg and Courtland Institutes* 43: (1980), 1–15.

Pinn, Anthony. *Varieties of African American Religious Experience*. Minneapolis: Fortress Press, 1998.

——. *Terror and Triumph: The Nature of Black Religion*. Minneapolis, Minneapolis: Fortress Press, 2003.

——. *African American Humanist Principles: Living and Thinking Like the Children of Nimrod*. New York: Palgrave Macmillan, 2004.

——. *Embodiment and the New Shape of Black Theological Thought*. New York: New York University Press, 2010.

——. *The End of God-Talk: An African American Humanist Theology*. New York: Oxford University Press, 2012.

Pitts, Walter F. "Physicking Priestess." *Time Magazine* 17: 16 (Apr. 20, 1931), 63–64.

——, ed. *What Is Humanism, and Why Does it Matter?* Durham, UK: Acumen Publishing, 2013.

Pinn, Anthony B. and Allen D. Callahan, eds. *African American Religious Life and the Story of Nimrod*. New York: Palgrave Macmillan, 2008.

——. *Old Ship of Zion: The Afro-Baptist Ritual in the African Diaspora*. New York: Oxford University Press, 1993.

Poe, Tracey N. "The Origins of Soul Food in Black Urban Identity: Chicago, 1915–1947." *American Studies International* 37: 1 (1999), 4–33.

——. "Pole Dancing For Jesus," last accessed December 14, 2011, http://www.huffingtonpost.com/2011/09/14/pole-dancing-for-jesus_n_962804.html.

Polk, P.A. "Other Books, Other Powers: The Sixth and Seventh Books of Moses in Afro-Atlantic Folk Belief." *Southern Folklore* 56: (1999), 115–133.

Pollard, Alton B. "African American Mysticism," in: *African American Religious Cultures*, Vol. 1, edited by Anthony B. Pinn, Stephen C. Finley, and Torin Alexander, 3–7. Santa Barbara: ABC-CLIO, 2009.

Pollard, M. *Personal Interview with Author*, 29 March, Winnsboro, Louisiana, 1997.

Primiano, Leonard Norman. "'Bringing Perfection in These Different Places': Father Divine's Vernacular Architecture of Intention." *Folklore* 115: (2004), 3–26.

Puckett, N.N. *Folk Beliefs of the Southern Negro*. Chapel Hill: University of North Carolina Press, 1926.

Raboteau, A.J. *Slave Religion: The "Invisible Institution" in the Antebellum South*. Update of original 1978 ed. Oxford, UK: Oxford University Press, 2004.

Randolph, Paschal Beverly. "New Work." *The Liberator*, August 14. American Periodicals Series Online, 1846.

——. "Letter from P. Beverly Randolph." *The Liberator*, November 12. American Periodicals Series Online, 1858.

——. *Dealings with the Dead; the Human Soul, Its Migration and Its Transmigrations.* Utica, NY: M.J. Randolph, 1862.

——. *Pre-adamite Man: Demonstrating the Existence of the Human Race upon this Earth 100,000 Years Ago!* New York, NY: S. Tousey, 1863a.

——. *The Wonderful Story of Ravalette. Also, Tom Clark and His Wife: Their Double Dreams and the Curious Things that Befell Them Therein; or, the Rosicrucian's Story.* New York, NY: S. Tousey, 1863b.

——. "Lloyd Garrison School – Colored." *The Liberator*, November 10. American Periodicals Series Online, 1865.

——. "Letter From Dr. Randolph." *The Christian Recorder*, August 25. Accessible Archives: African American Newspapers, 1866.

——. *P.B. Randolph, the "Learned Pundit," and "Man with Two Souls," His Curious Life, Works, and Career. The Great Free-Love Trial.* Boston, MA: Randolph Publishing House, 1872.

——. *Ravalette: The Rosicrucian's Story.* Quakertown, PA: Philosophical Publishing Company, 1939.

Ragar, Cheryl R. "The Douglas Legacy." *American Studies* 49: 1/2 (2008), 131–145.

Reed, Christopher Robert. *Black Chicago's First Century: Volume I, 1833–1900.* Columbia: University of Missouri Press, 2005.

Reed, Ishmael. *Mumbo Jumbo.* New York: Atheneum, 1988.

Rivera, Jason David, and DeMond Shondell Miller. "Continually Neglected: Situating Natural Disasters in the African American Experience." *Journal of Black Studies* 37: 4 (2007), 502–522.

Roediger, David R. "And Die in Dixie: Funerals, Death and Heaven in the Slave Community 1700–1895." *The Massachusetts Review* 22: (1981), 163–183.

Rollefson, J.G. The "Robot Voodoo Power" Thesis: Afrofuturism and Anti-Anti-essentialism from sun ra to kool keith. *Black Music Research Journal* 28: 1 (2008), 83–109.

Rosenbaum, Art. *Shout Because You're Free: The African American Ring Shout Tradition in Coastal Georgia.* Athens: University of Georgia Press, 1998.

Ruble, Blair A. *Second Metropolis: Pragmatic Pluralism in Gilded Age Chicago, Silver Age Moscow, and Meiji Osaka.* Cambridge: Cambridge University Press, 2001.

Rusch, Frederik L., ed. *A Jean Toomer Reader: Selected Unpublished Writings.* New York: Oxford University Press, 1993.

Sahib, Hatim A. "The Nation of Islam." *Contributions in Black Studies* 13: (1995), 3.

Sanders, Cheryl J. *Saints in Exile: The Holiness-Pentecostal Experience in African American Religion and Culture*. Oxford: Oxford University Press, 1996.

Schwaller de Lubicz, R.A. *The Temple of Man: Apet of the South at Luxor*. Rochester: Inner Traditions, 1998.

Segal, Judah Benzion. "The Sabian Mysteries: The Planet Cult of Ancient Harran," in: *Vanished Civilizations*, 24–37, edited by E. Bacon. London: Thames and Hudson, 1963.

Societatis Rosicruianae Banford America. *Rituals of the First Order* Original manuscript, 1881.

Sernett, Milton C. *Bound for the Promised Land: African American Religion and the Great Migration*. Durham, N.C.: Duke University Press, 1997.

Simmel, Georg. *The Sociology of Georg Simmel*. Berlin: Marquart, 1906.

Singh, Amritjit. *Introduction to The Collected writings of Wallace Thurman: A Harlem Renaissance Reader*, edited by Amritjit Singh and Daniel M. Scott III. Rutgers, New Jersey: Rutgers University Press, 2003.

Smith, Theophus. *Conjuring Culture*. New York: Oxford University Press. "The Picatrix or Ghayat al Hikam" accessed December 7, 2011, 1995, http://www.renaissance astrology.com/picatrix.html.

Sobel, M. *Trabelin On: The Slave Journey to an Afro-Baptist Faith*. Westport, Conn.: Greenwood Press, 1979.

Southern, Eileen. *The Music of Black Americans: A History*, 3rd ed. NY: W.W. Norton & Co, 1999.

Sovatsky, Stuart. *Eros, Consciousness, and Kundalini: Deepening Sensuality Through Tantric Celibacy and Spiritual Intimacy*. Rochester, VT: Rock Street Press, 1999.

Spangler, Ann. *Praying the Names of God*. Grand Rapids, MI: Zondervan, 2004.

Spence, Verona and Dalian Adofo. *Ancestral Voices: Esoteric African Knowledge*. Longbelly Entertainment, DVD, 2011.

Spencer, Jon Michael. *Sacred Music in the Secular City From Blues to Rap*. Texas: Duke University Press, 1992.

Steiner, Rudolf. *The Gospel of Saint John*. Hudson, NY: The Anthroposophic Press, 1940.

Steingroot, Ira. "Sun Ra's Magical Kingdom." *Reality Hackers* 6 (Winter 1988), 46–51.

Soitos, Stephen. *The Blues Detective: A Study of African American Detective Fiction*. Amherst: University of Massachusetts Press, 1996.

Stone, Dan. *Breeding Superman: Nietzsche, Race and Eugenics in Edwardian and Interwar Britain*. (Studies in Social and Political Thought.) Liverpool: Liverpool University Press, 2002.

Strabo, Mikhail. *The Guiding Light to Power and Success: A Study in the Use of Candles in the Search for Truth*. Buena Park, CA: Jaguar Books, 2006.

Stratton-Kent, Jake. *The True Grimoire*. London: Scarlet Imprint, 2010.

——. *Geosophia: The Argo of Magic, Volumes I and II*. London: Scarlet Imprint, 2011.

Strother, Thomas. "Convention of Colored Men." *The Christian Recorder*, November 10. Accessible Archives: African American Newspapers, 1866.

Stuckey, Sterling. *Slave Culture: Nationalist Theory and the Foundations of Black America*. New York: Oxford University Press, 1987.

———. "African Spirituality in Colonial New York, 1700–1770," in: *Inequality in Early America*, 160–181. Hanover, NH: University Press of New England, 1999.

Sturman, Janet. Asserting Tradition: The Building and Maintenance of African-American Baptist Rock Ceremony in Northeast Louisiana. *Louisiana Folklife* 17: (1993), 24–45.

Sun Ra. *The Immeasurable Equation: The Collected Poetry and Prose*, edited by James Wolf and Hartmut Geerken. Wartaweil: Waitawhile, 2005.

Sweet, James H. "The Evolution of Ritual in the African Diaspora: Central African Kilundu in Brazil, St. Domingue, and the United States, Seventeenth-Nineteenth Centuries," in: *Diasporic Africa: A Reader*, edited by Michael A. Gomez. New York: New York University Press, 2006.

Swimme, Brian. *The Universe Is a Green Dragon: A Cosmic Creation Story*. Rochester: Vermont, Bear & Company, 2001.

Szwed, John. *Space Is the Place: The Lives and Times of Sun Ra*. New York: Da Capo Press, 1998.

Taylor, Clarence. *Black Religious Intellectuals: The Fight for Equality from Jim Crow to the 21st Century*. New York: Routledge, 2002.

Taylor, Paul Beekman. *Gurdjieff and Orage: Brothers in Elysium*. York Beach: Weiser Books, 2001.

Tertullian. *The Ante-Nicene Fathers: Translations of the Writings of the Fathers Down to A.D. 325*. Alexander Roberts and James Donaldson, eds., *Arthur Cleveland Coxe, Revised*. Buffalo: The Christian Literature Publishing Company. American Reprint, 1896.

Thompson, Robert Farris. *The Four Moments of the Sun*. Washington, D.C.: National Gallery of Art, 1981.

———. *Flash of the Spirit: African and Afro-American Art and Philosophy*. New York: Random House, 1984.

———. "Bighearted Power: Kongo Presence in the Landscape and Art of Black America," in *Keep Your Head to the Sky: Interpreting African American Home Ground*, edited by G. Gundaker, 37–64. Charlotesville/London: University Press of Virginia, 1998.

Thornton, John K. *African and Afro-Americans in the Making of the Atlantic World, 1400–1680*. Cambridge: Cambridge University Press, 1992.

Thurman, Howard. *Meditations of the Heart*. New York, NY: Harper & Row, 1953.

———. *The Luminous Darkness*. Richmond: Friends United Press, 1965.

———. *Jesus and the Disinherited*. Richmond: Friends United Press, 1976.

——. *A Strange Freedom: The Best of Howard Thurman on Religious Experience and Public Life*. Boston: Beacon Press, 1998.

Thurman, Wallace. *The Conjure Man Dies: A Mystery Tale of Dark Harlem*. Ann Arbor: University of Michigan Press, 1932.

——. *Infants of the Spring* (1932), *The Northeastern Library of Black Literature*, edited by Richard Yarborough. Boston: Northeastern UP,1992.

Tidwell, John E. and Cheryl R. Ragar, eds. *Montage of a Dream: The Art and Life of Langston Hughes*. Columbia: University of Missouri Press, 2007.

Tolnay, Stewart E. and E.M. Beck. "Black Flight: Lethal Violence and the Great Migration, 1900–1930." *Social Science History* 14: 3 (1990), 347–370.

Tolson, Melvin B. "The Wine of Ecstasy," in: *Negro Voices*, edited by Beatrice Murphy, 153. New York: Henry Harrison, 1938.

——. *Harlem Gallery: Book !, The Curator*, with an introd. by Karl Shapiro. New York: Twayne, 1965.

——. *A Gallery of Harlem Portraits*, edited with afterword by Robert M. Farnsworth. Columbia, MO: University of Missouri Press, 1982.

Toomer, Jean. *The Collected Poems of Jean Toomer*, edited by Robert B. Jones and Margery Toomer Latimer. Chapel Hill: University of North Carolina Press, 1988.

Townes, Emilie. *Womanist Ethics and the Cultural Production of Evil*. New York: Palgrave Macmillan, 2006.

Tracy, Steven C. "Langston Hughes: Poetry, Blues, and Gospel—Somewhere to Stand," in: *Langston Hughes: The Man, His Art, and His Continuing Influence*, edited by C. James Trotman. New York: Taylor & Francis, 1995.

Trafton, Scott. *Egypt Land: Race and Nineteenth-Century American Egyptomania*. Durham, NC: Duke UP, 2004.

Turner, Bryan S. "Cosmopolitan Virtue: Loyalty and the City," in: *Democracy, Citizenship and the Global City*, edited by Engin F. Isin, 129–147. London and New York: Routledge, 2000.

Turner, Richard Brent. "What Shall We Call Him?: Islam and African American Identity, *Journal of Religious Thought* 51: 1 (1994), 25–52.

Tuttle, William M. *Race Riot: Chicago in the Red Summer of 1919*. New York: Atheneum, 1970.

Urban, Hugh B. "Elitism and Esotericism: Strategies of Secrecy and Power in South Indian Tantra and French Freemasonry." *Numen* 44: (1997), 1–38.

——. "The Torment of Secrecy: Ethical and Epistemological Problems in the Study of Esoteric Traditions." *History of Religions* 37: 3 (1998), 209–248.

——. "The Adornment of Silence: Secrecy and Symbolic Capital in American Freemasonry." *Journal of Religion and Society* 3: (2001), 1–29.

——. *Magia Sexualis: Sex, Magic, and Liberation in Modern Western Esotericism*. Berkeley, CA: California UP, 2006.

——. "Secrecy and New Religious Movements." *Religion Compass* 2: 1 (2008), 66–83.

——. "The Secrets of Scientology: Concealment, Information Control and Esoteric Knowledge in the World's Most Controversial New Religion," in: *Contemporary Esotericism*, edited by Egil Asprem and Kennet Granholm, 181–199. London: Acumen Publishing, 2012.

Van Deburg, William L. *Modern Black Nationalism: From Marcus Garvey to Louis Farrakhan.* New York: New York University Press, 1996.

Versluis, Arthur. "What Is Esoteric? Methods in the Study of Western Esotericism." *Esoterica* 4: (2002), 1–15.

——. *Restoring Paradise: Western Esotericism, Literature, Art, and Consciousness.* Albany, NY: New York State UP, 2004.

Vincenti, Marissa. "A Matter of Spirit: Aaron Douglas, Gurdjieffian Thought, and the Expression of 'Conscious Art,'" *The International Review of African American Art* 21: 3 (2007), 11–15.

von Nettesheim, Henry Cornelius Agrippa. *Three Books of Occult Philosophy*, edited by Freake, James and Tyson, Donald. Woodbury: Llewellyn Publications, 1992.

von Stuckrad, Kocku. "'Voodoo' Is Held for Murder." *Camden Courier* (April 9, 1925a), retrieved from http://www.dvrbs.com/people/CamdenPeople-DrHyghcock .htm.

——. "Voodoo Man Confesses Bigamy." *Camden Courier* (April 10, 1925b), retrieved from http://www.dvrbs.com/people/CamdenPeople-DrHyghcock.htm.

——. "Voodoo Doctor Is Held." *Oregonian* (April 11, 1925c) Retrieved from www .newsinhistory.com.

——. "Reenchanting Nature: Modern Western Shamanism and Nineteenth-Century Thought." *Journal of the American Academy of Religion* 70: 4 (2002), 771–799.

——. Western Esotericism: A Brief History of Secret Knowledge. London: Equinox Publishing, 2005.

——. *Locations of Knowledge in Medieval and Early Modern Europe: Esoteric Discourse and Western Identities*, Leiden: Brill, 2010.

Wakeel Allah. *In the Name of Allah a History of Clarence 13x and the Five Percenters.* A-Team Pub Inc, 2009.

Walker, Alice. *Overcoming Speechlessness: A Poet Encounters Horror in Rwanda, Eastern Congo, and Palestine/Israel,* New York: Seven Stories Press, 2010.

Wardle, Huon. "A Groundwork for West Indian Cultural Openness." *Journal of the Royal Anthropological Institute* 13: 3 (2007), 567–583.

Wardle, Huon. "Ambiguation, Disjuncture, Commitment: A Social Analysis of Caribbean Cultural Creativity." *Journal of the Royal Anthropological Institute* 8: 3 (2002), 493–508.

Washington, Joseph Jr. *Black Religion: The Negro and Christianity in the United States.* Boston: Beacon Press, 1964.

Washington, Mary Helen. Lives of the Exiles." Review of *The Forging of the Mid-Twentieth-Century Literary Left* by Alan Wald. *Solidarity*, 2002, http://www.solidarity-us.org/node/761.

Wehmeyer, Stephen C. "Indian Altars of the Spiritual Churches." *African Arts* 33: 4 (2000), 62–69.

———. "'Indians at the Door': Power and Placement on New Orleans Spiritual Church Altars." *Western Folklore* 66: 1/2 (2007), 15–44.

———. "Indian Spirits on the Rock Island Line: Chicago as 'Gate of Tradition' for African American Spiritualism in the Gulf South." American Academy of Religion panel, "Gateway of the Spirits: African Diaspora Religions in Chicago," 2008.

———. "Marching Bones and Invisible Indians: African American Spiritualism in New Orleans, Past and Present." *Southern Quarterly* 47: 4 (Summer 2010), 43–60.

Wesley, John. *Primitive Physic: An Easy and Natural Method of Curing Most Diseases.* Eugene, OR: Wipf and Stock Publishers, 1993.

West, Cornel. *The American Evasion of Philosophy: A Genealogy of Pragmatism.* Madison: University of Wisconsin Press, 1989.

———. *Race Matters*, 22. New York, Vintage Press, 1994.

Westfield, Nancy Lynn, Ray, Stephen G., Duncan, Carol B., Floyd-Thomas, Stacey and Floyd-Thomas, J eds. *Black Church Studies: An Introduction.* Nashville, TN: Abingdon Press, 2007.

———. "What is Esotericism?" Association for the Study of Esotericism, http://www.aseweb.org/?page_id=6, accessed January 5, 2012.

Wilkerson, David. *Knowing God by Name: Names of God That Bring Hope and Healing.* Grand Rapids, MI: Chosen, 2003.

Wilkinson, Bruce. *The Prayer of Jabez: Breaking through to the Blessed Life, the Break Through Series.* Sisters, OR: Multnomah, 2000.

William-Jones, Pearl. "The Musical Quality of Black Religious Folk Ritual." *Spirit* 1: (1977), 21

Wilmore, Gayraud S. *Black Religion and Black Radicalism: An Interpretation of the Religious History of African Americans.* New York: Orbis Books, 1999.

Wilson, Harriet. *Our Nig; Or, Sketches from the Life of a Free Black*, edited and introduced by P. Gabrielle Foreman. New York, NY: Penguin, 2009.

Wilson, Peter L. *Sacred Drift: Essays on the Margins of Islam.* San Francisco: City of Lights Books, 1993.

Wood, Sharon. "Feminist Writing in the Twentieth Century," in: *The Cambridge Companion to the Italian Novel*, edited By Peter E. Bondanella, Andrea Ciccarelli. New York: Cambridge UP, 2003.

Woodson, Jon. *To Make a New Race: Gurdjieff, Toomer, and the Harlem Renaissance.* Jackson: University Press of Mississippi, 1999.

——. "Woman offers Christian Pole Dancing Class in Houston," http://theurbandaily .com/special-features/wtf-special-features/theurbandailystaff2/christian-pole -dancing-class-houston-video, last accessed December 14, 2011.

York, Malachi York. *The Paleman.* Monticello, NY: The Original Tents of Kedar, 1990.

——. *The Holy Tablets.* Eatonton, GA: The Holy Tabernacle Ministries, n.d, 1996.

——. *Actual Facts Series.* Eatonton, Georgia: The Holy Tabernacle Ministries.

——. *Who Was Jesus' Father?* Eatonton, Georgia: The Holy Tabernacle Ministries, 1994.

——. *The Resurrection.* Eatonton, Georgia: The Holy Tabernacle Ministries, 1994.

——. *Who Was Jesus Sent To?* Eatonton, Georgia: The Holy Tabernacle Ministries, 1988.

——. *Could Jesus Transform Himself.* Eatonton, Georgia: The Holy Tabernacle Ministries, 1994.

——. *Be Prepared for the Anti-Christ.* Eatonton, Georgia: The Holy Tabernacle Ministries, 1994.

——. *666 – Mark of the Beast.* Eatonton, Georgia: The Holy Tabernacle Ministries, 1992.

——. *Man from Planet Rizq.* Eatonton, Georgia: The Holy Tabernacle Ministries, 1996.

——. *Science of Creation.* Eatonton, Georgia: The Holy Tabernacle Ministries, 1986.

——. *Mission Earth.* Eatonton, Georgia: The Holy Tabernacle Ministries, 1991.

——. *Who Lived before the Adam and Eve Story.* Eatonton, Georgia: The Holy Tabernacle Ministries, 1995.

——. *Shamballah And Aghaarta Cities Within the Earth.* Eatonton, Georgia: The Holy Tabernacle Ministries, 1995.

——. *Are There (UFO's) Extraterrestrials in Your Midst?* Eatonton, Georgia: The Holy Tabernacle Ministries, 1995.

——. *Actual Fact # 5: The Celtics.* Eatonton, Georgia: The Holy Tabernacle Ministries.

——. *Actual Fact # 21: Image of the Beast.* Eatonton, Georgia: The Holy Tabernacle Ministries.

——. *El Maguraj.* Eatonton, Georgia: The Holy Tabernacle Ministries, 1999.

——. *Human Reptile,* http://www.youtube.com/watch?v=-HozIcOxqjI, accessed October, 2012.

——. *Holy Tablets,* http://holytablets.nuwaubianfacts.com/, accessed October, 2012.

Yronwode, Catherine. The Enduring Occult Mystery of Lewis de Claremont, Louis de Clermont, Godfrey Spencer, Henri Gamache, Joe Kay, Joseph Spitalnick, Black Herman, Benjamin Rucker, and the Elusive Mr. Young, 1995–2003, http://www .luckymojo.com/young.html.

——. "Candle Magic for the Home Practitioner," in: *The Art of Hoodoo Candle Magic in Rootwork, Conjure, and Spiritual Church Services,* edited by C.Y.a.M. Strabo. Forrestville, CA: Missionary Independent Spiritual Church, 2013.

Zorbaugh, Harvey Warren. *The Gold Coast and The Slum: A Sociological Study of Chicago's Near North Side.* Chicago: University of Chicago Press, 1929.

Index